Disney | SQUARE ENIX

KINGDOM HEARTS

Volume 2
Adapted by
Shiro Amano

HAMBURG // LONDON // LOS ANGELES // TOKYO

Kingdom Hearts II Volume 2
Adapted by Shiro Amano

Assistant Editor - Jessica Chavez
Copy Editor - Shannon Watters
Retouch and Lettering - Michael Paolilli
Cover Design - James Lee

Editor - Bryce P. Coleman
Digital Imaging Manager - Chris Buford
Pre-Production Supervisor - Lucas Rivera
Art Director - Al-Insan Lashley
Production Manager - Elisabeth Brizzi
Managing Editor - Vy Nguyen
Creative Director - Anne Marie Horne
Editor-in-Chief - Rob Tokar
Publisher - Mike Kiley
President and C.O.O. - John Parker
C.E.O. and Chief Creative Officer - Stu Levy

A TOKYOPOP Manga

TOKYOPOP and are trademarks or registered trademarks of TOKYOPOP Inc.

TOKYOPOP Inc.
5900 Wilshire Blvd. Suite 2000
Los Angeles, CA 90036

E-mail: info@TOKYOPOP.com
Come visit us online at www.TOKYOPOP.com

ISBN: 978-1-4278-0059-6

First TOKYOPOP printing: May 2008

10 9 8 7 6 5 4 3 2 1

Printed in the USA

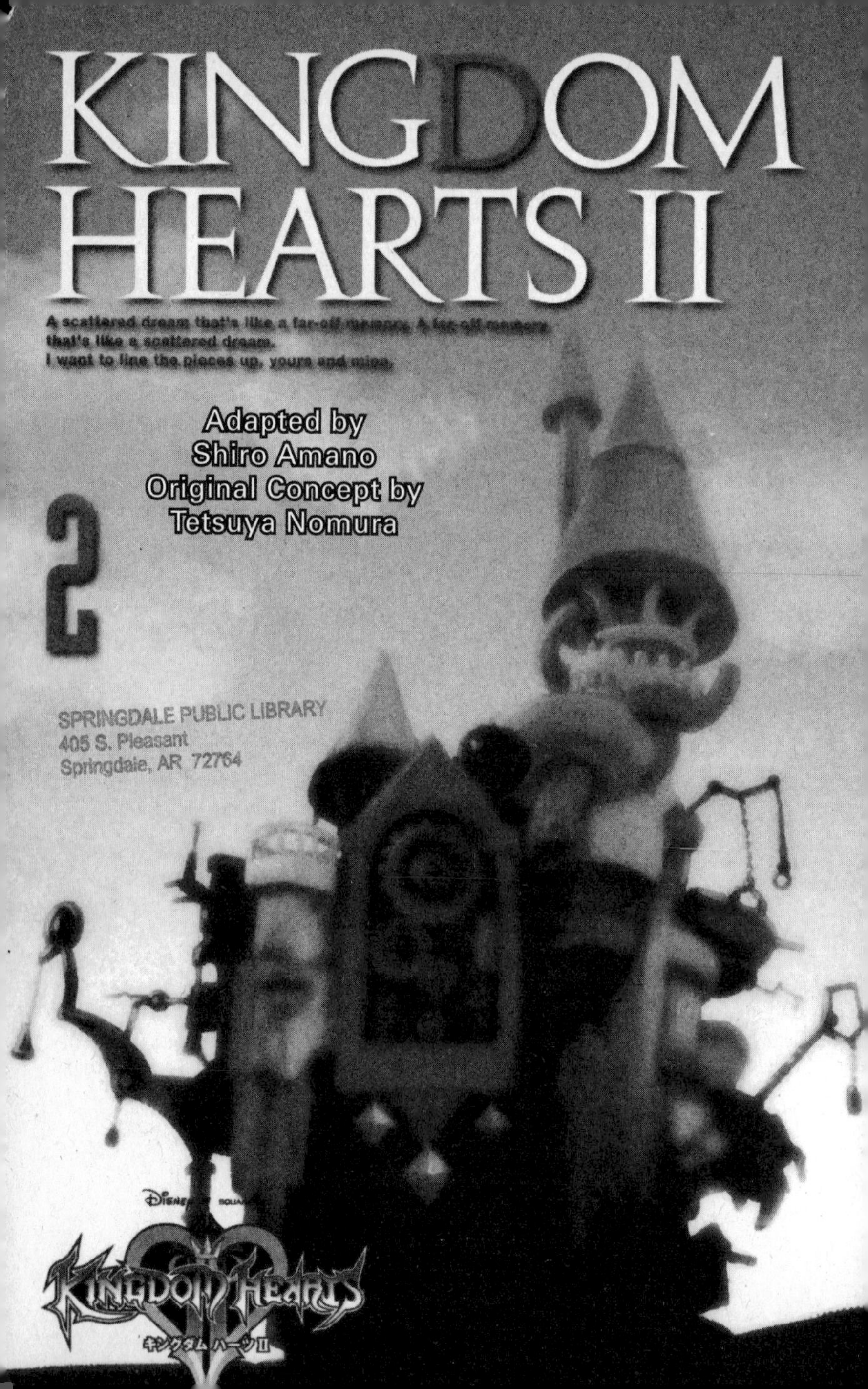

KINGDOM HEARTS II
A scattered dream that's like a far-off memory. A far-off memory
that's like a scattered dream.
I want to line the pieces up, yours and mine.
Adapted by
Shiro Amano
Original Concept by
Tetsuya Nomura
2
SPRINGDALE PUBLIC LIBRARY
405 S. Pleasant
Springdale, AR 72764
KINGDOM HEARTS
キングダム ハーツII

CONTENTS

KINGDOM HEARTS II

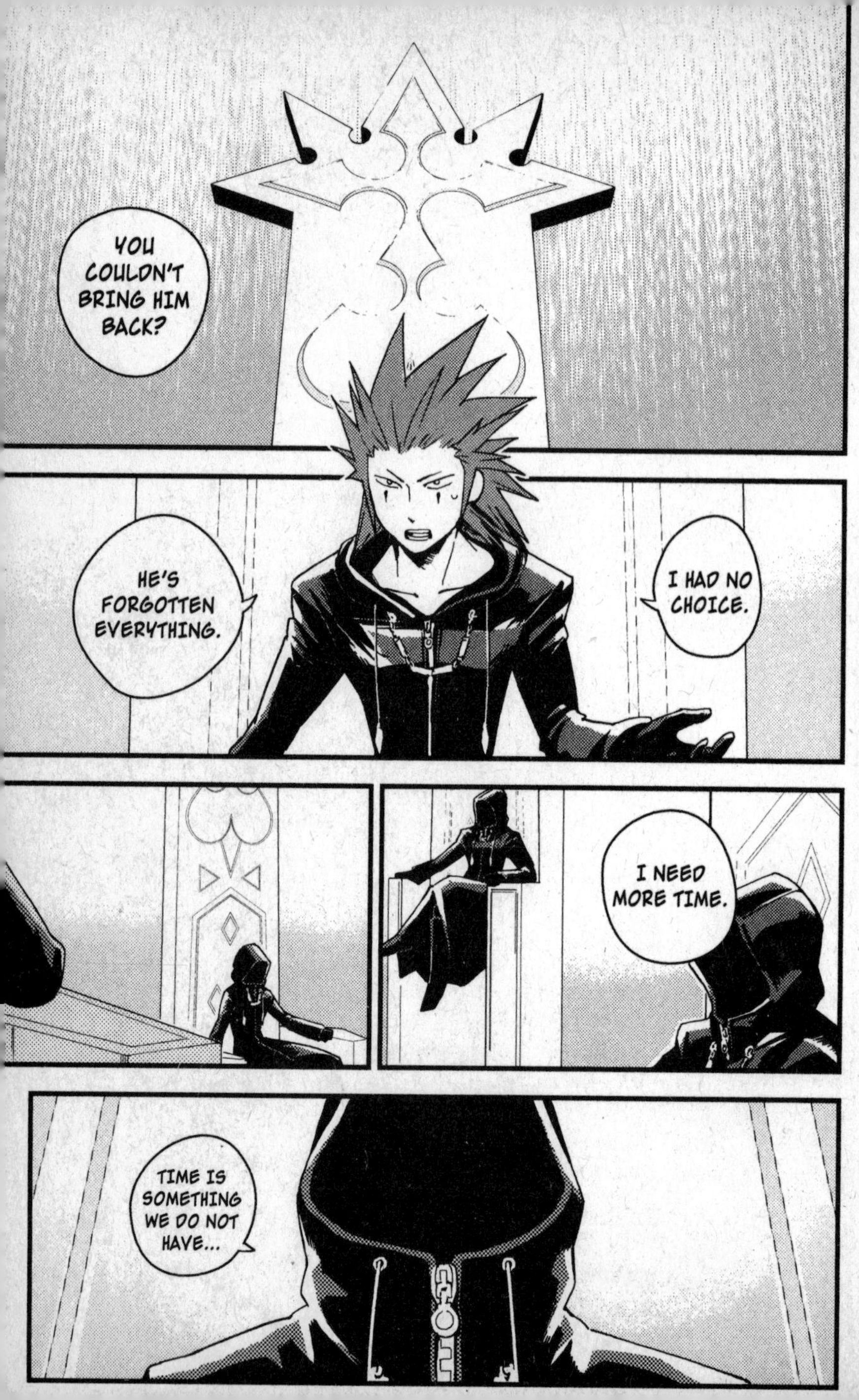
YOU COULDN'T BRING HIM BACK?
I HAD NO CHOICE.
HE'S FORGOTTEN EVERYTHING.
I NEED MORE TIME.
TIME IS SOMETHING WE DO NOT HAVE...

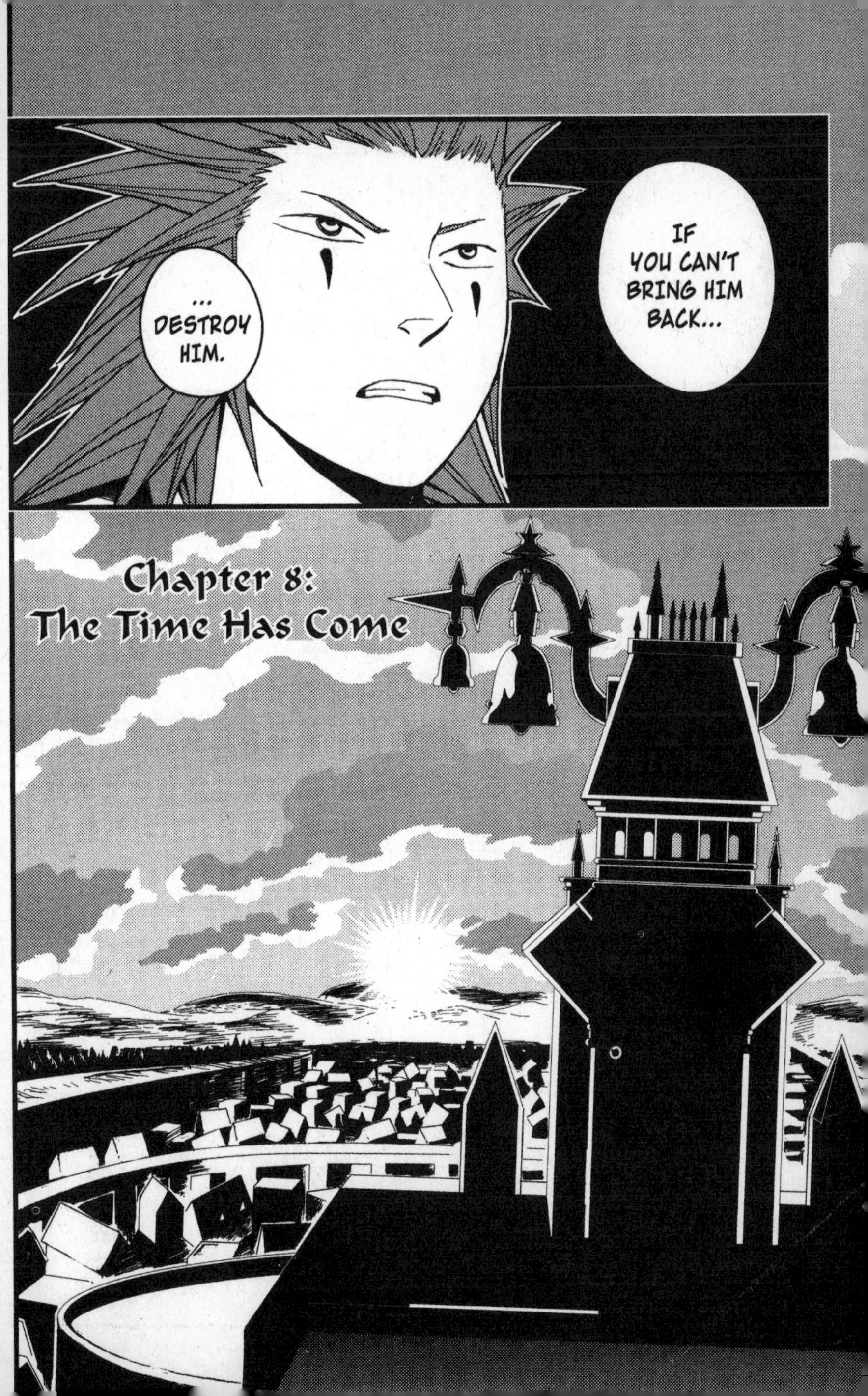
IF YOU CAN'T BRING HIM BACK...
...DESTROY HIM.
Chapter 8: The Time Has Come

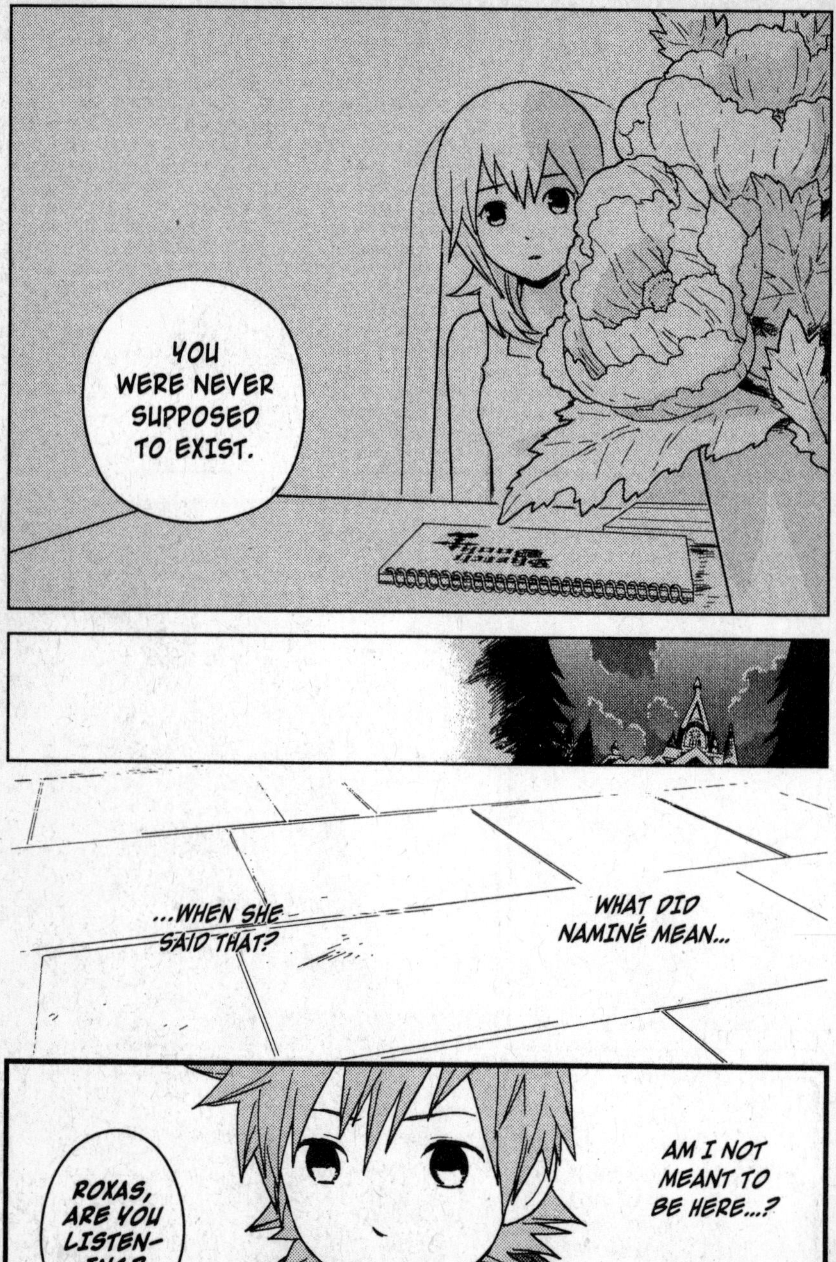
YOU WERE NEVER SUPPOSED TO EXIST.
WHAT DID NAMINÉ MEAN...
...WHEN SHE SAID THAT?
AM I NOT MEANT TO BE HERE...?
ROXAS, ARE YOU LISTEN-ING?

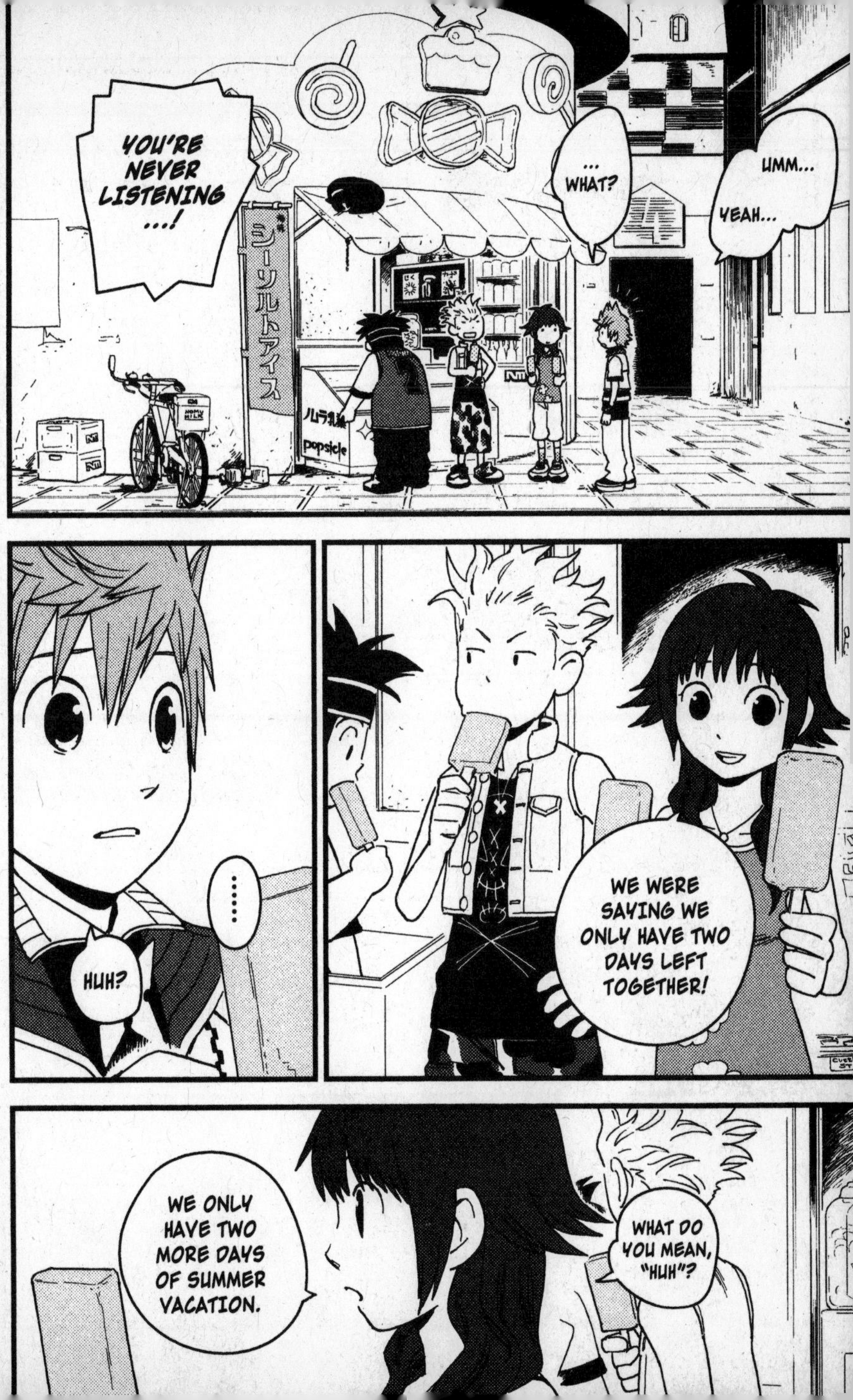
UMM... YEAH...
... WHAT?
YOU'RE NEVER LISTENING ...!
シーソルトアイス
ノムラ乳業
popsicle
WE WERE SAYING WE ONLY HAVE TWO DAYS LEFT TOGETHER!
......
HUH?
WHAT DO YOU MEAN, "HUH"?
WE ONLY HAVE TWO MORE DAYS OF SUMMER VACATION.

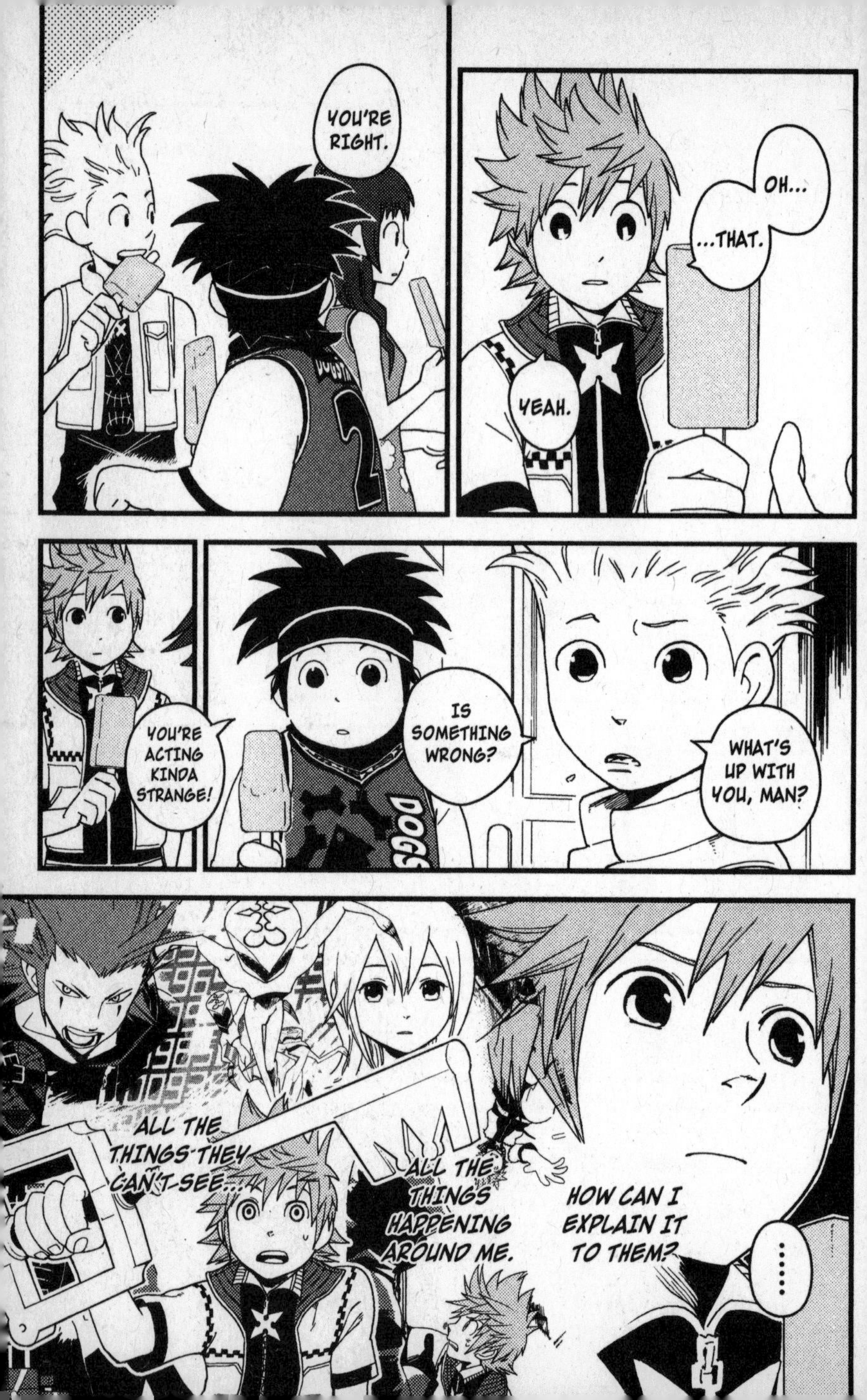
OH...
...THAT.
YEAH.
YOU'RE RIGHT.
WHAT'S UP WITH YOU, MAN?
IS SOMETHING WRONG?
YOU'RE ACTING KINDA STRANGE!
......
HOW CAN I EXPLAIN IT TO THEM?
ALL THE THINGS HAPPENING AROUND ME.
ALL THE THINGS THEY CAN'T SEE...

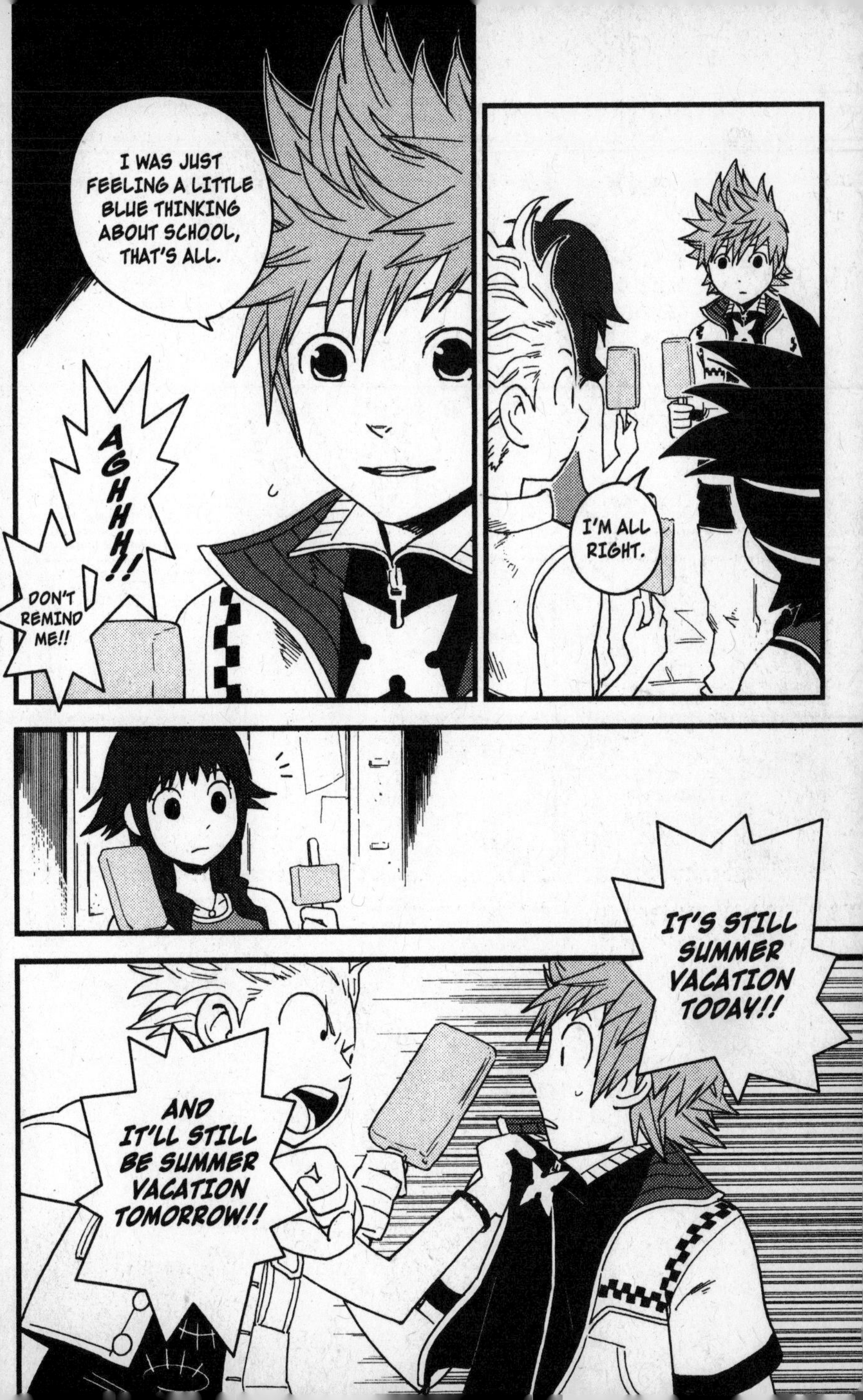
I'M ALL RIGHT.
I WAS JUST FEELING A LITTLE BLUE THINKING ABOUT SCHOOL, THAT'S ALL.
AGHHH!!
DON'T REMIND ME!!
IT'S STILL SUMMER VACATION TODAY!!
AND IT'LL STILL BE SUMMER VACATION TOMORROW!!

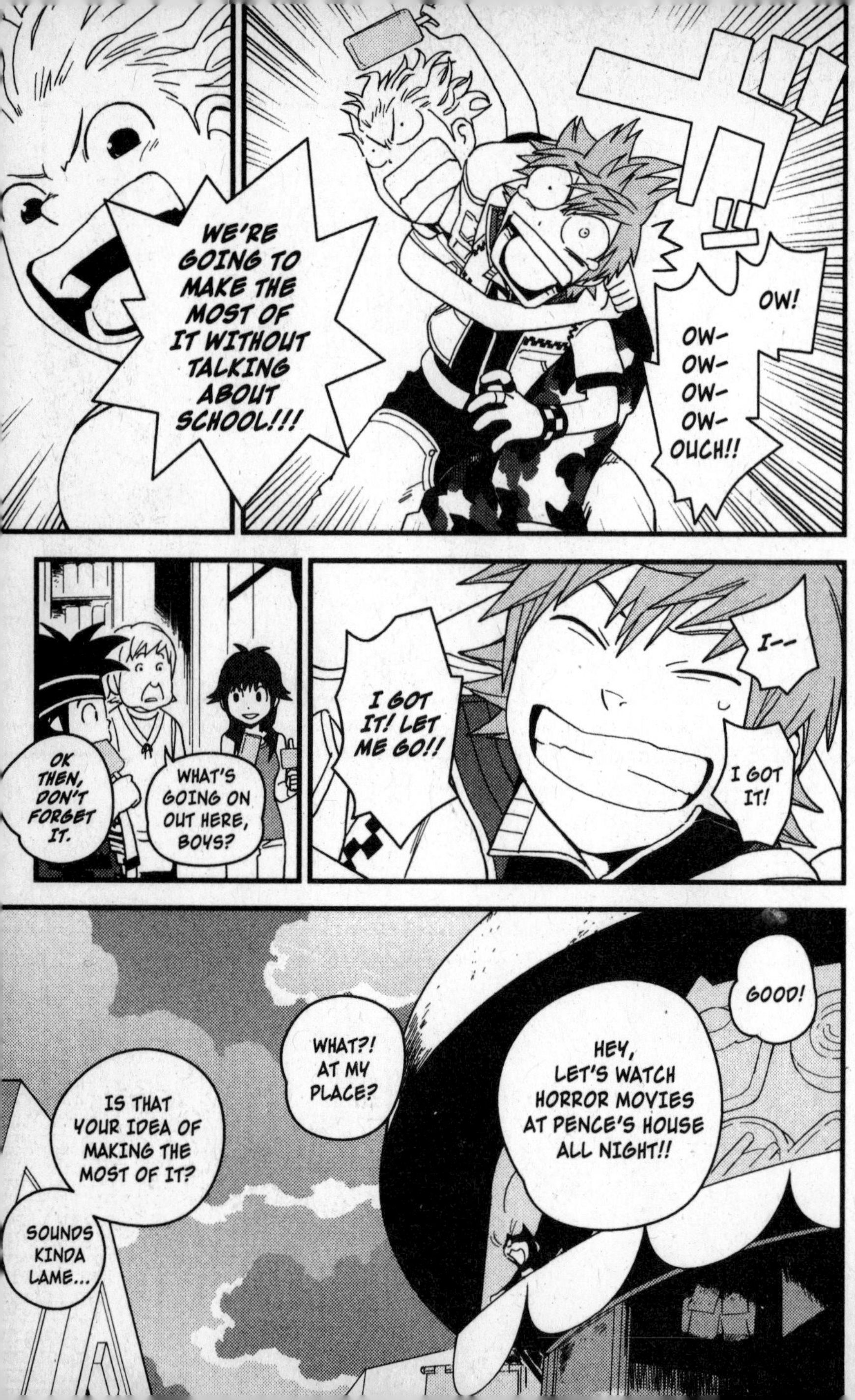
OW! OW-OW-OW-OW-OUCH!!
WE'RE GOING TO MAKE THE MOST OF IT WITHOUT TALKING ABOUT SCHOOL!!!
I--
I GOT IT!
I GOT IT! LET ME GO!!
WHAT'S GOING ON OUT HERE, BOYS?
OK THEN, DON'T FORGET IT.
GOOD!
HEY, LET'S WATCH HORROR MOVIES AT PENCE'S HOUSE ALL NIGHT!!
WHAT?! AT MY PLACE?
IS THAT YOUR IDEA OF MAKING THE MOST OF IT?
SOUNDS KINDA LAME...

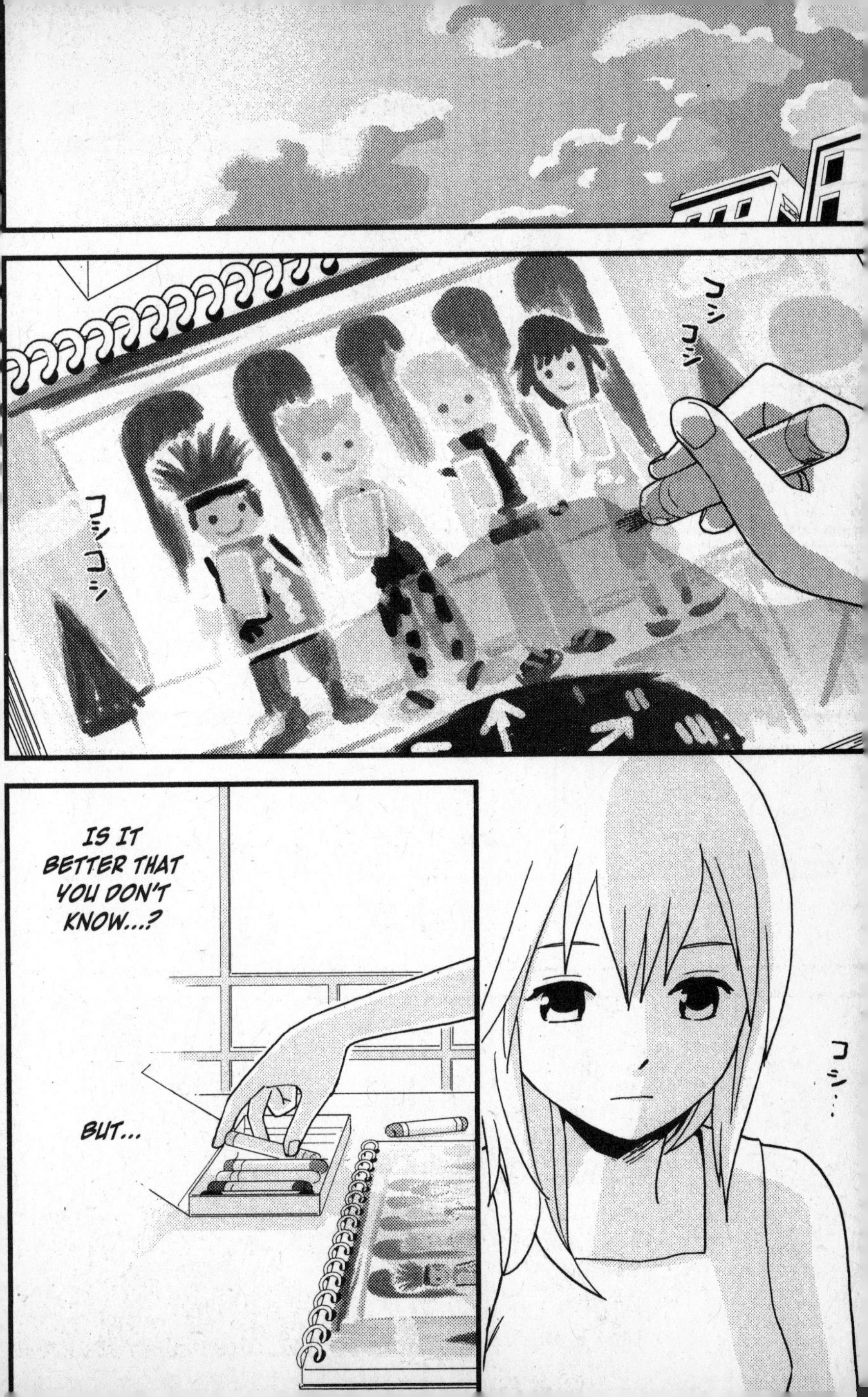

コシ コシ
コシ コシ
コシ…
IS IT BETTER THAT YOU DON'T KNOW...?
BUT...

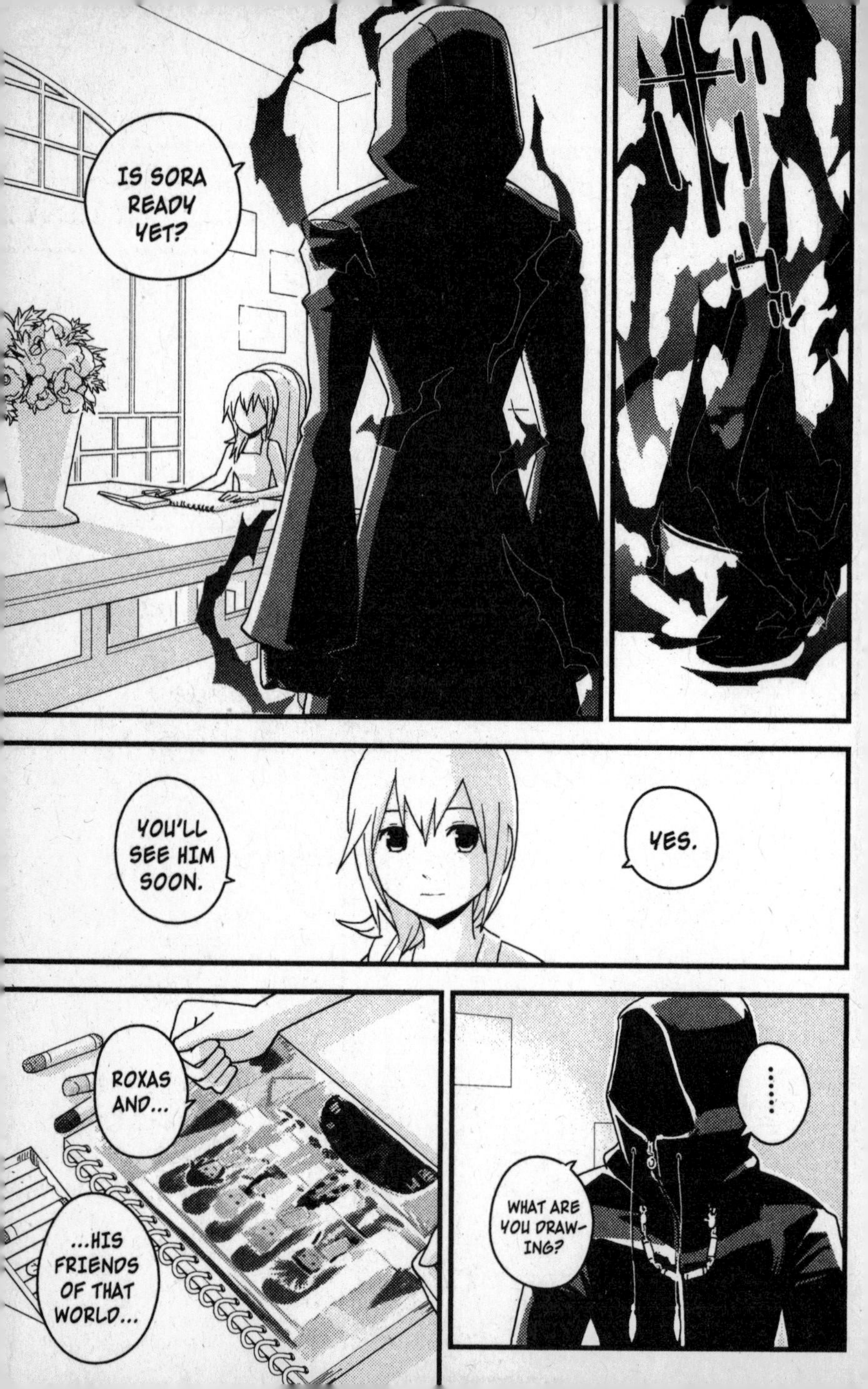
IS SORA READY YET?
YES.
YOU'LL SEE HIM SOON.
......
WHAT ARE YOU DRAWING?
ROXAS AND...
...HIS FRIENDS OF THAT WORLD...

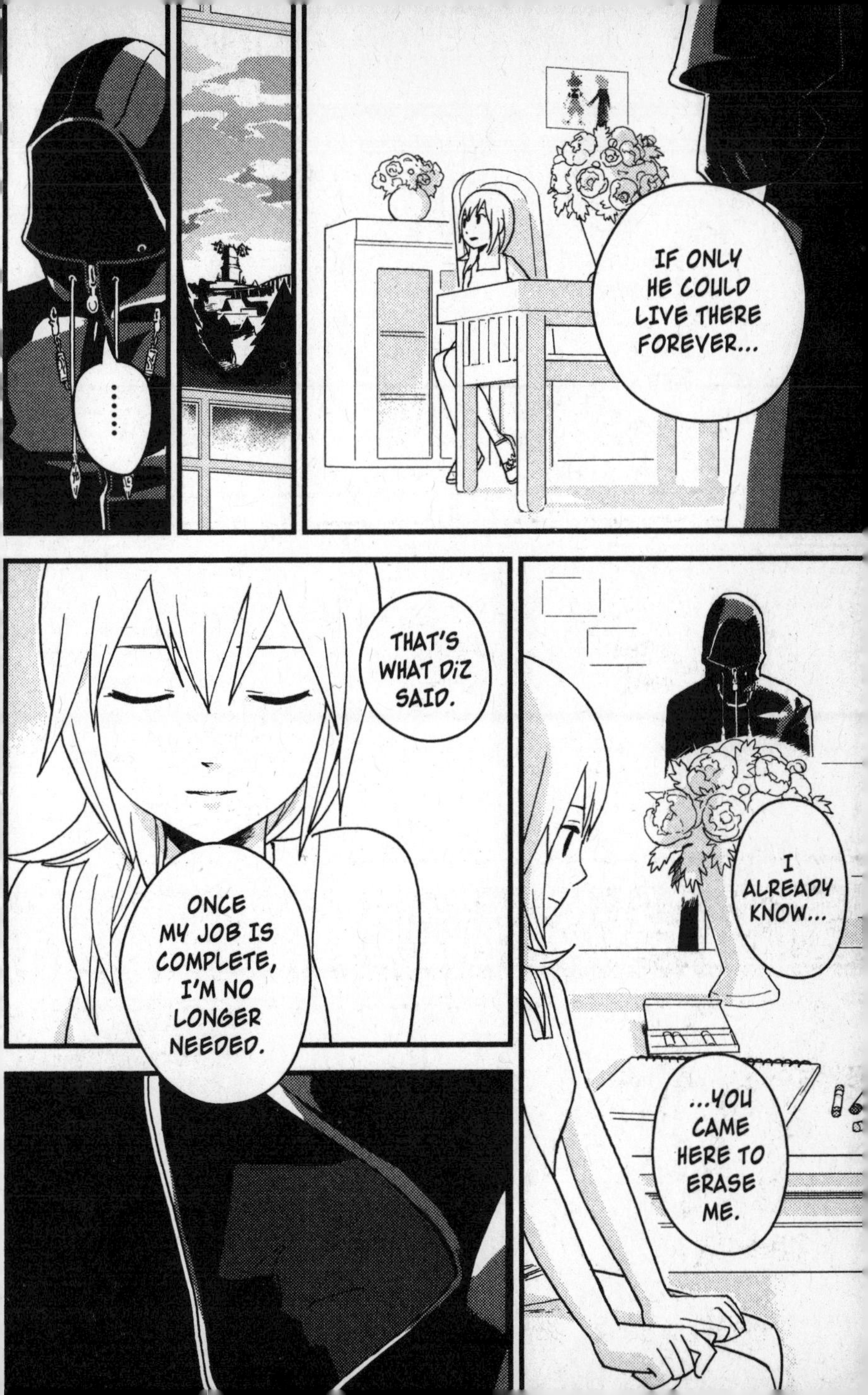
IF ONLY HE COULD LIVE THERE FOREVER...
......
I ALREADY KNOW...
...YOU CAME HERE TO ERASE ME.
THAT'S WHAT DiZ SAID.
ONCE MY JOB IS COMPLETE, I'M NO LONGER NEEDED.

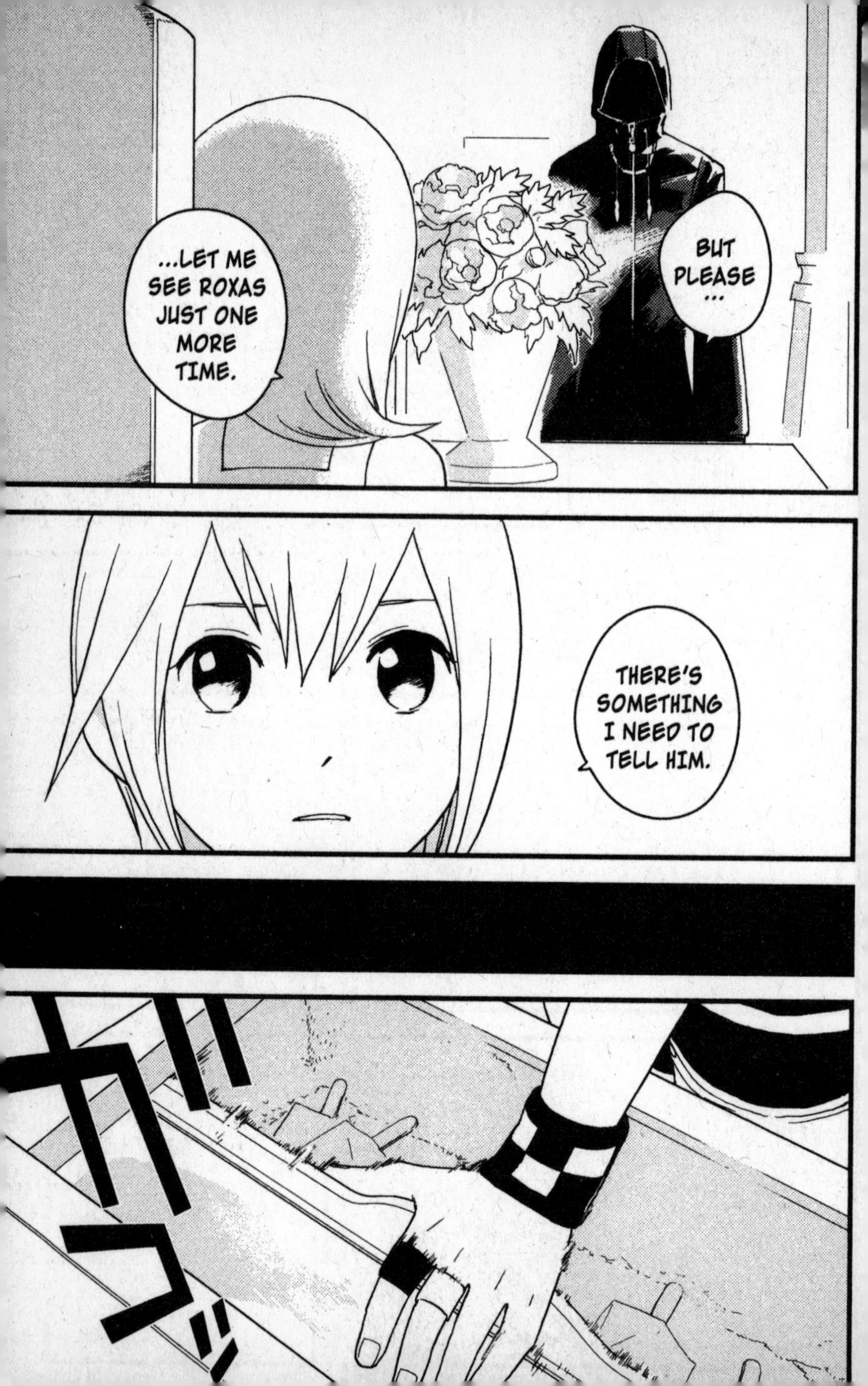
BUT PLEASE...
...LET ME SEE ROXAS JUST ONE MORE TIME.
THERE'S SOMETHING I NEED TO TELL HIM.

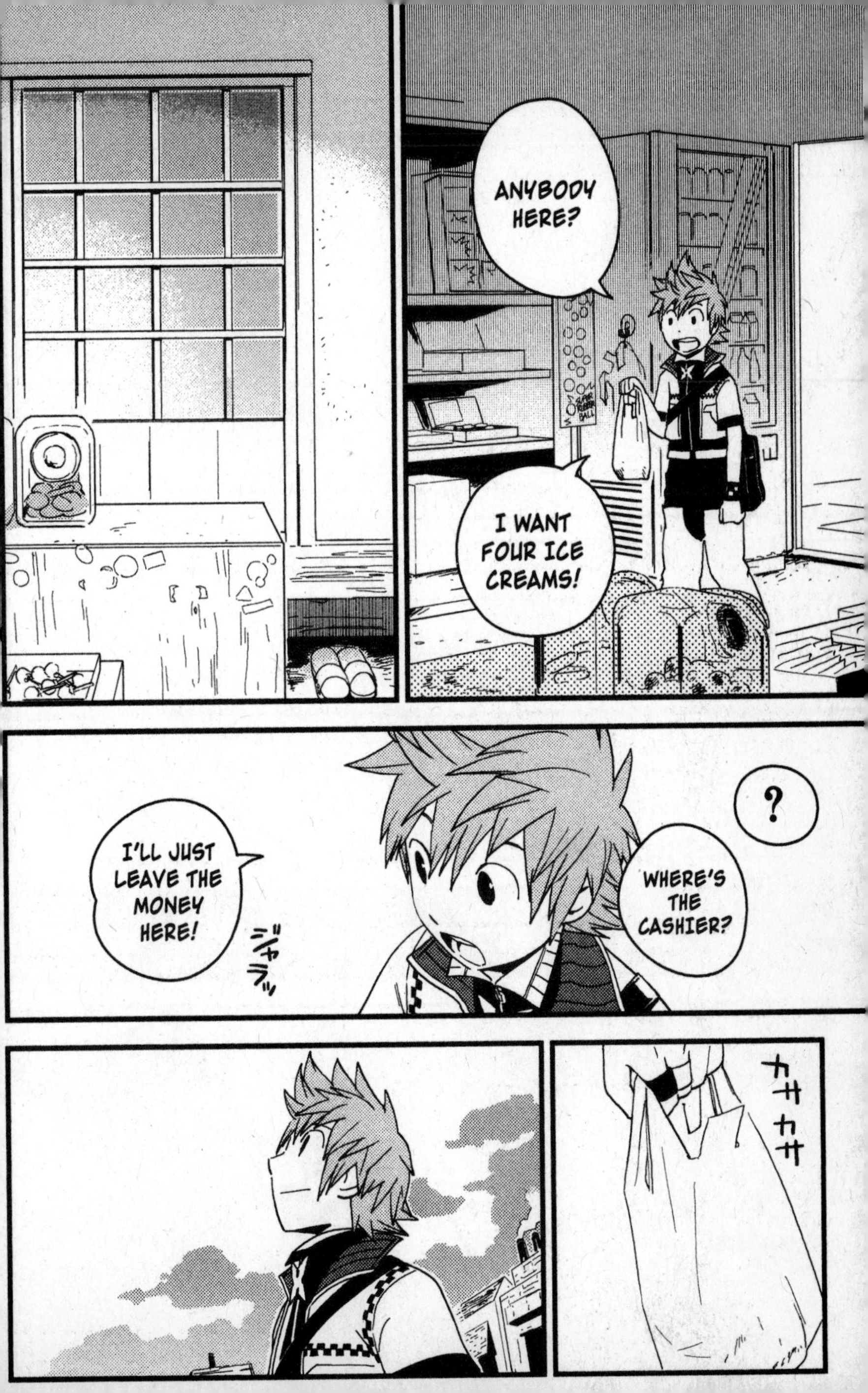
ANYBODY HERE?
I WANT FOUR ICE CREAMS!
?
WHERE'S THE CASHIER?
ジャラッ
I'LL JUST LEAVE THE MONEY HERE!
カサ カサ

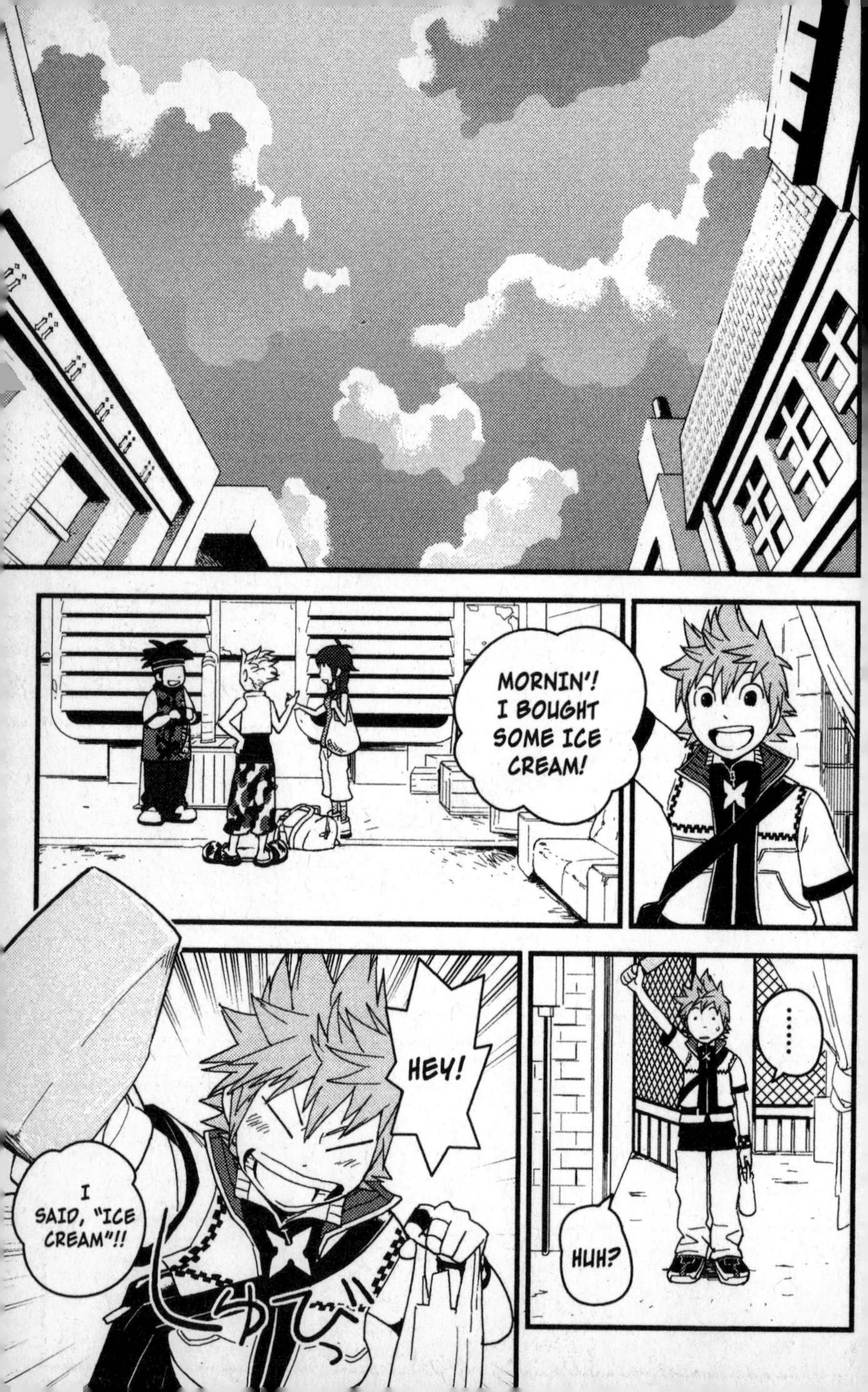
MORNIN'! I BOUGHT SOME ICE CREAM!
......
HUH?
HEY!
I SAID, "ICE CREAM"!!

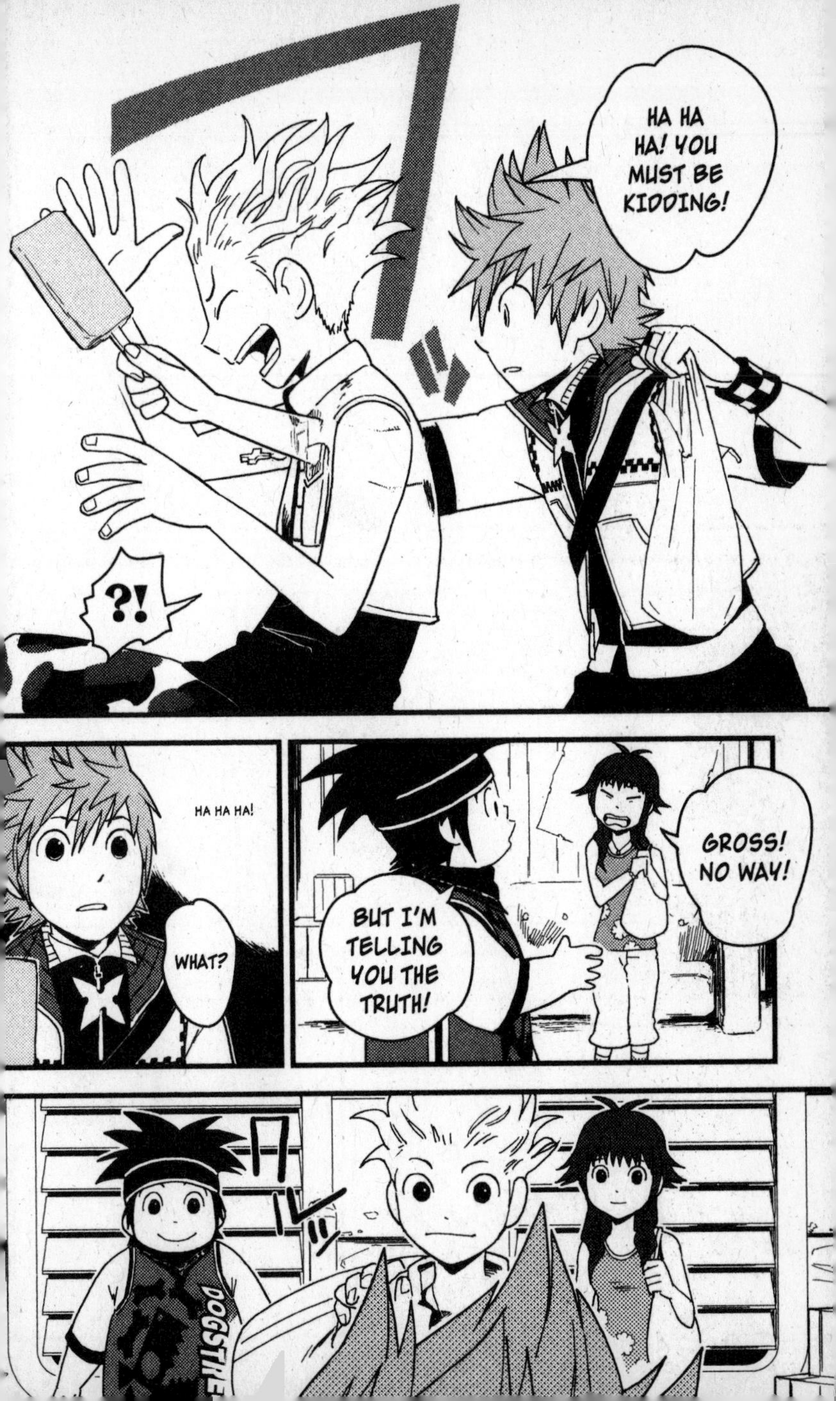
HA HA HA! YOU MUST BE KIDDING!
?!
GROSS! NO WAY!
BUT I'M TELLING YOU THE TRUTH!
HA HA HA!
WHAT?

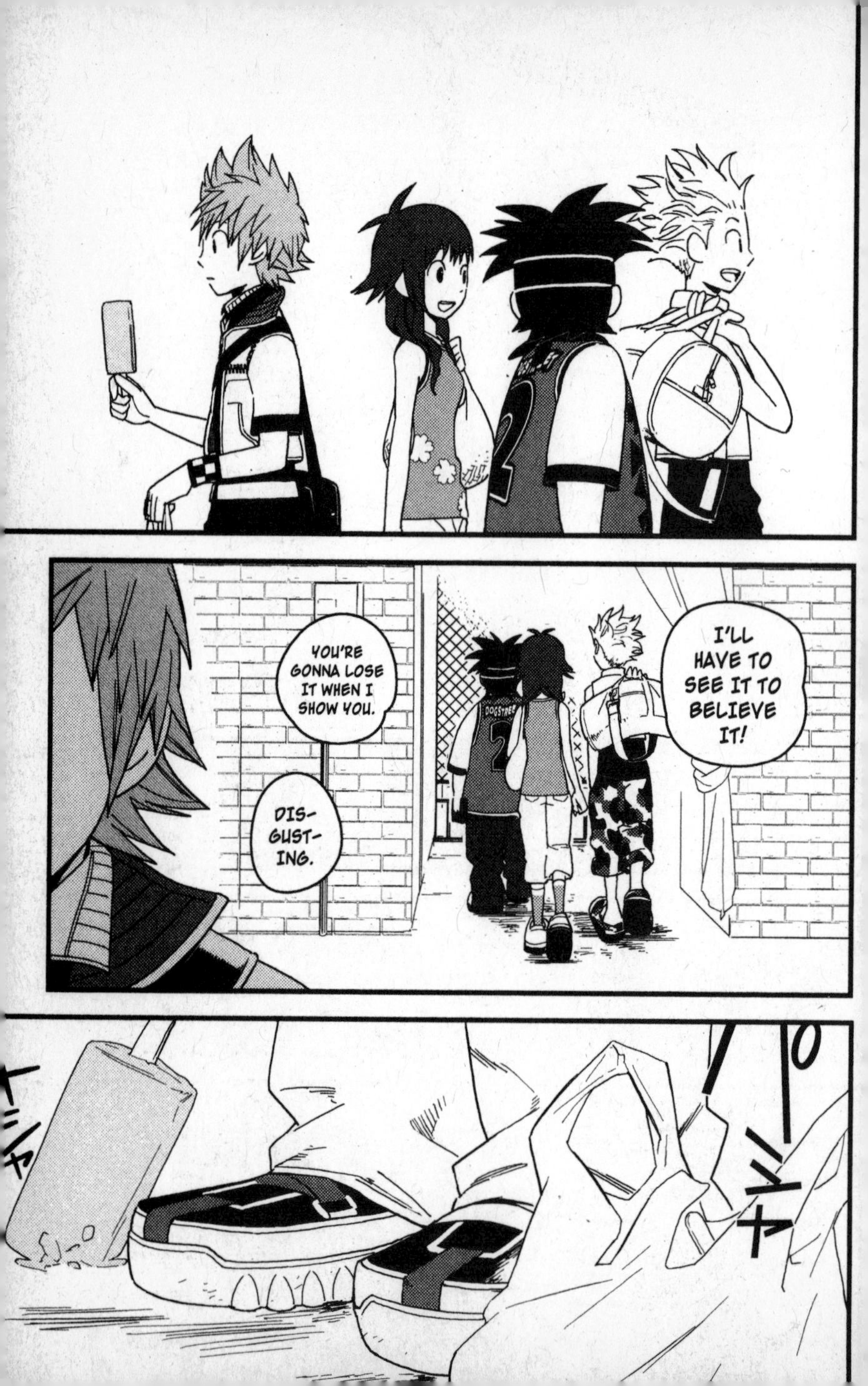
I'LL HAVE TO SEE IT TO BELIEVE IT!
YOU'RE GONNA LOSE IT WHEN I SHOW YOU.
DIS-GUST-ING.

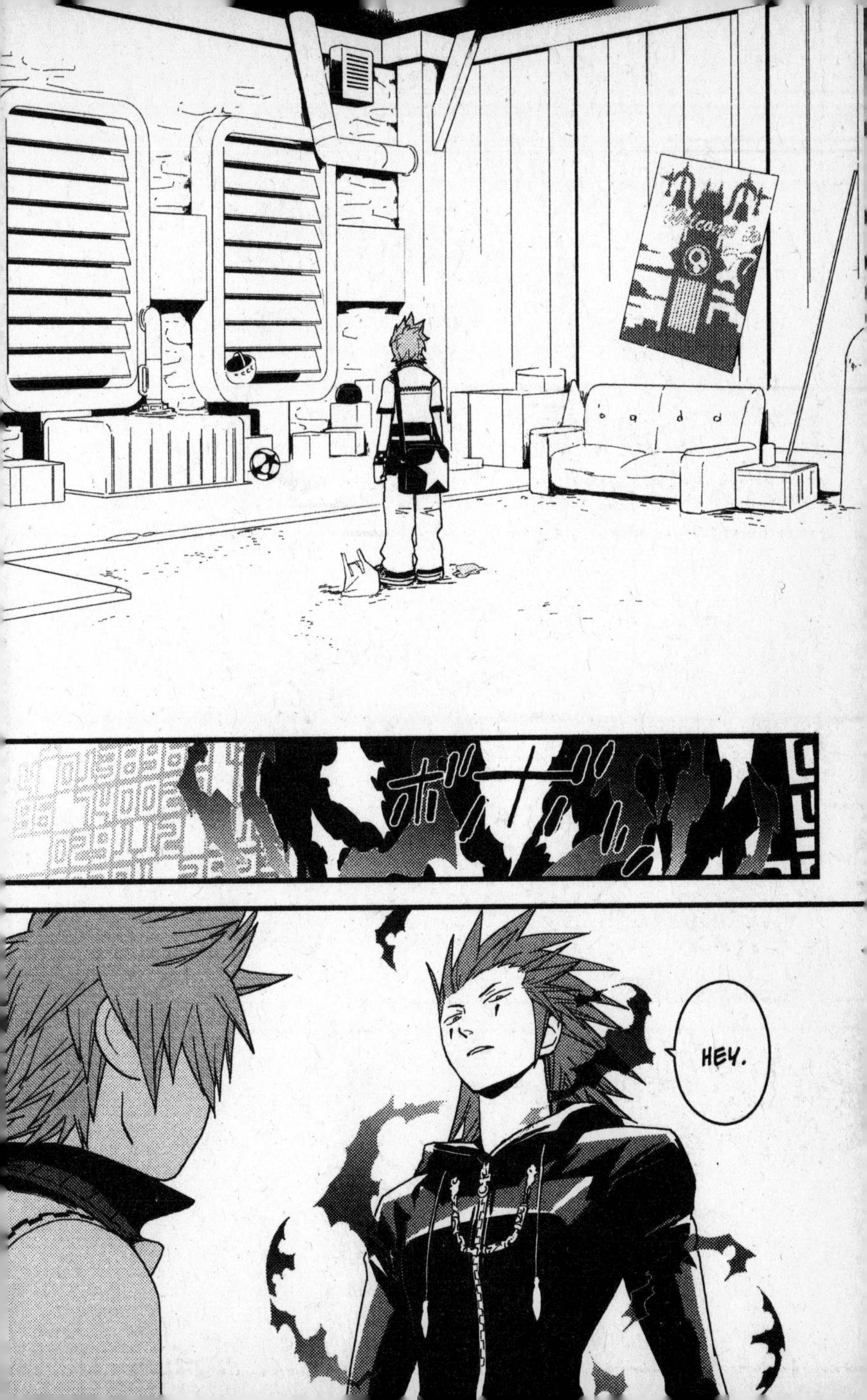
HEY.

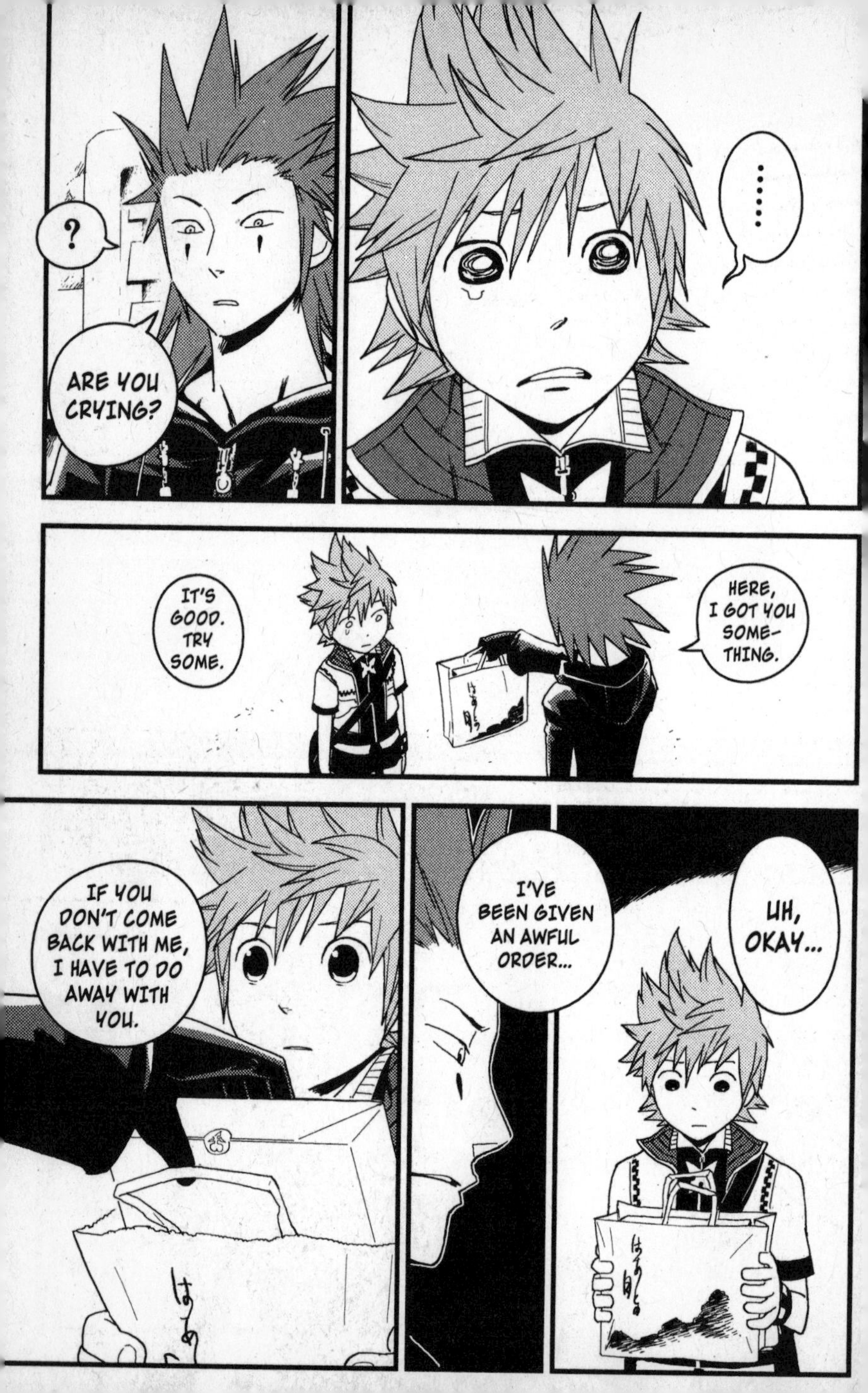
......
?
ARE YOU CRYING?
HERE, I GOT YOU SOME-THING.
IT'S GOOD. TRY SOME.
UH, OKAY...
I'VE BEEN GIVEN AN AWFUL ORDER...
IF YOU DON'T COME BACK WITH ME, I HAVE TO DO AWAY WITH YOU.

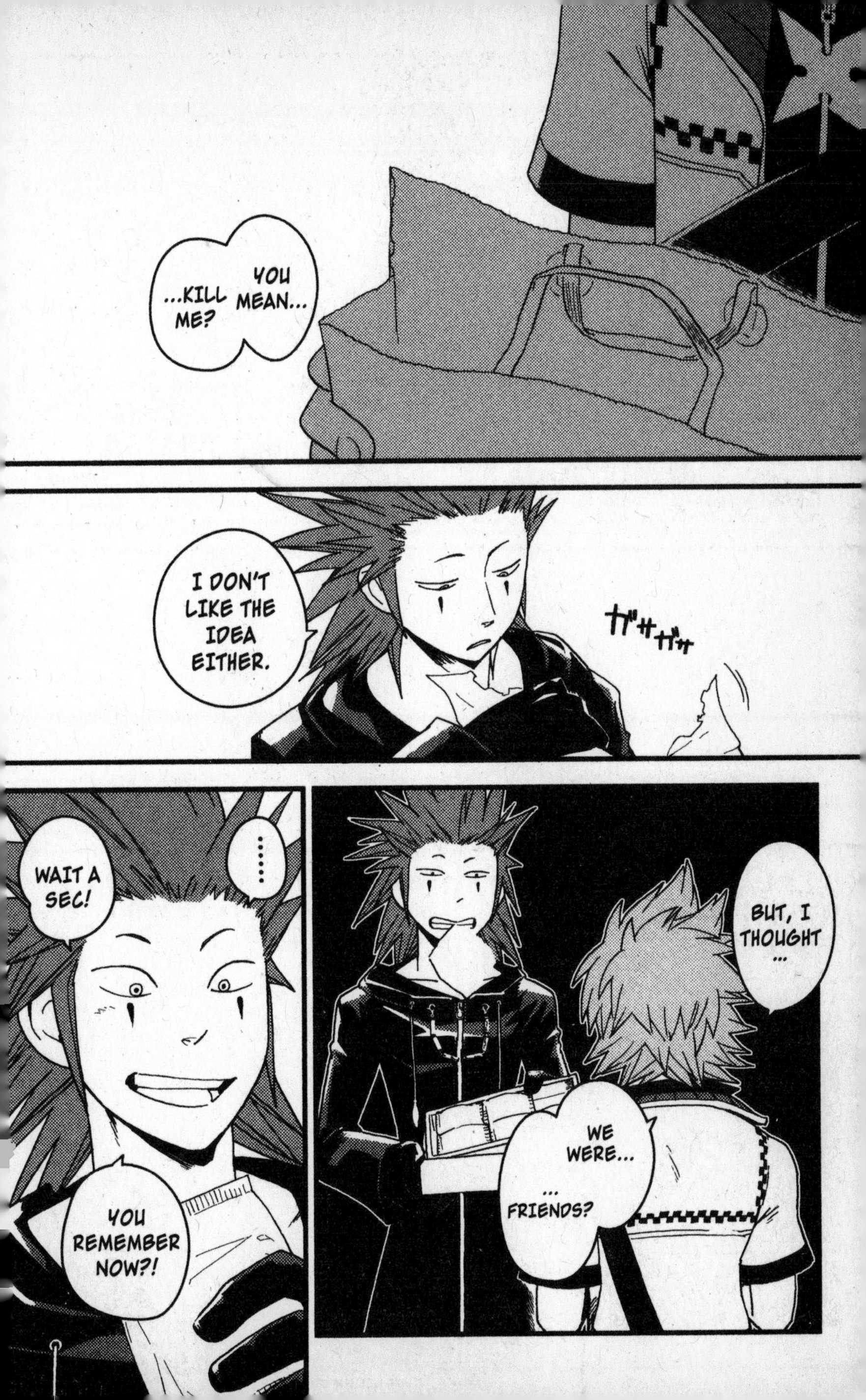
YOU MEAN...
...KILL ME?
I DON'T LIKE THE IDEA EITHER.
ガサガサ
BUT, I THOUGHT ...
WE WERE...
... FRIENDS?
......
WAIT A SEC!
YOU REMEMBER NOW?!

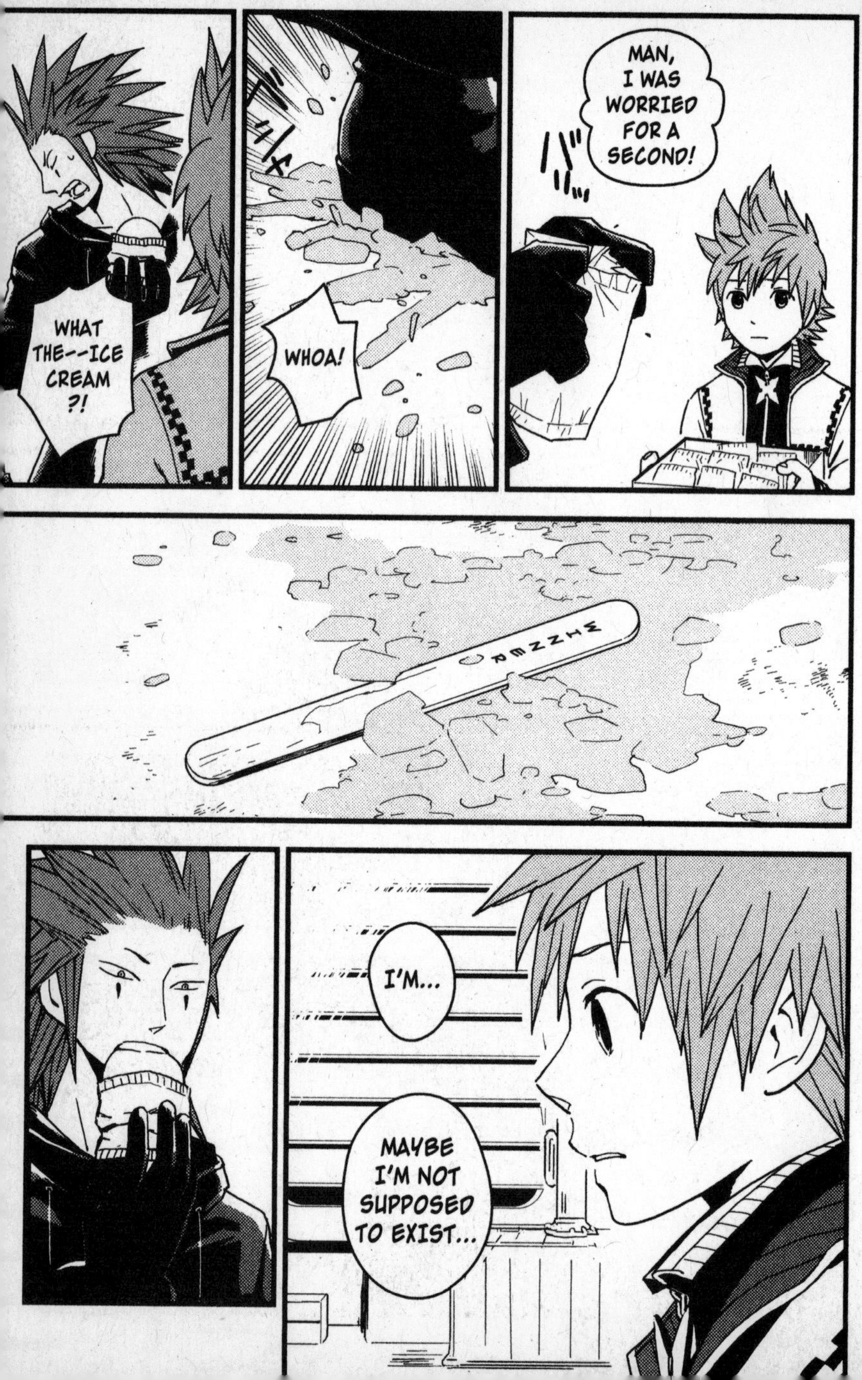

MAN, I WAS WORRIED FOR A SECOND!
WHOA!
WHAT THE--ICE CREAM ?!
I'M...
MAYBE I'M NOT SUPPOSED TO EXIST...

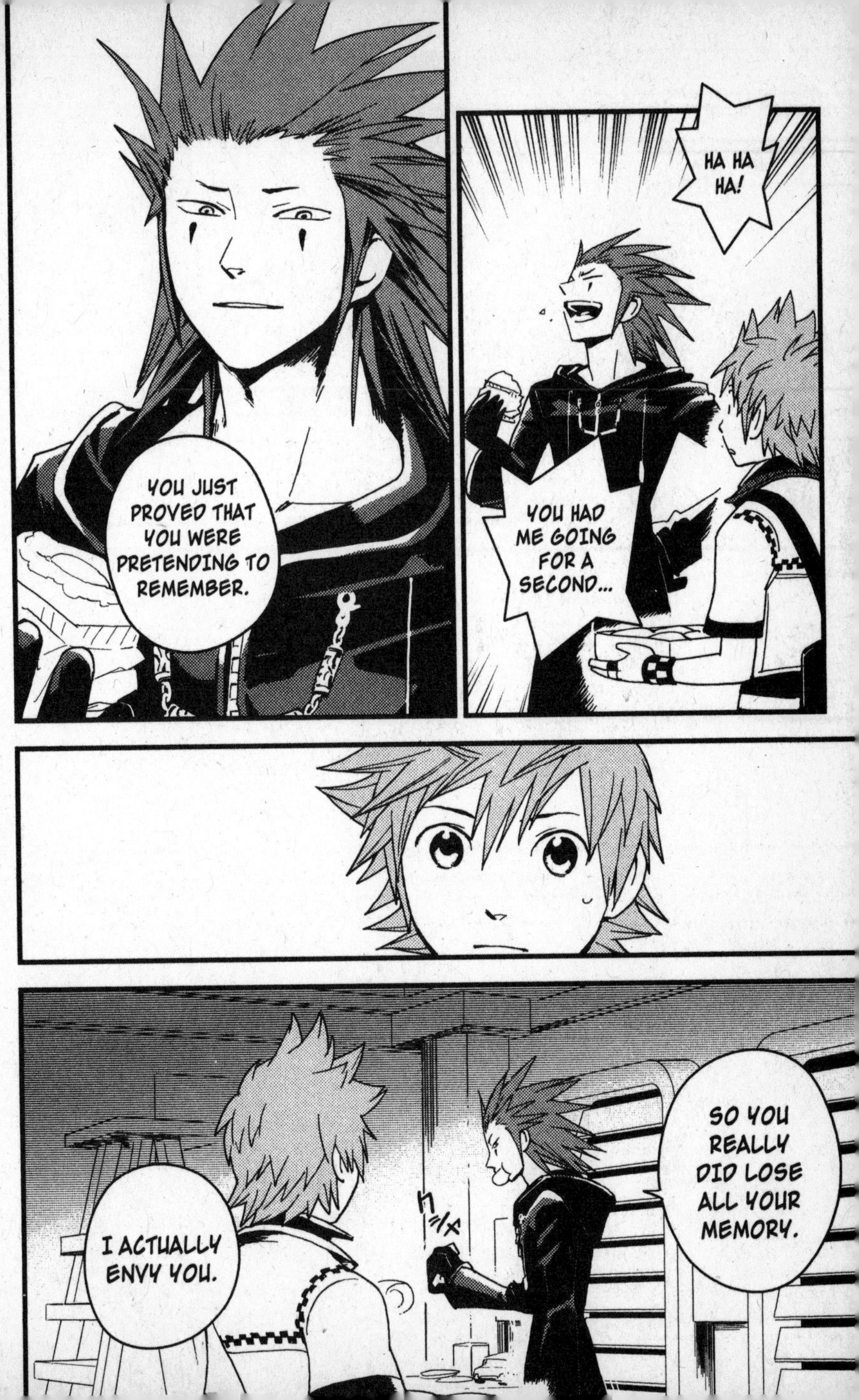
HA HA HA!
YOU HAD ME GOING FOR A SECOND...
YOU JUST PROVED THAT YOU WERE PRETENDING TO REMEMBER.
SO YOU REALLY DID LOSE ALL YOUR MEMORY.
I ACTUALLY ENVY YOU.

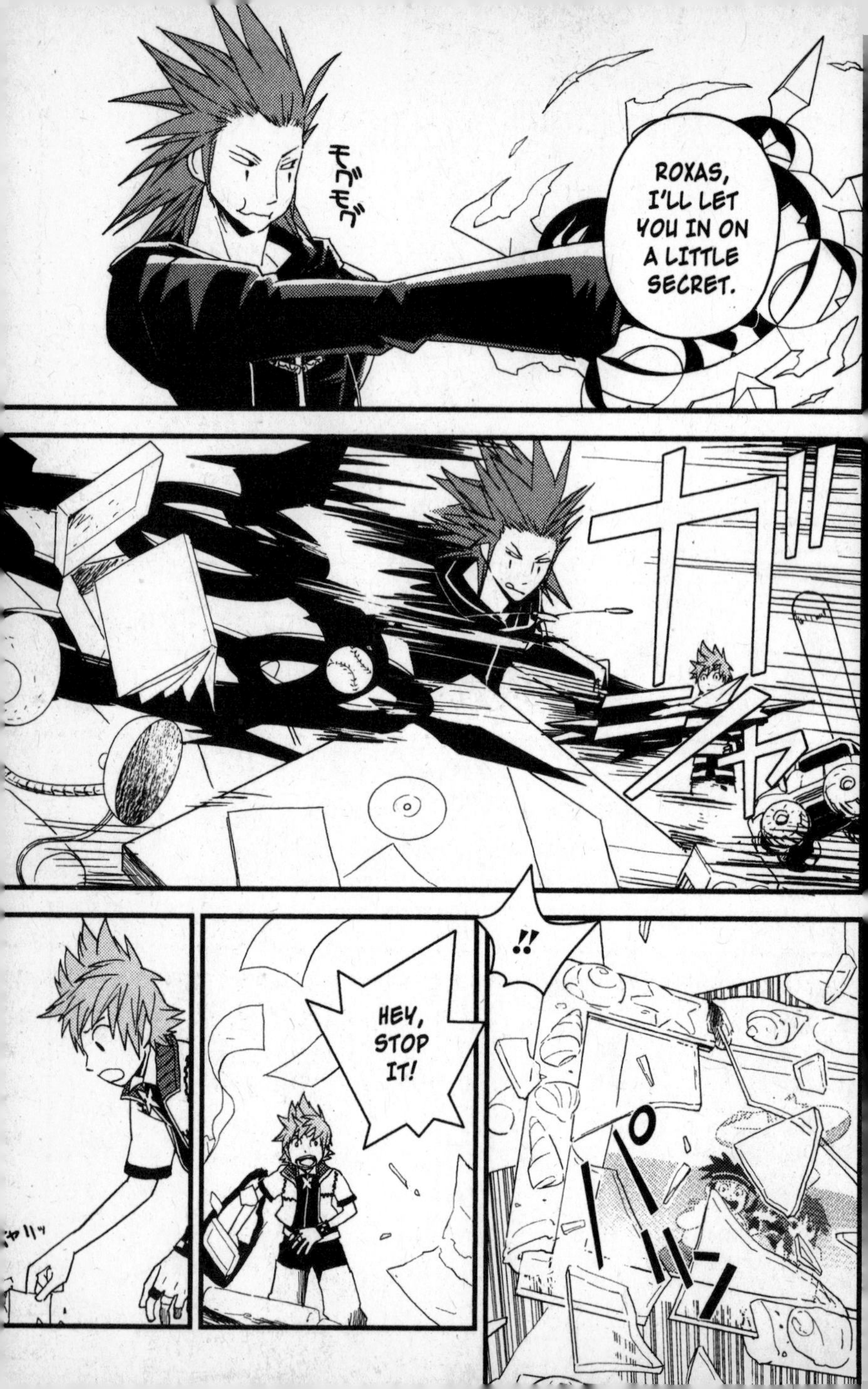

ROXAS, I'LL LET YOU IN ON A LITTLE SECRET.
モグモグ
!!
HEY, STOP IT!

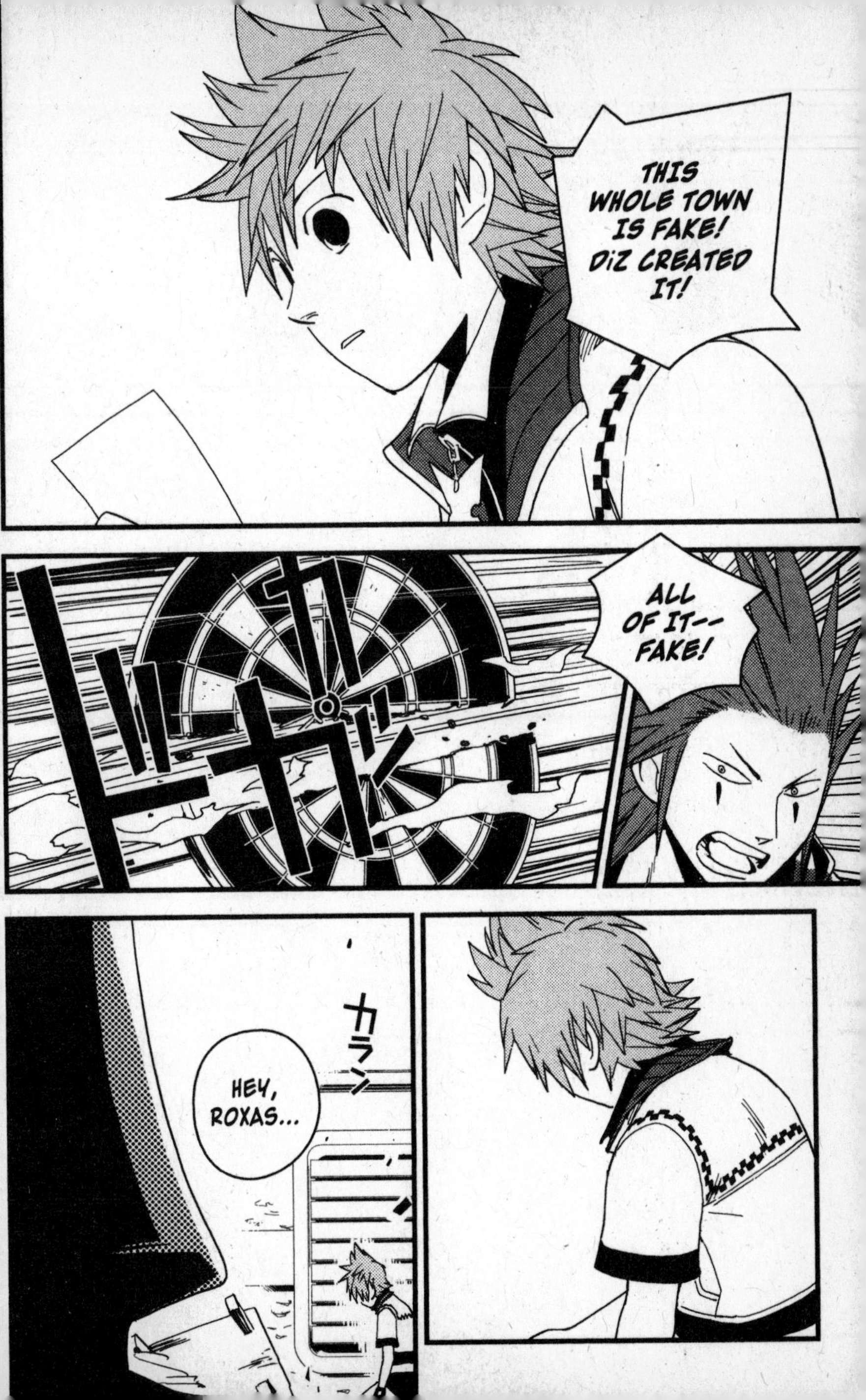
THIS WHOLE TOWN IS FAKE! DiZ CREATED IT!
ALL OF IT--FAKE!
ドカッ
ドギャ
カラン
HEY, ROXAS...

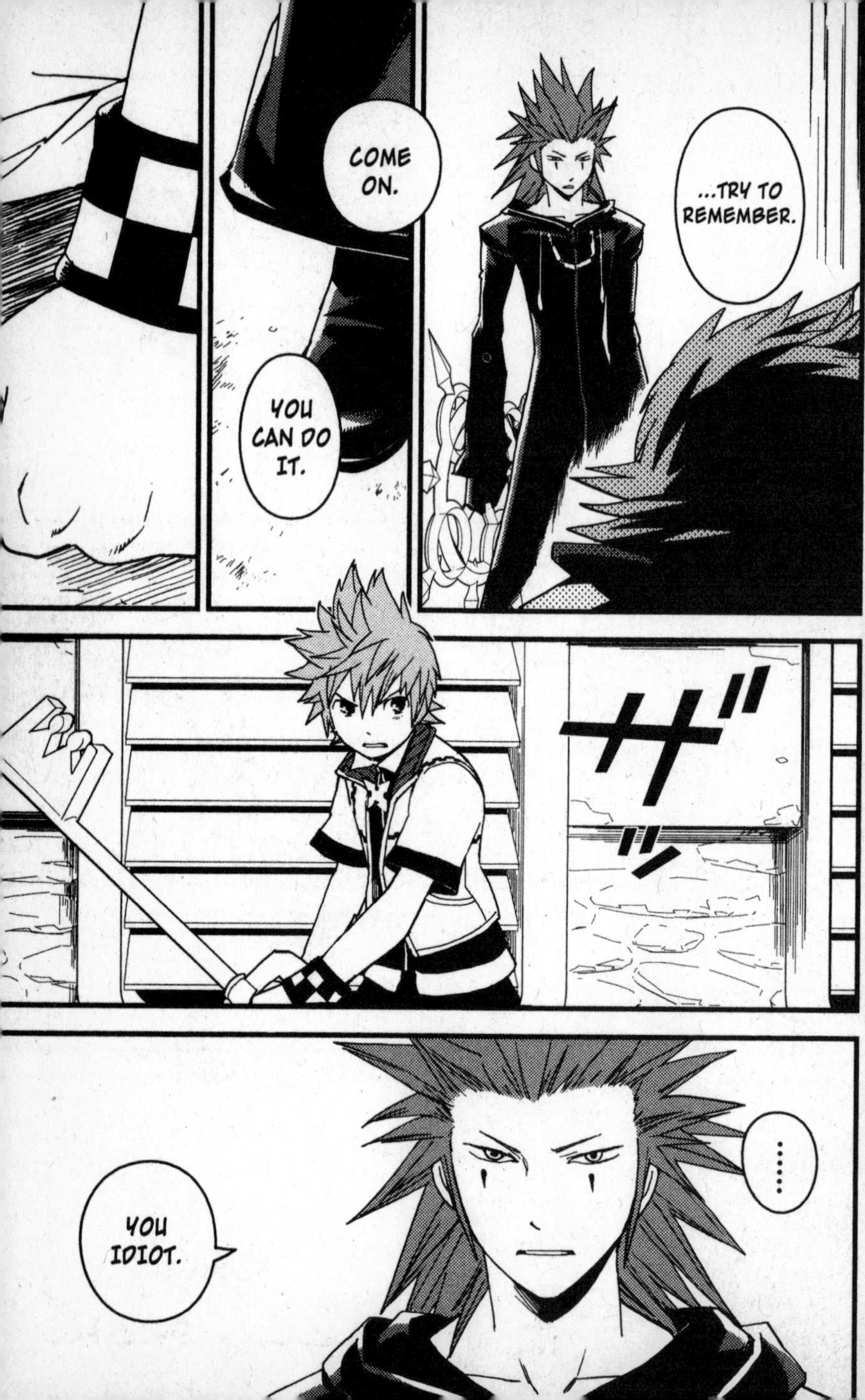
...TRY TO REMEMBER.
COME ON.
YOU CAN DO IT.
ザッ
......
YOU IDIOT.

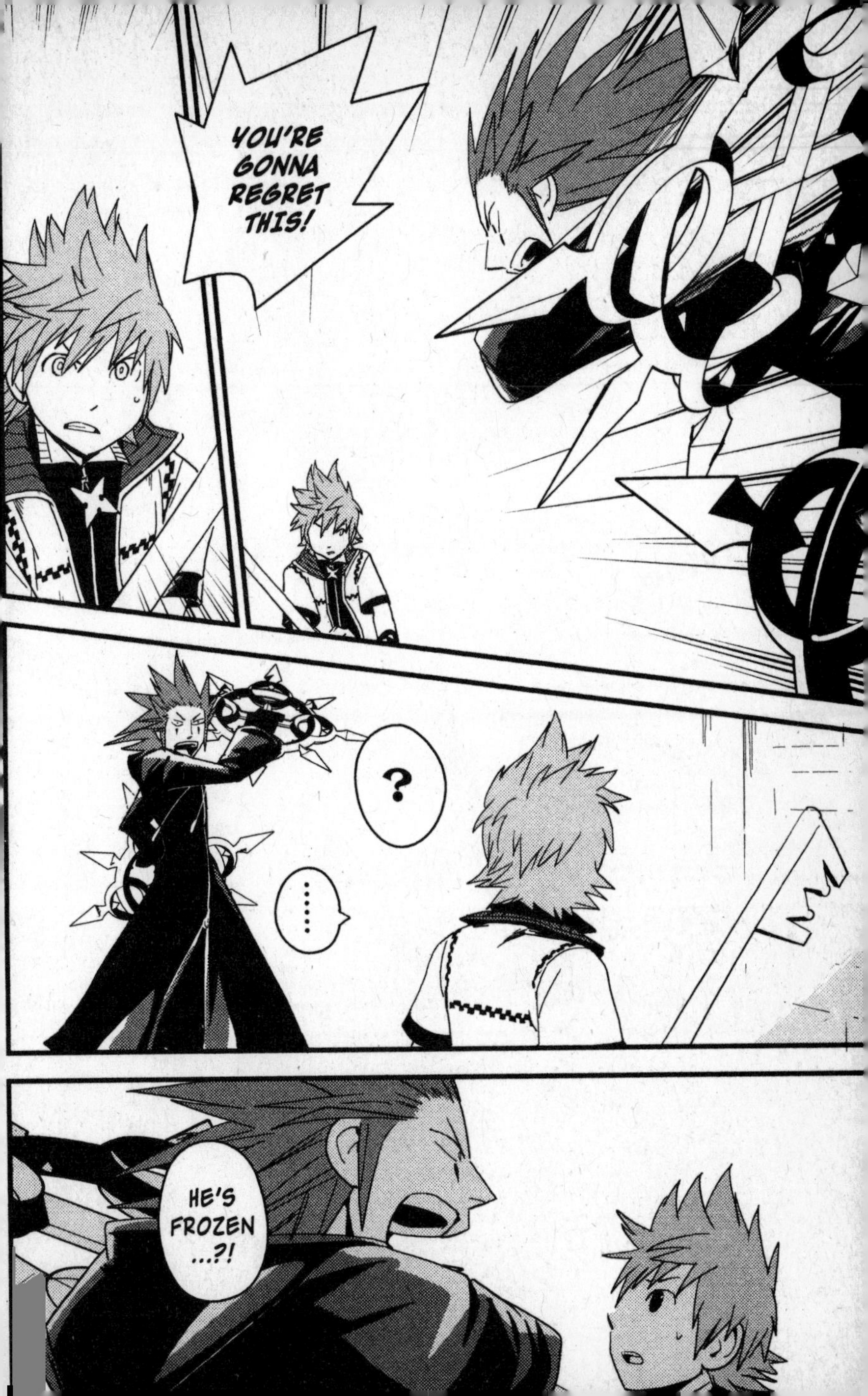
YOU'RE GONNA REGRET THIS!
?
......
HE'S FROZEN ...?!

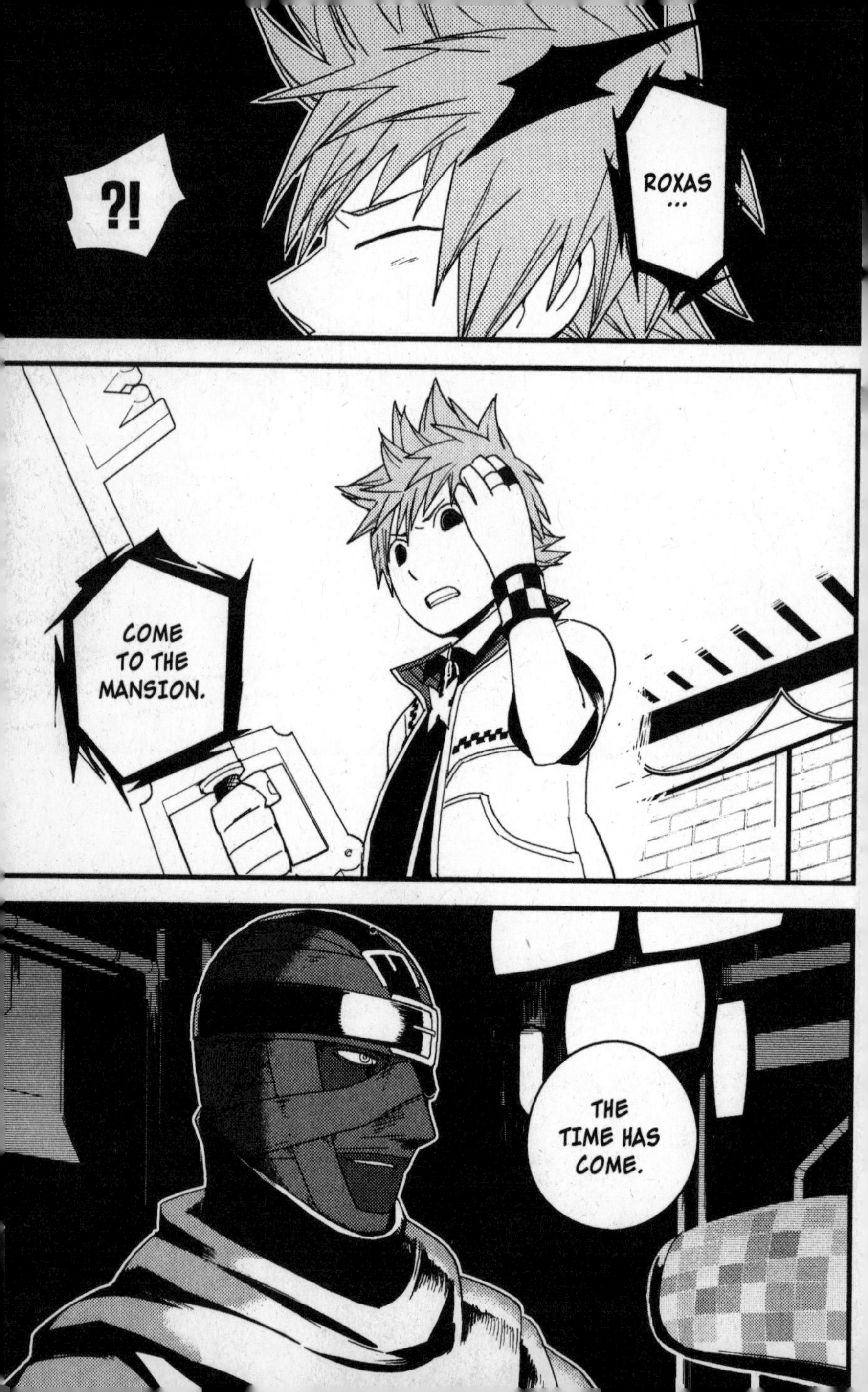
ROXAS ...
?!
COME TO THE MANSION.
THE TIME HAS COME.

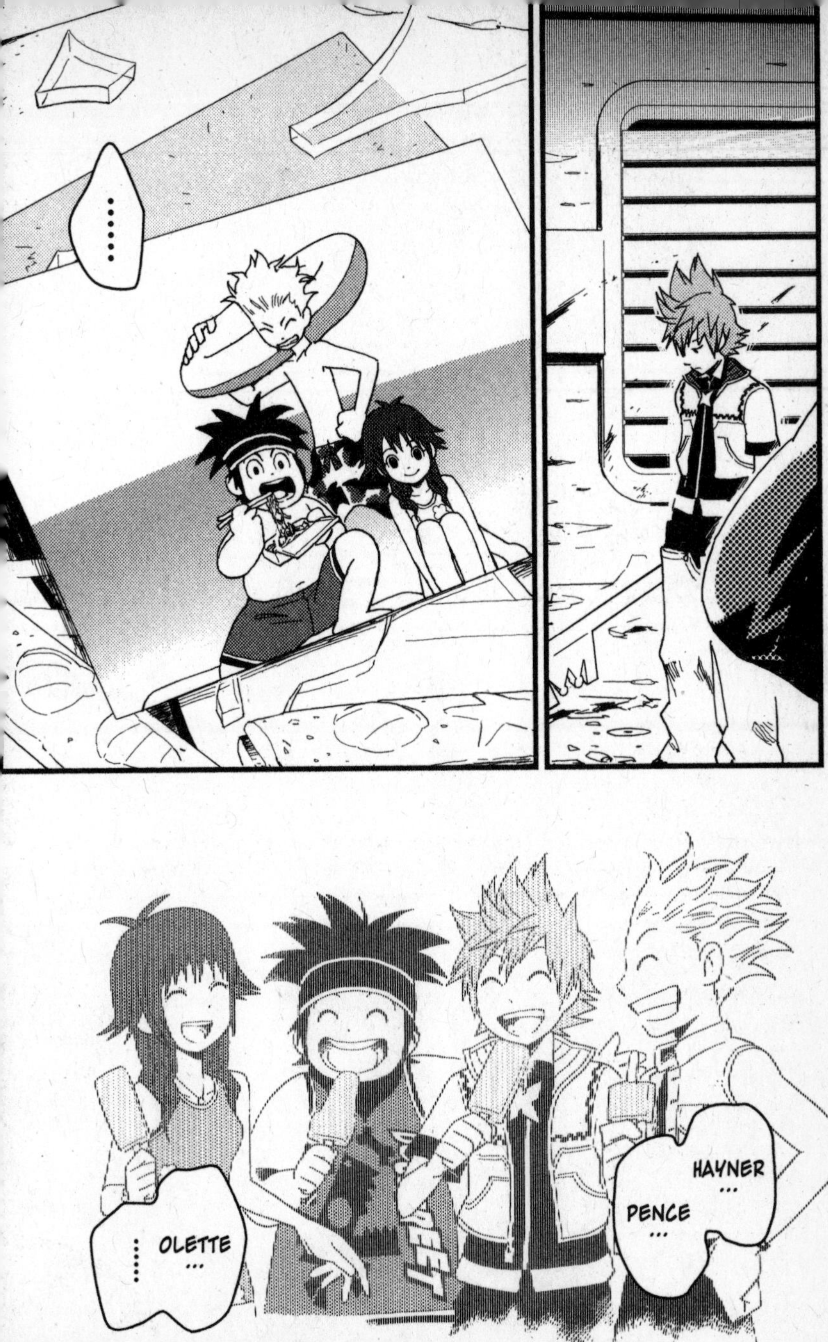
......
HAYNER ... PENCE ...
OLETTE ... .

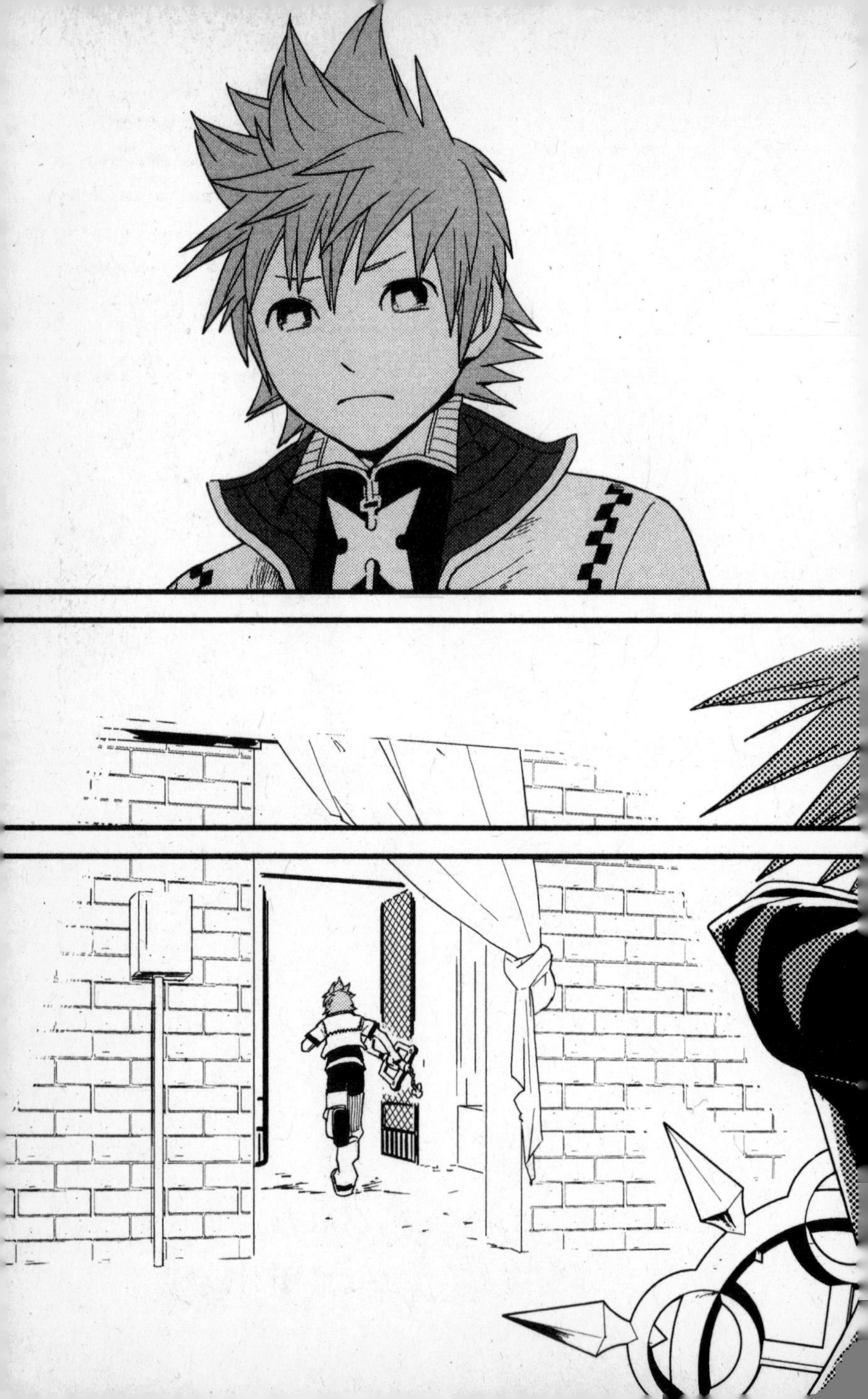

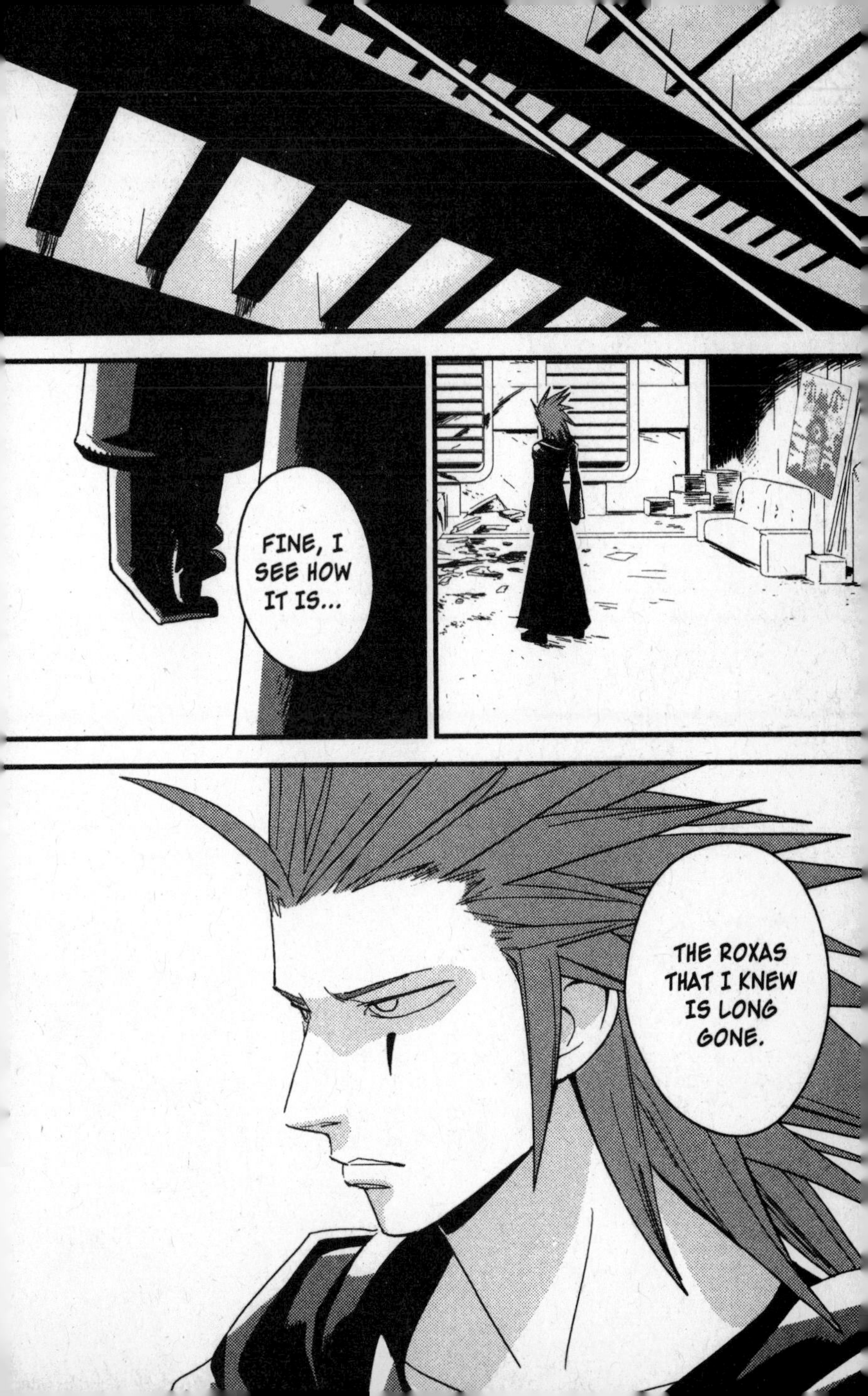
FINE, I SEE HOW IT IS...
THE ROXAS THAT I KNEW IS LONG GONE.

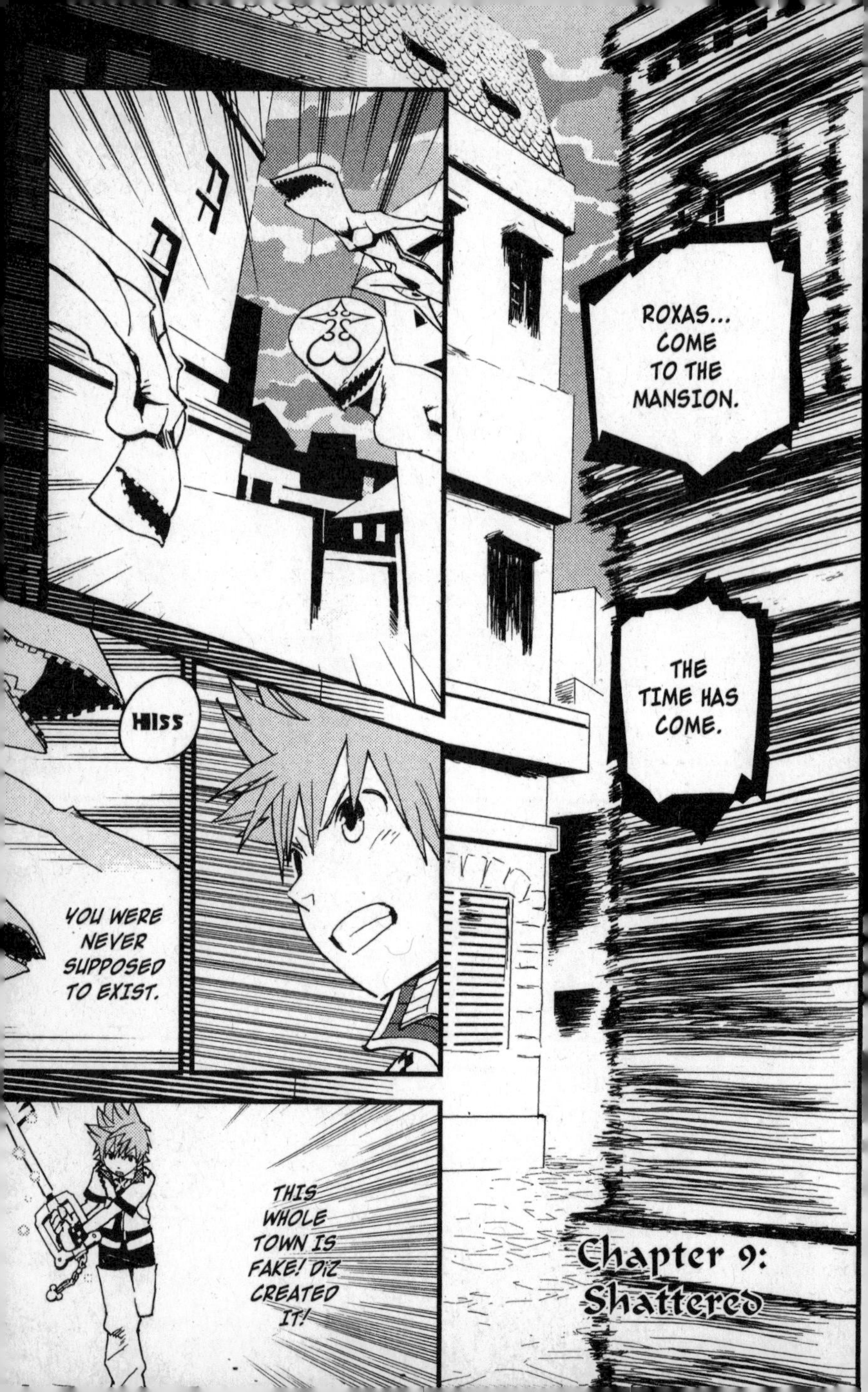
ROXAS... COME TO THE MANSION.
THE TIME HAS COME.
HISS
YOU WERE NEVER SUPPOSED TO EXIST.
THIS WHOLE TOWN IS FAKE! DiZ CREATED IT!
Chapter 9: Shattered

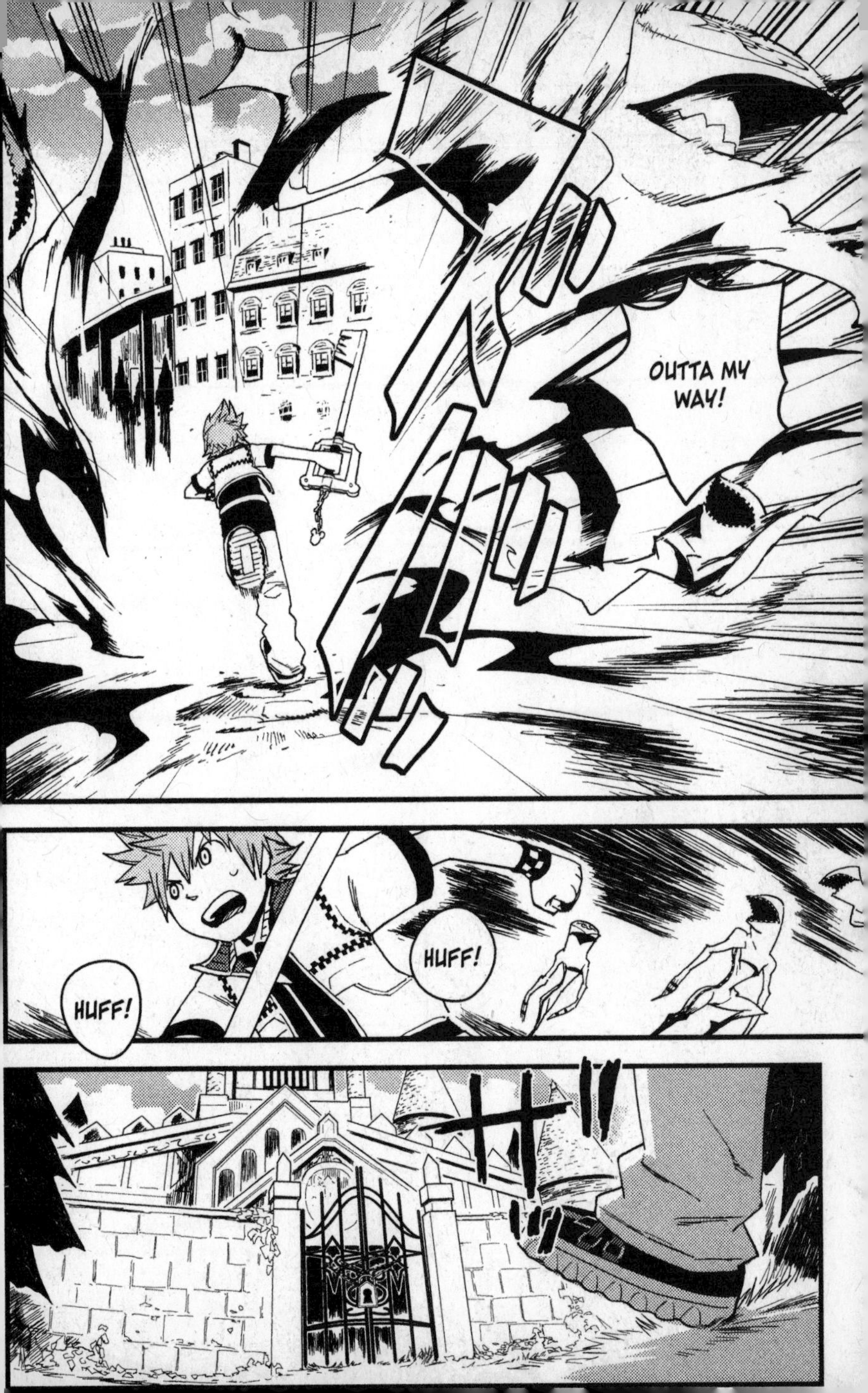
OUTTA MY WAY!
HUFF!
HUFF!

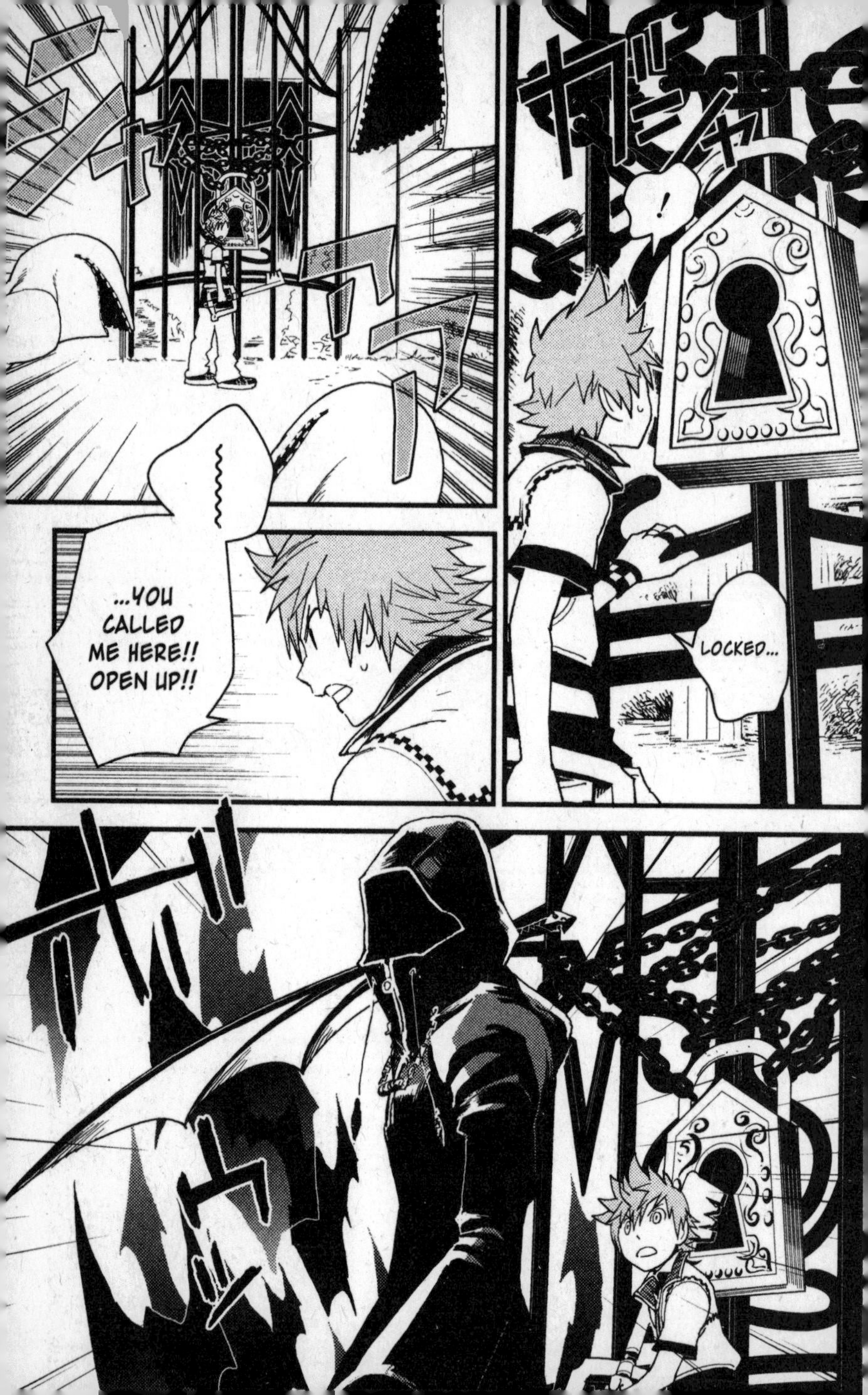
!
LOCKED...
...YOU CALLED ME HERE!! OPEN UP!!

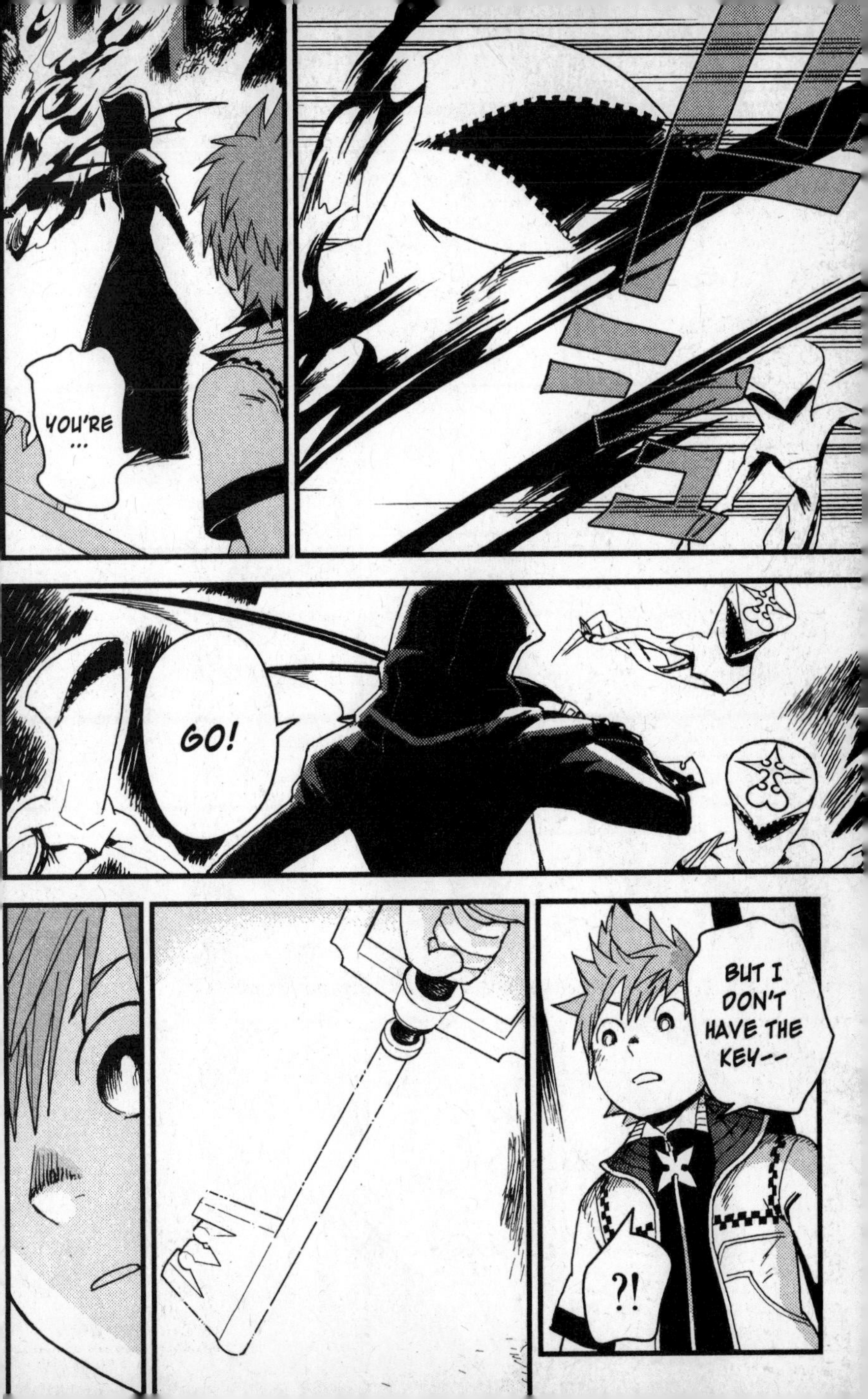
YOU'RE ...
GO!
BUT I DON'T HAVE THE KEY--
?!

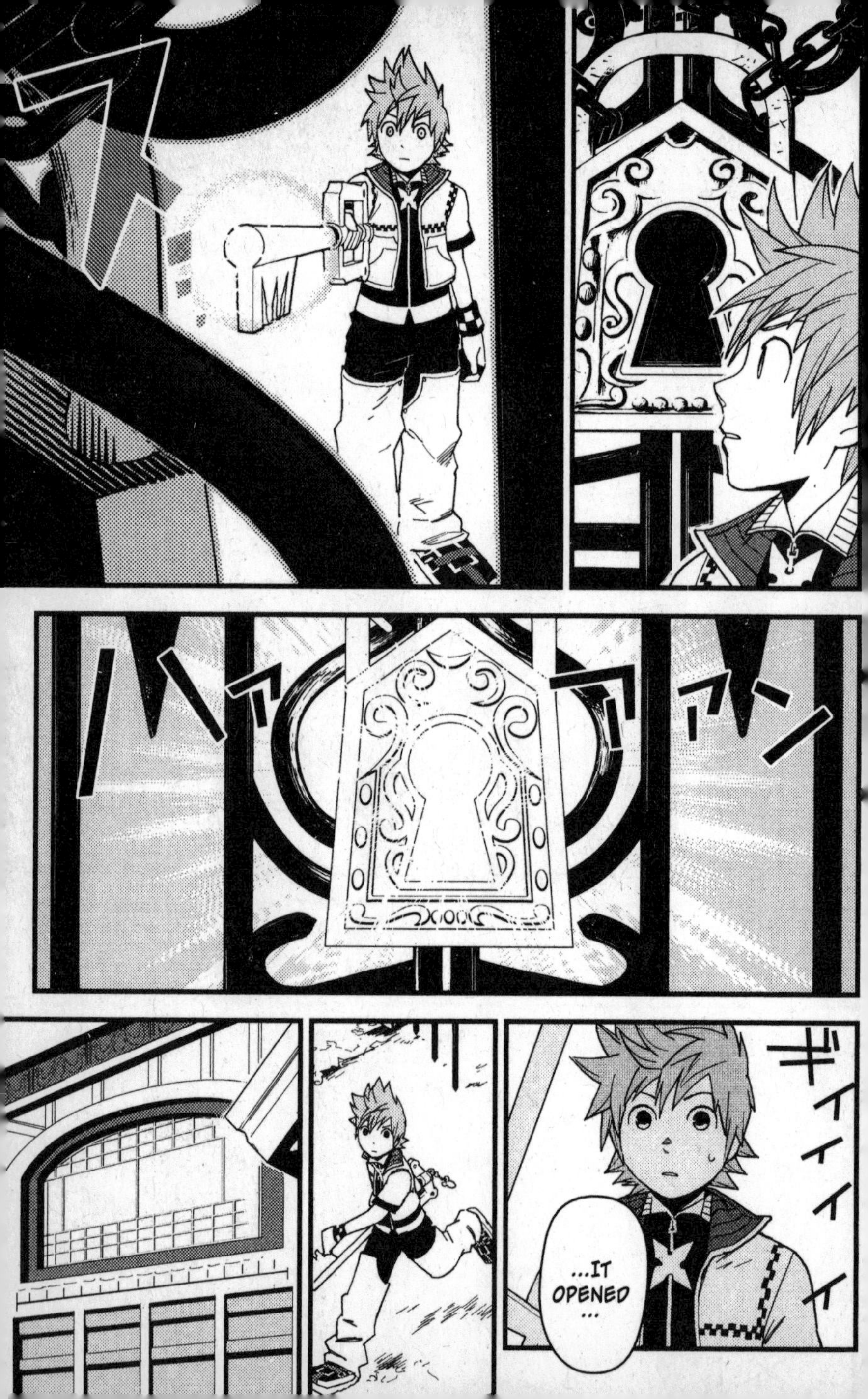
ハアアアン
ギイイイイ
...IT OPENED ...

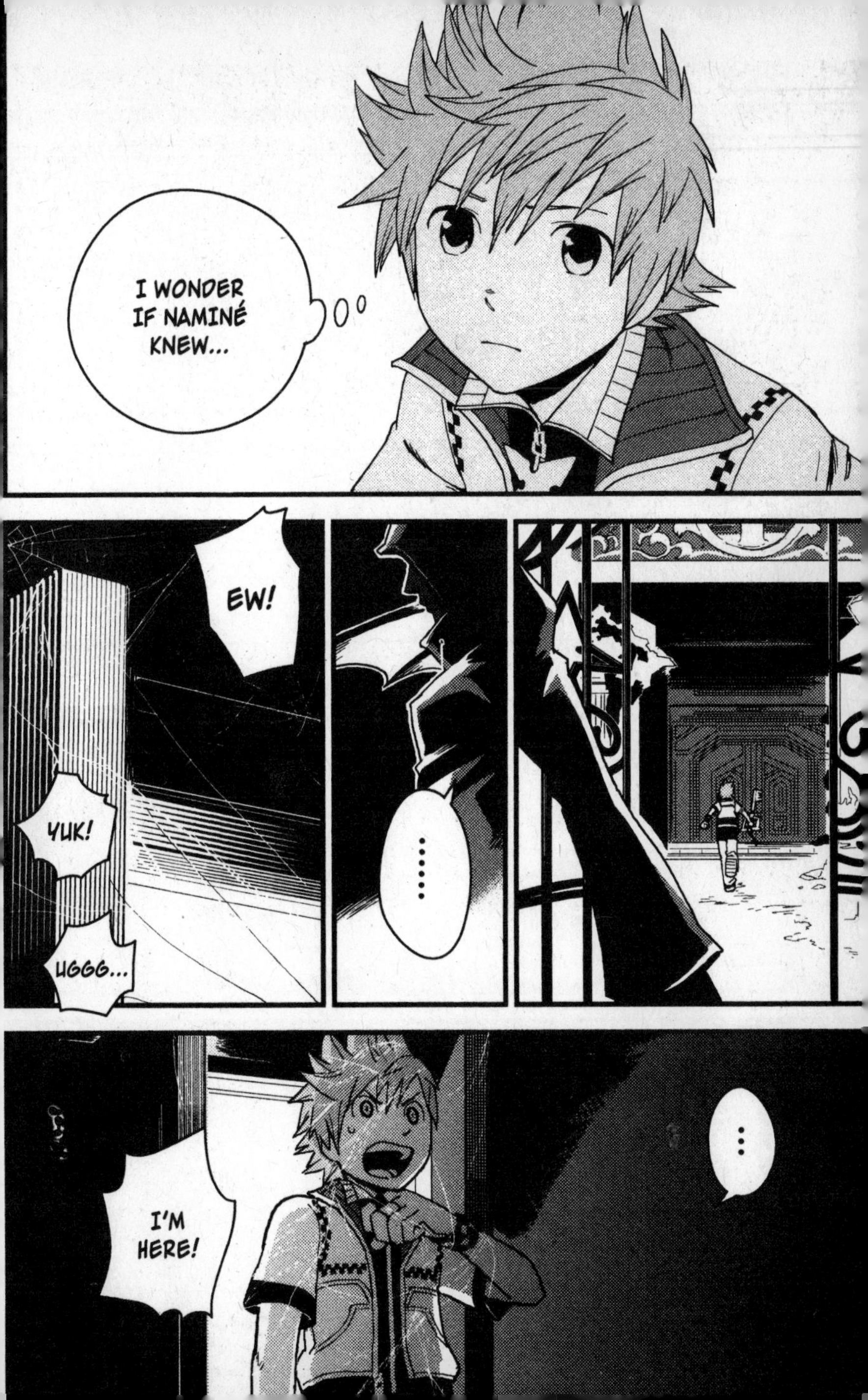
I WONDER IF NAMINÉ KNEW...
......
EW!
YUK!
UGGG...
...
I'M HERE!

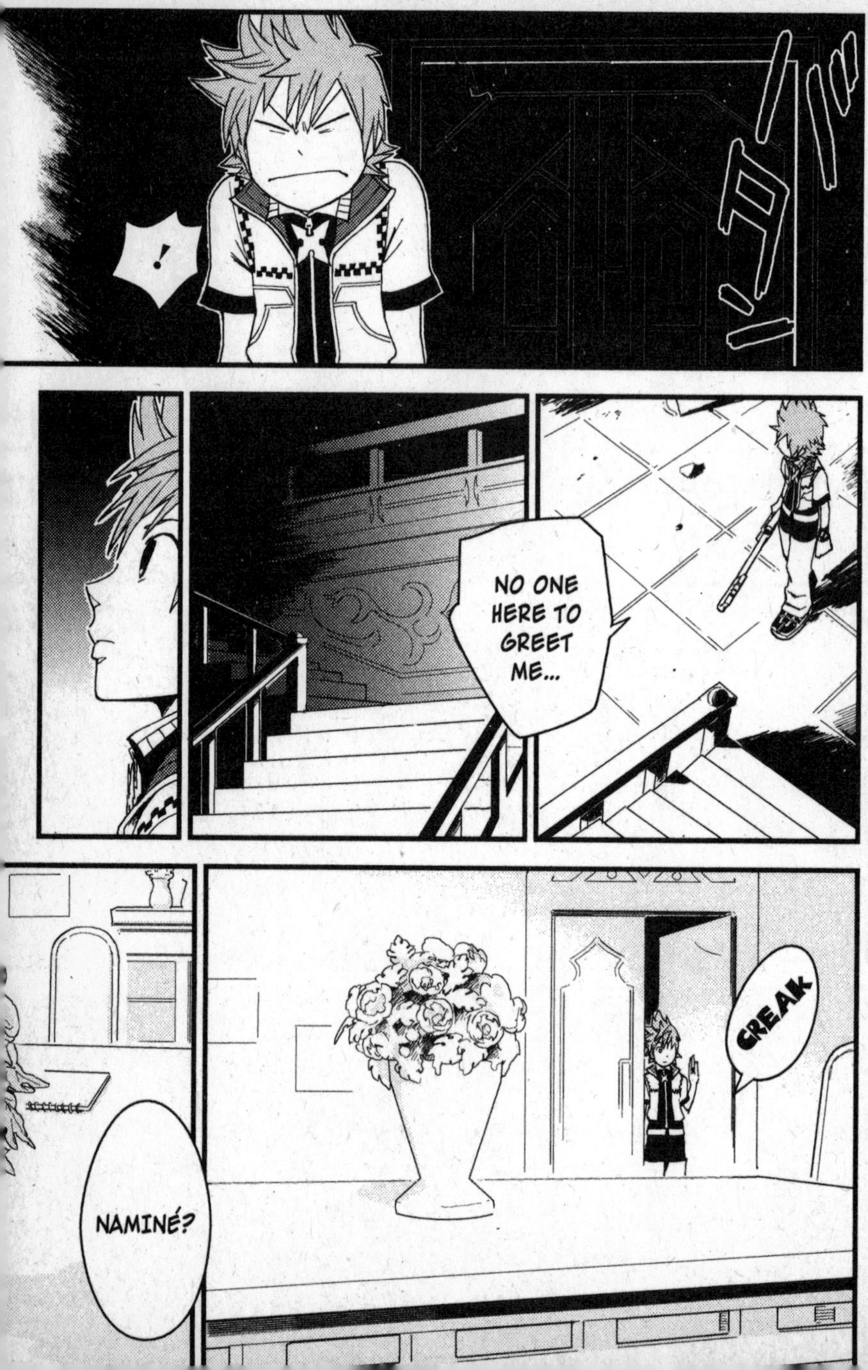
!
NO ONE HERE TO GREET ME...
CREAK
NAMINÉ?

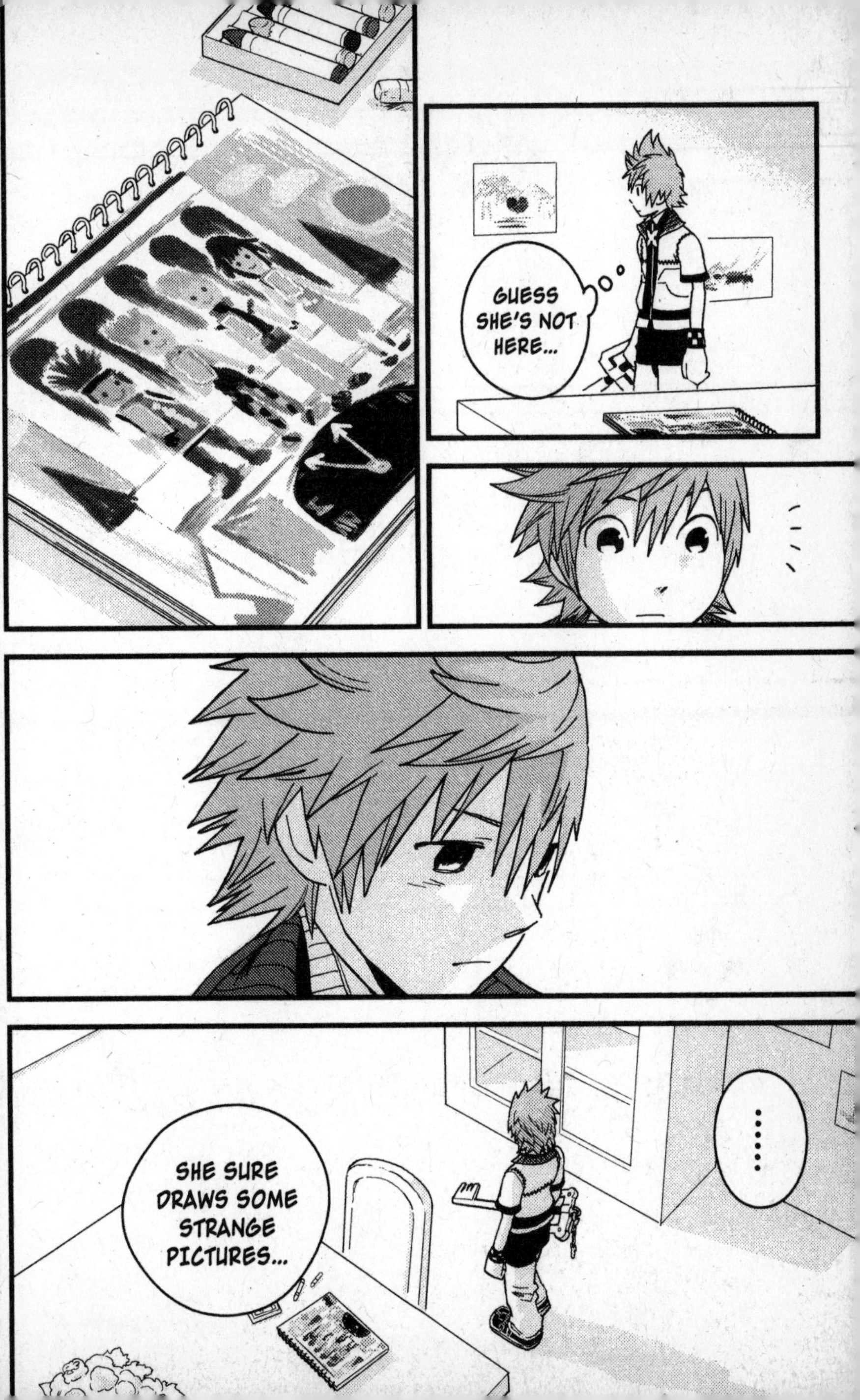
GUESS SHE'S NOT HERE...
......
SHE SURE DRAWS SOME STRANGE PICTURES...

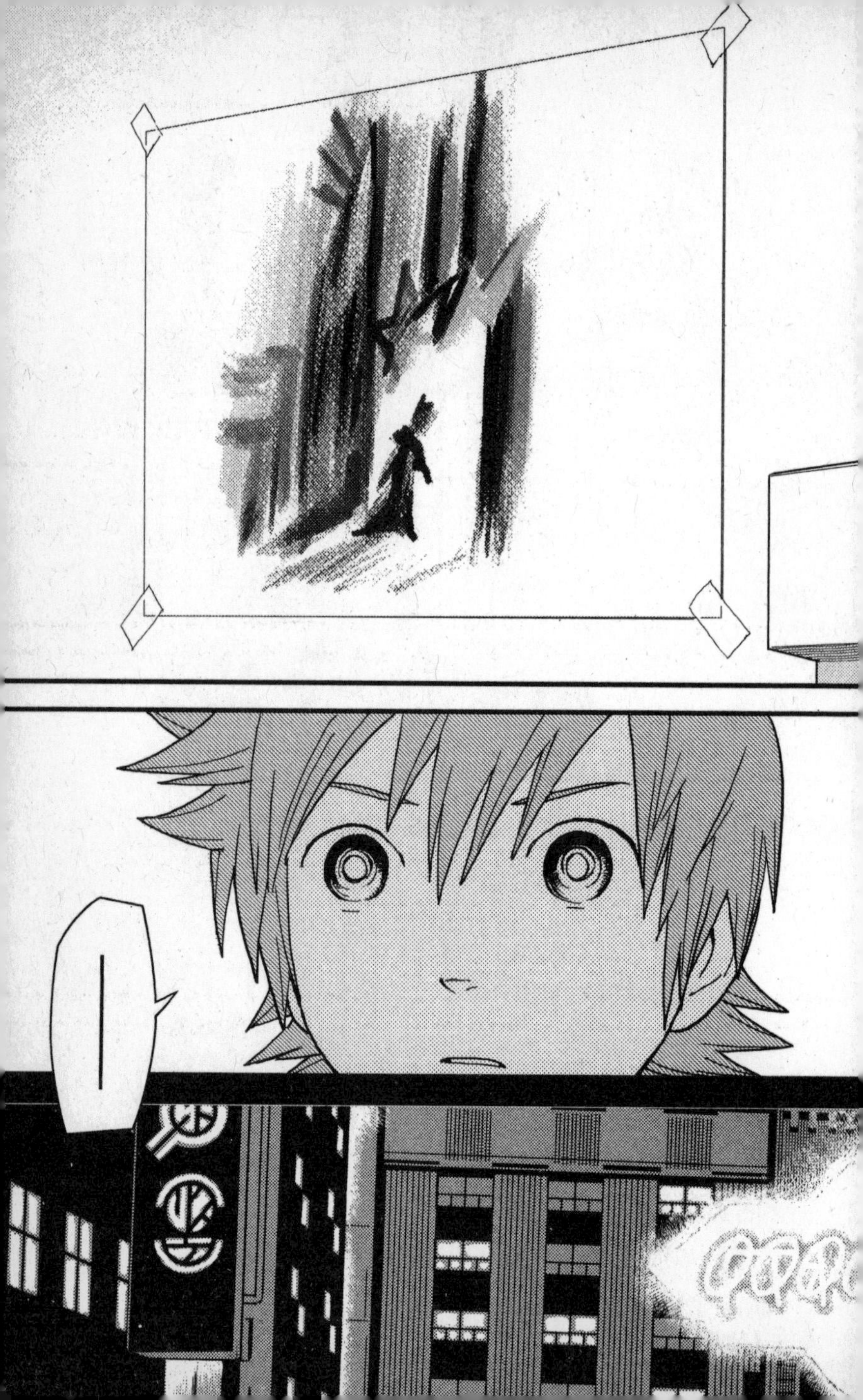

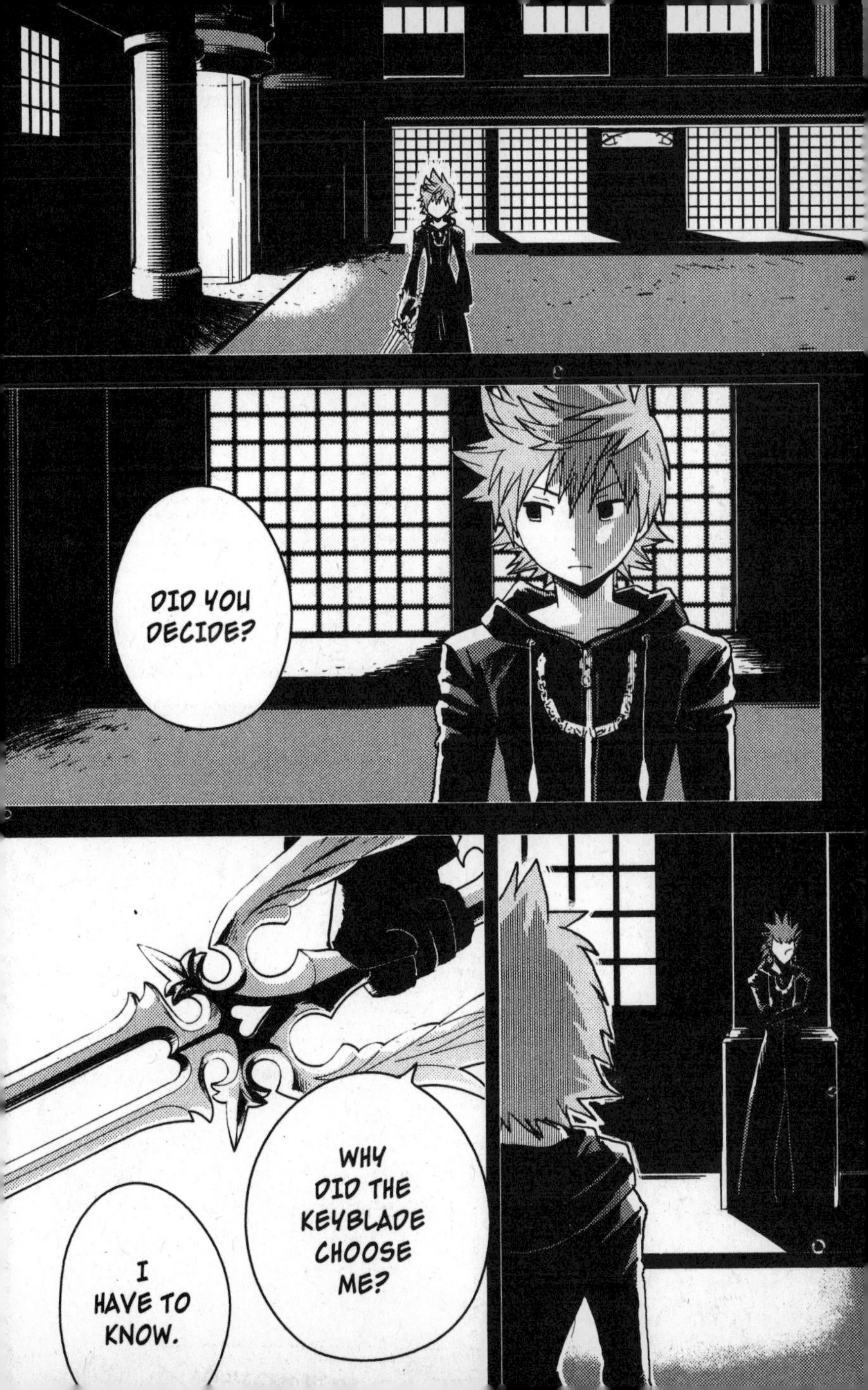
DID YOU DECIDE?
WHY DID THE KEYBLADE CHOOSE ME?
I HAVE TO KNOW.

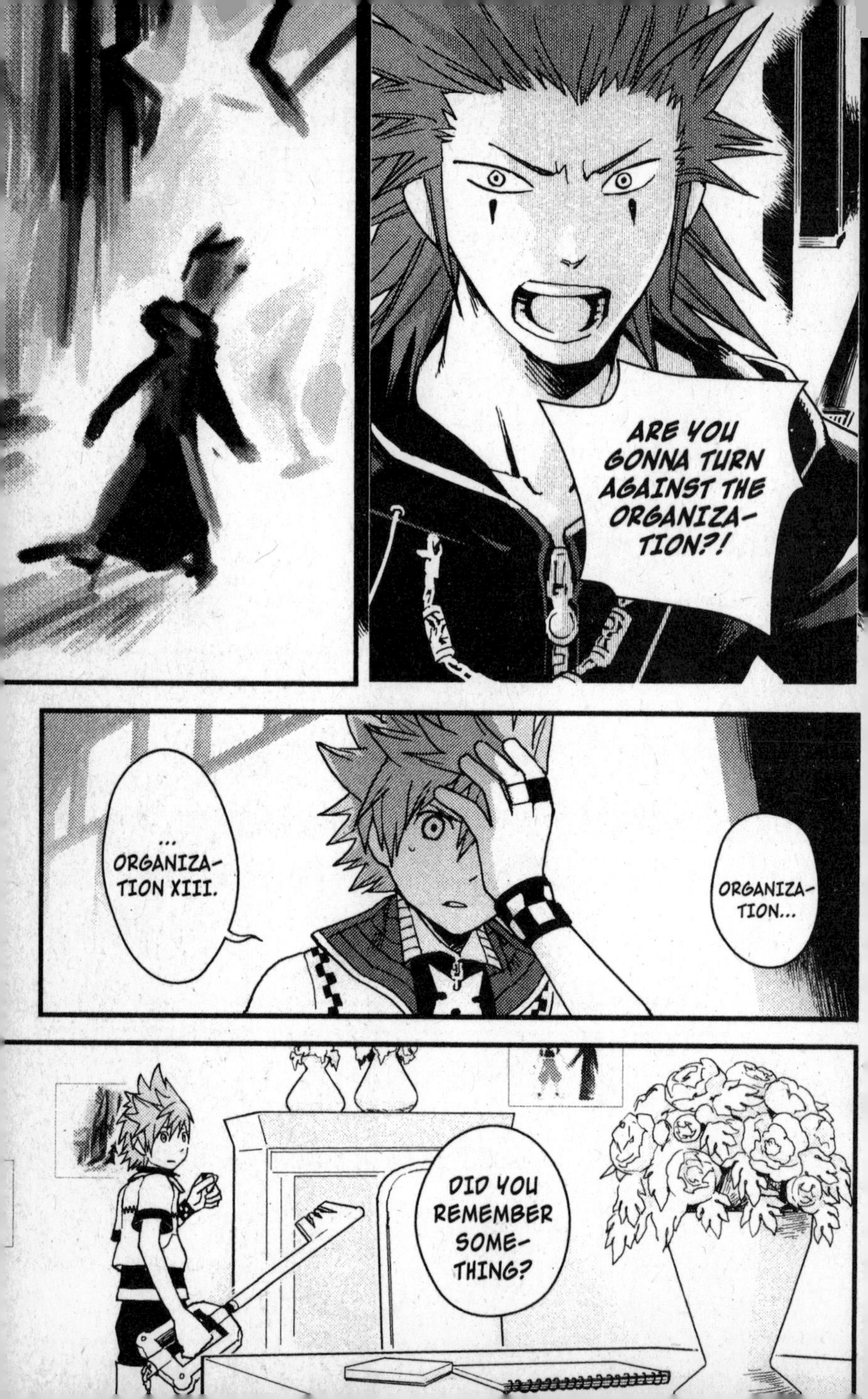
ARE YOU GONNA TURN AGAINST THE ORGANIZATION?!
ORGANIZATION...
...ORGANIZATION XIII.
DID YOU REMEMBER SOMETHING?

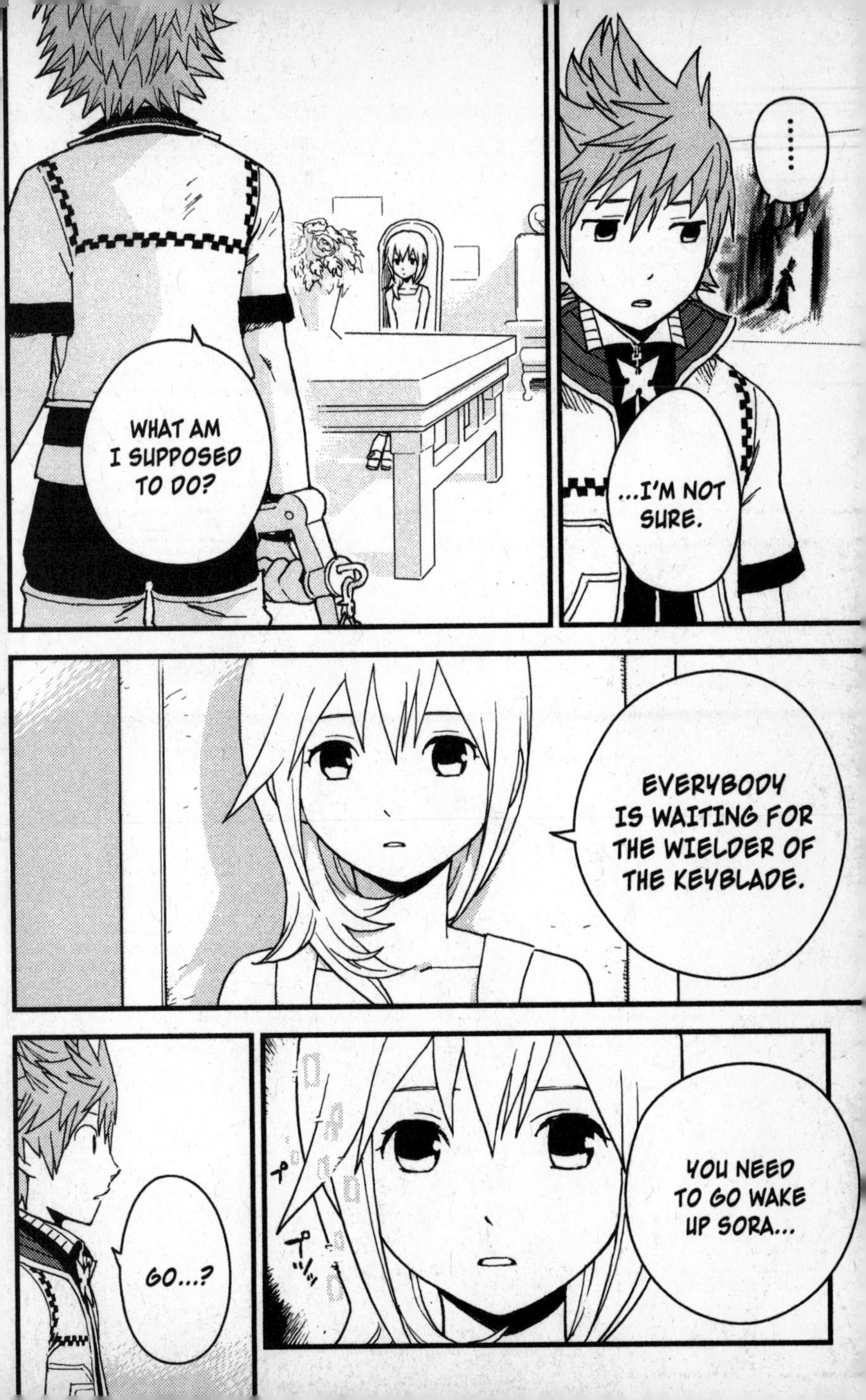
......
...I'M NOT SURE.
WHAT AM I SUPPOSED TO DO?
EVERYBODY IS WAITING FOR THE WIELDER OF THE KEYBLADE.
YOU NEED TO GO WAKE UP SORA...
GO...?

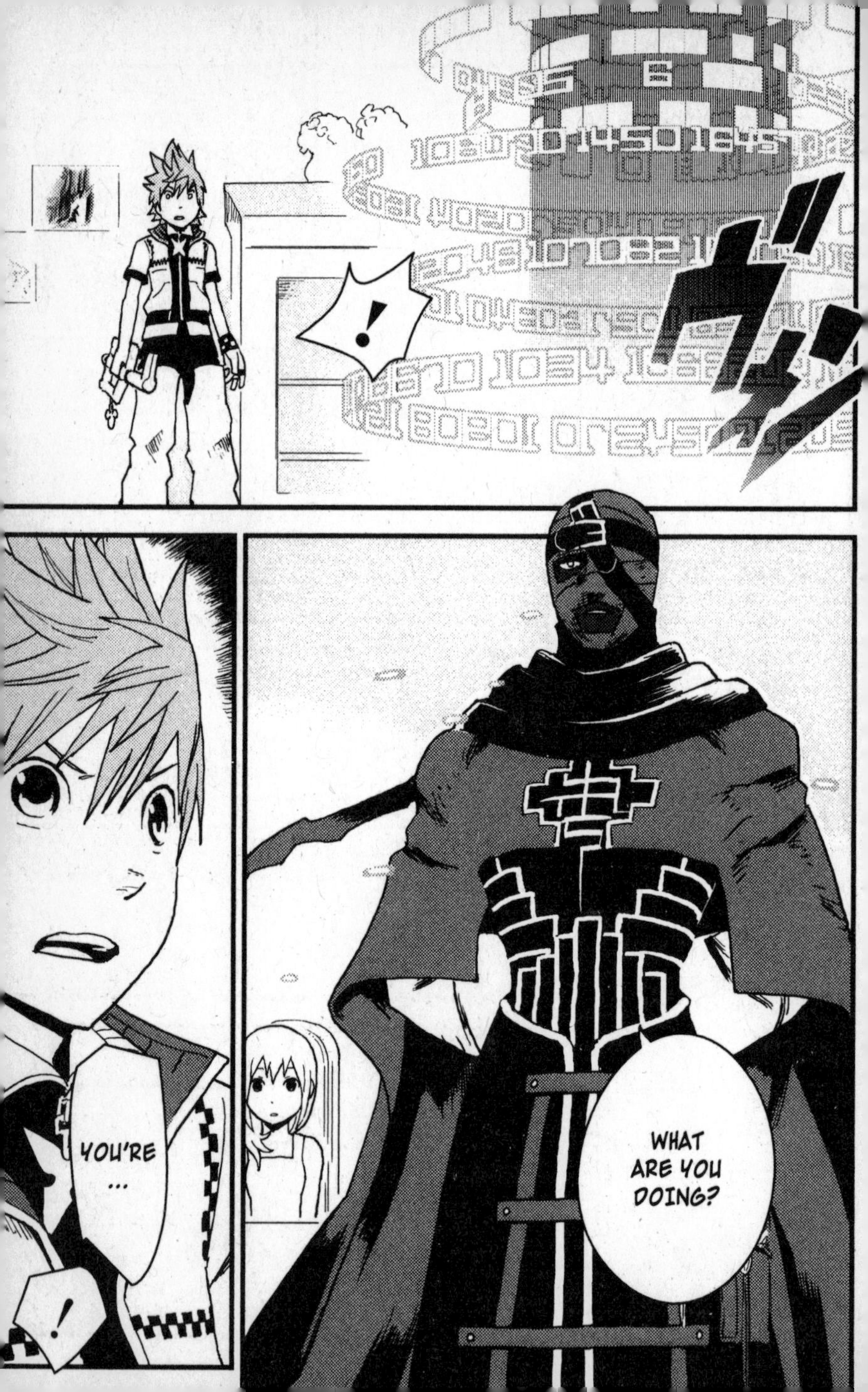
!
ヴン
WHAT ARE YOU DOING?
YOU'RE ...
!

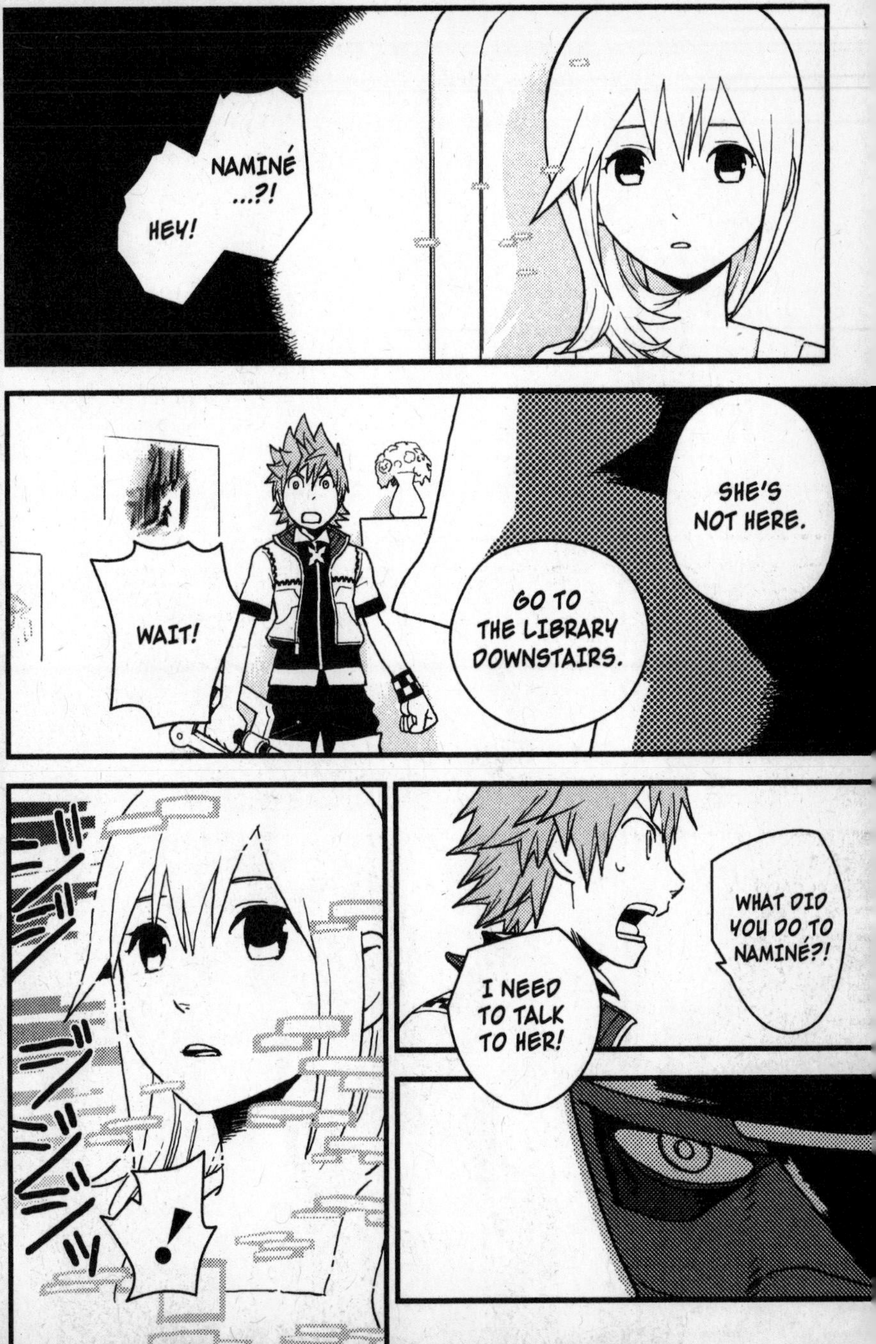
NAMINÉ ...?!
HEY!
SHE'S NOT HERE.
GO TO THE LIBRARY DOWNSTAIRS.
WAIT!
WHAT DID YOU DO TO NAMINÉ?!
I NEED TO TALK TO HER!
!

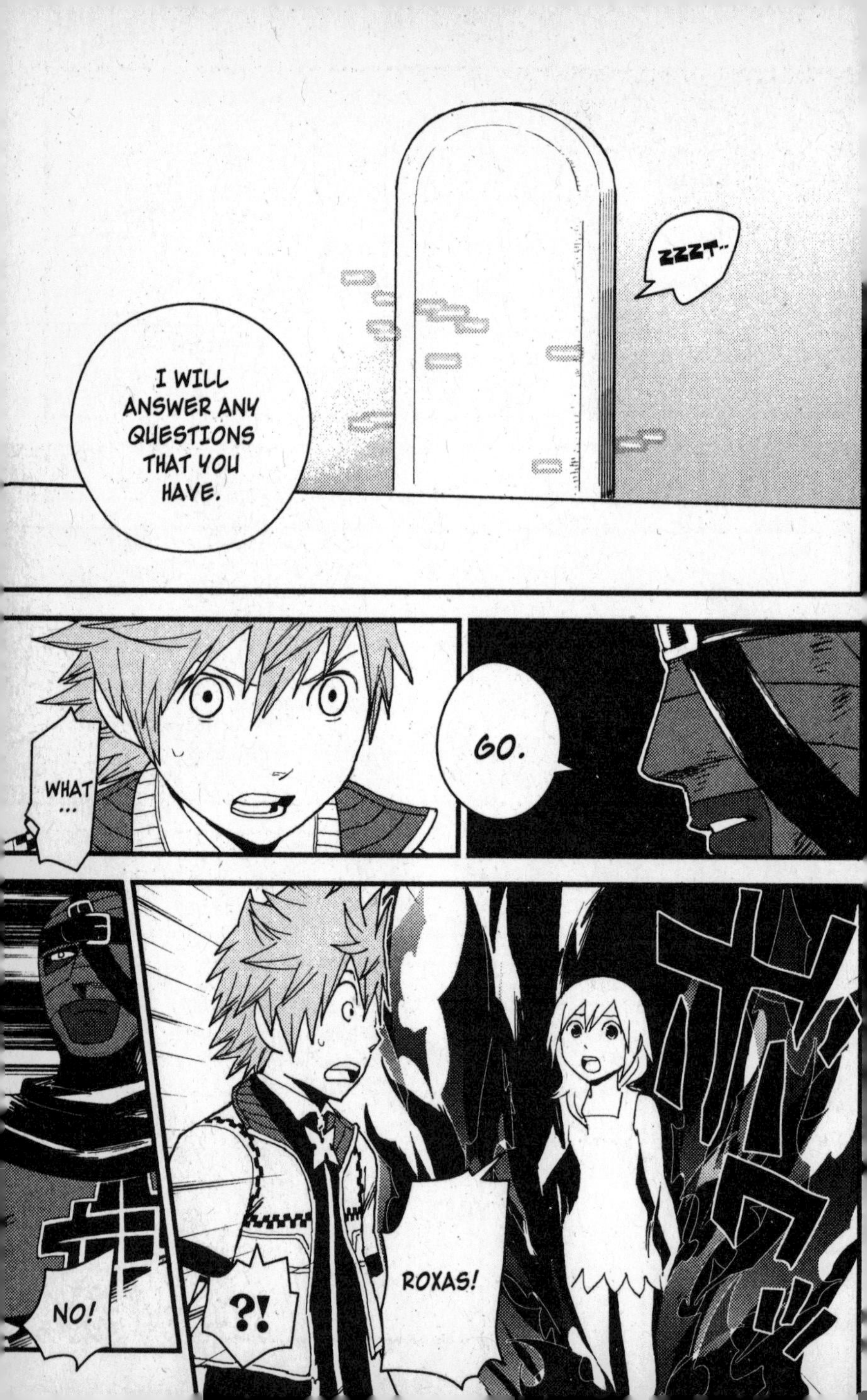
ZZZT..
I WILL ANSWER ANY QUESTIONS THAT YOU HAVE.
GO.
WHAT...
ROXAS!
?!
NO!

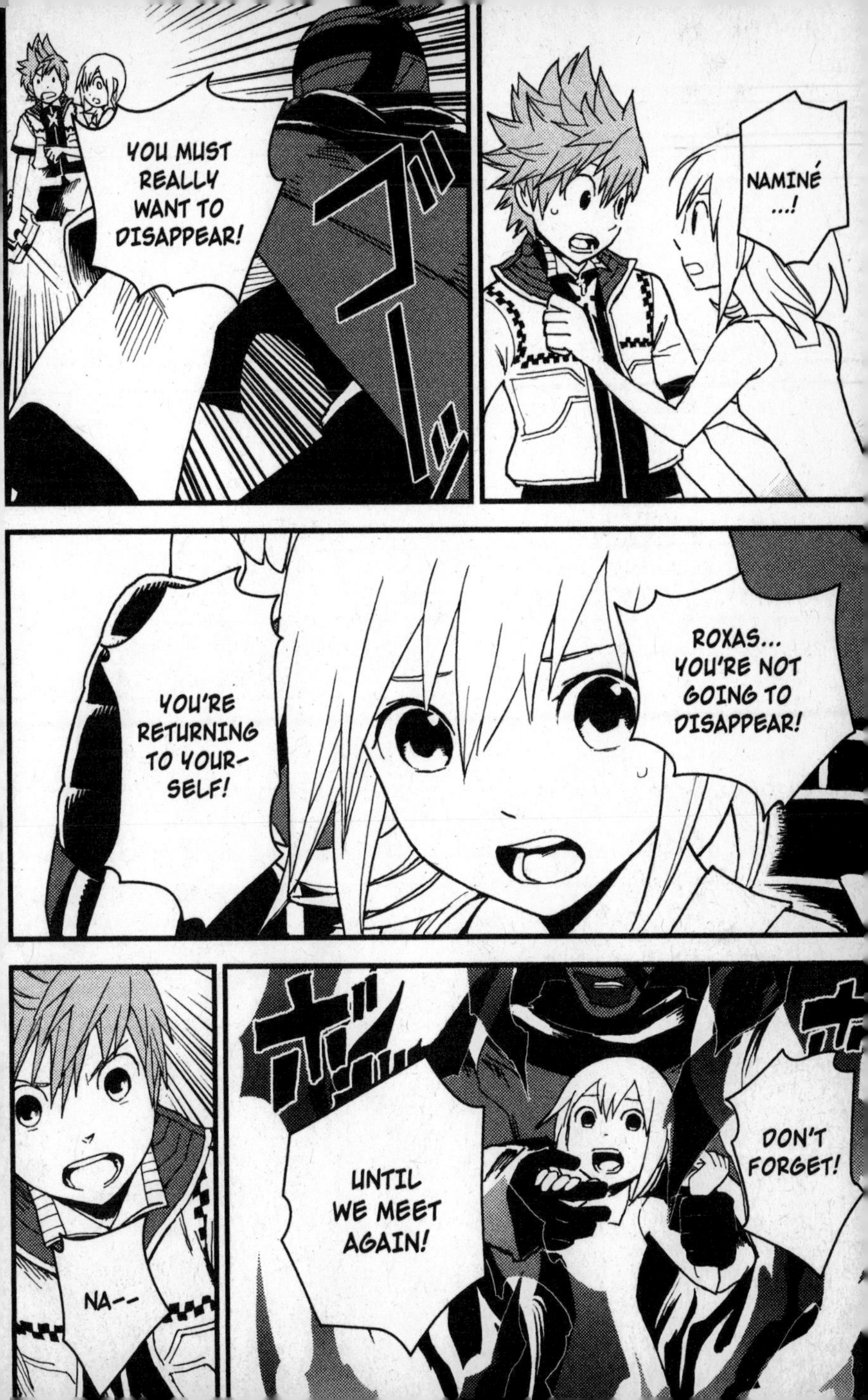
NAMINÉ ...!
YOU MUST REALLY WANT TO DISAPPEAR!
ROXAS... YOU'RE NOT GOING TO DISAPPEAR!
YOU'RE RETURNING TO YOUR-SELF!
DON'T FORGET!
UNTIL WE MEET AGAIN!
NA--

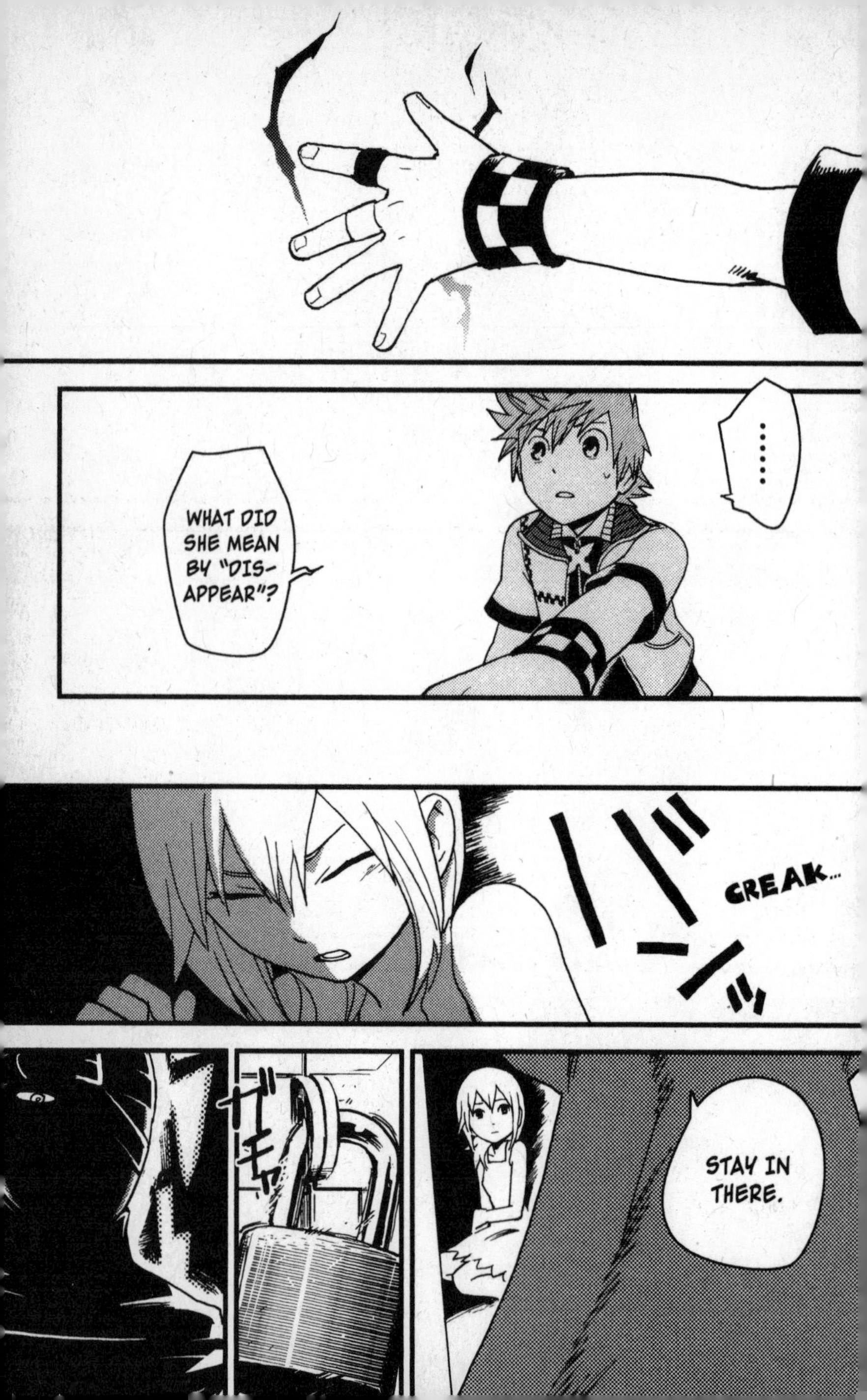
......
WHAT DID SHE MEAN BY "DIS-APPEAR"?
CREAK...
STAY IN THERE.

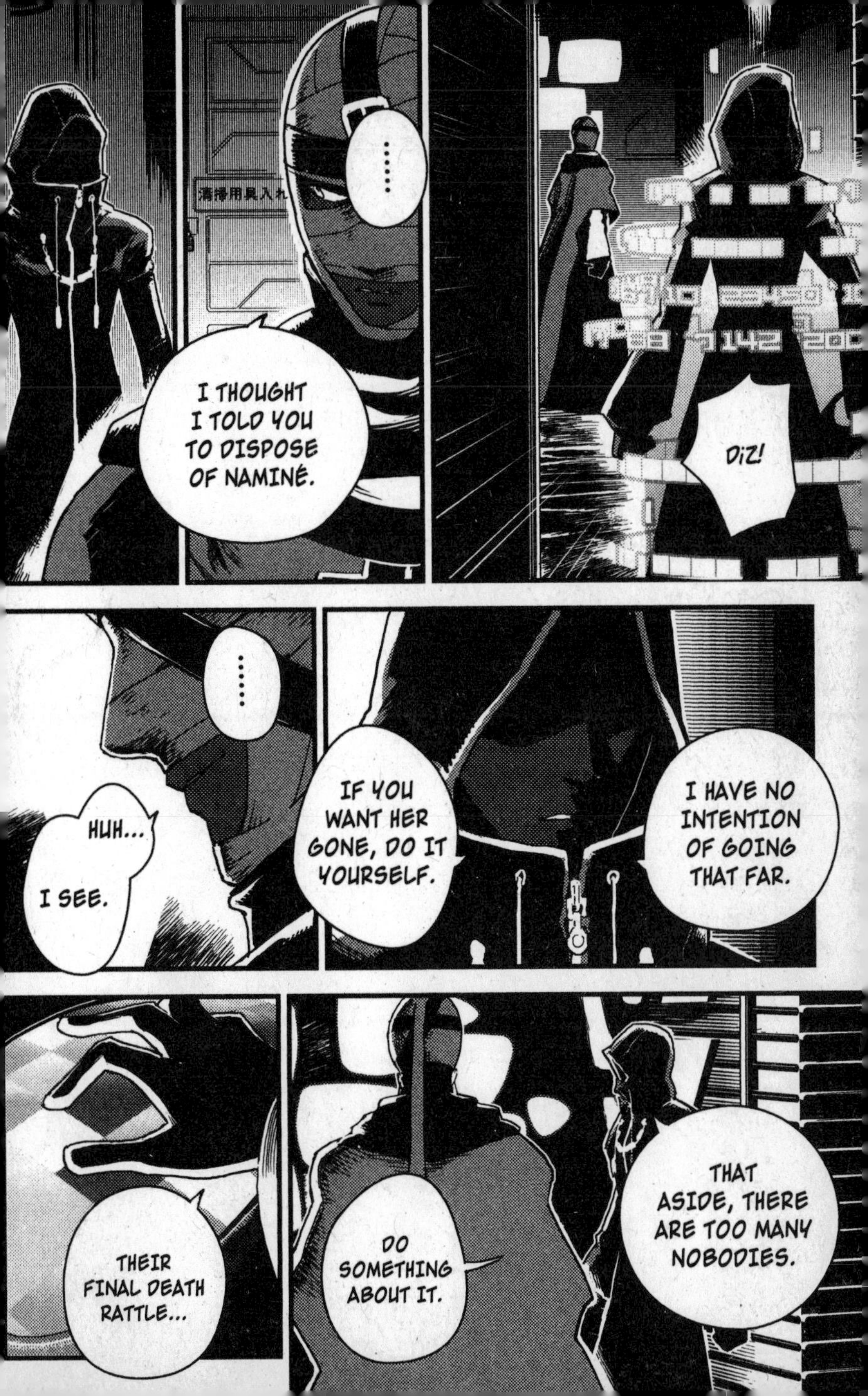
DiZ!
......
清掃用具入れ
I THOUGHT I TOLD YOU TO DISPOSE OF NAMINÉ.
I HAVE NO INTENTION OF GOING THAT FAR.
IF YOU WANT HER GONE, DO IT YOURSELF.
......
HUH...
I SEE.
THAT ASIDE, THERE ARE TOO MANY NOBODIES.
DO SOMETHING ABOUT IT.
THEIR FINAL DEATH RATTLE...

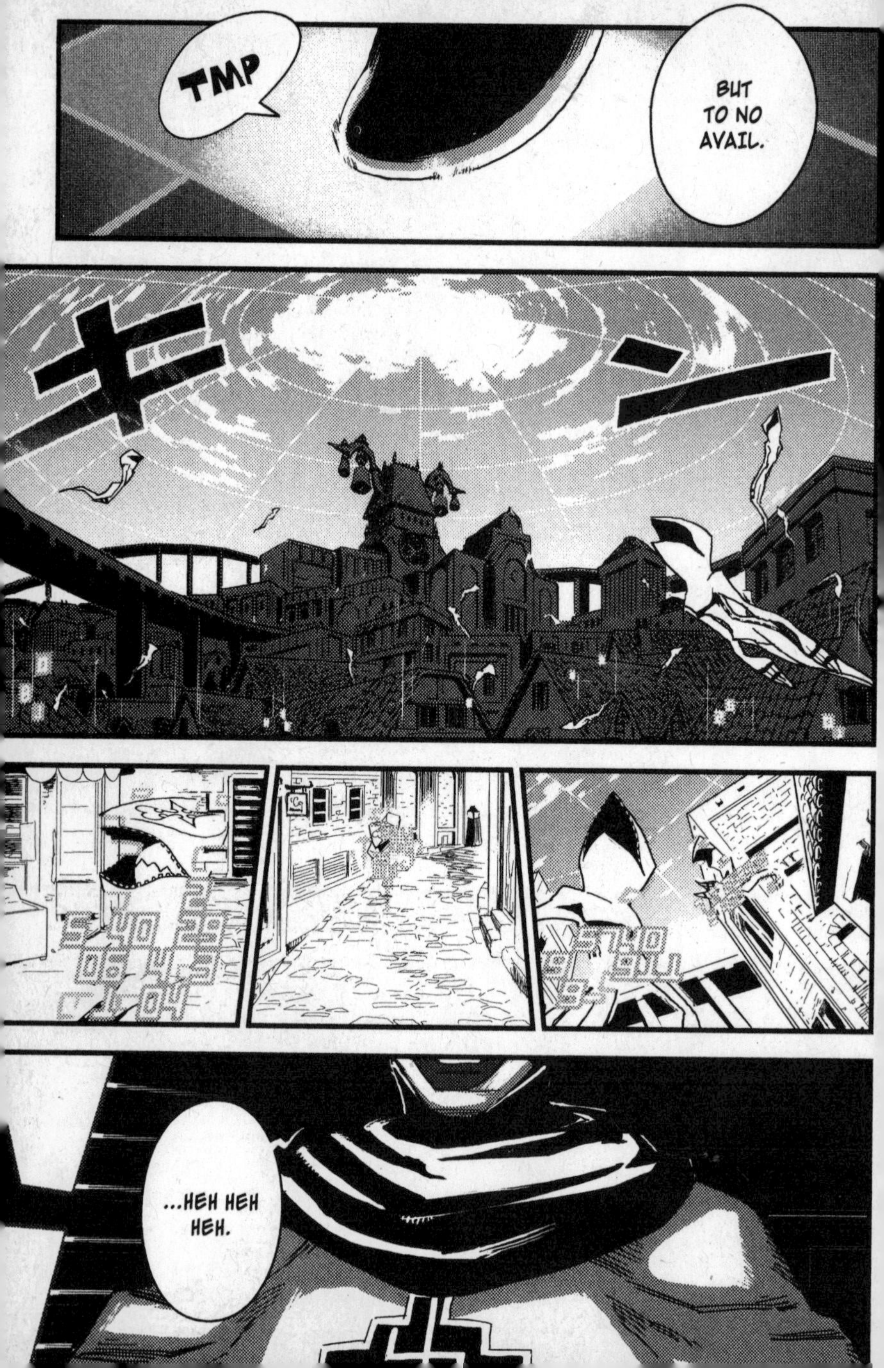
BUT TO NO AVAIL.
TMP
キーン
...HEH HEH HEH.

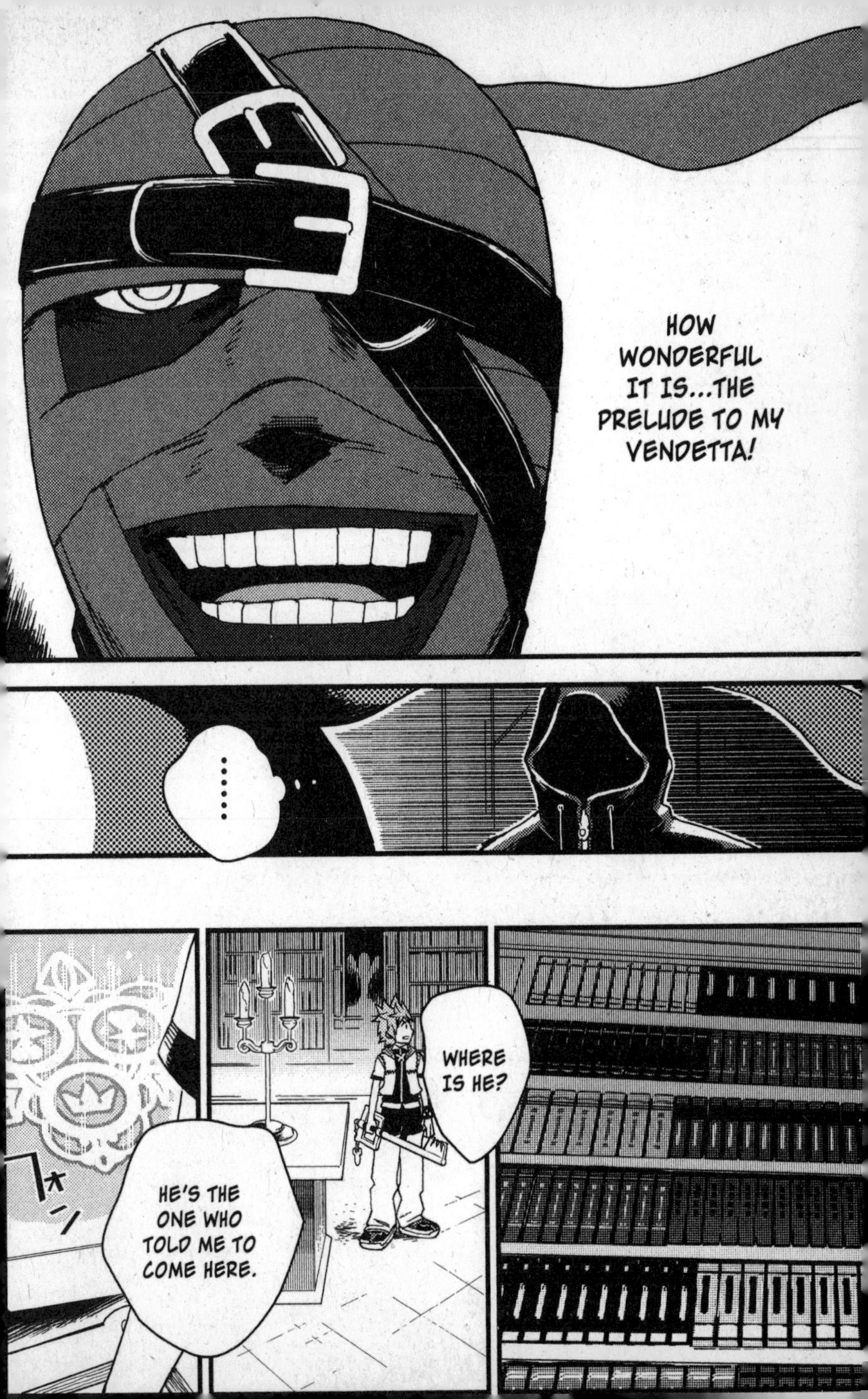
HOW WONDERFUL IT IS...THE PRELUDE TO MY VENDETTA!
......
WHERE IS HE?
HE'S THE ONE WHO TOLD ME TO COME HERE.

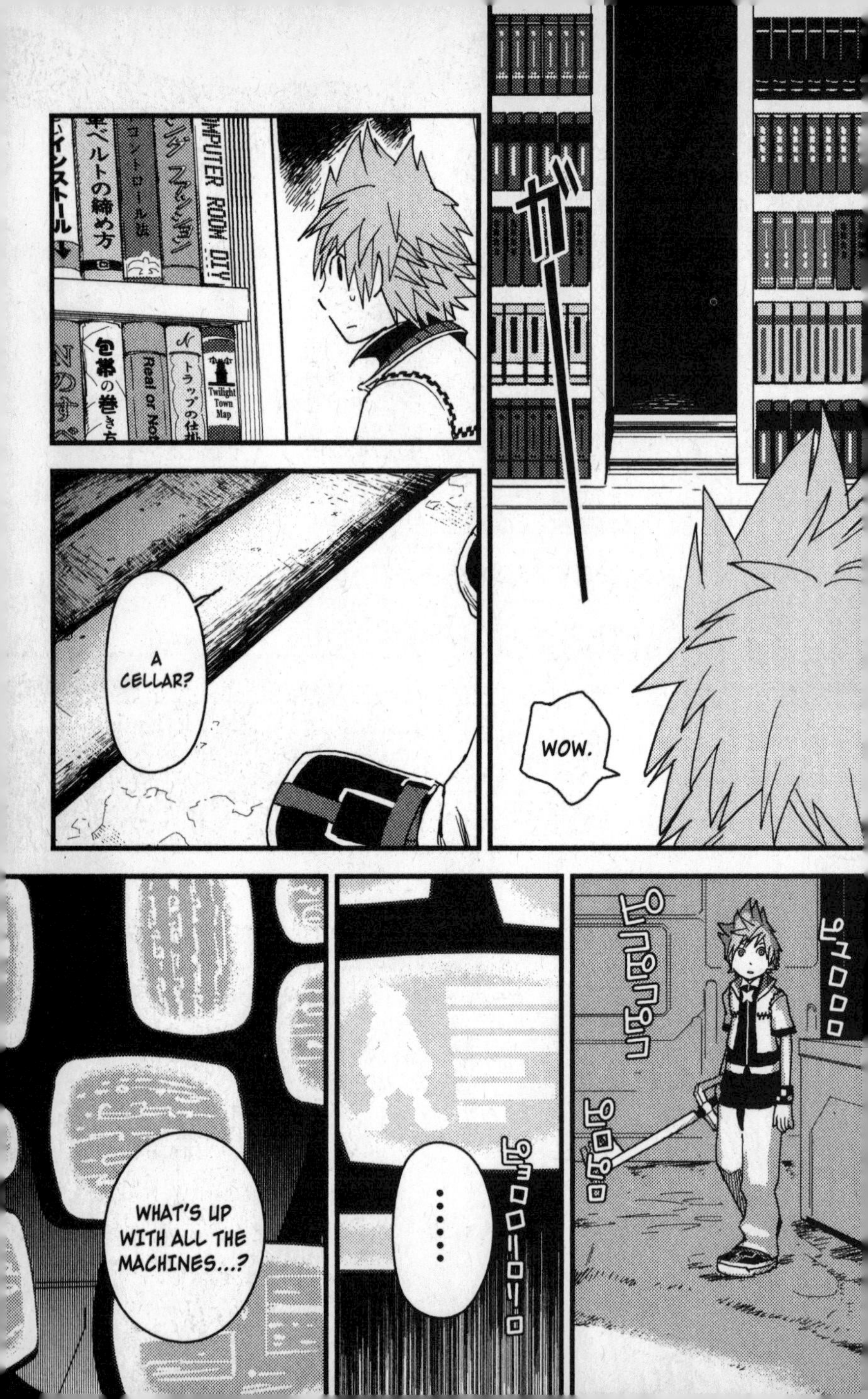

ガ
WOW.
コントロール法
Twilight Town Map
A CELLAR?
......
WHAT'S UP WITH ALL THE MACHINES...?

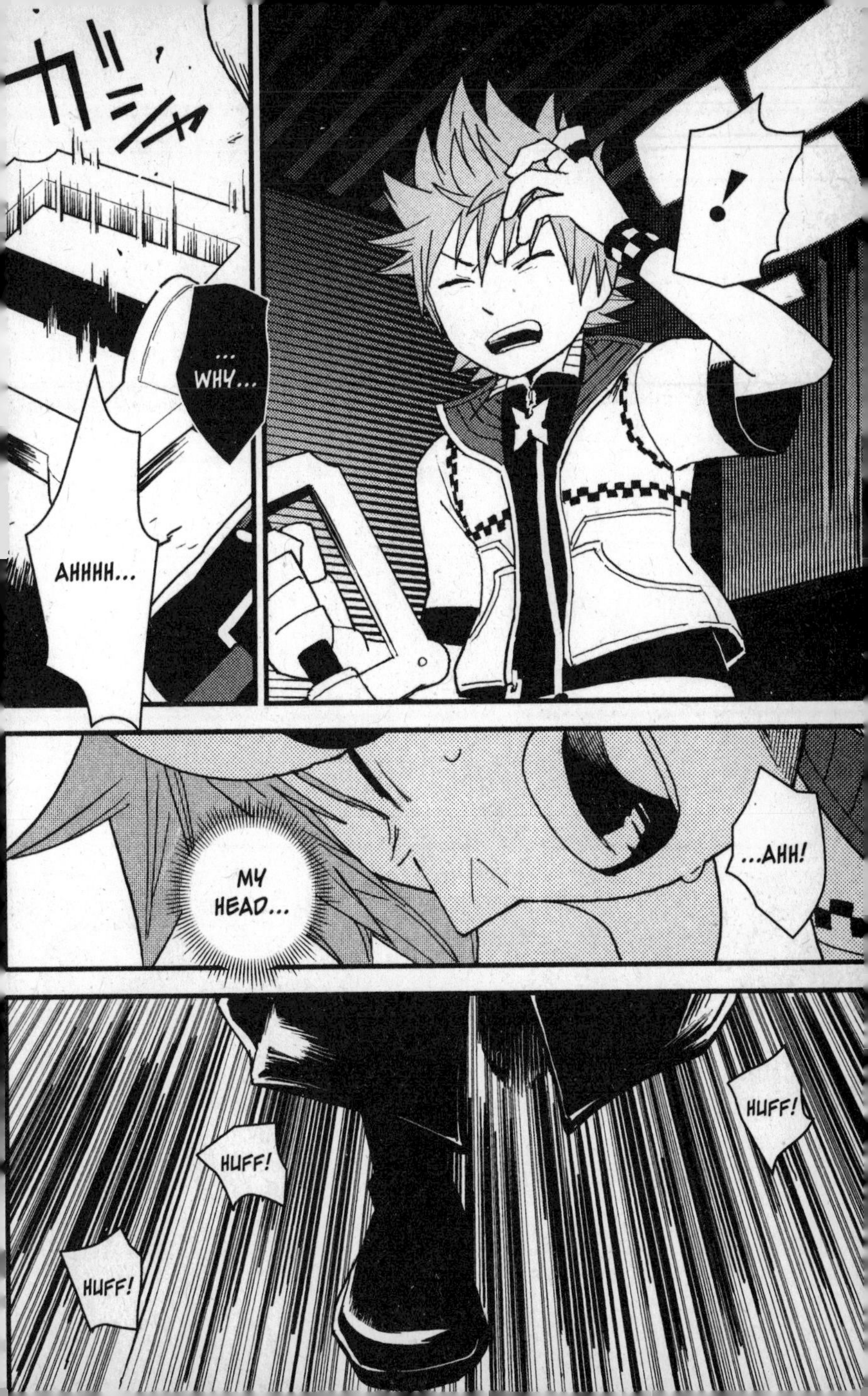
!
ガシャ
... WHY...
AHHHH...
...AHH!
MY HEAD...
HUFF!
HUFF!
HUFF!

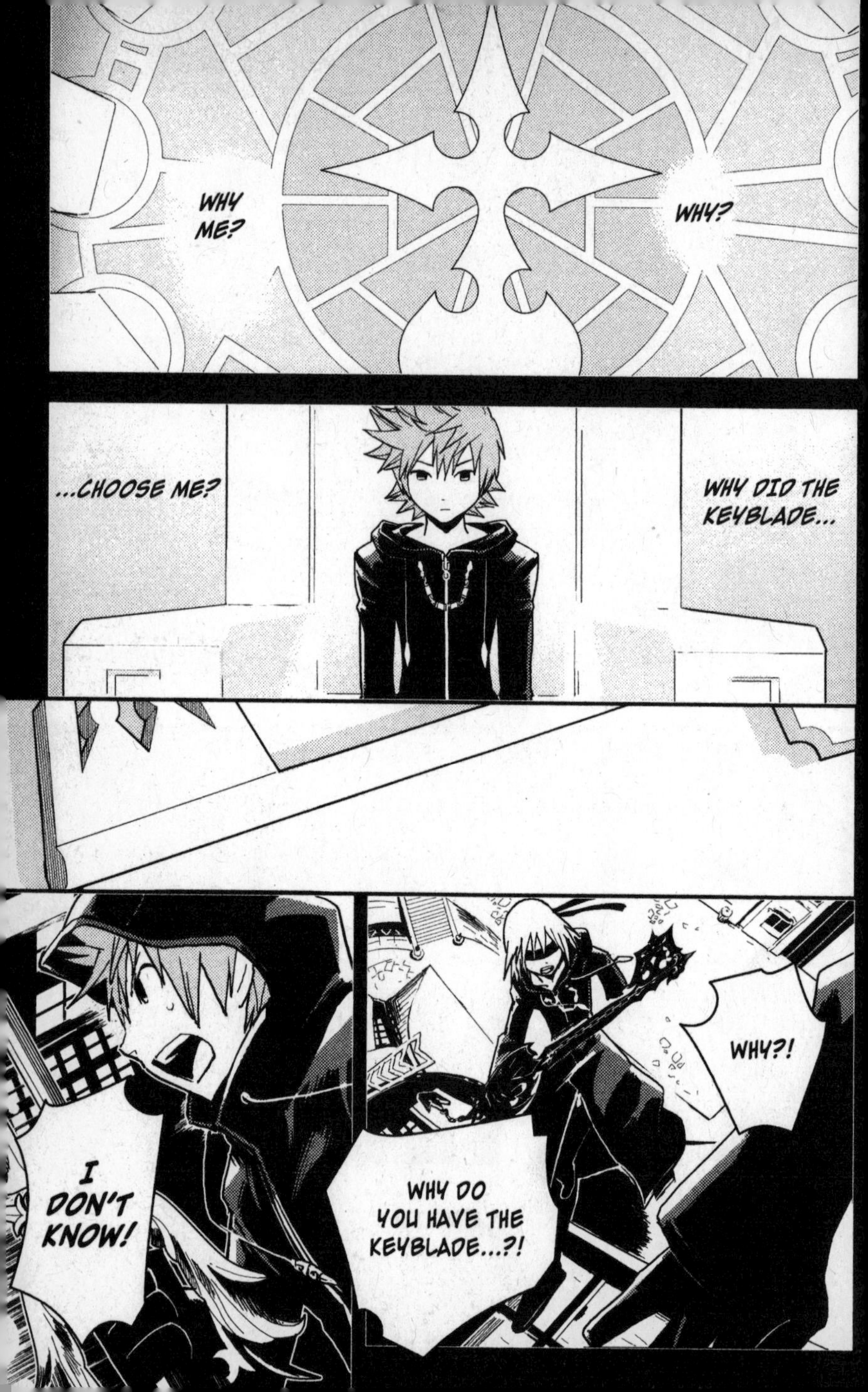
WHY?
WHY ME?
WHY DID THE KEYBLADE...
...CHOOSE ME?
WHY?!
WHY DO YOU HAVE THE KEYBLADE...?!
I DON'T KNOW!

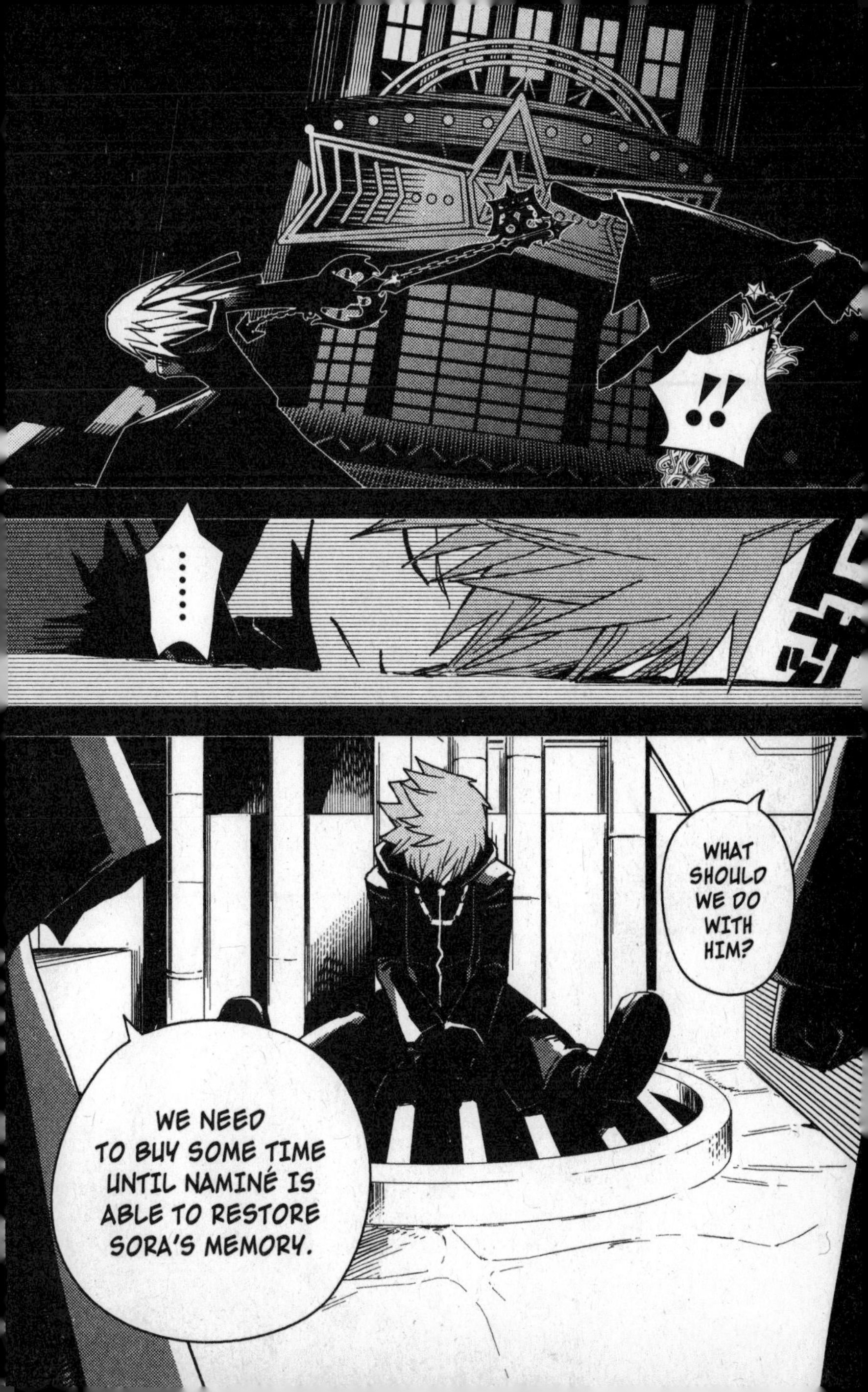
!!
......
WHAT SHOULD WE DO WITH HIM?
WE NEED TO BUY SOME TIME UNTIL NAMINÉ IS ABLE TO RESTORE SORA'S MEMORY.

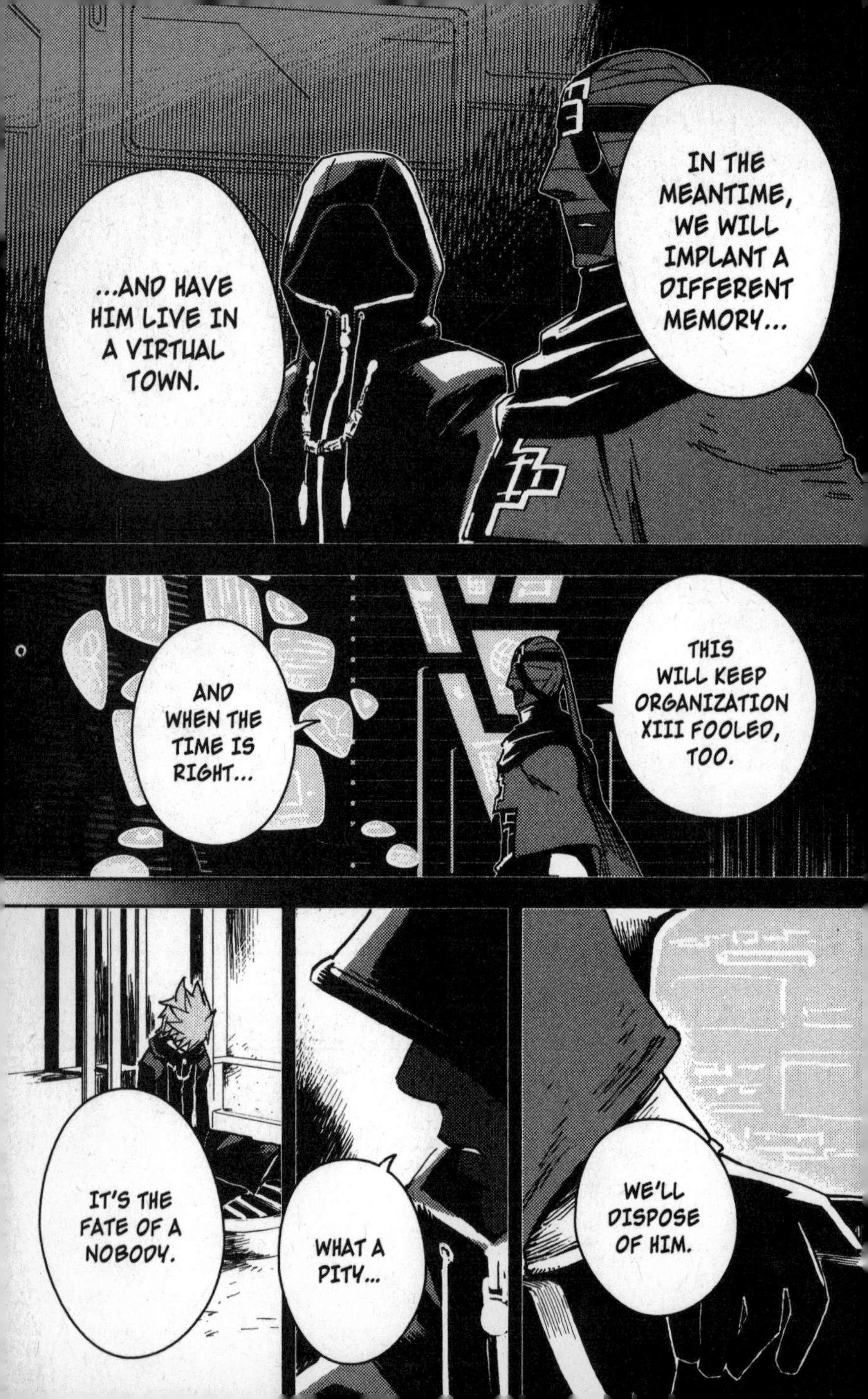
IN THE MEANTIME, WE WILL IMPLANT A DIFFERENT MEMORY...
...AND HAVE HIM LIVE IN A VIRTUAL TOWN.
THIS WILL KEEP ORGANIZATION XIII FOOLED, TOO.
AND WHEN THE TIME IS RIGHT...
WE'LL DISPOSE OF HIM.
WHAT A PITY...
IT'S THE FATE OF A NOBODY.

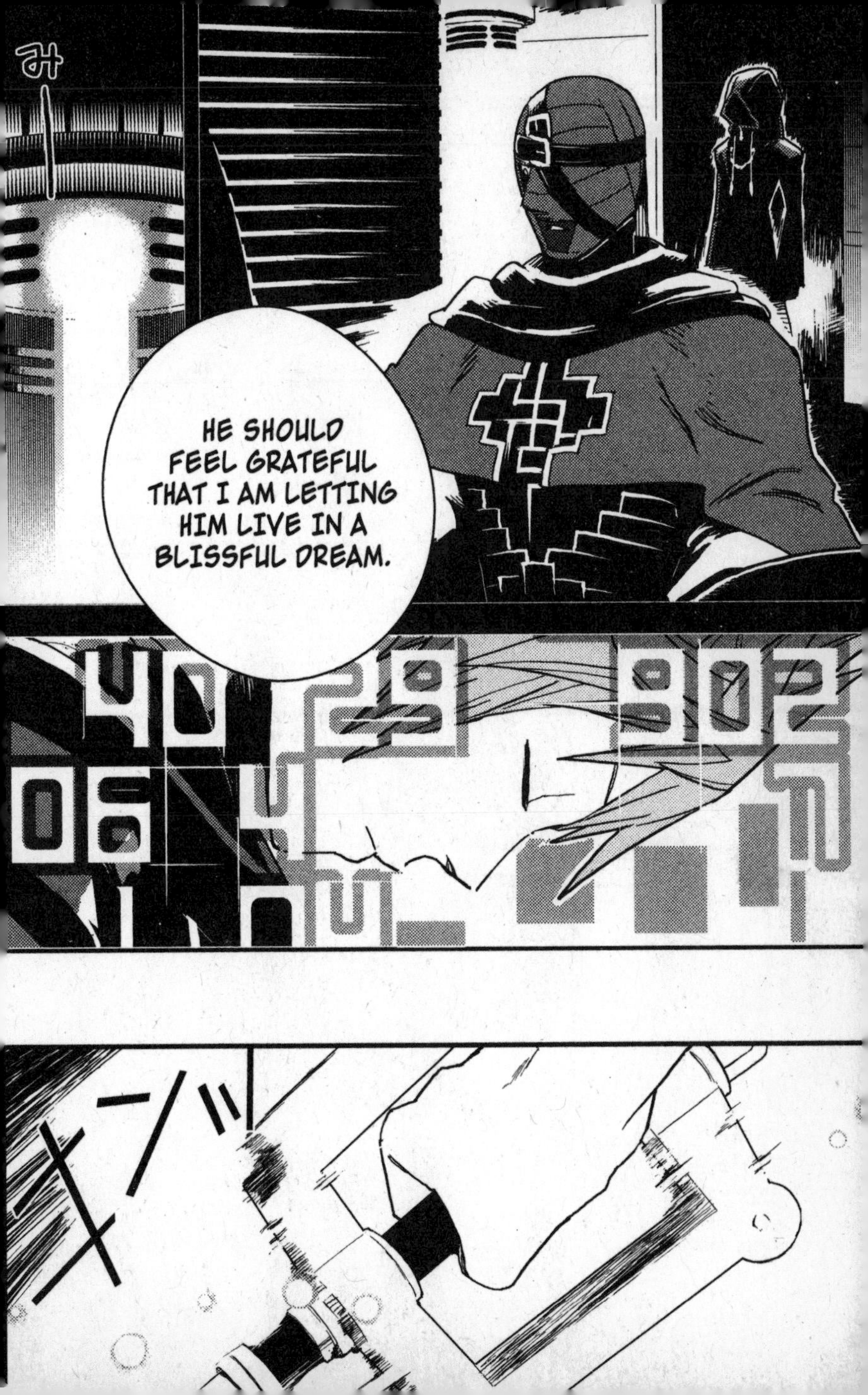
みー
HE SHOULD FEEL GRATEFUL THAT I AM LETTING HIM LIVE IN A BLISSFUL DREAM.
ギーー

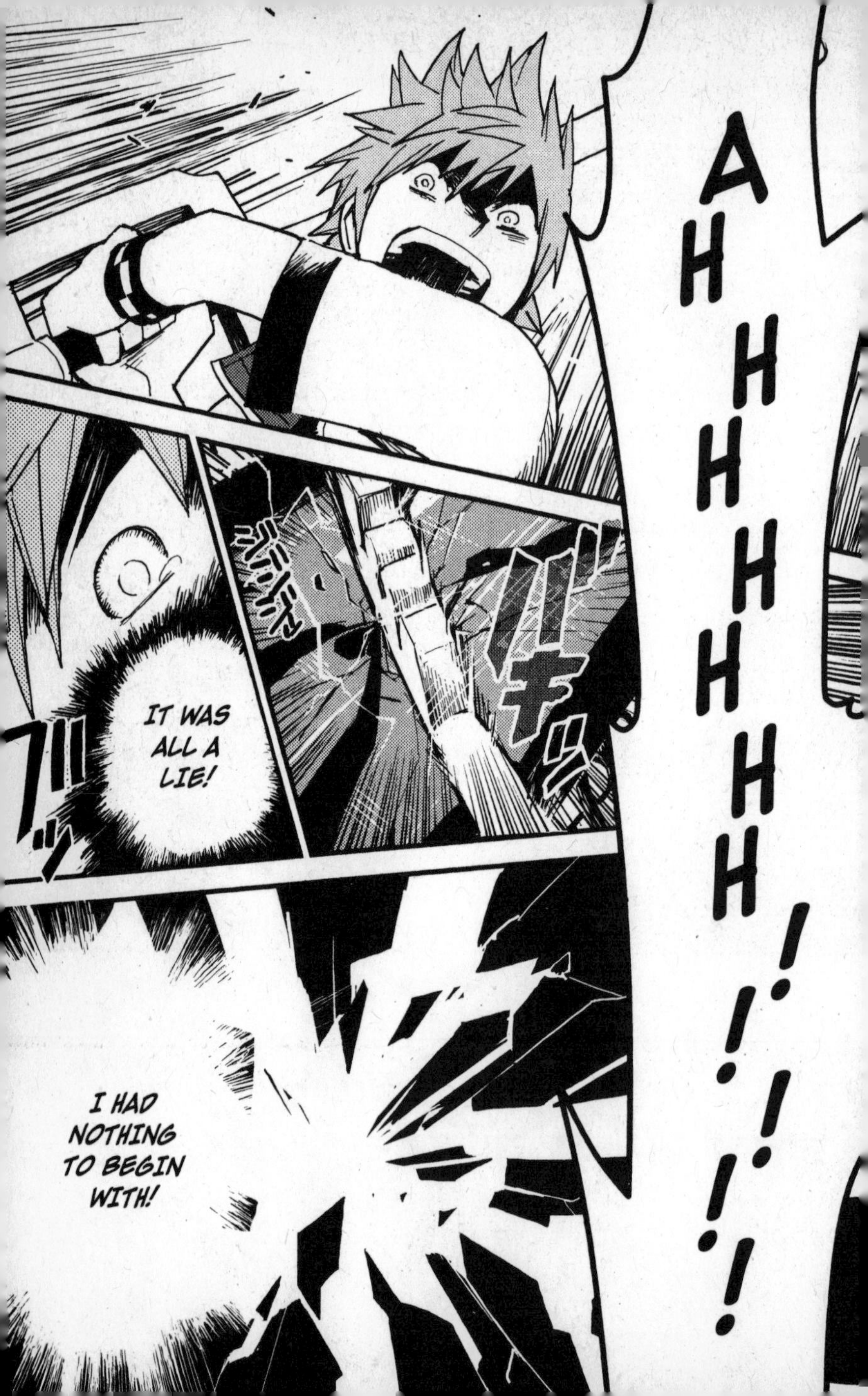
AHHHHHHH!!!!!
IT WAS ALL A LIE!
I HAD NOTHING TO BEGIN WITH!

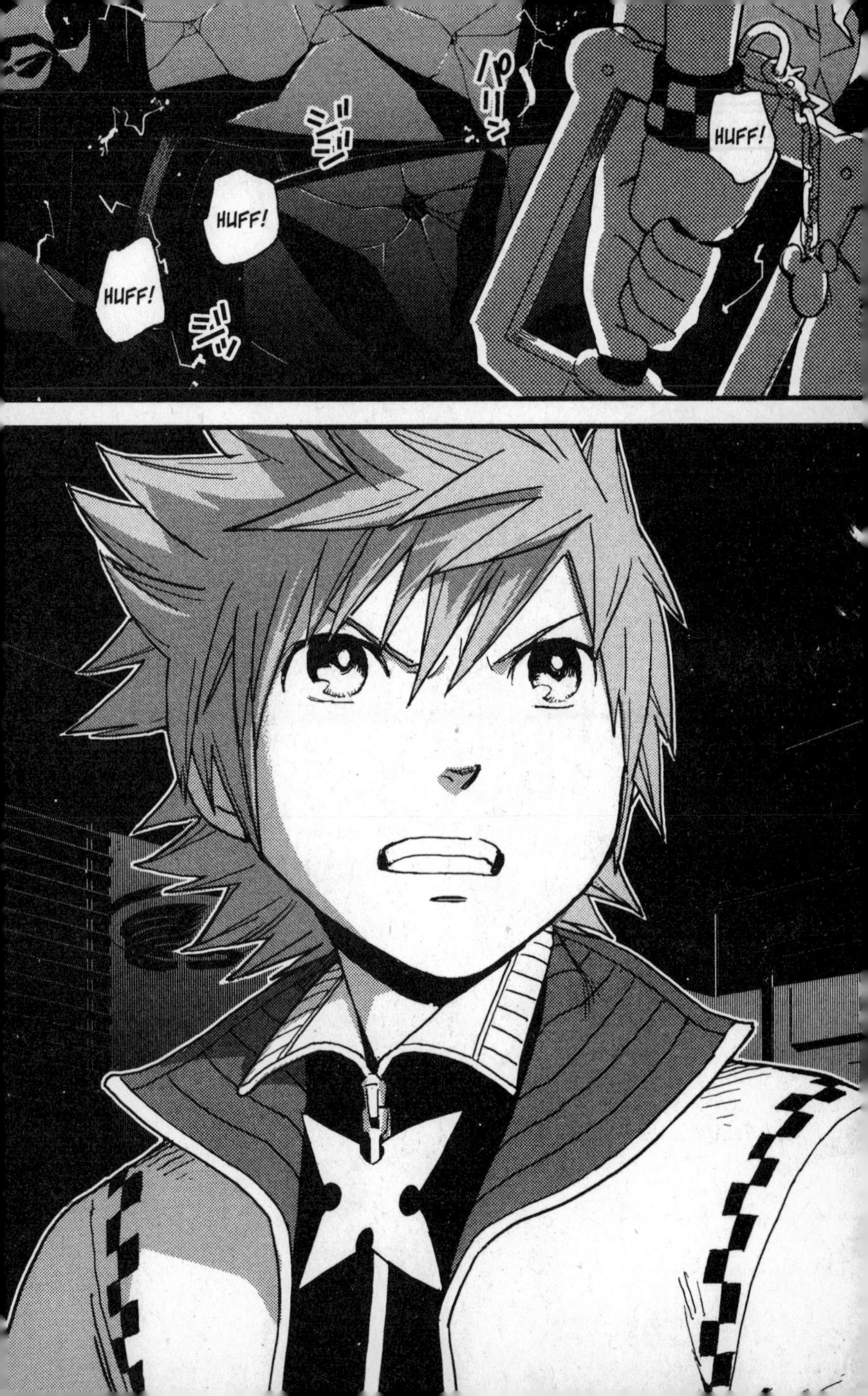
HUFF!
HUFF!
HUFF!

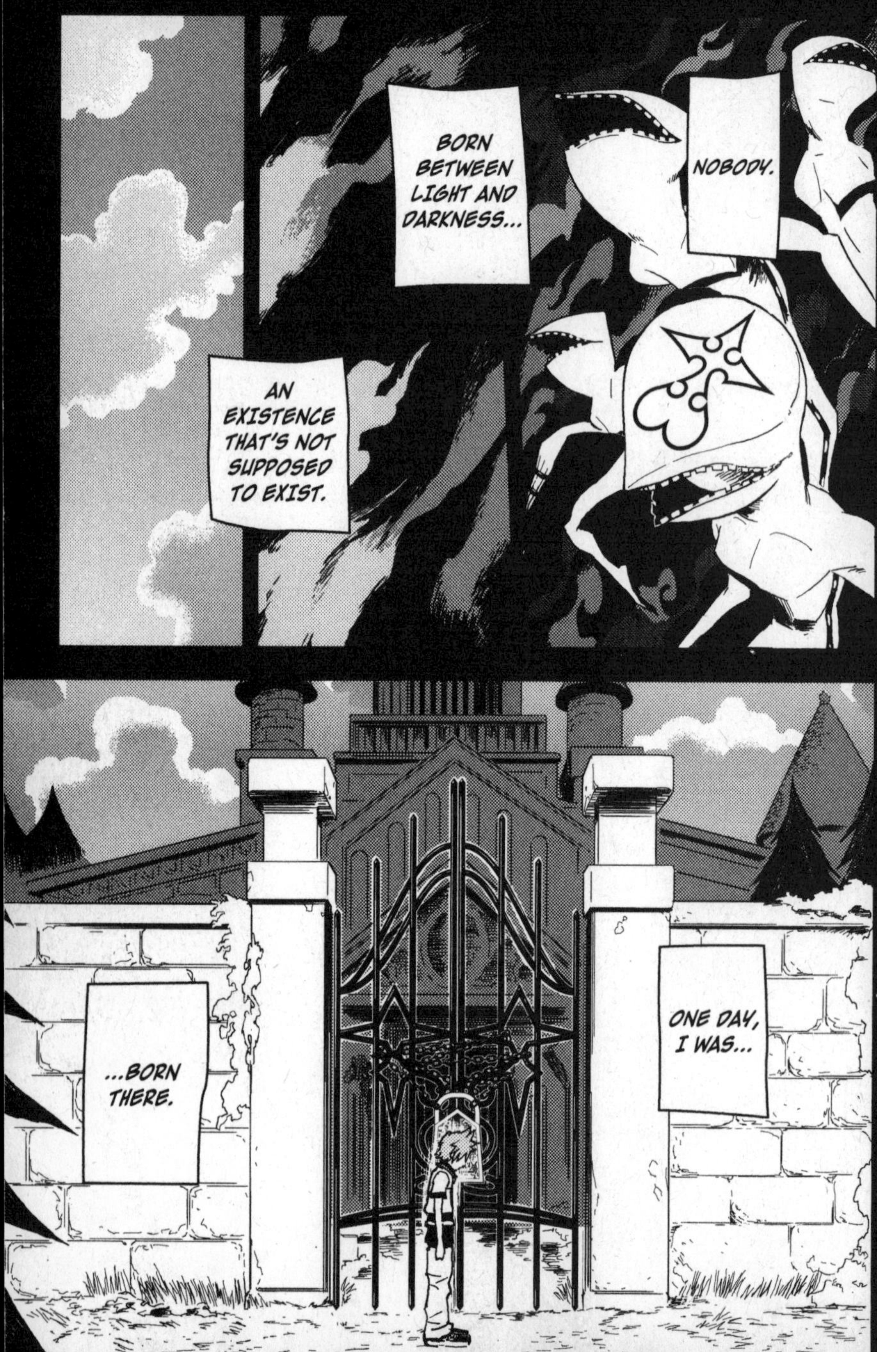

BORN BETWEEN LIGHT AND DARKNESS...
NOBODY.
AN EXISTENCE THAT'S NOT SUPPOSED TO EXIST.
ONE DAY, I WAS...
...BORN THERE.

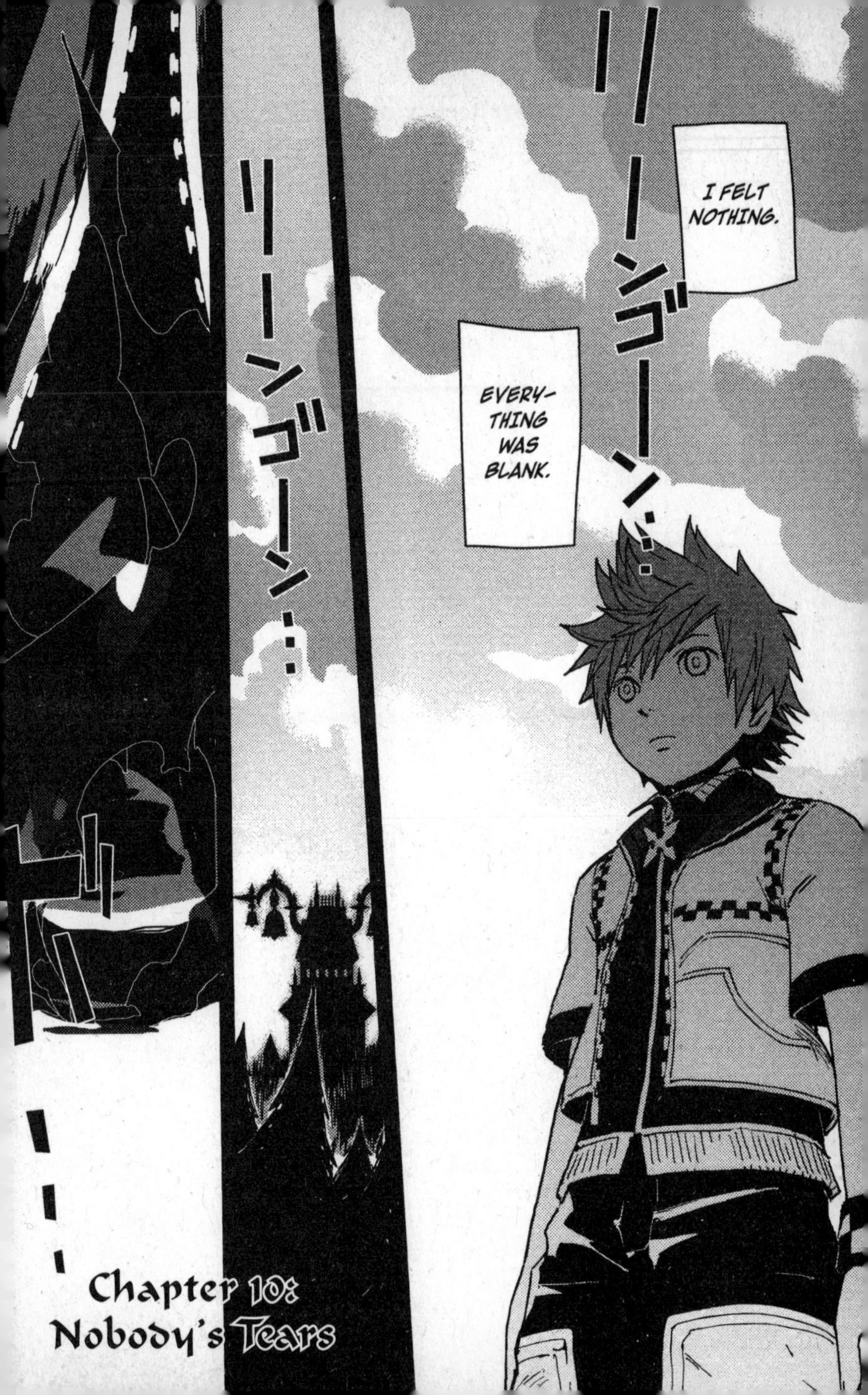
リーーンゴーーン…
I FELT NOTHING.
EVERY-THING WAS BLANK.
リーーンゴーーン…

Chapter 10: Nobody's Tears

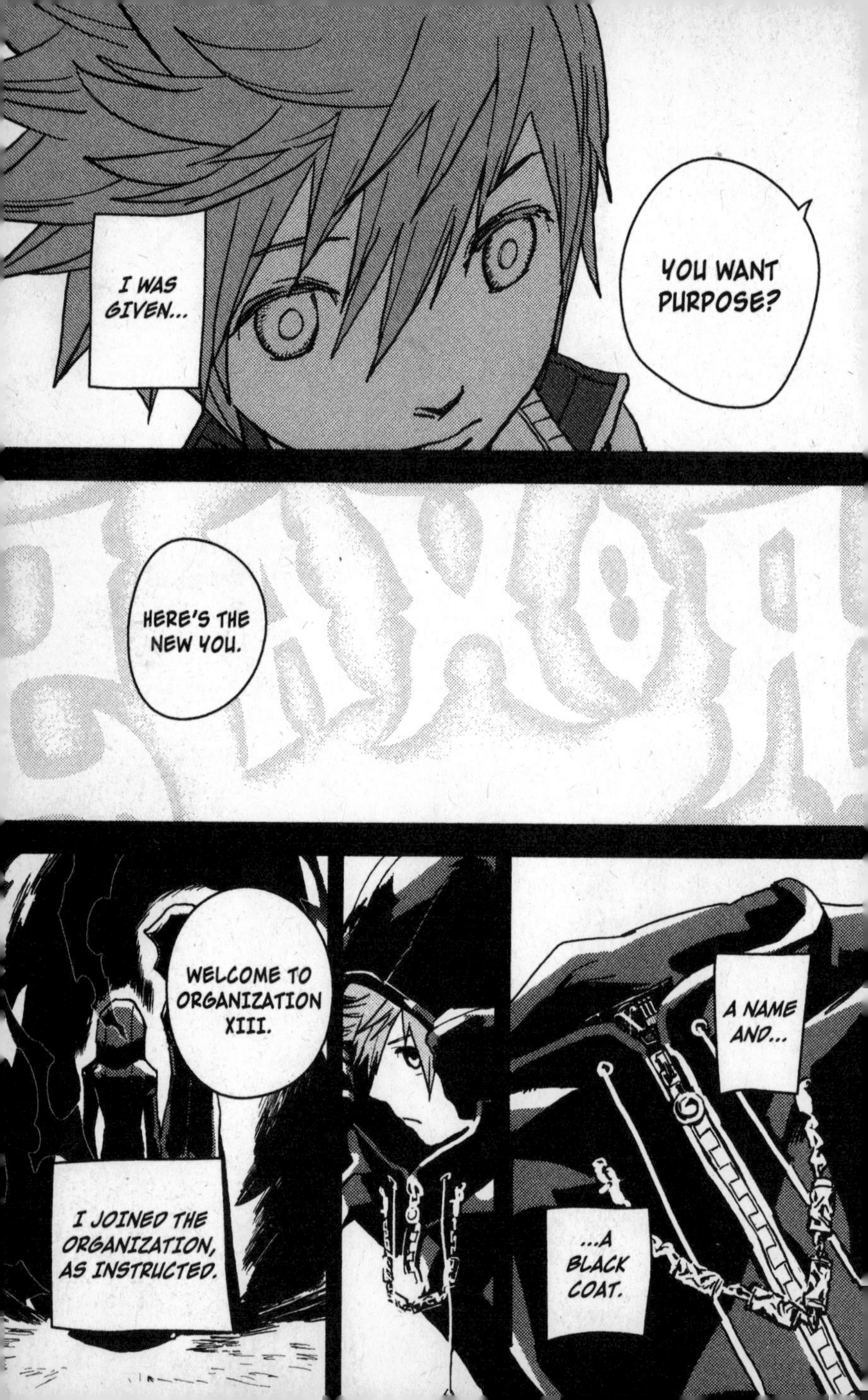
YOU WANT PURPOSE?
I WAS GIVEN...
HERE'S THE NEW YOU.
A NAME AND...
...A BLACK COAT.
WELCOME TO ORGANIZATION XIII.
I JOINED THE ORGANIZATION, AS INSTRUCTED.

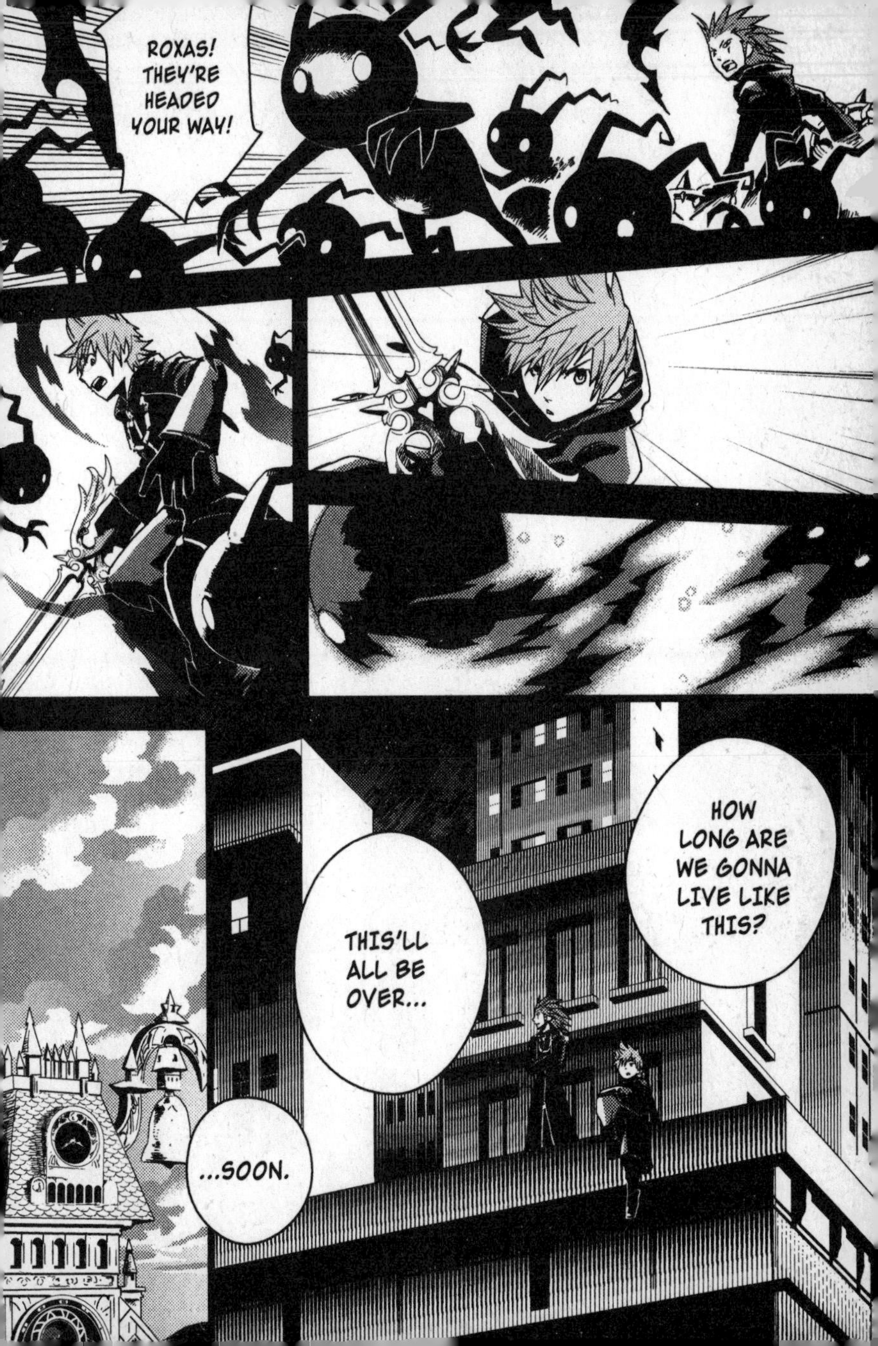
ROXAS! THEY'RE HEADED YOUR WAY!
HOW LONG ARE WE GONNA LIVE LIKE THIS?
THIS'LL ALL BE OVER...
...SOON.

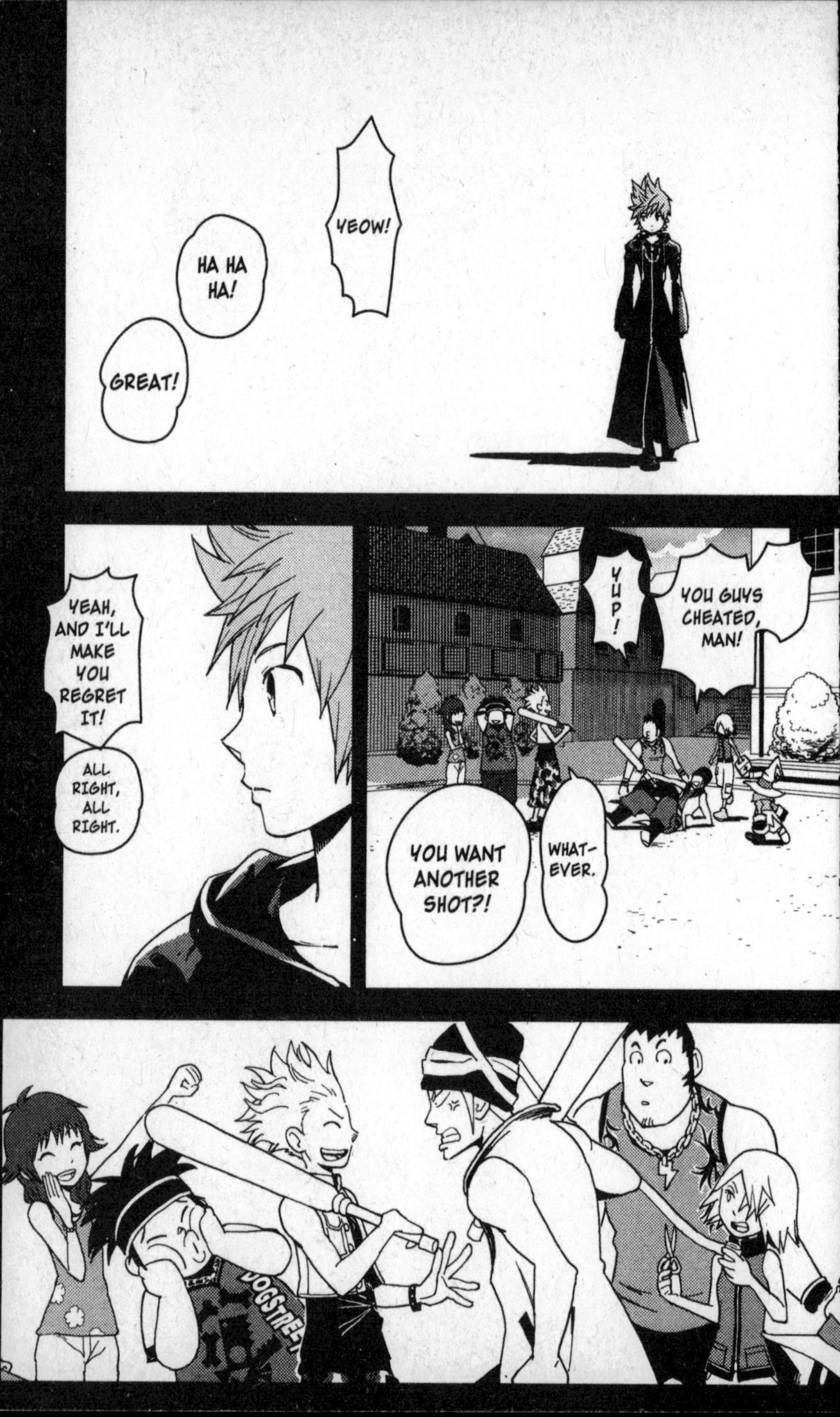
YEOW!
HA HA HA!
GREAT!
YOU GUYS CHEATED, MAN!
YUP!
WHAT-EVER.
YOU WANT ANOTHER SHOT?!
YEAH, AND I'LL MAKE YOU REGRET IT!
ALL RIGHT, ALL RIGHT.

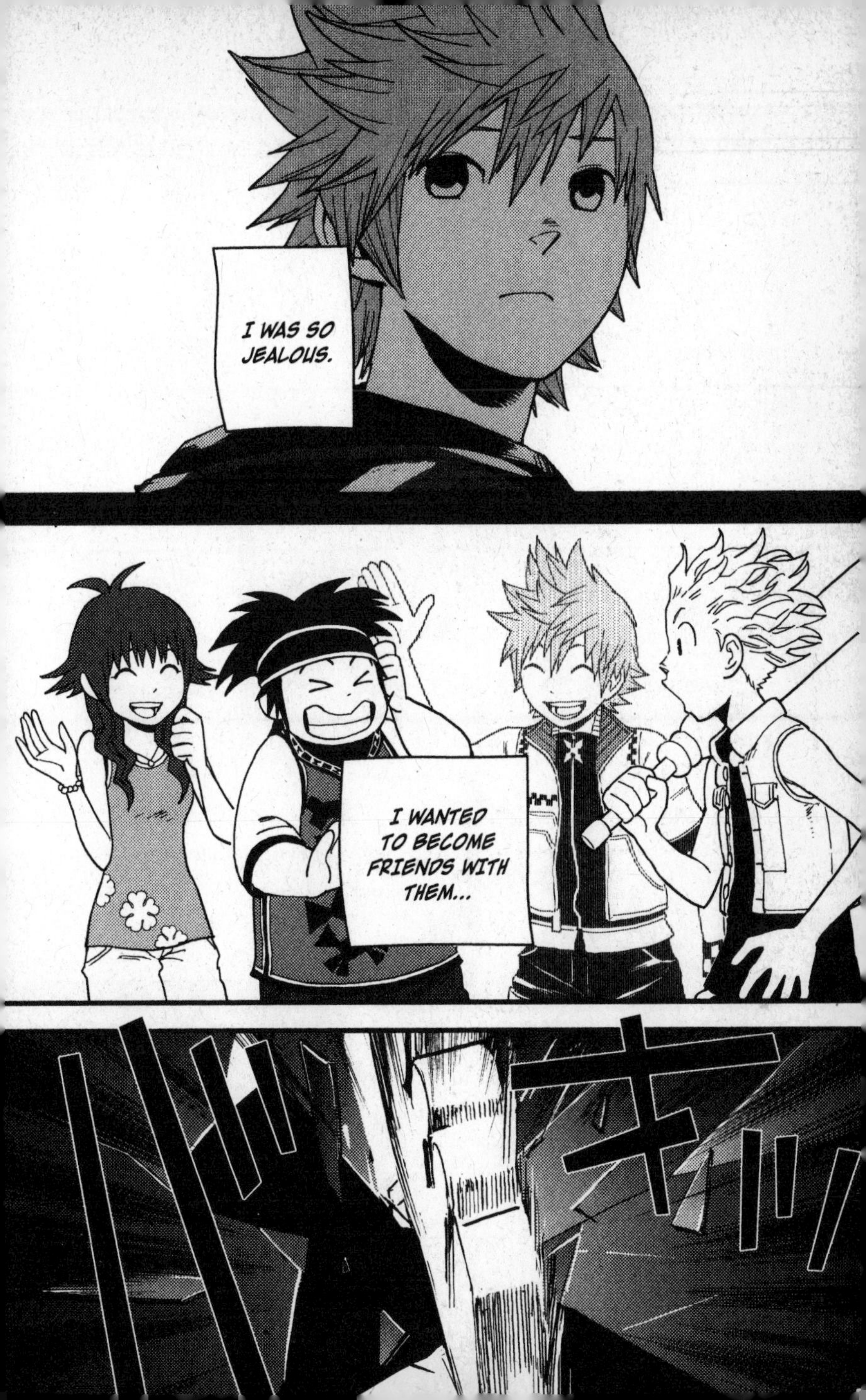
I WAS SO JEALOUS.
I WANTED TO BECOME FRIENDS WITH THEM...

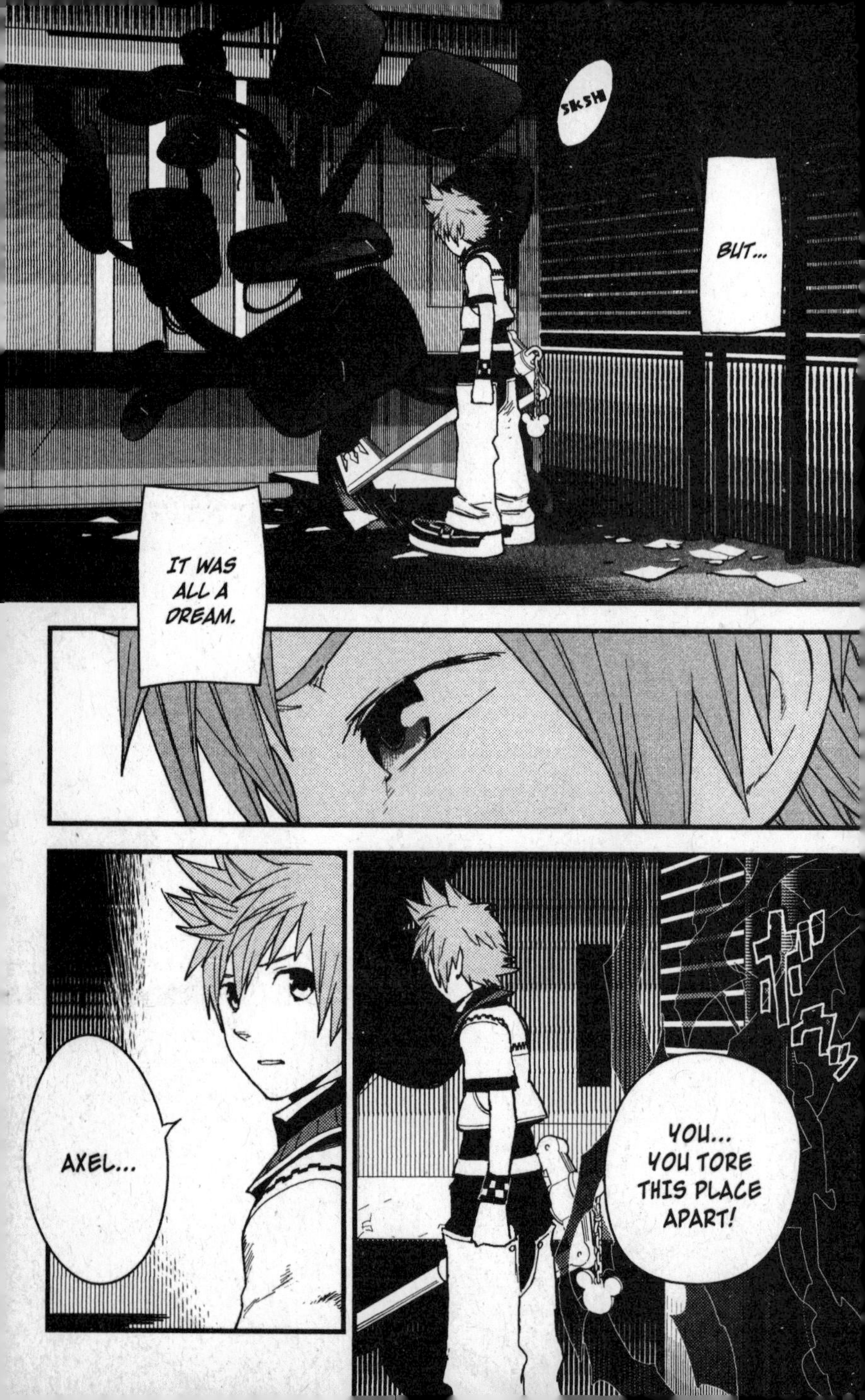
SKSH
BUT...
IT WAS ALL A DREAM.
YOU... YOU TORE THIS PLACE APART!
AXEL...

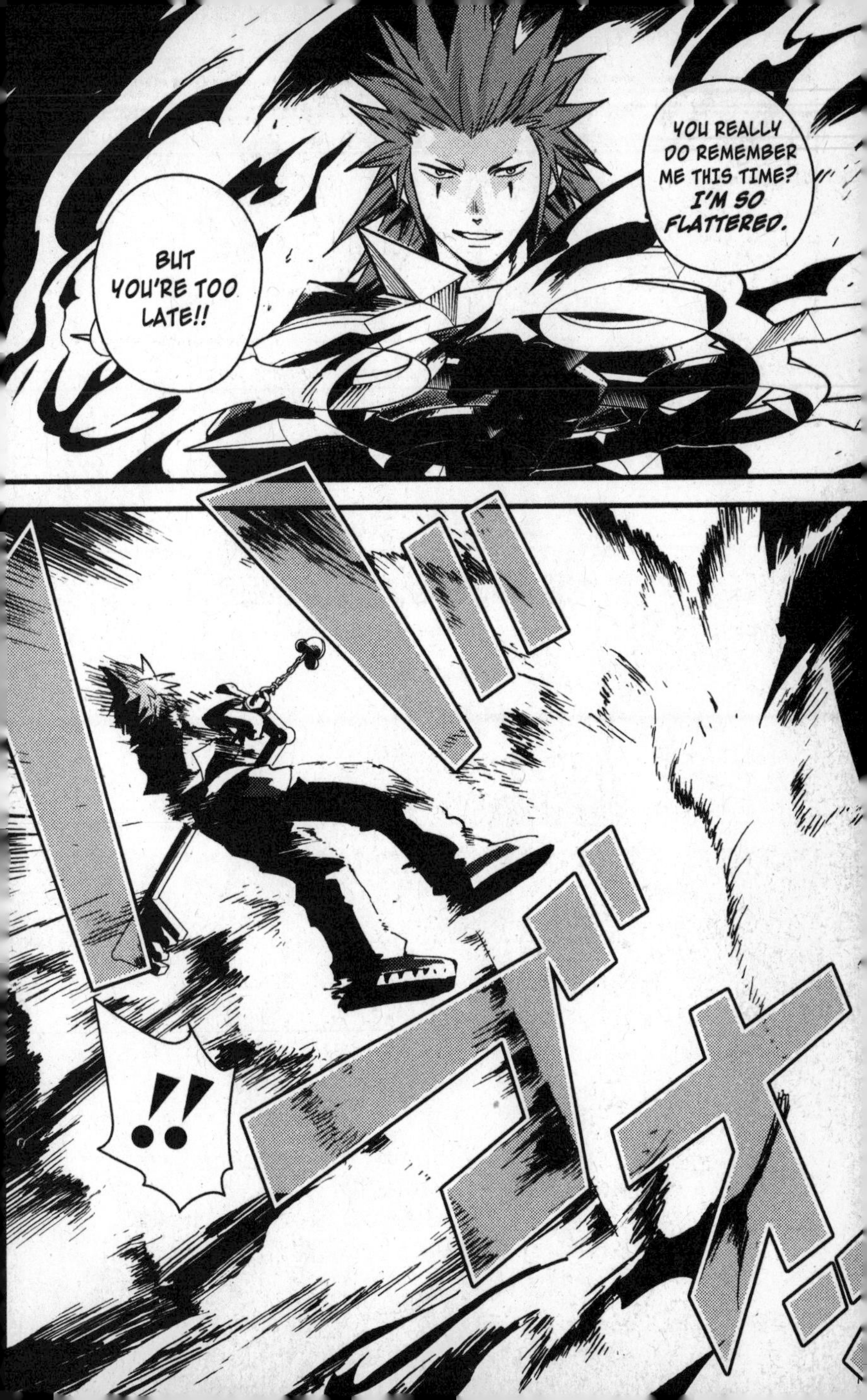
YOU REALLY DO REMEMBER ME THIS TIME? I'M SO FLATTERED.
BUT YOU'RE TOO LATE!!
!!

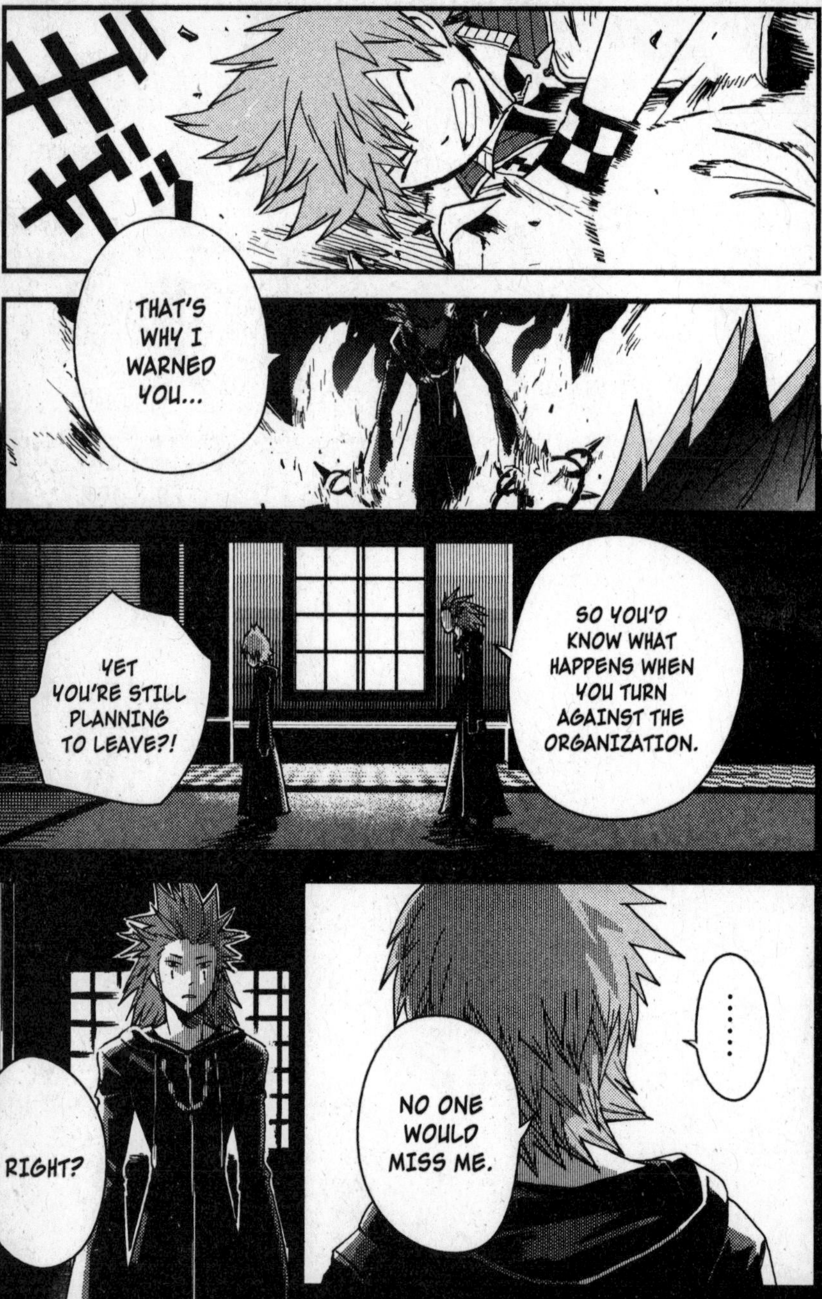
THAT'S WHY I WARNED YOU...
SO YOU'D KNOW WHAT HAPPENS WHEN YOU TURN AGAINST THE ORGANIZATION.
YET YOU'RE STILL PLANNING TO LEAVE?!
......
NO ONE WOULD MISS ME.
RIGHT?

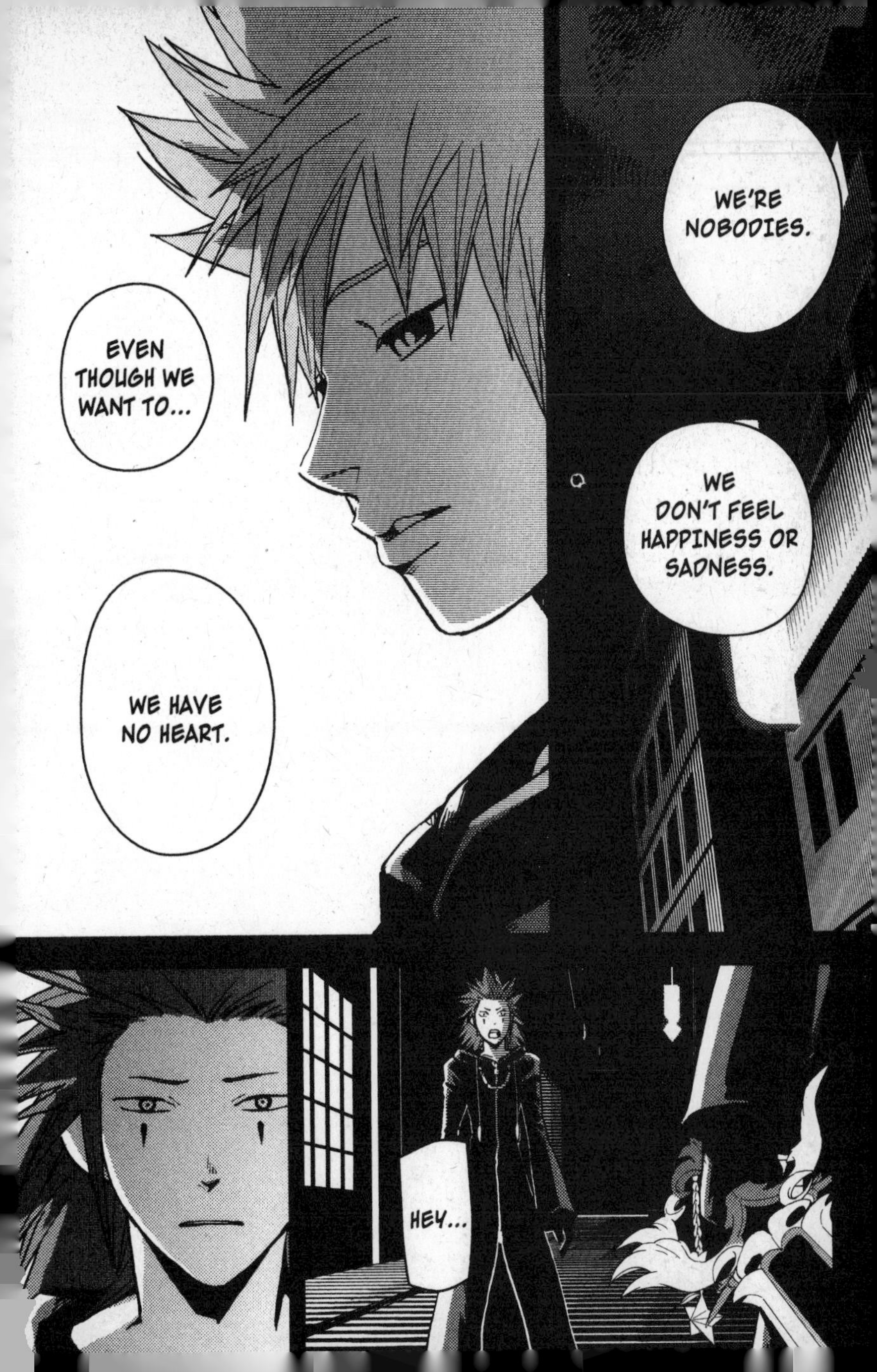
WE'RE NOBODIES.
WE DON'T FEEL HAPPINESS OR SADNESS.
EVEN THOUGH WE WANT TO...
WE HAVE NO HEART.
HEY...

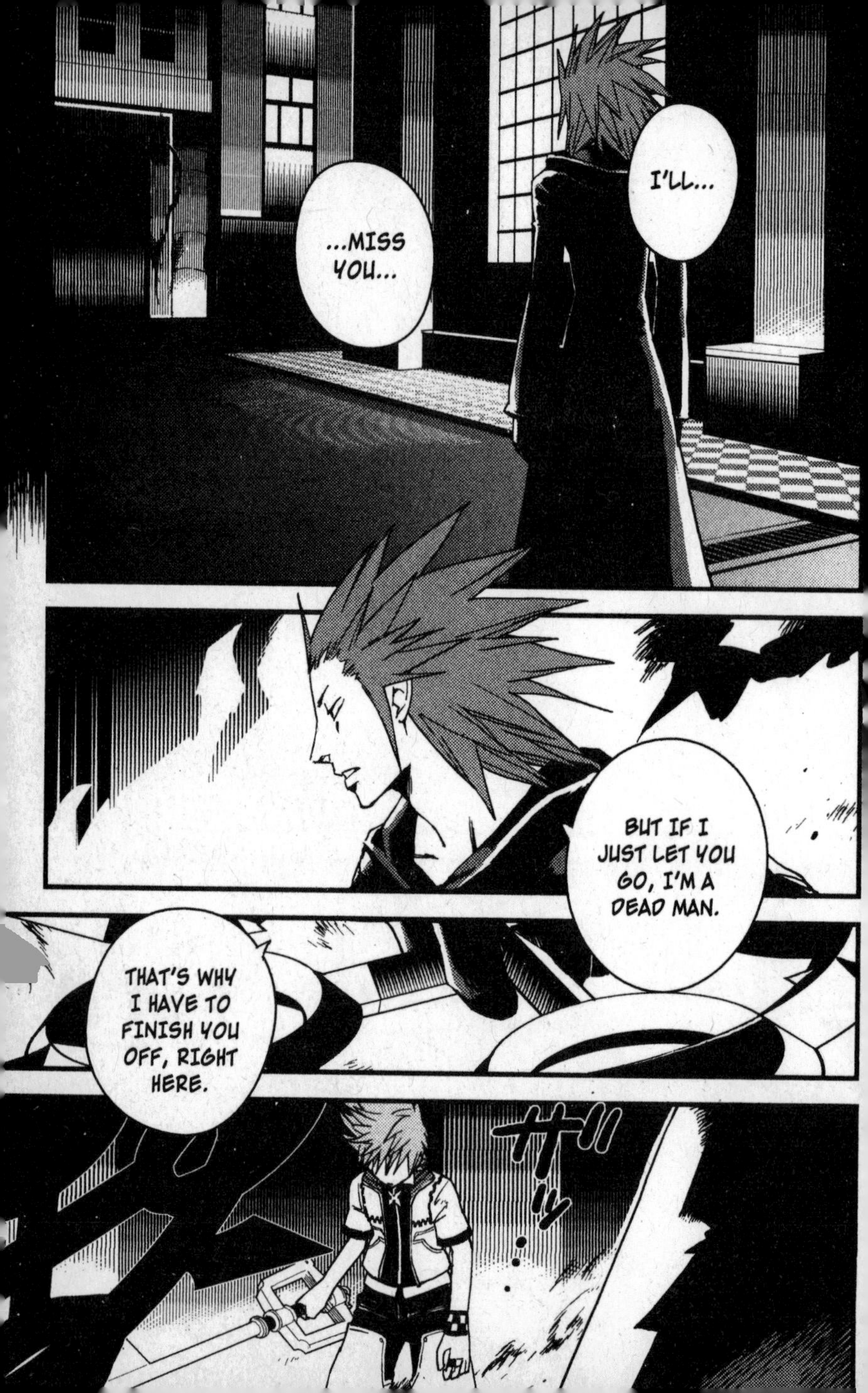
I'LL...
...MISS YOU...
BUT IF I JUST LET YOU GO, I'M A DEAD MAN.
THAT'S WHY I HAVE TO FINISH YOU OFF, RIGHT HERE.

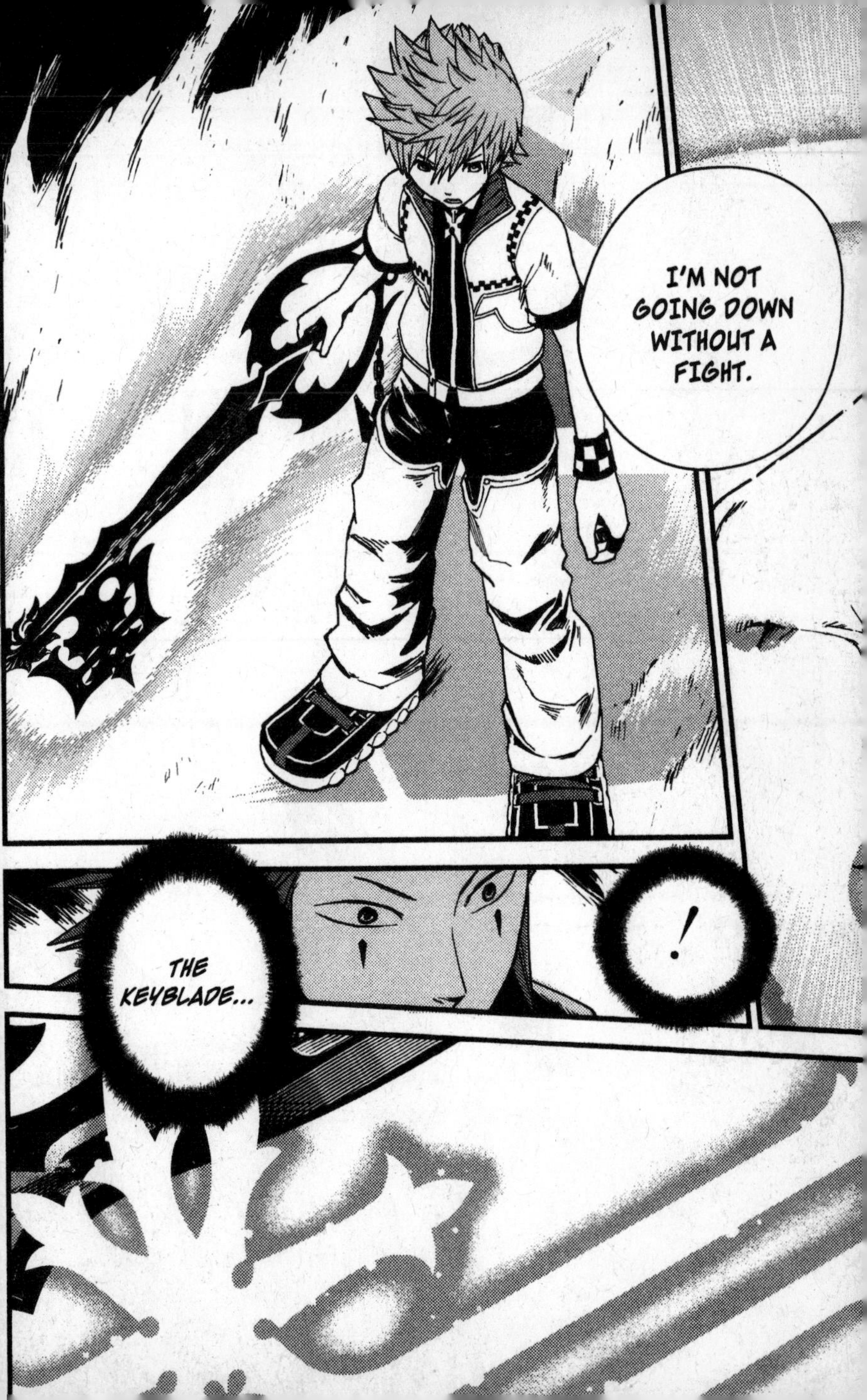
I'M NOT GOING DOWN WITHOUT A FIGHT.
!
THE KEYBLADE...

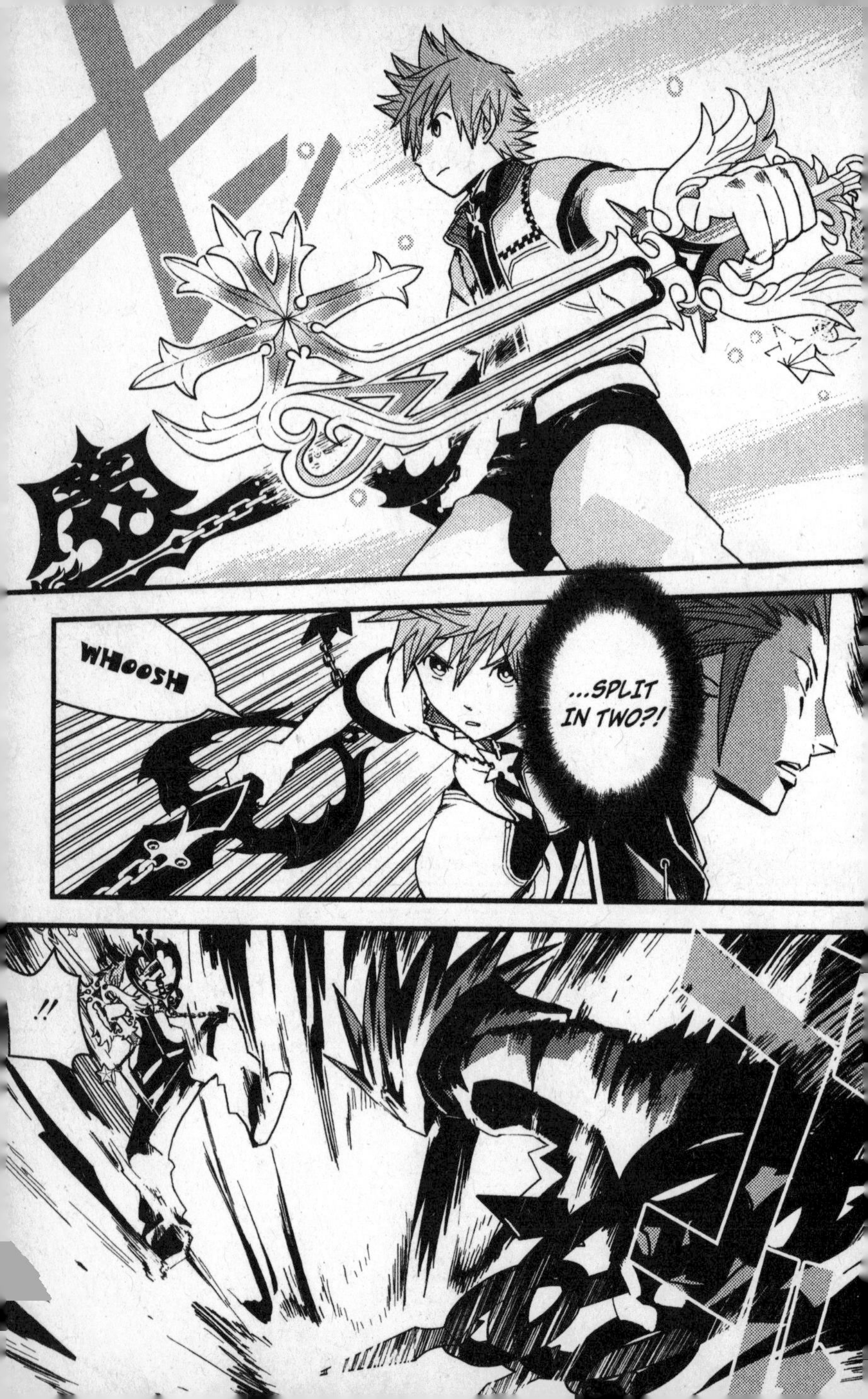
...SPLIT IN TWO?!
WHOOSH
!!

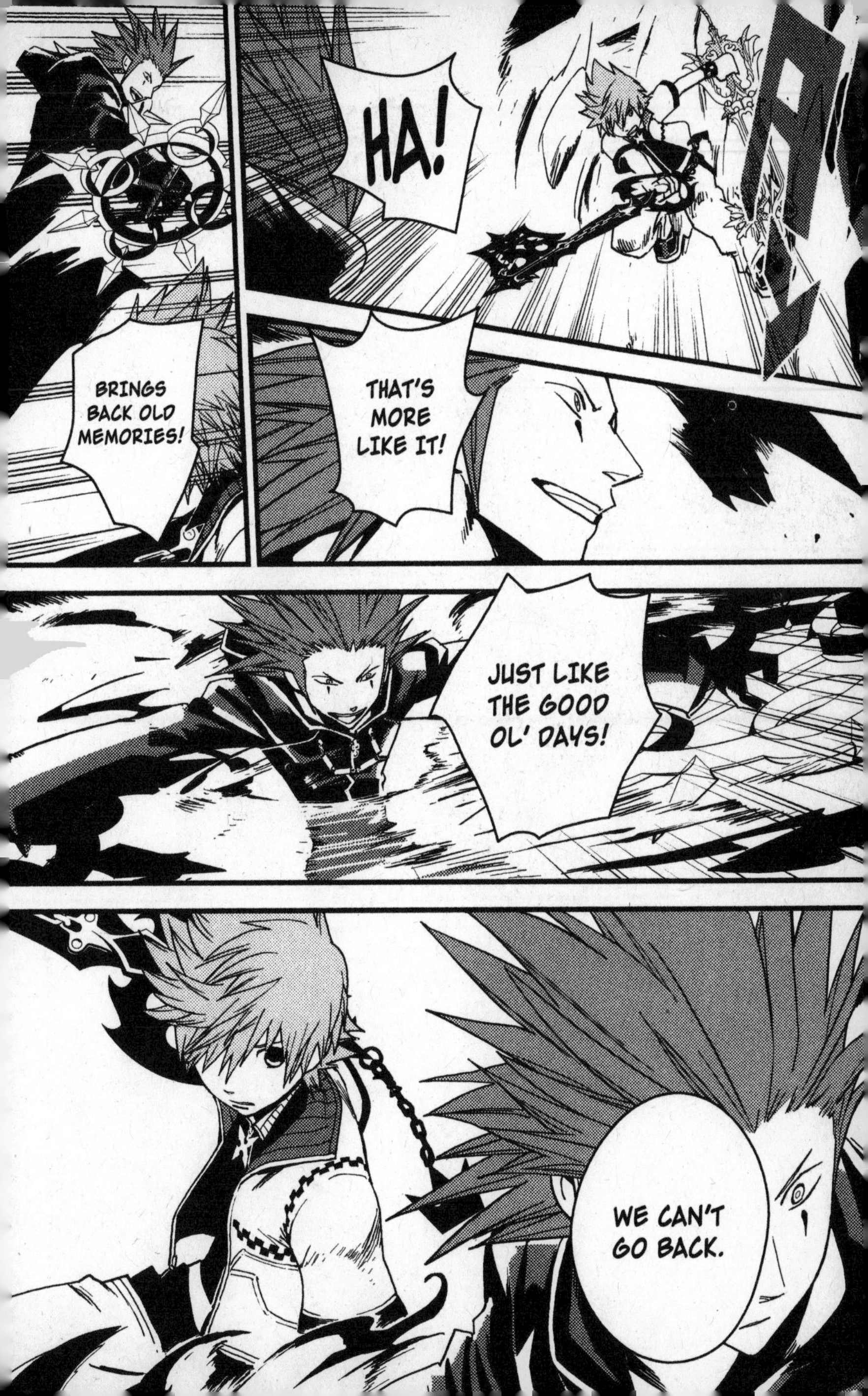
HA!
THAT'S MORE LIKE IT!
BRINGS BACK OLD MEMORIES!
JUST LIKE THE GOOD OL' DAYS!
WE CAN'T GO BACK.

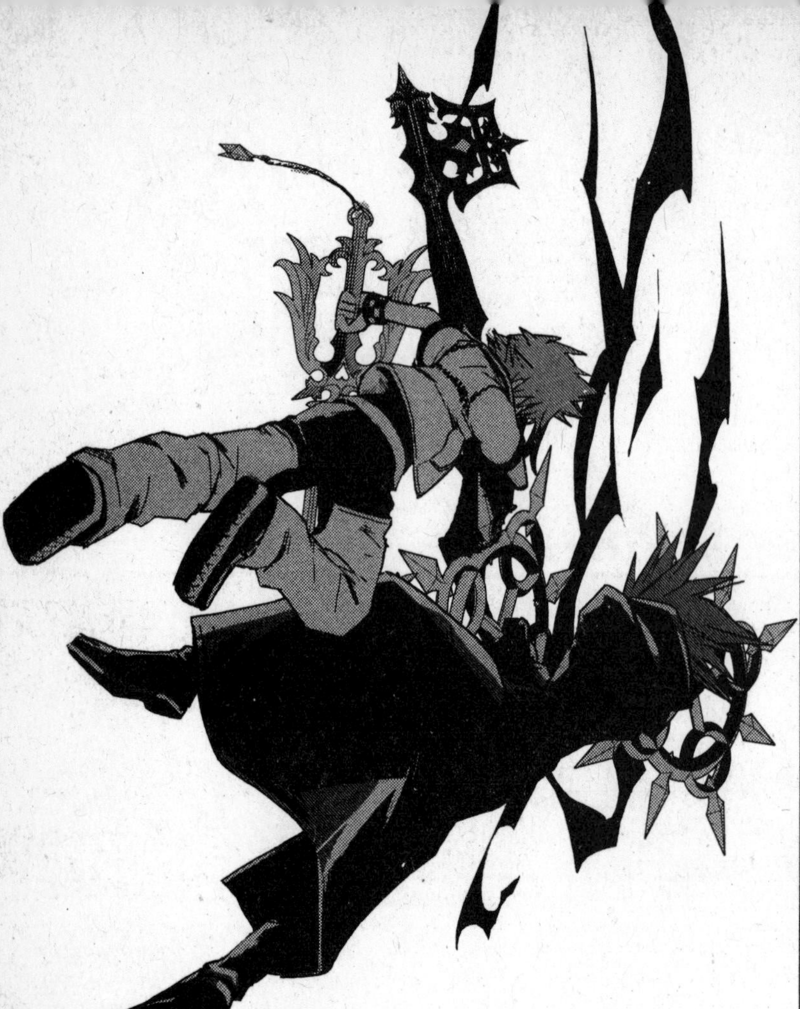

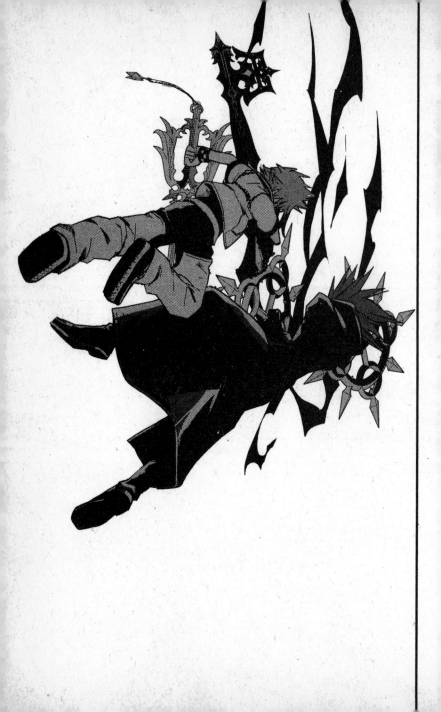

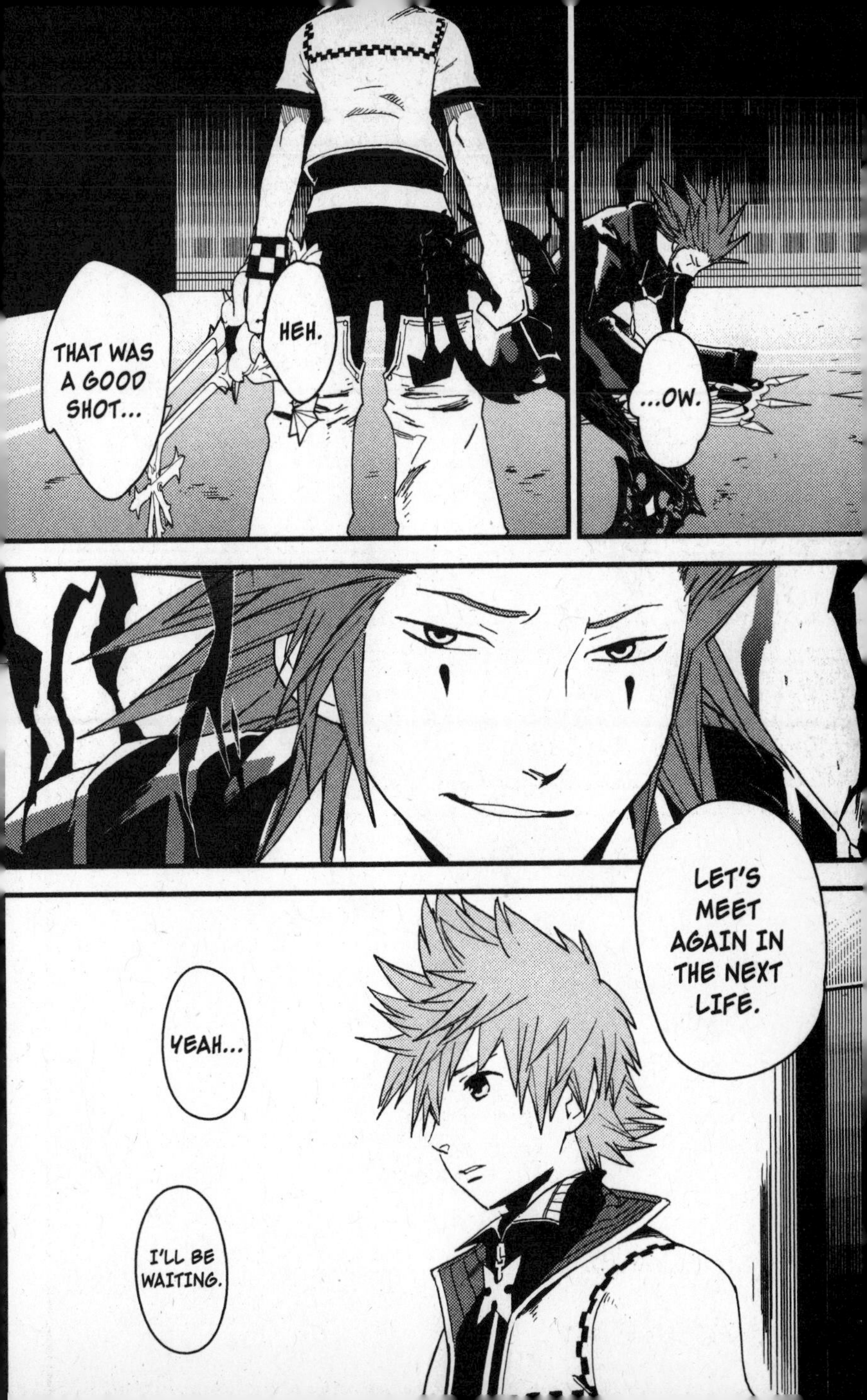
...OW.
HEH.
THAT WAS A GOOD SHOT...
LET'S MEET AGAIN IN THE NEXT LIFE.
YEAH...
I'LL BE WAITING.

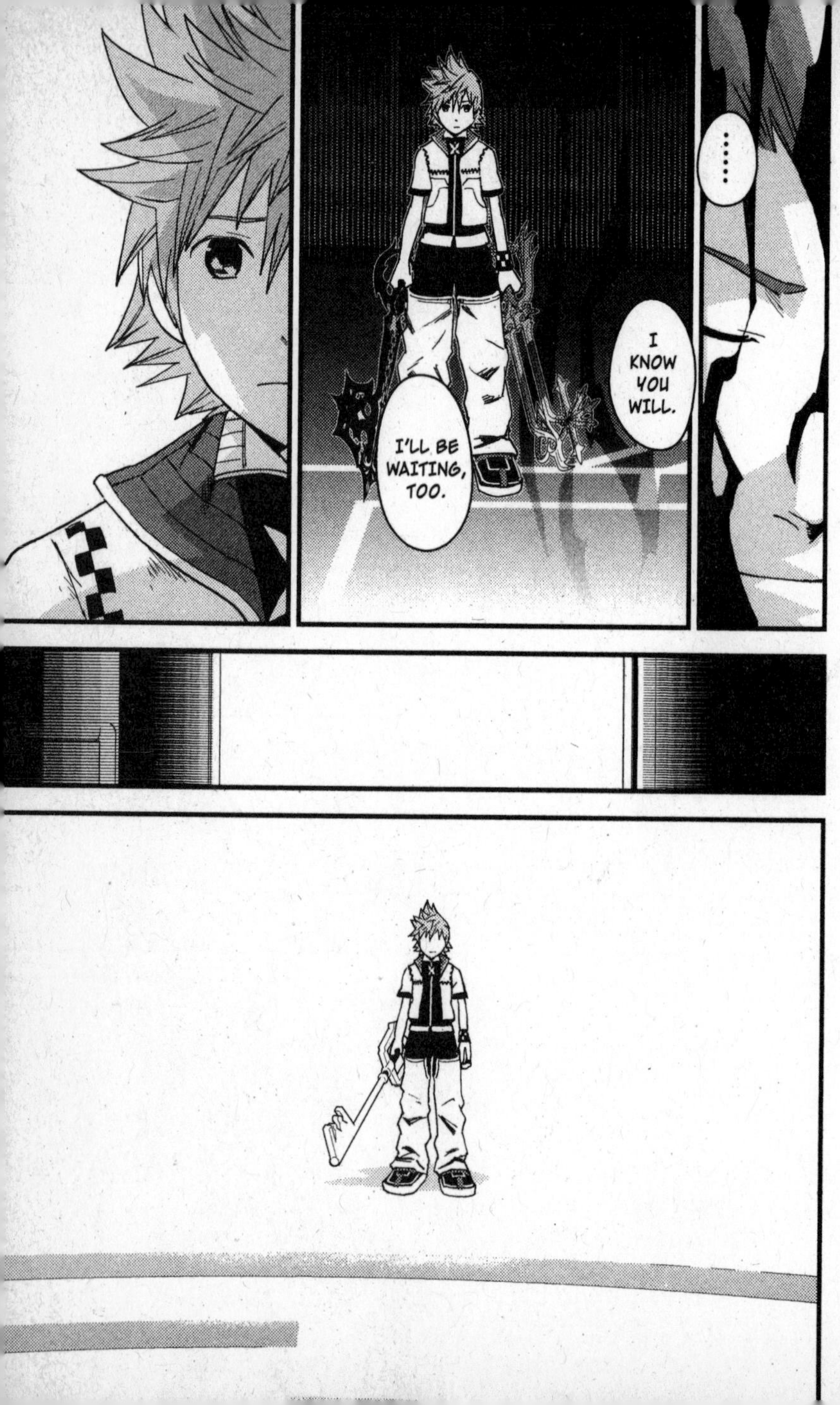
……
I KNOW YOU WILL.
I'LL BE WAITING, TOO.

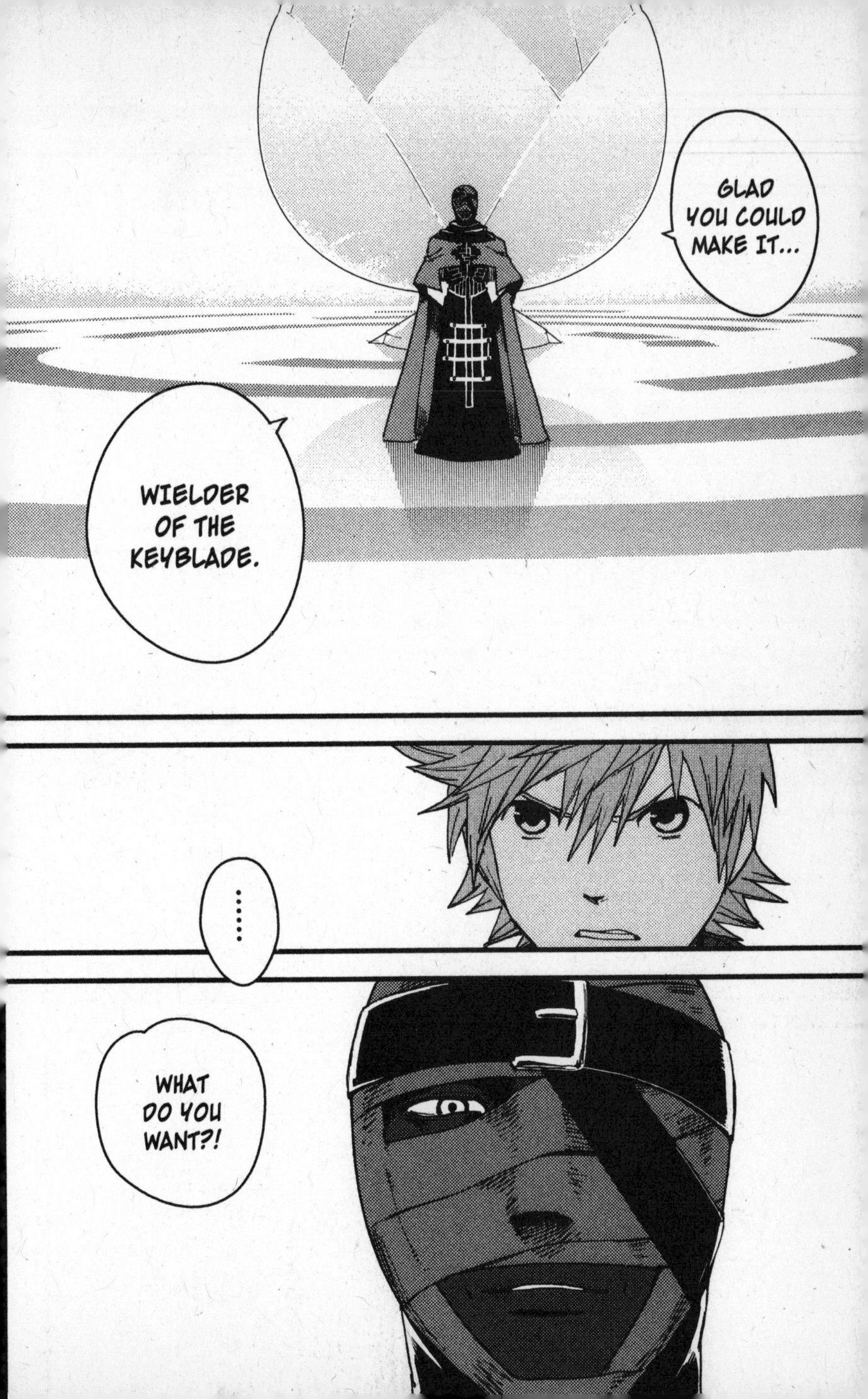
GLAD YOU COULD MAKE IT...
WIELDER OF THE KEYBLADE.
......
WHAT DO YOU WANT?!

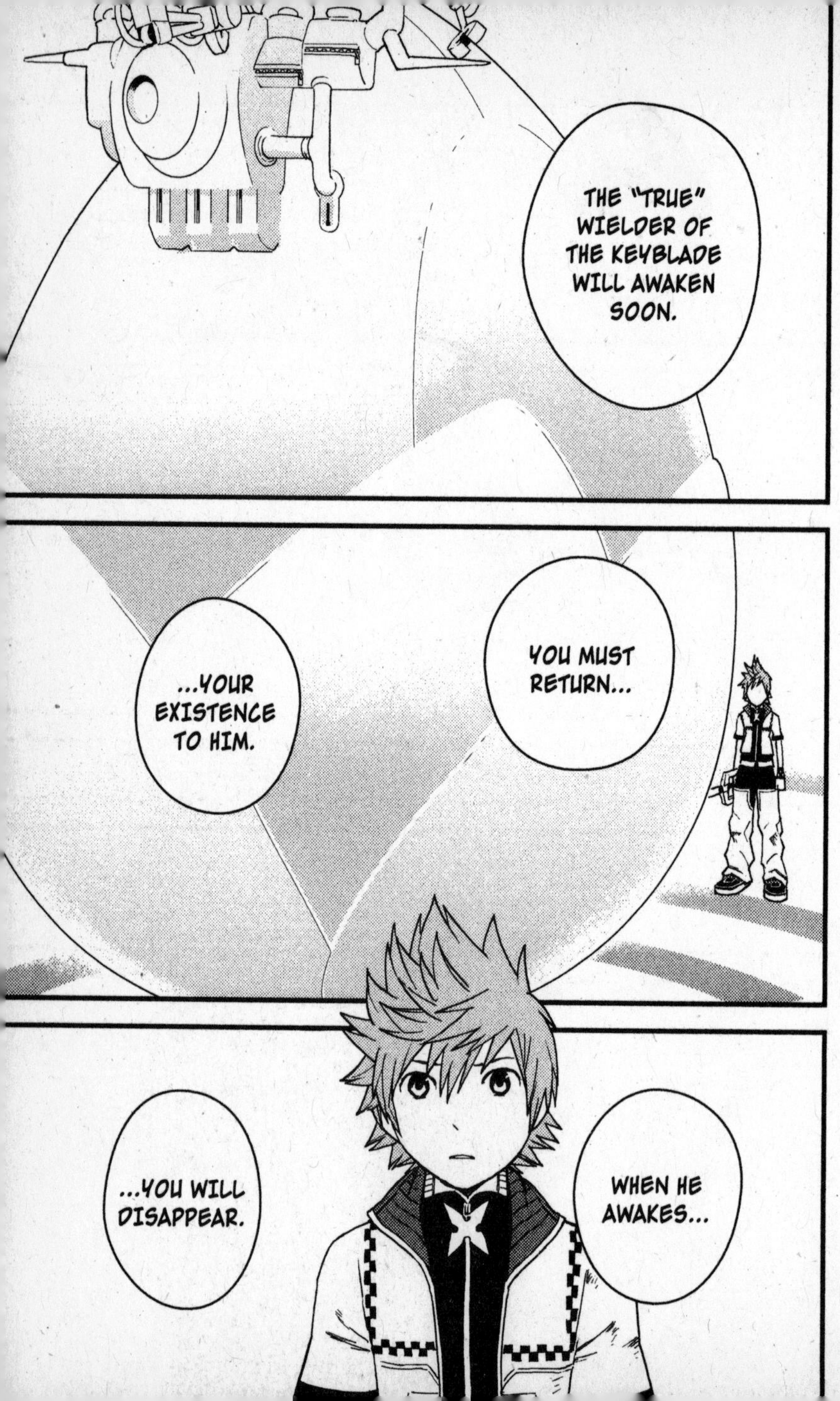
THE "TRUE" WIELDER OF THE KEYBLADE WILL AWAKEN SOON.
YOU MUST RETURN...
...YOUR EXISTENCE TO HIM.
WHEN HE AWAKES...
...YOU WILL DISAPPEAR.

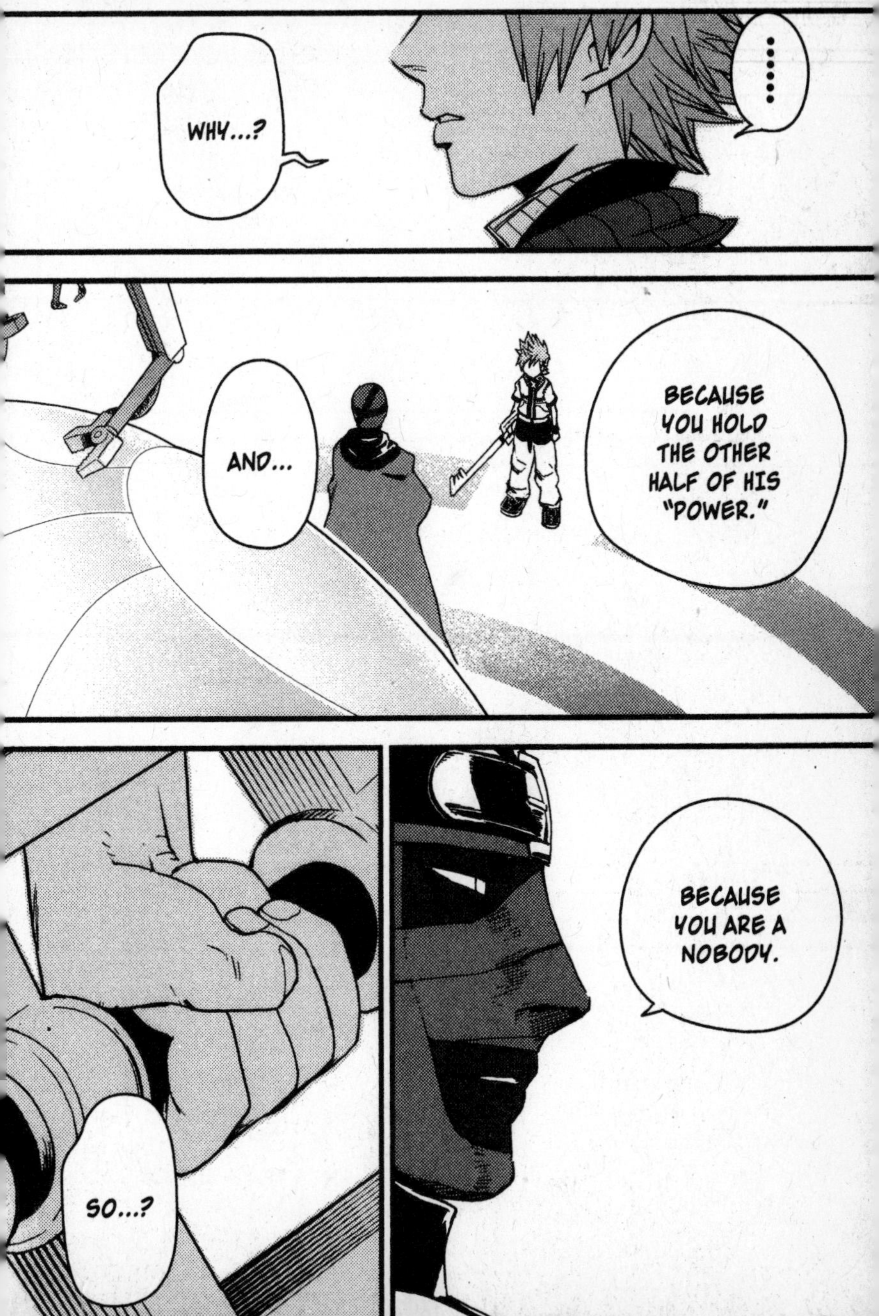
......
WHY...?
BECAUSE YOU HOLD THE OTHER HALF OF HIS "POWER."
AND...
BECAUSE YOU ARE A NOBODY.
SO...?

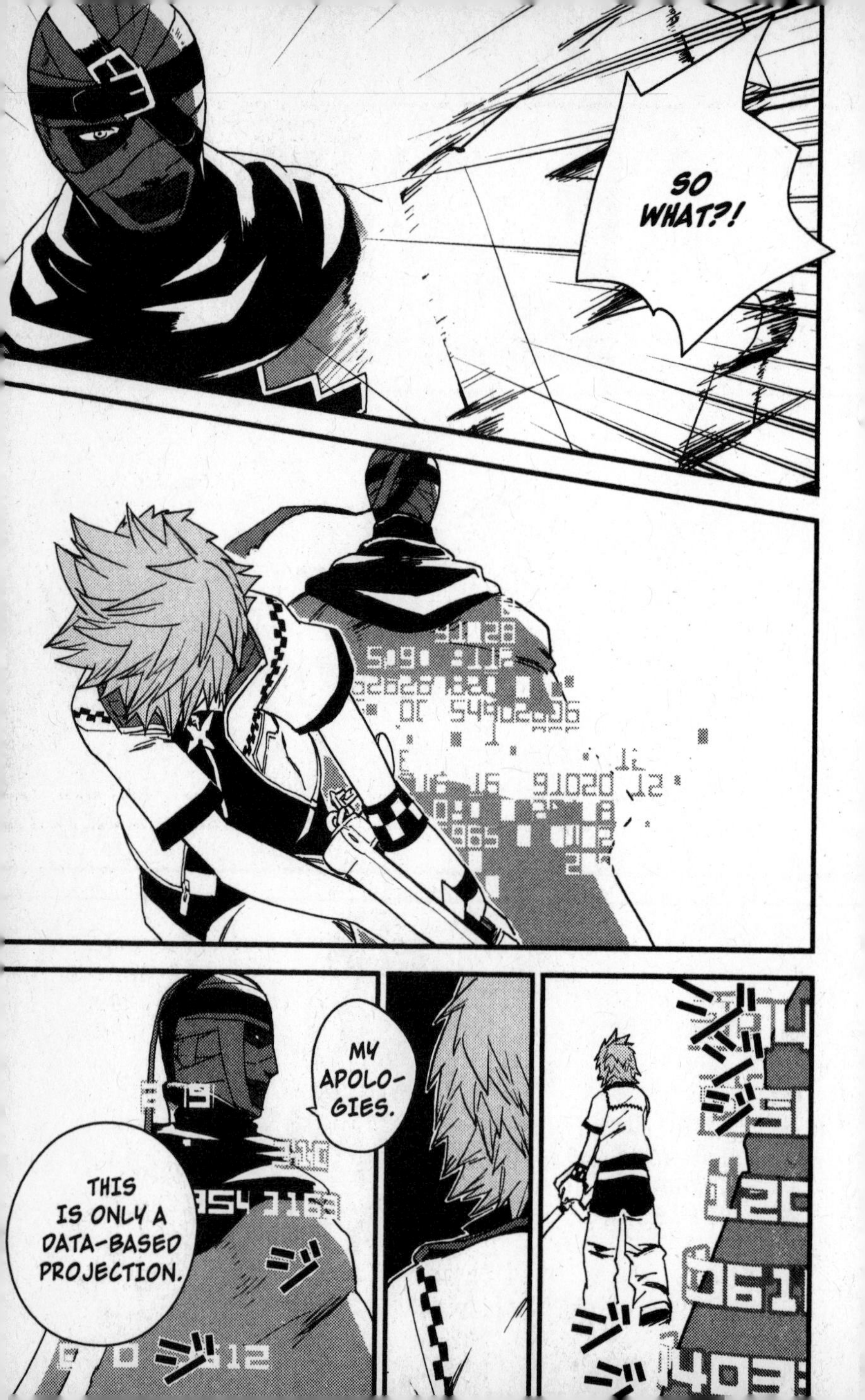
SO WHAT?!
MY APOLOGIES.
THIS IS ONLY A DATA-BASED PROJECTION.

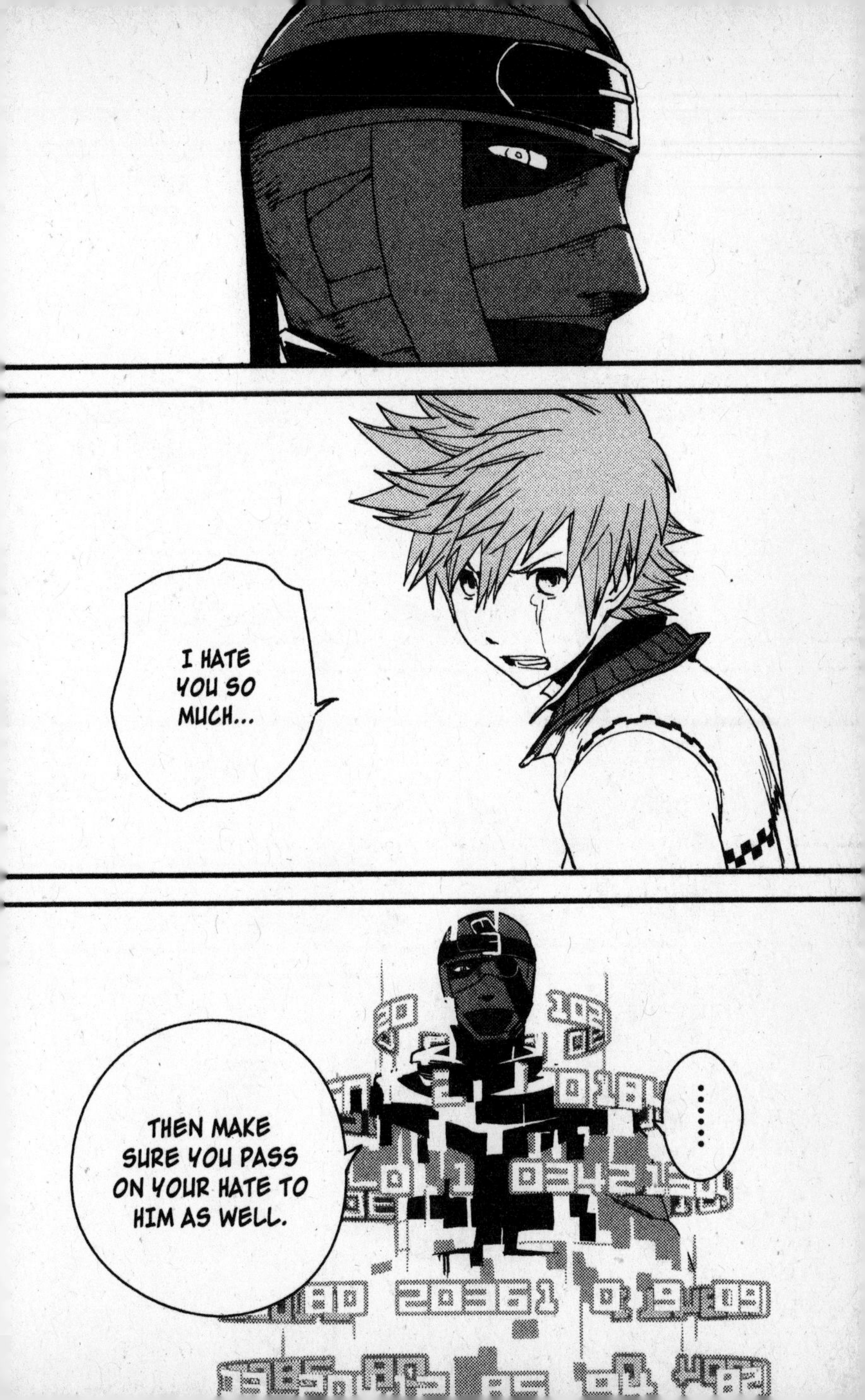
I HATE YOU SO MUCH...
......
THEN MAKE SURE YOU PASS ON YOUR HATE TO HIM AS WELL.

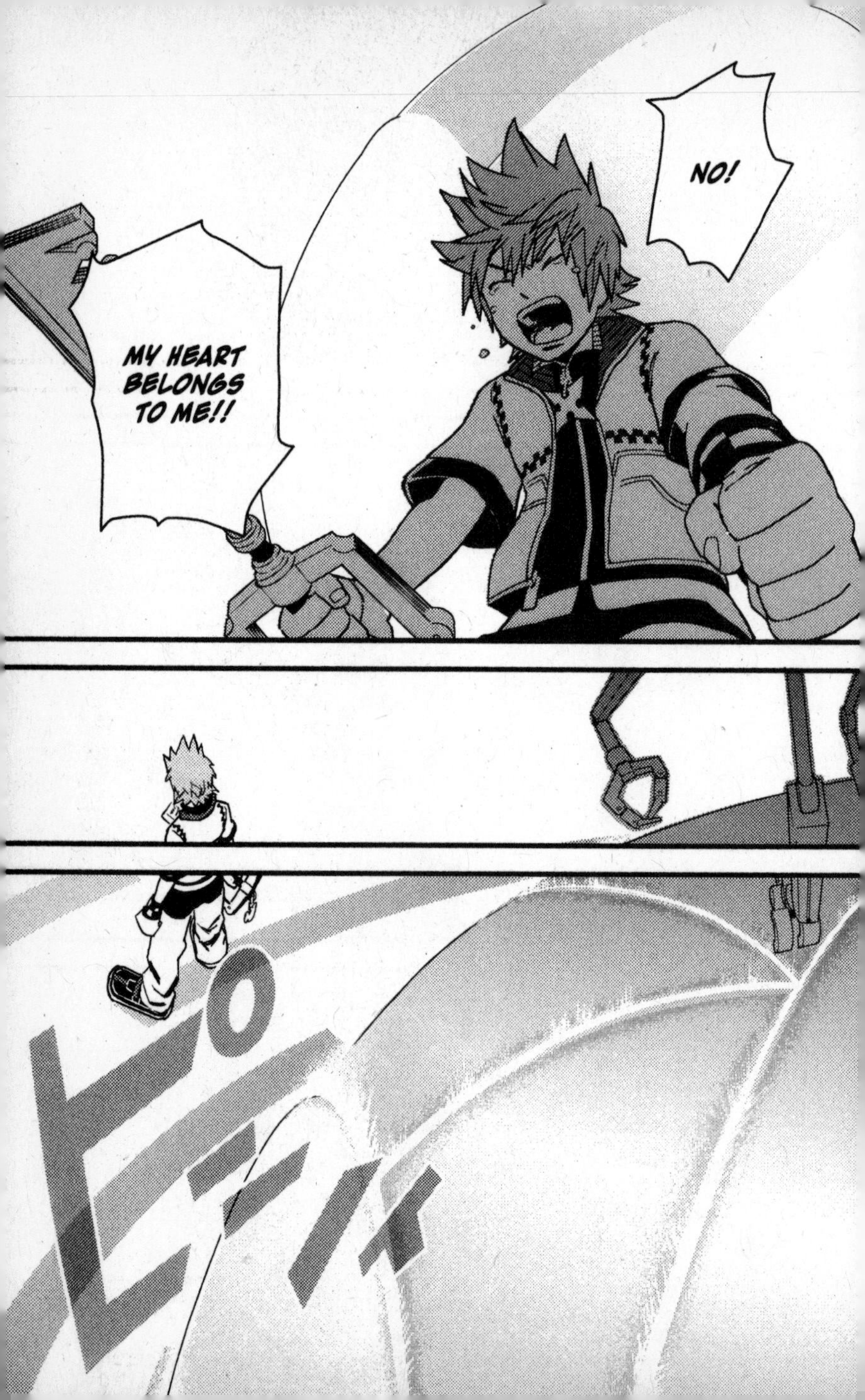
NO!
MY HEART BELONGS TO ME!!

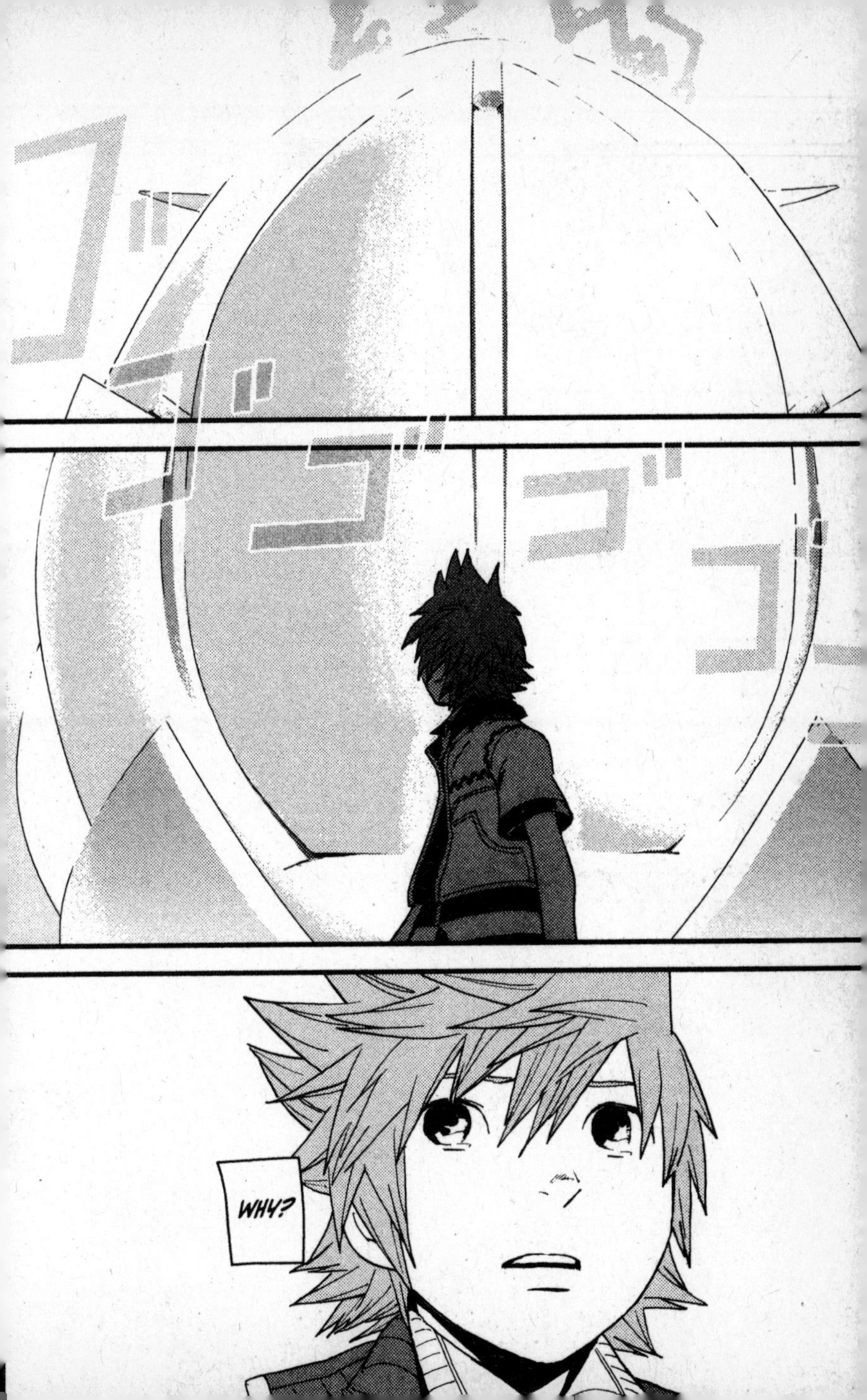
WHY?

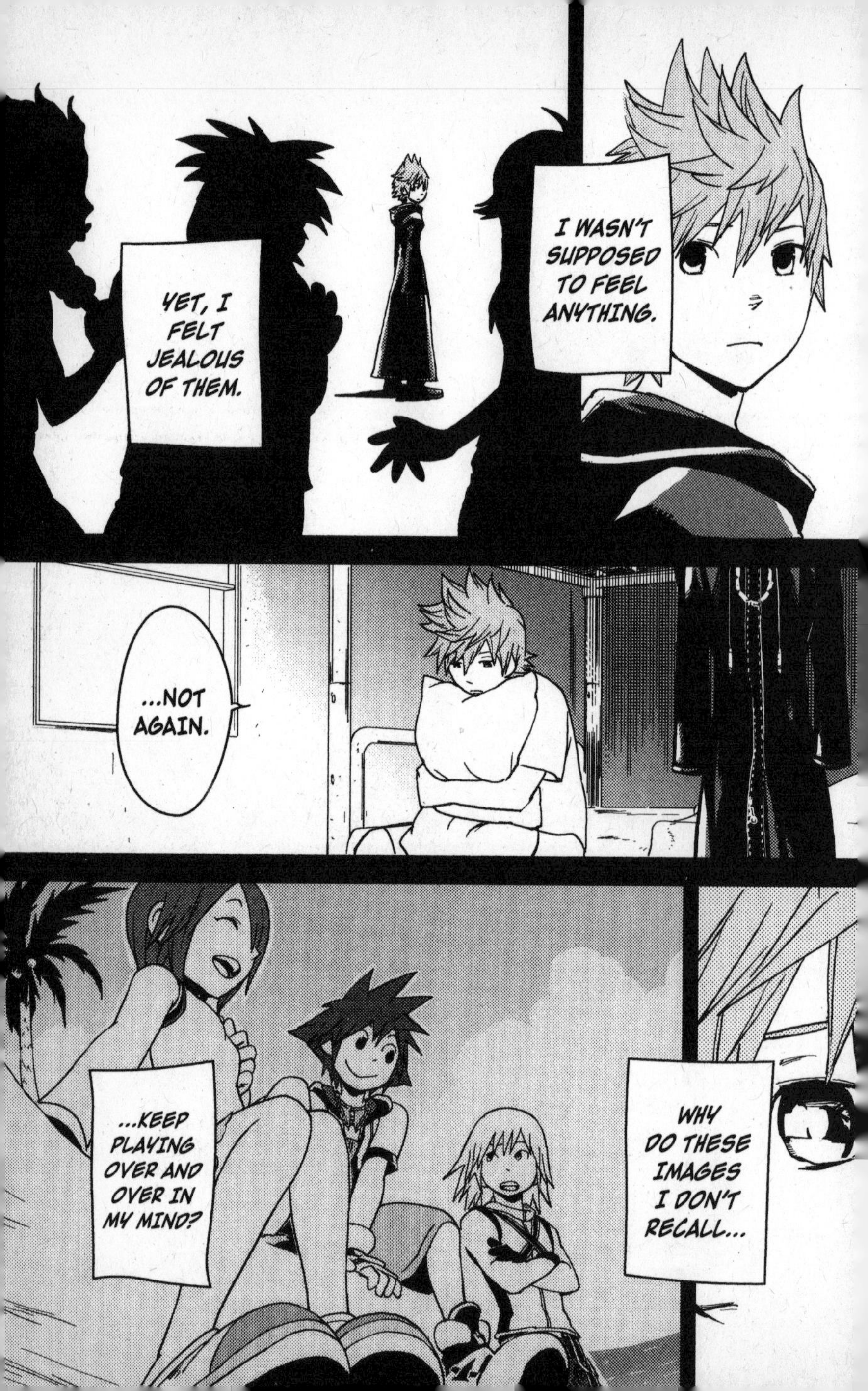
I WASN'T SUPPOSED TO FEEL ANYTHING.
YET, I FELT JEALOUS OF THEM.
...NOT AGAIN.
WHY DO THESE IMAGES I DON'T RECALL...
...KEEP PLAYING OVER AND OVER IN MY MIND?

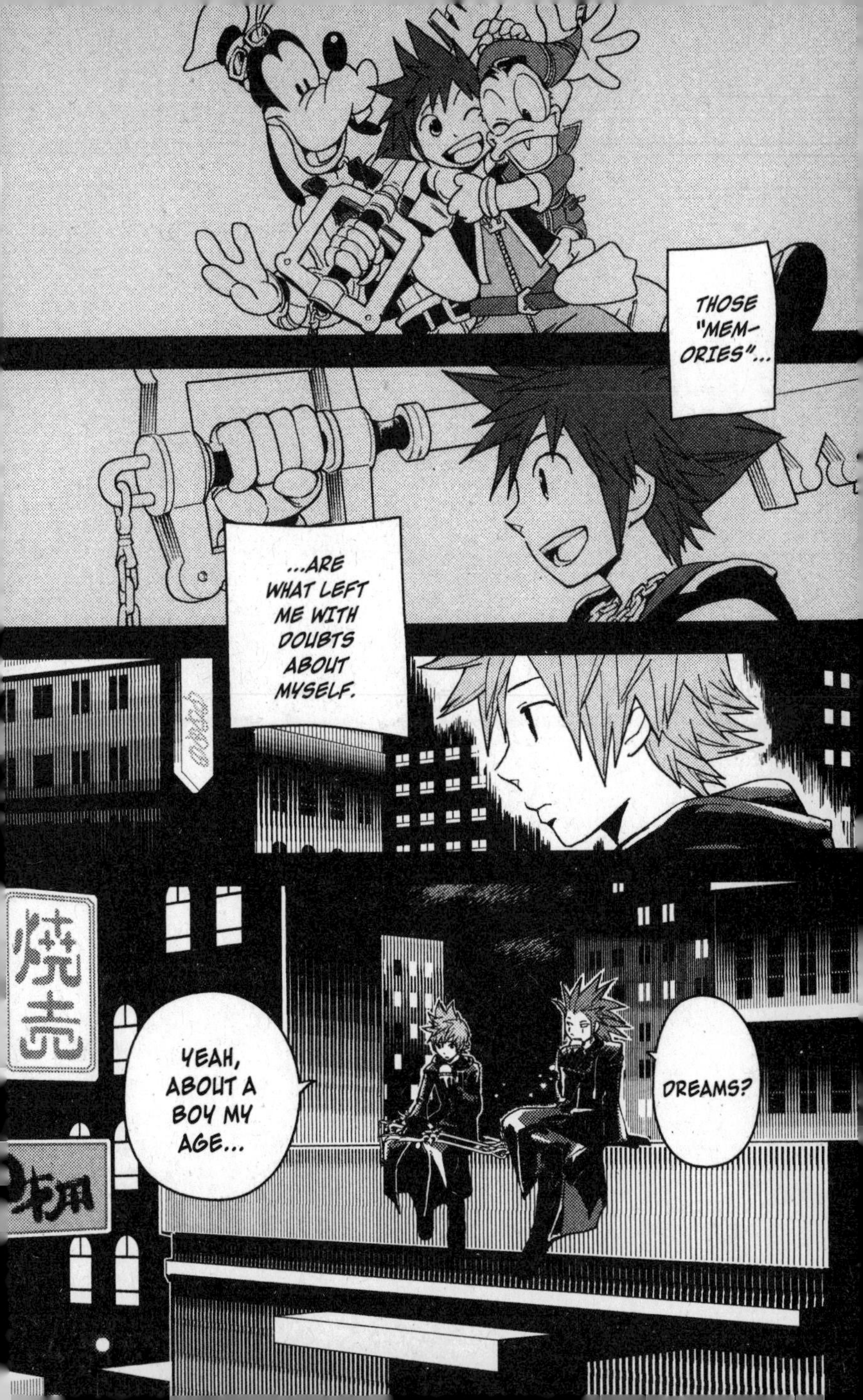
THOSE "MEM-ORIES"...
...ARE WHAT LEFT ME WITH DOUBTS ABOUT MYSELF.
DREAMS?
YEAH, ABOUT A BOY MY AGE...
焼売

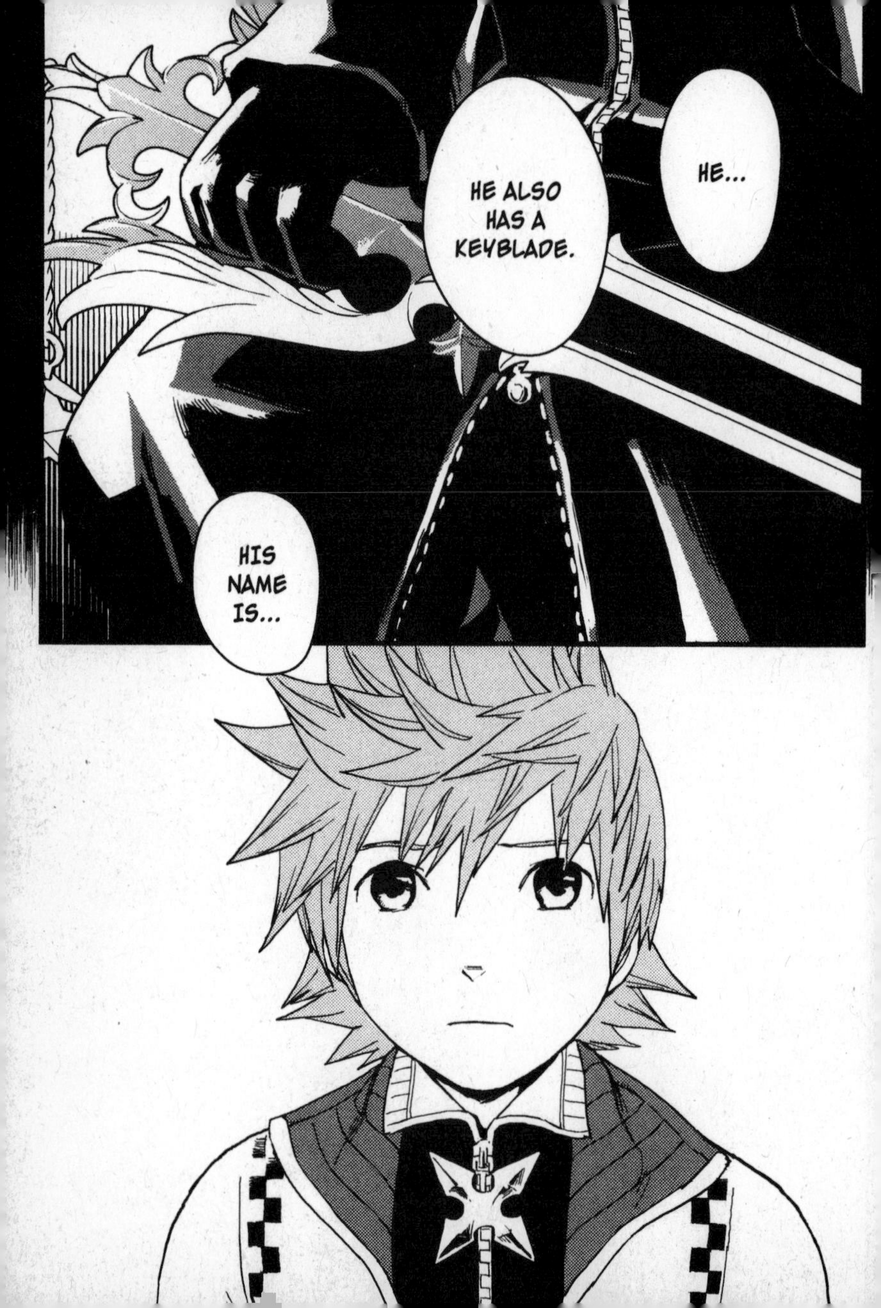
HE...
HE ALSO HAS A KEYBLADE.
HIS NAME IS...

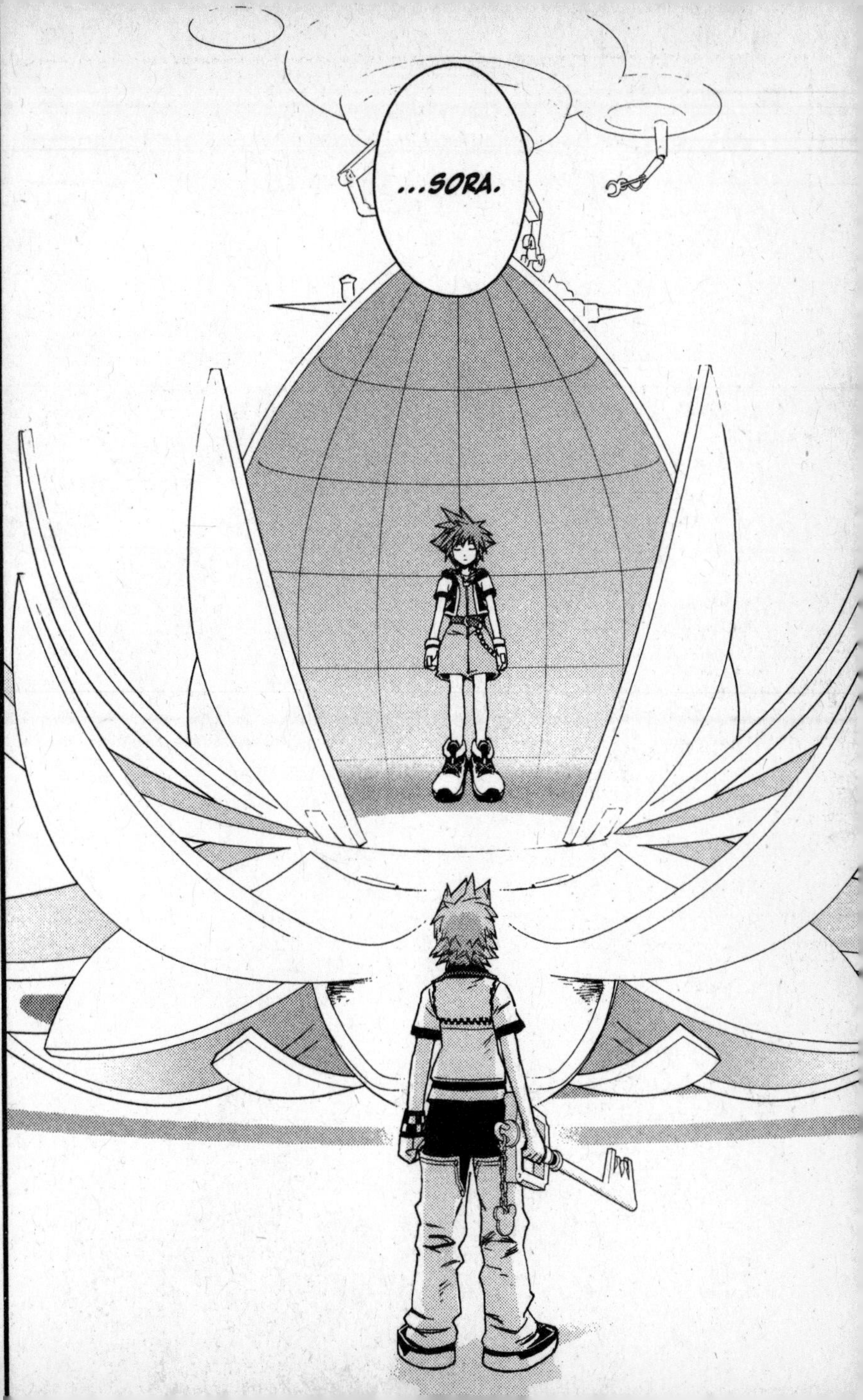
...SORA.

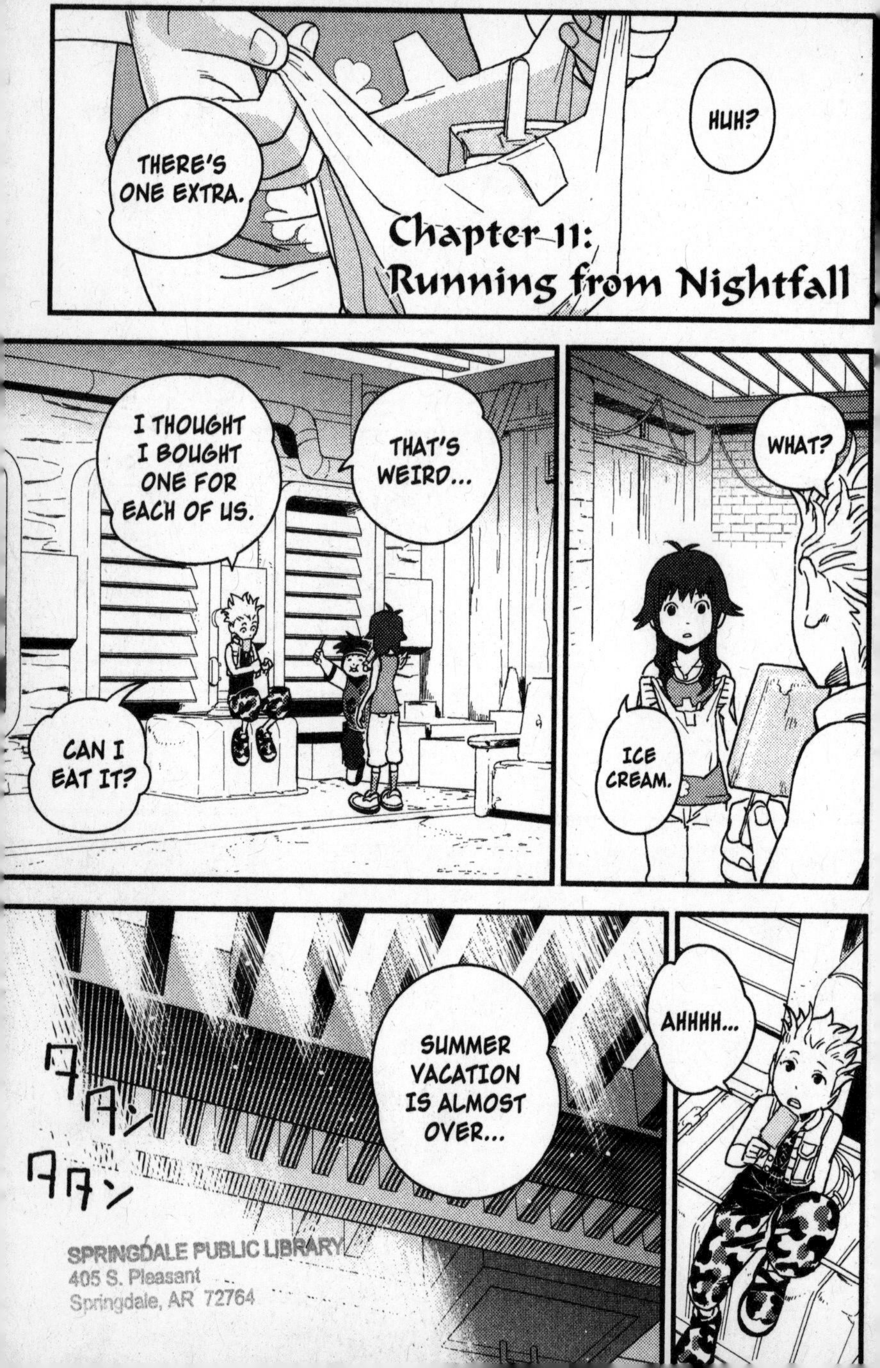
HUH?
THERE'S ONE EXTRA.
Chapter 11: Running from Nightfall
WHAT?
ICE CREAM.
THAT'S WEIRD...
I THOUGHT I BOUGHT ONE FOR EACH OF US.
CAN I EAT IT?
AHHHH...
SUMMER VACATION IS ALMOST OVER...

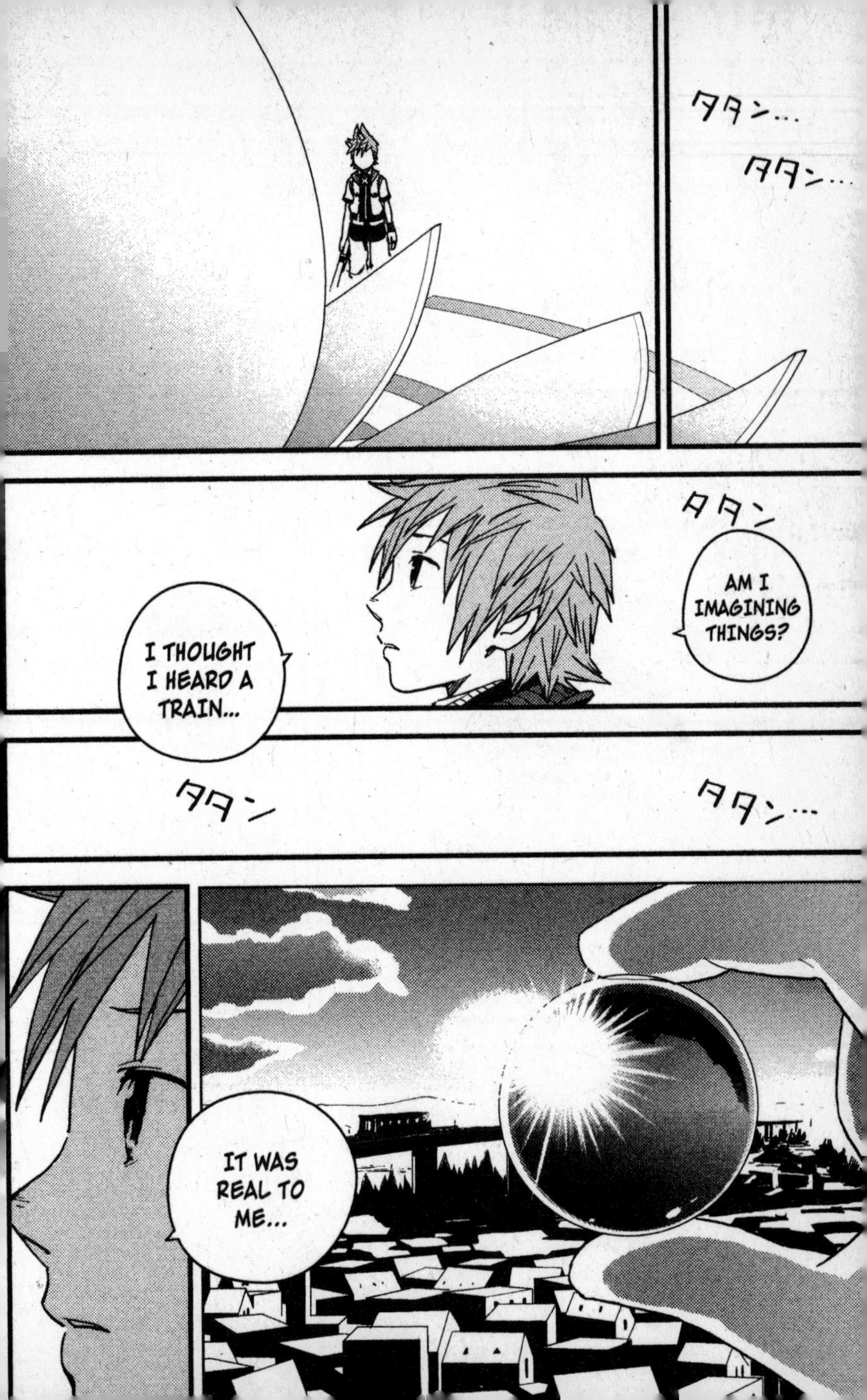
タタン…
タタン…
タタン
AM I IMAGINING THINGS?
I THOUGHT I HEARD A TRAIN...
タタン…
タタン
IT WAS REAL TO ME...

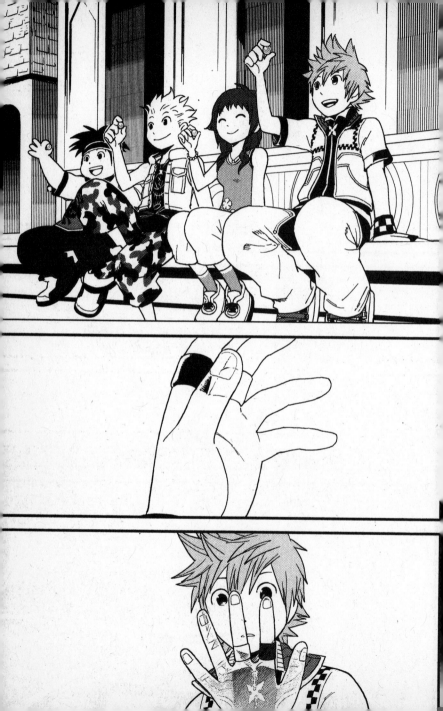

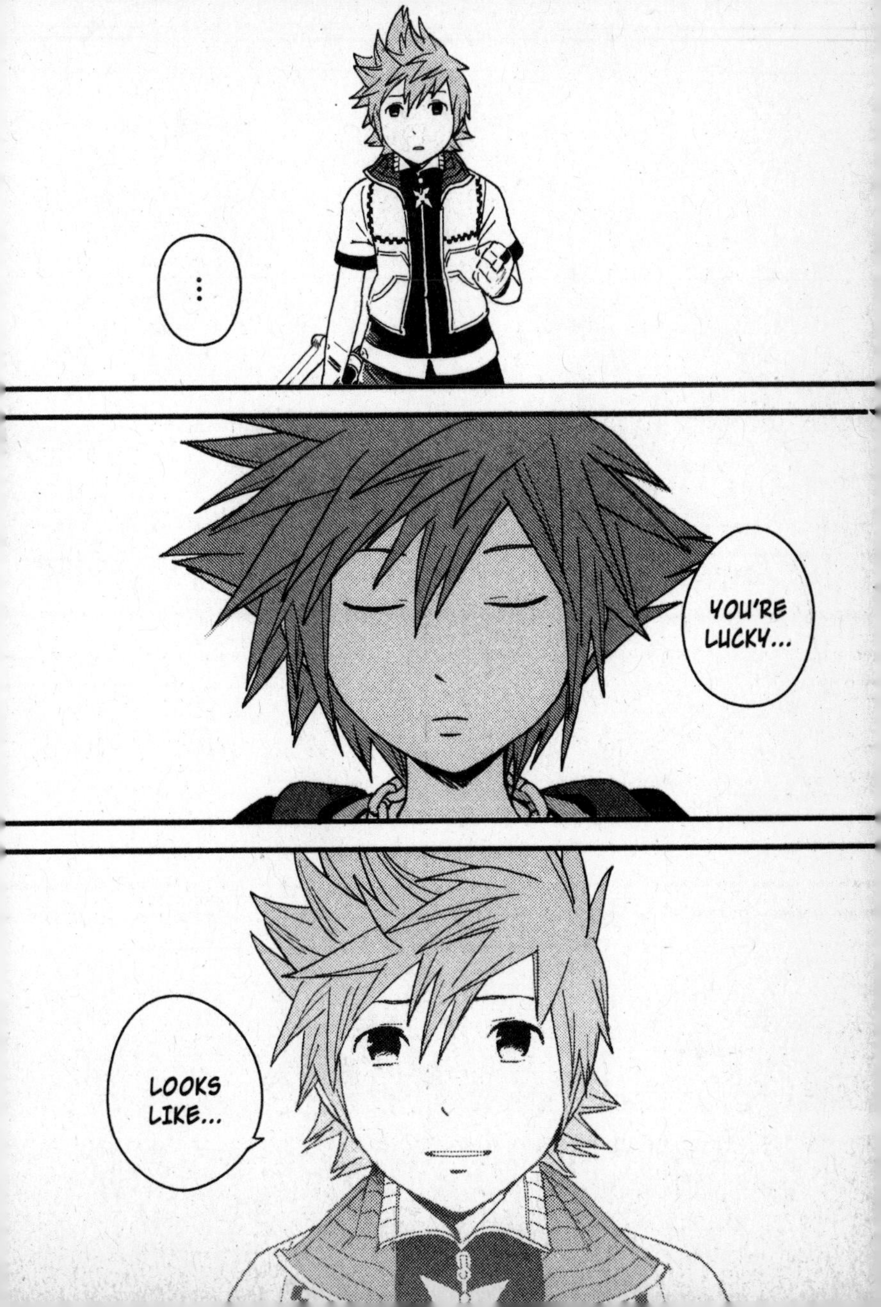
...
YOU'RE LUCKY...
LOOKS LIKE...

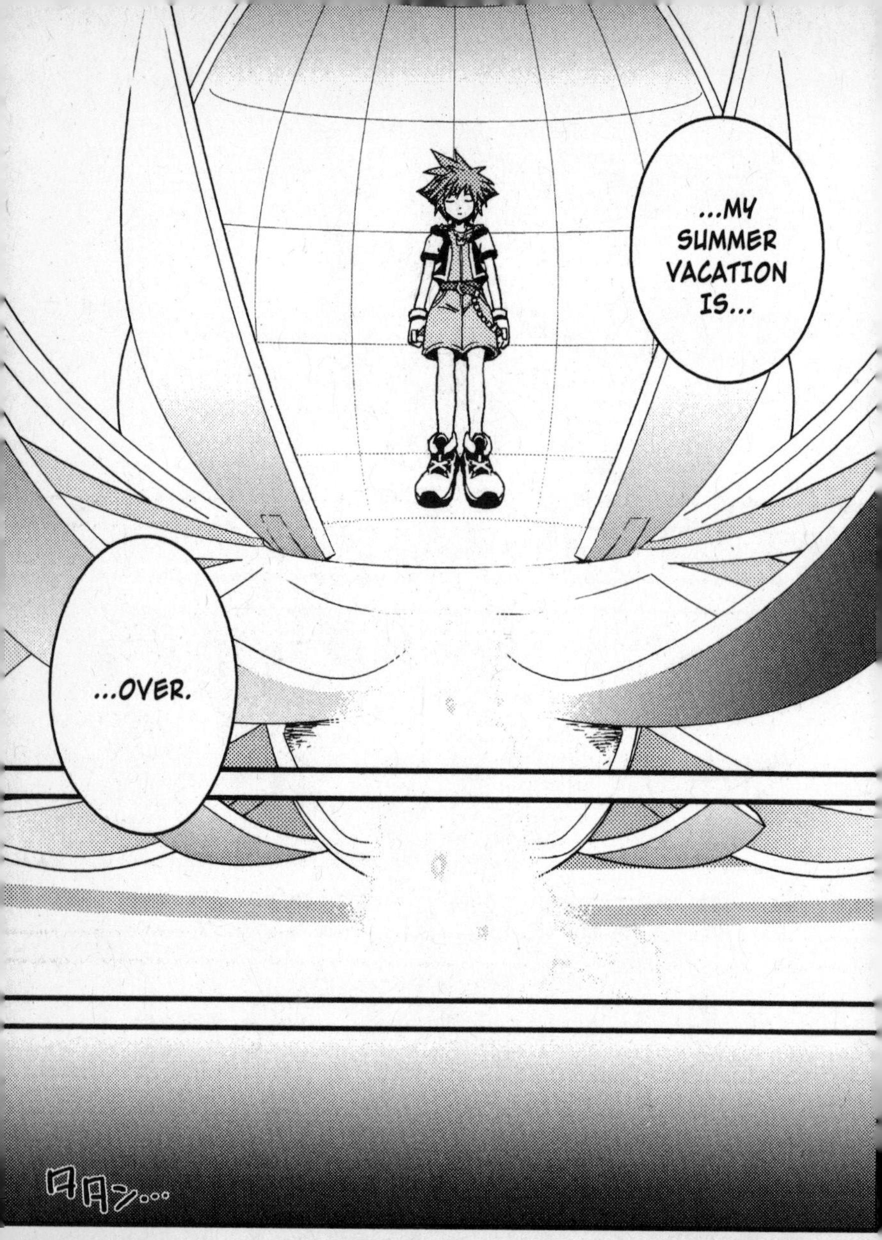
...MY SUMMER VACATION IS...
...OVER.

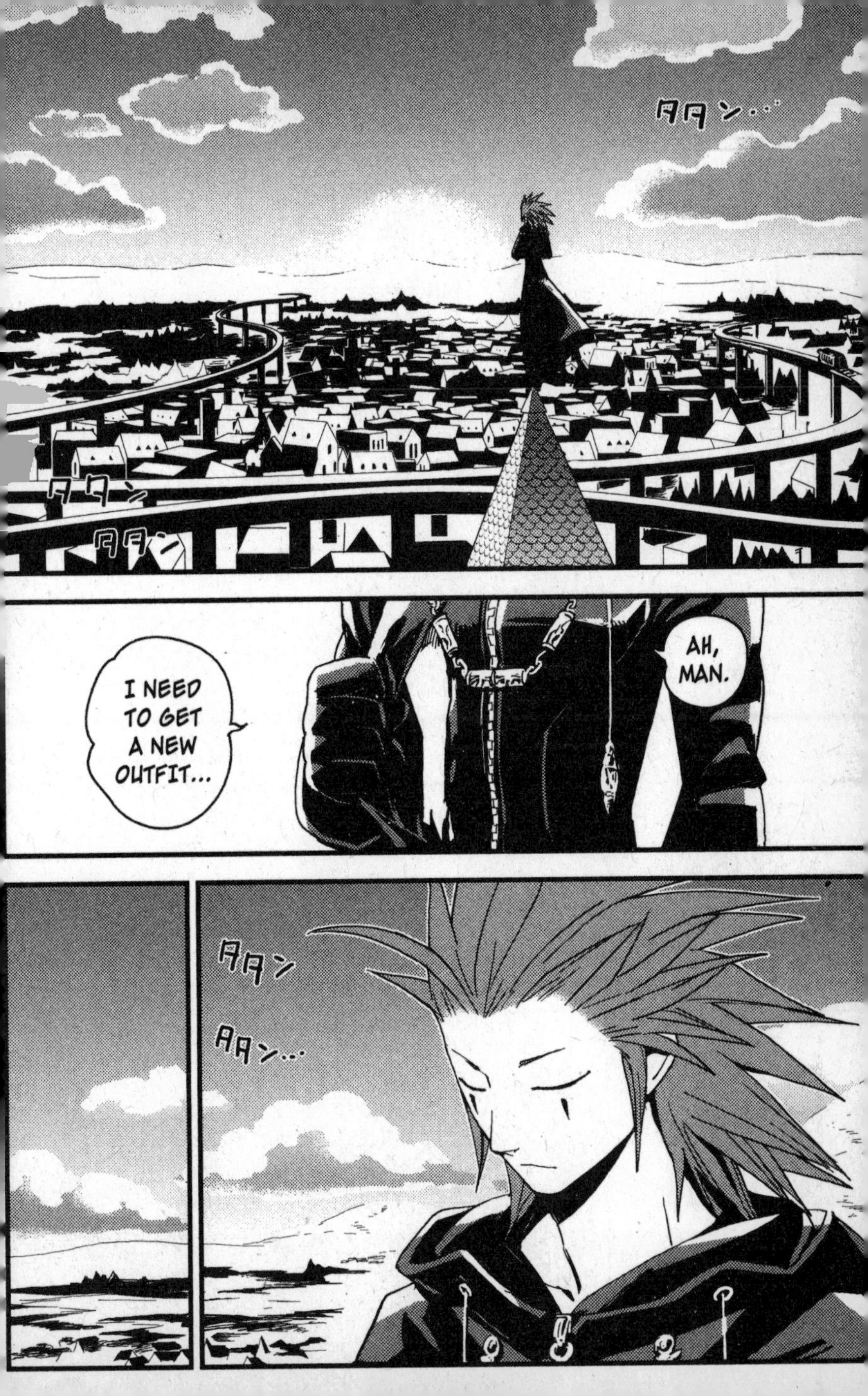
タタン…
タタン
タタン
AH, MAN.
I NEED TO GET A NEW OUTFIT...
タタン
タタン…

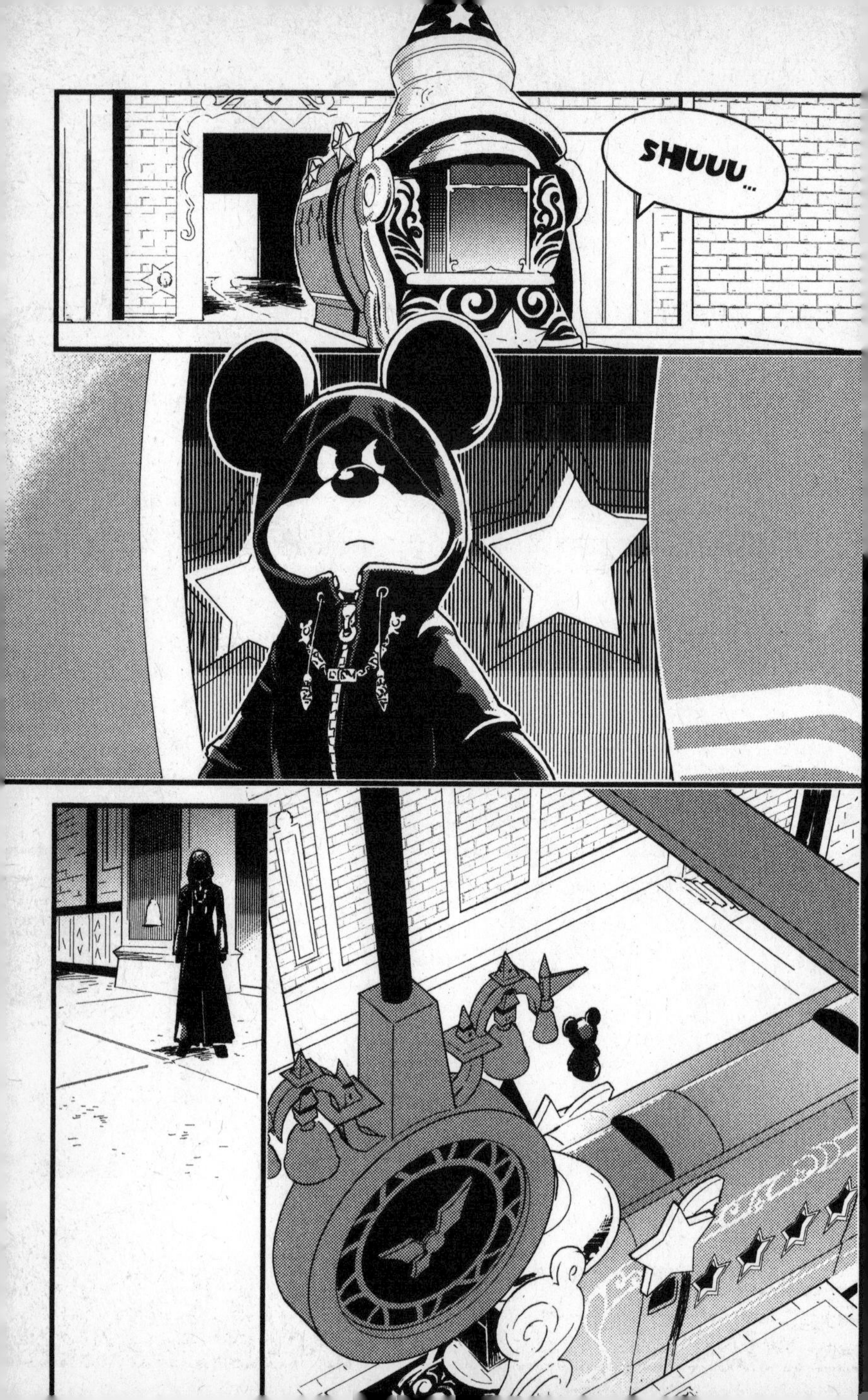
SHUUU...

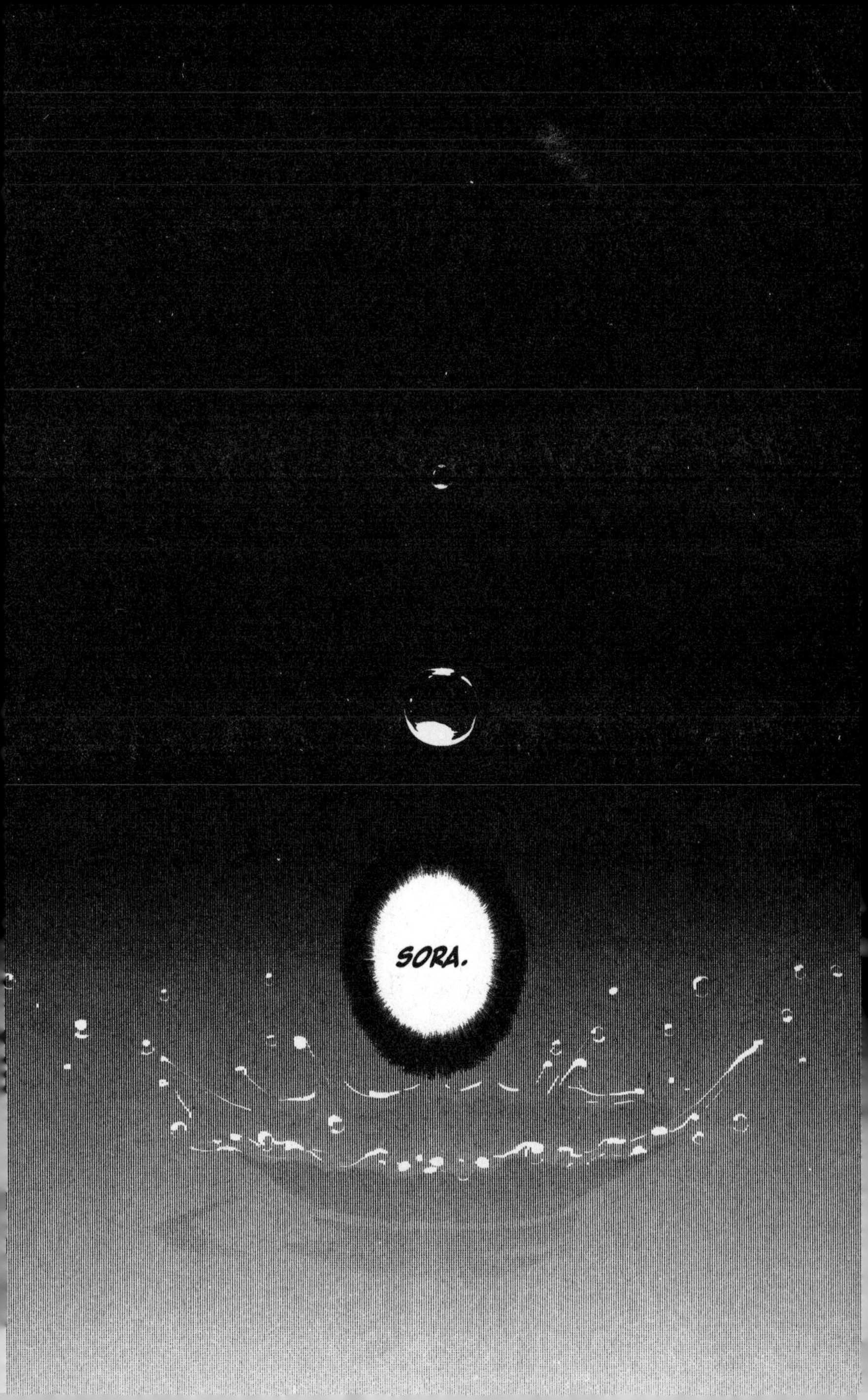
SORA.

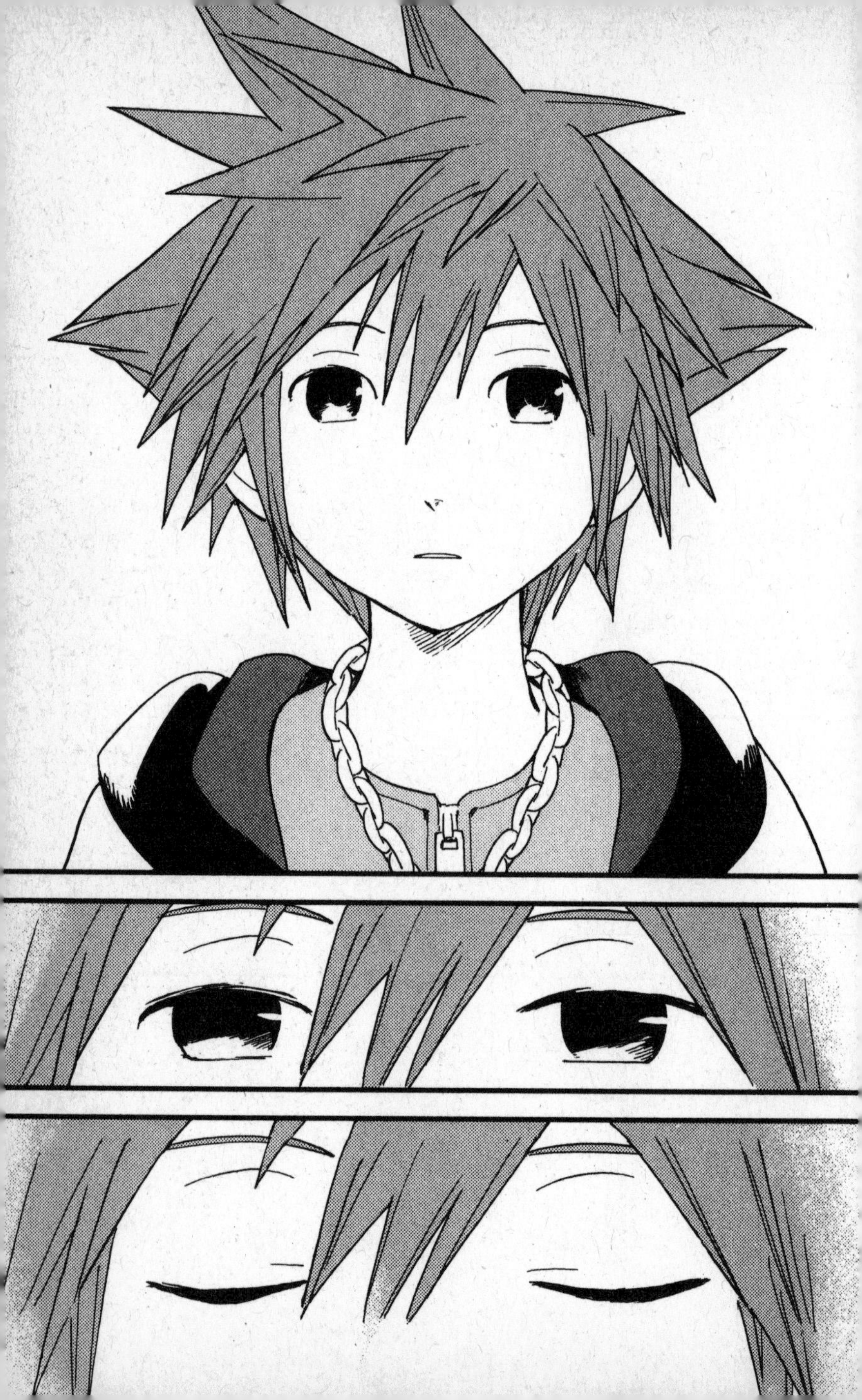

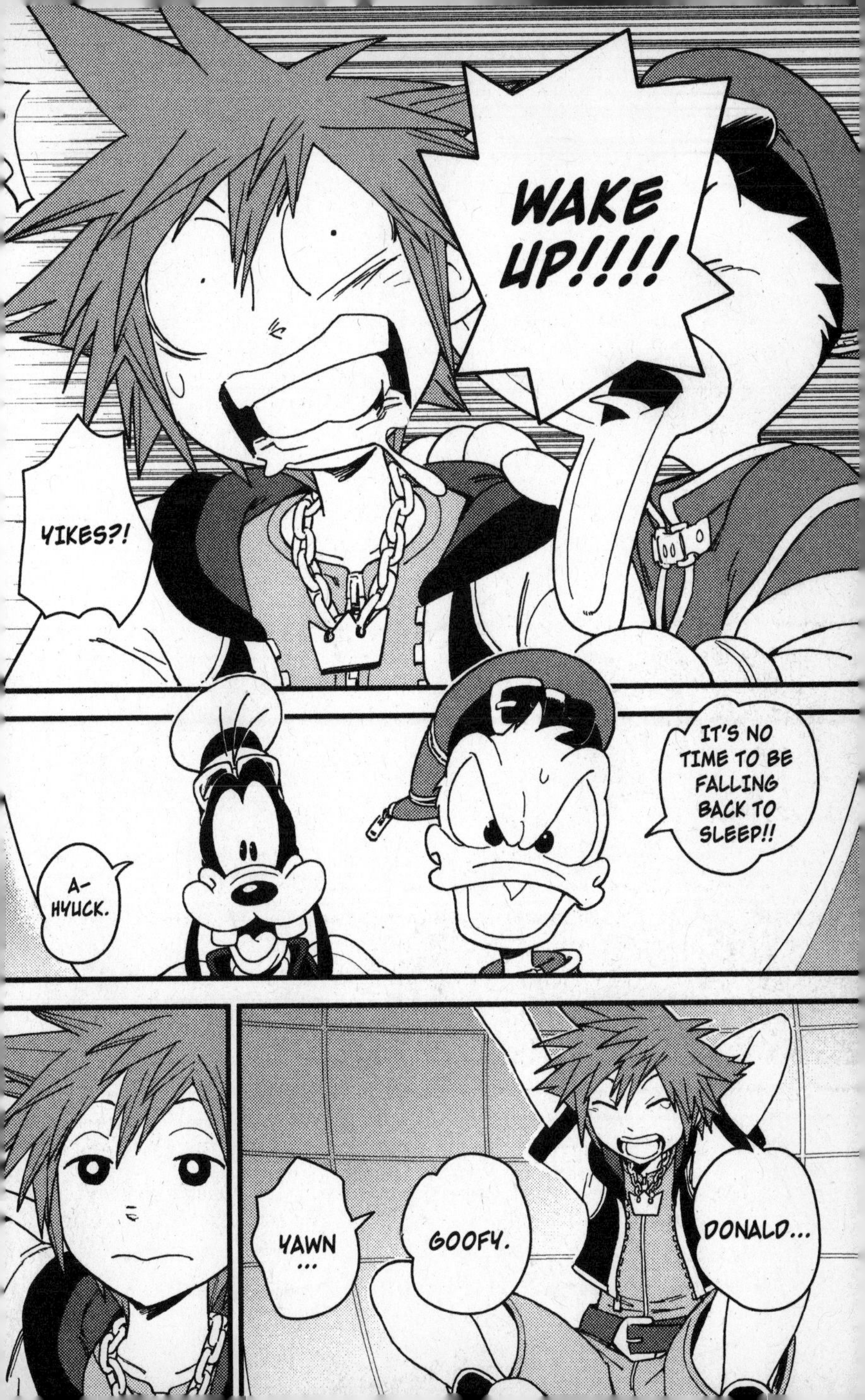
WAKE UP!!!!
YIKES?!
IT'S NO TIME TO BE FALLING BACK TO SLEEP!!
A-HYUCK.
DONALD...
GOOFY.
YAWN ...

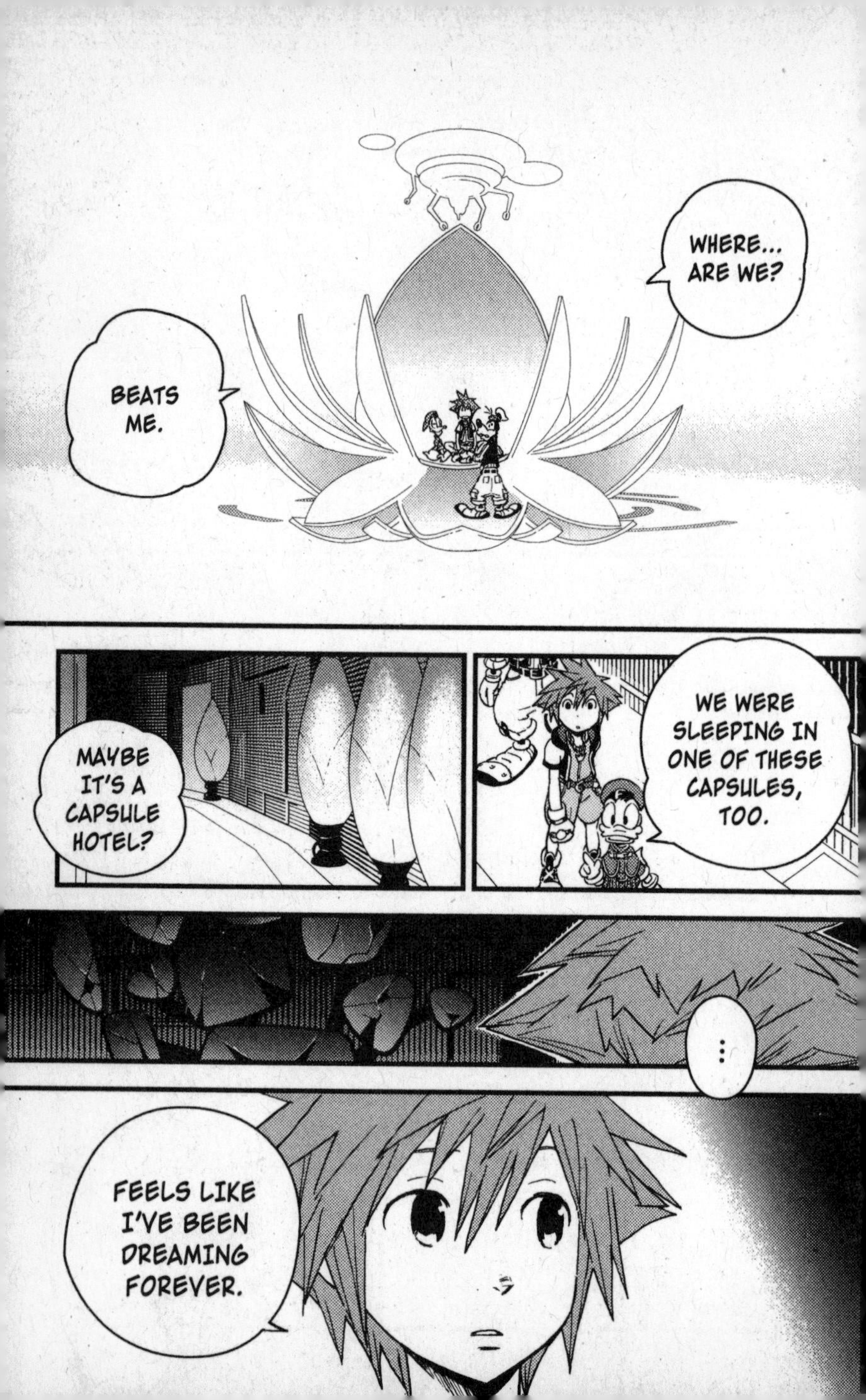
WHERE... ARE WE?
BEATS ME.
WE WERE SLEEPING IN ONE OF THESE CAPSULES, TOO.
MAYBE IT'S A CAPSULE HOTEL?
...
FEELS LIKE I'VE BEEN DREAMING FOREVER.

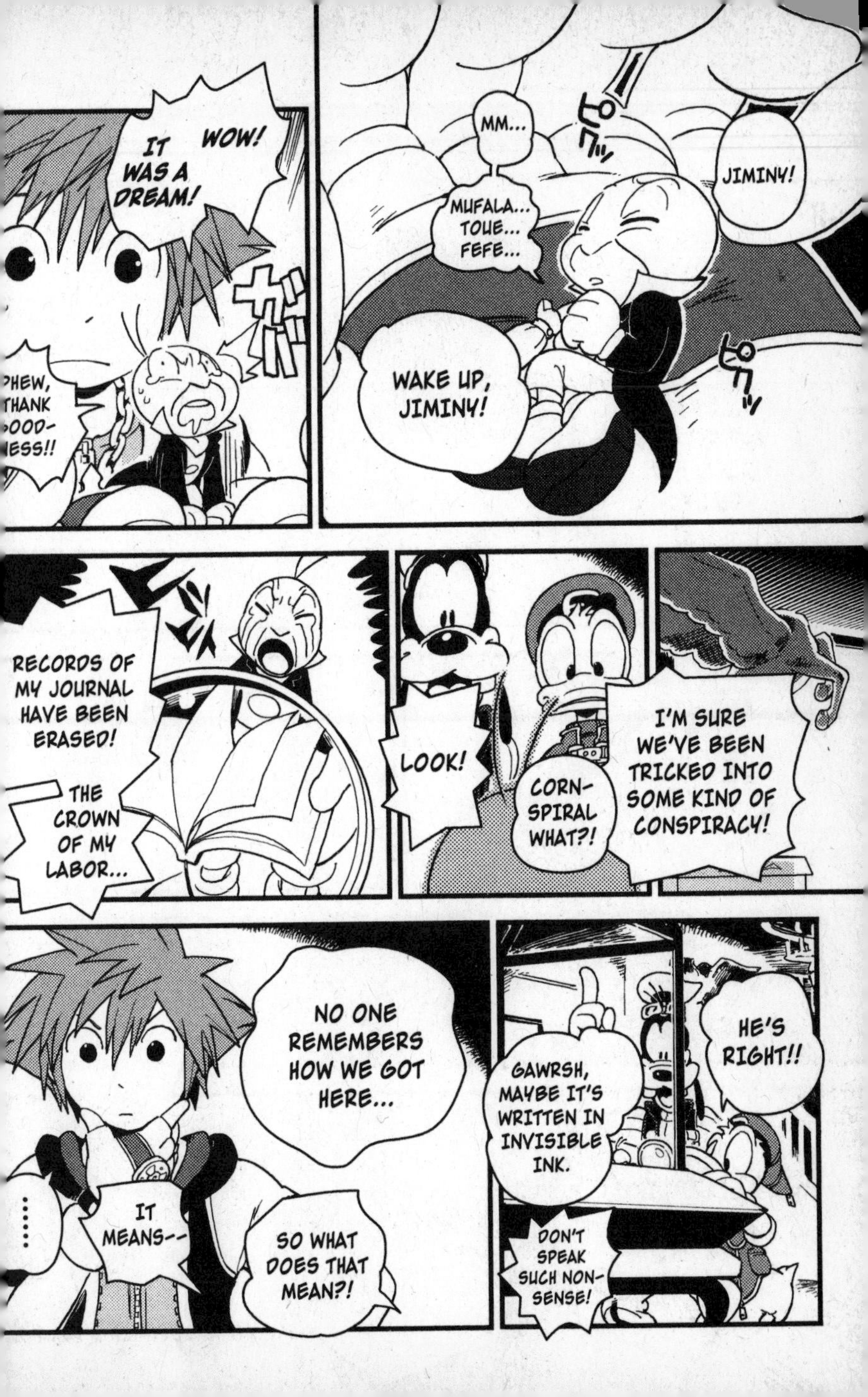

JIMINY!
MM...
MUFALA... TOUE... FEFE...
WAKE UP, JIMINY!
WOW!
IT WAS A DREAM!
PHEW, THANK
I'M SURE WE'VE BEEN TRICKED INTO SOME KIND OF CONSPIRACY!
CORN-SPIRAL WHAT?!
LOOK!
RECORDS OF MY JOURNAL HAVE BEEN ERASED!
THE CROWN OF MY LABOR...
HE'S RIGHT!!
GAWRSH, MAYBE IT'S WRITTEN IN INVISIBLE INK.
DON'T SPEAK SUCH NONSENSE!
NO ONE REMEMBERS HOW WE GOT HERE...
SO WHAT DOES THAT MEAN?!
IT MEANS--
......

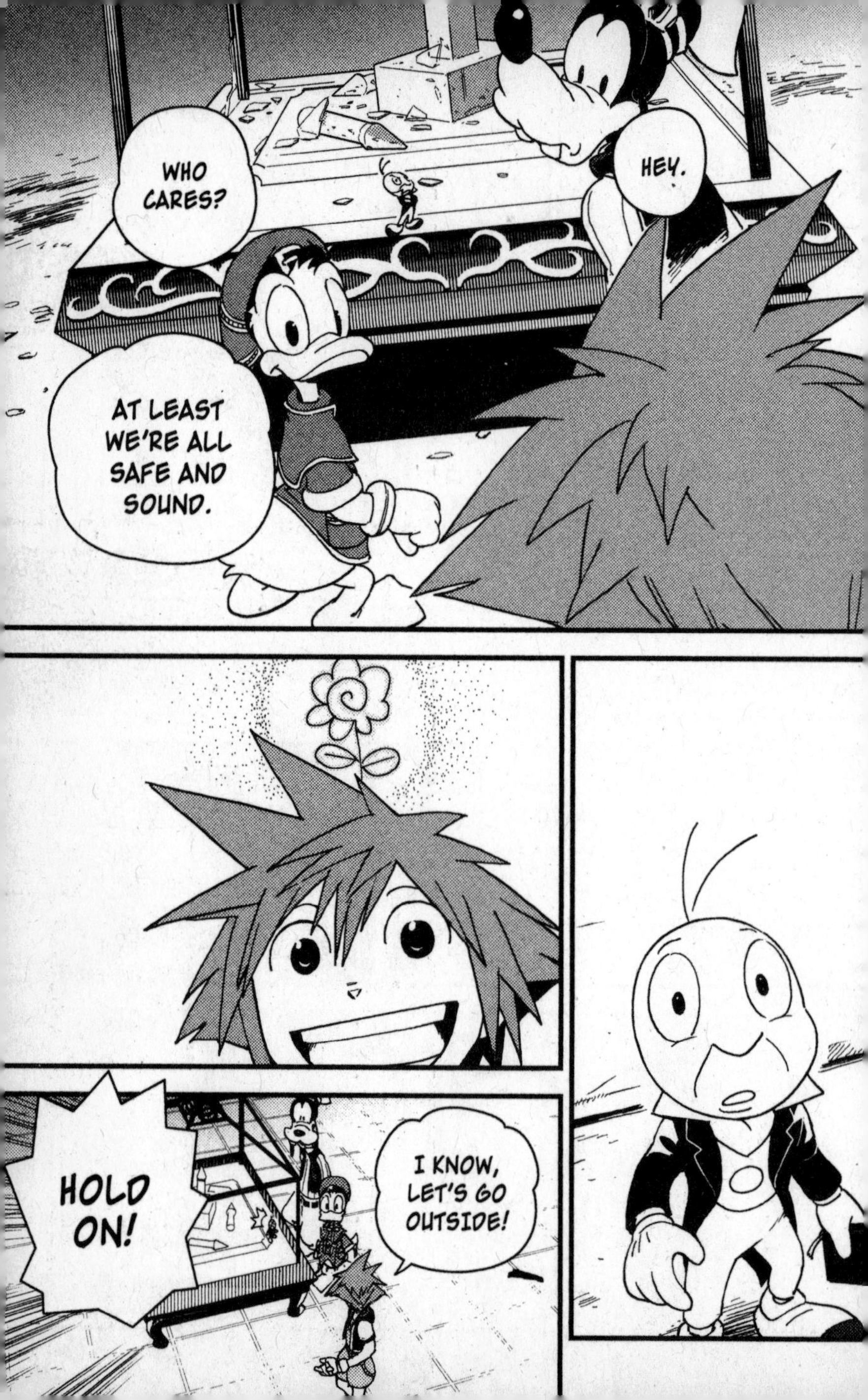
HEY.
WHO CARES?
AT LEAST WE'RE ALL SAFE AND SOUND.
I KNOW, LET'S GO OUTSIDE!
HOLD ON!

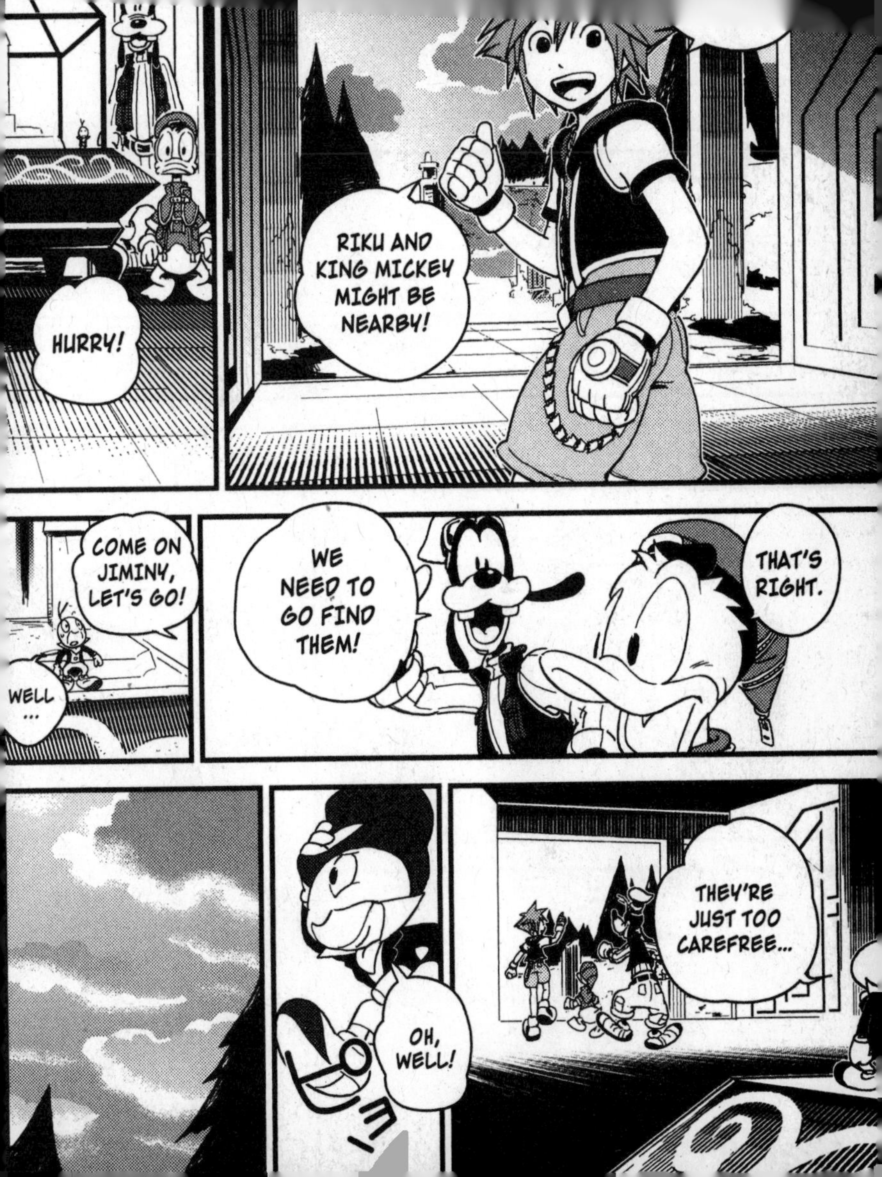
RIKU AND KING MICKEY MIGHT BE NEARBY!
HURRY!
THAT'S RIGHT.
WE NEED TO GO FIND THEM!
COME ON JIMINY, LET'S GO!
WELL ...
THEY'RE JUST TOO CAREFREE...
OH, WELL!

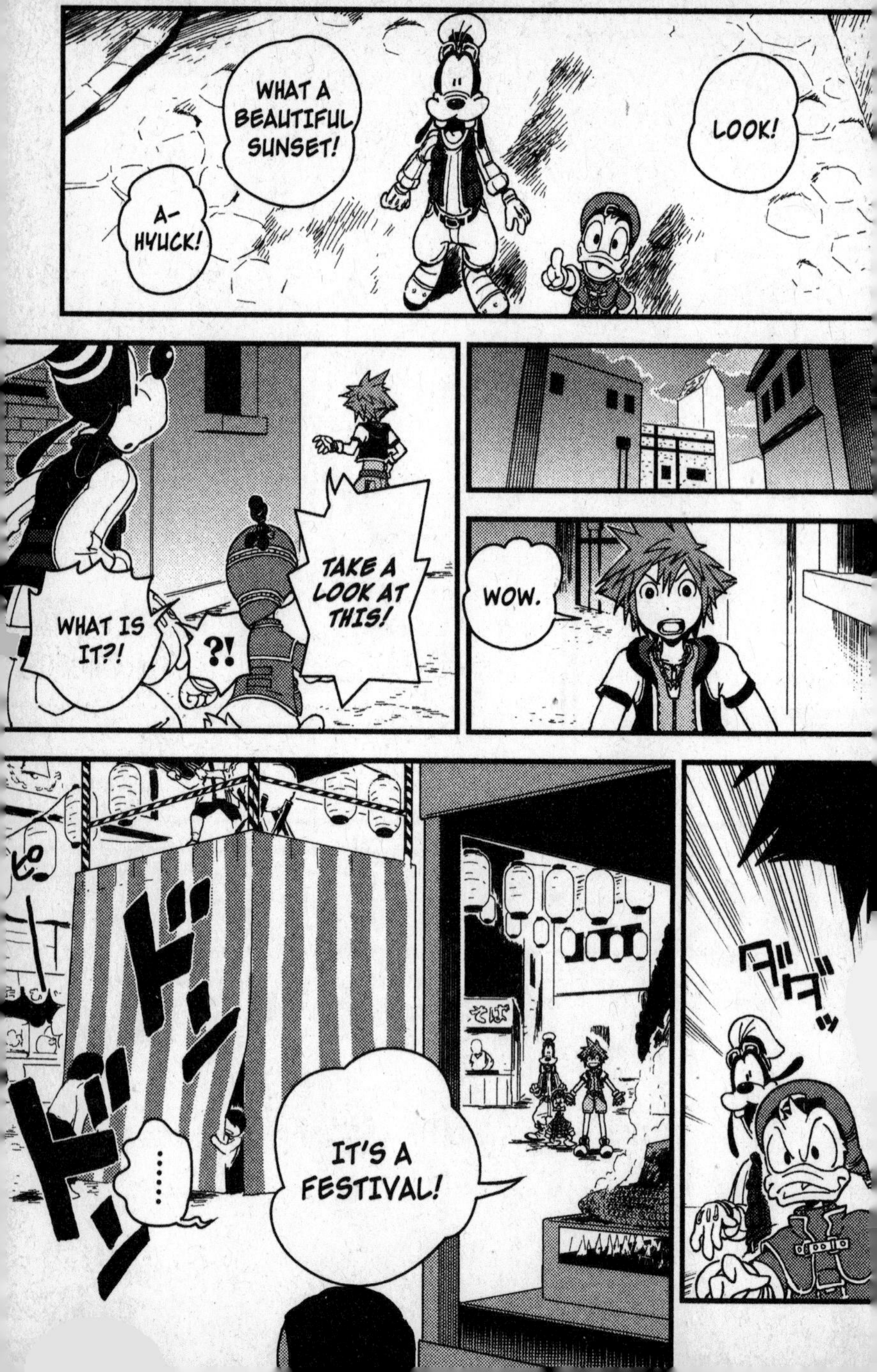

LOOK!
WHAT A BEAUTIFUL SUNSET!
A-HYUCK!
WOW.
TAKE A LOOK AT THIS!
?!
WHAT IS IT?!
ダダッ
そば
IT'S A FESTIVAL!
......
ドドン

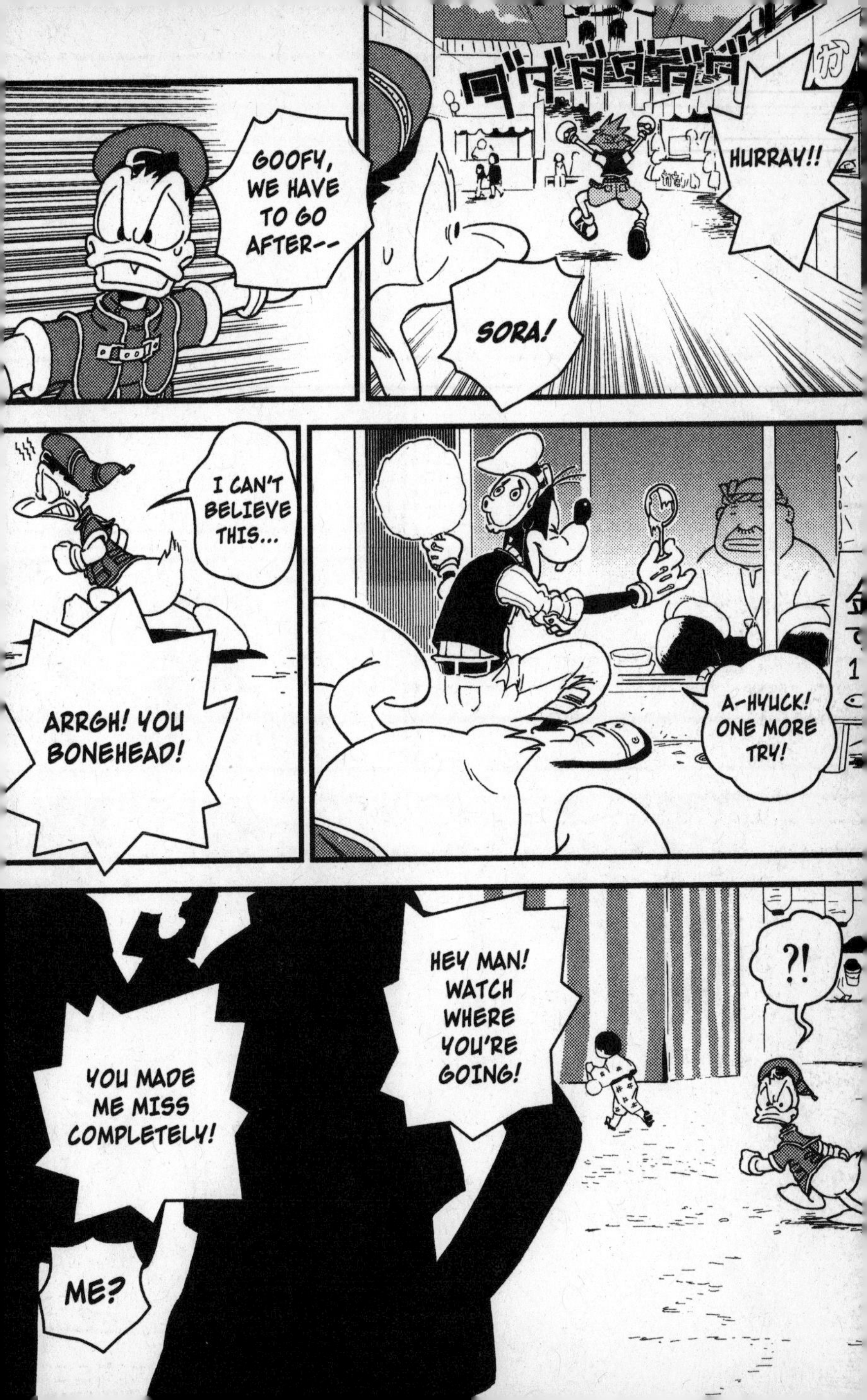
ダダダダダダ
HURRAY!!
SORA!
GOOFY, WE HAVE TO GO AFTER--
A-HYUCK! ONE MORE TRY!
I CAN'T BELIEVE THIS...
ARRGH! YOU BONEHEAD!
?!
HEY MAN! WATCH WHERE YOU'RE GOING!
YOU MADE ME MISS COMPLETELY!
ME?

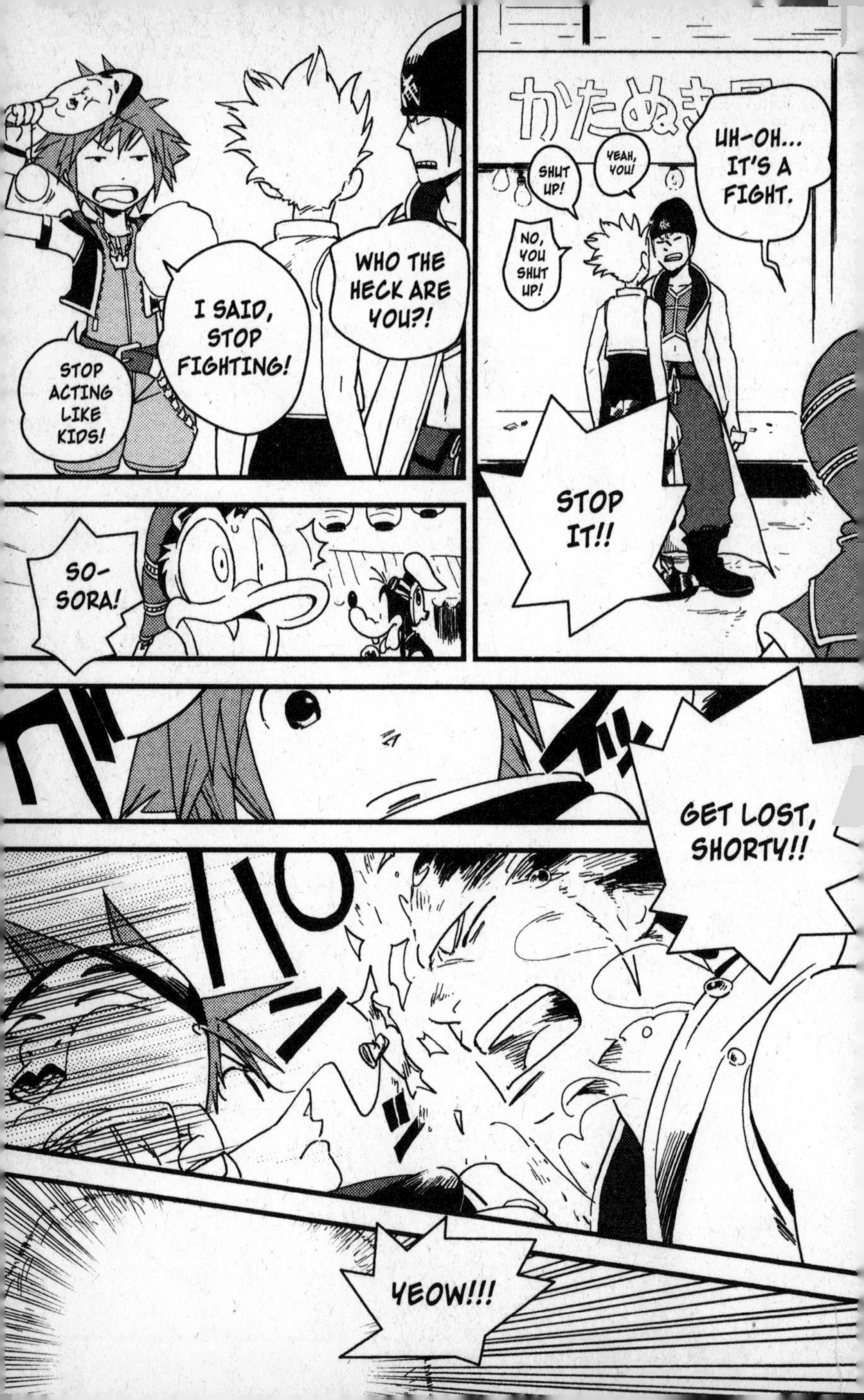
かためぬき
UH-OH... IT'S A FIGHT.
YEAH, YOU!
SHUT UP!
NO, YOU SHUT UP!
STOP IT!!
WHO THE HECK ARE YOU?!
I SAID, STOP FIGHTING!
STOP ACTING LIKE KIDS!
SO-SORA!
GET LOST, SHORTY!!
YEOW!!!

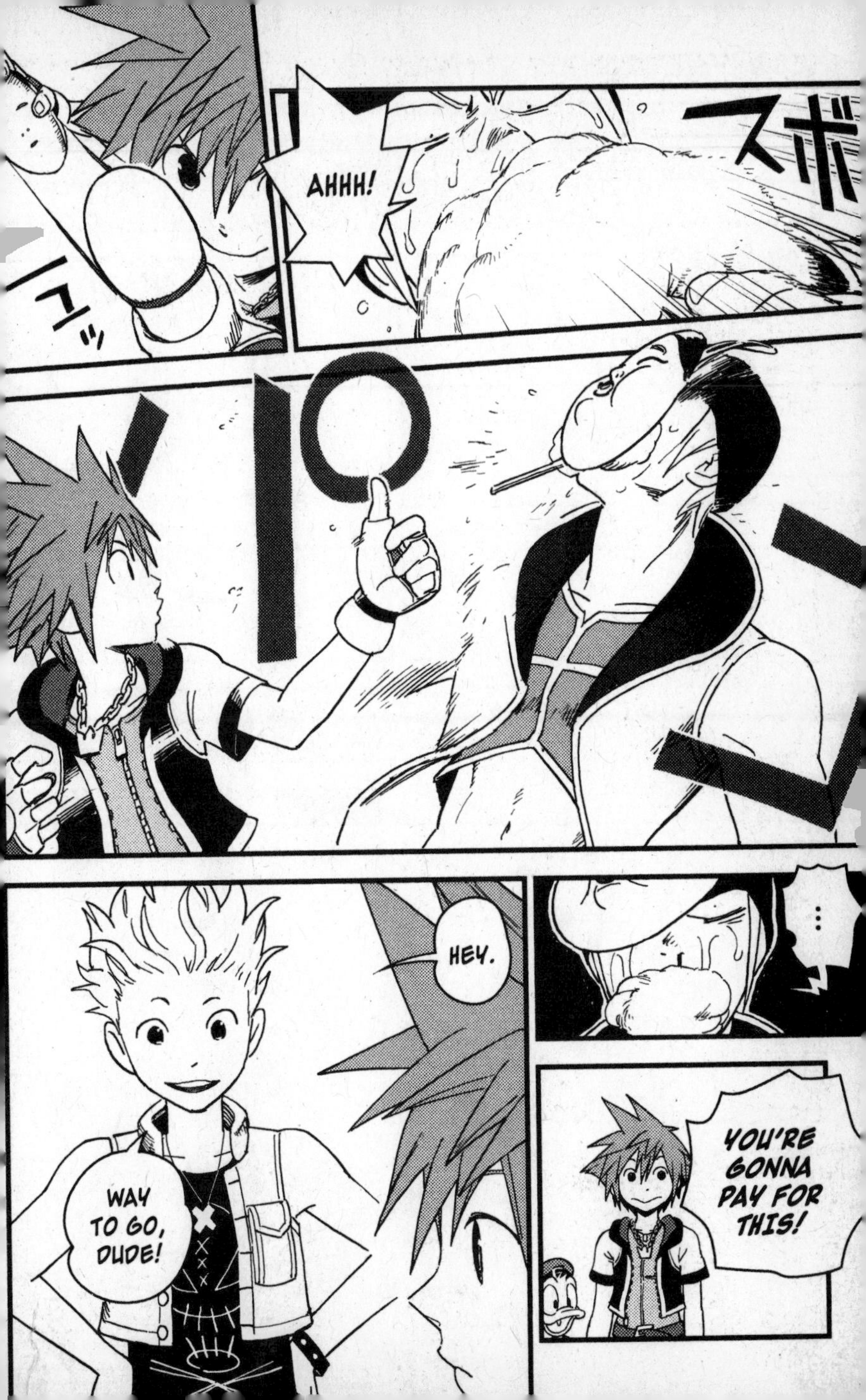

スボ
AHHH!
ゴッ
...
YOU'RE GONNA PAY FOR THIS!
HEY.
WAY TO GO, DUDE!

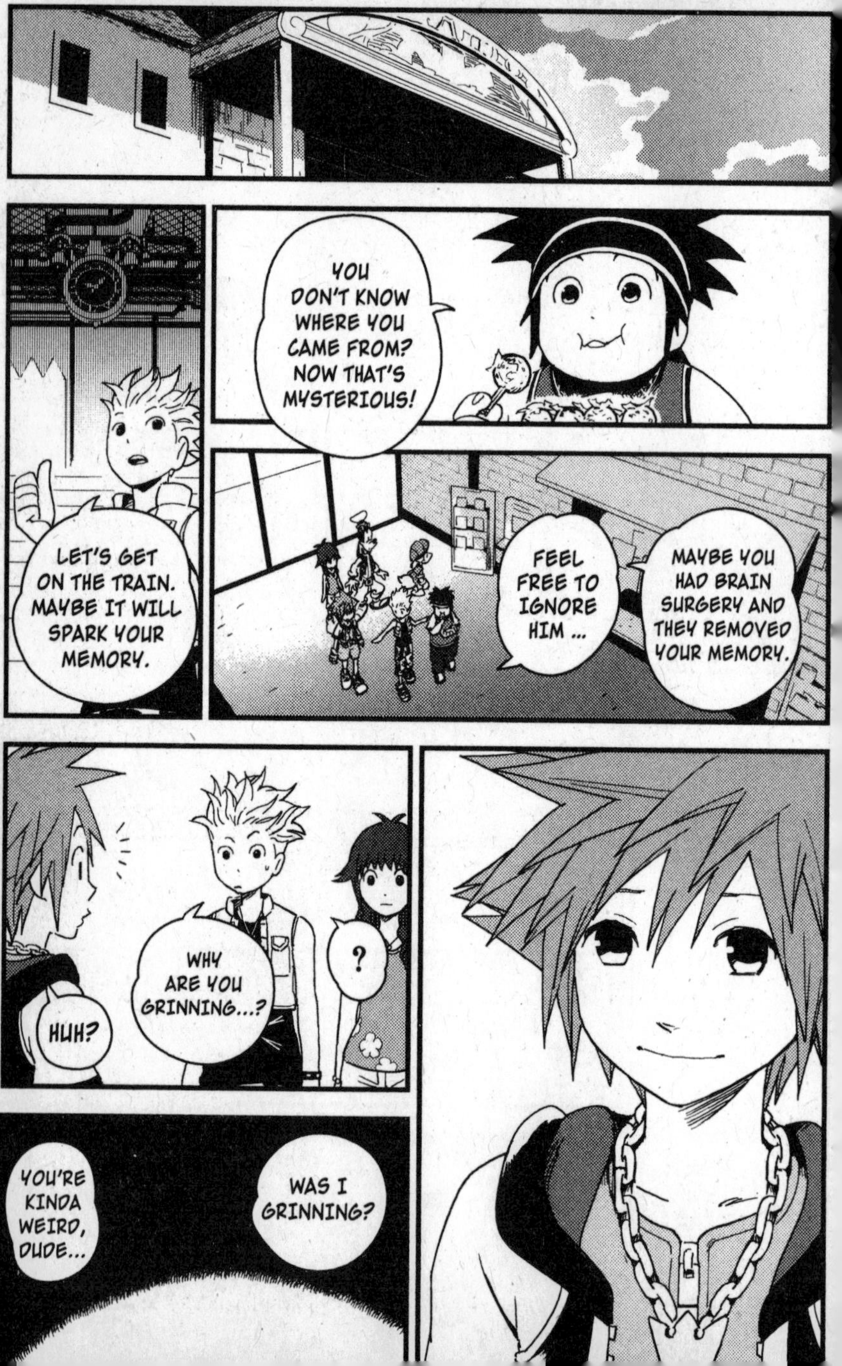
YOU DON'T KNOW WHERE YOU CAME FROM? NOW THAT'S MYSTERIOUS!
MAYBE YOU HAD BRAIN SURGERY AND THEY REMOVED YOUR MEMORY.
FEEL FREE TO IGNORE HIM ...
LET'S GET ON THE TRAIN. MAYBE IT WILL SPARK YOUR MEMORY.
?
WHY ARE YOU GRINNING...?
HUH?
WAS I GRINNING?
YOU'RE KINDA WEIRD, DUDE...

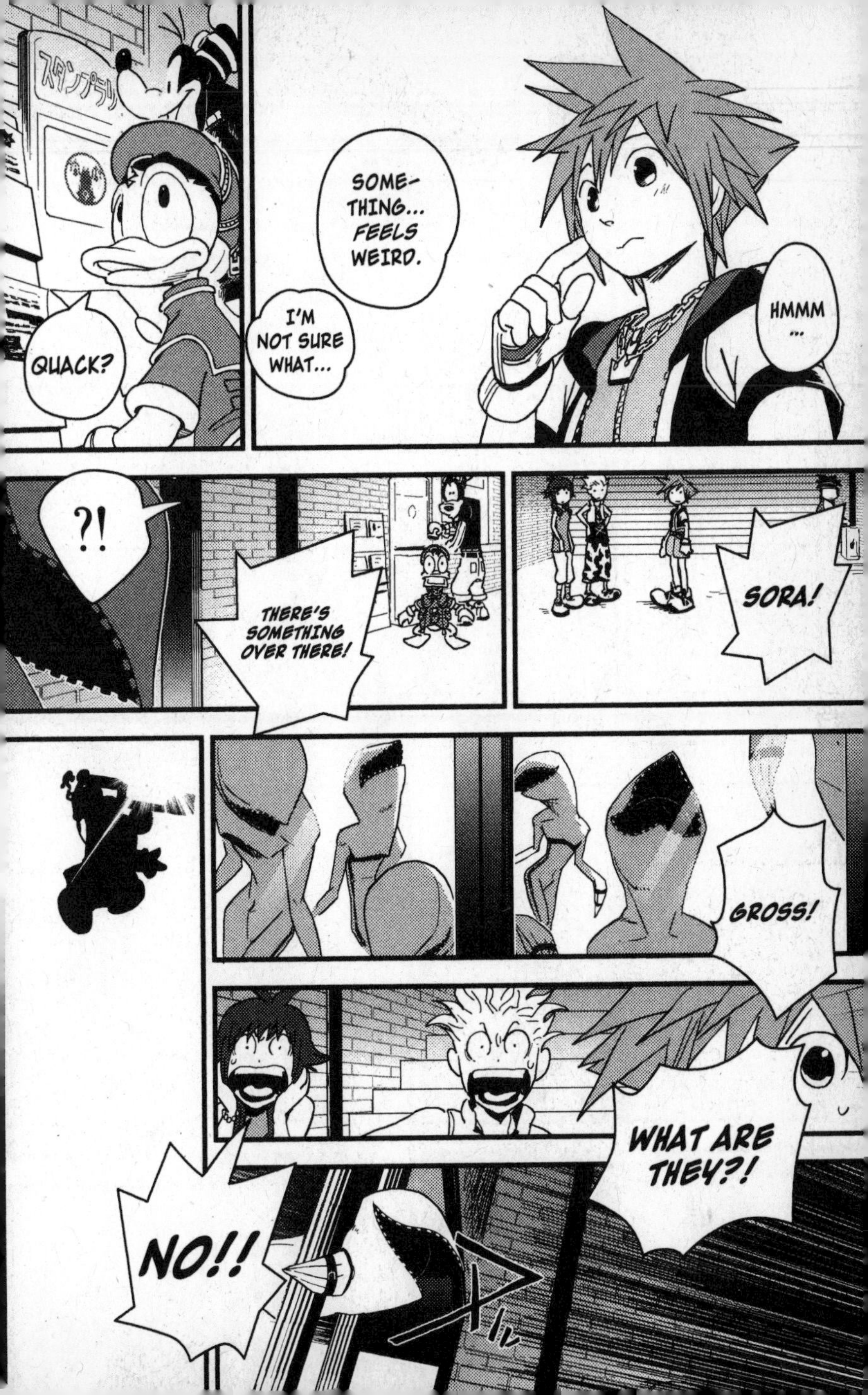
HMMM ...
SOME-THING... FEELS WEIRD.
I'M NOT SURE WHAT...
スタンプラリ
QUACK?
SORA!
THERE'S SOMETHING OVER THERE!
?!
GROSS!
WHAT ARE THEY?!
NO!!

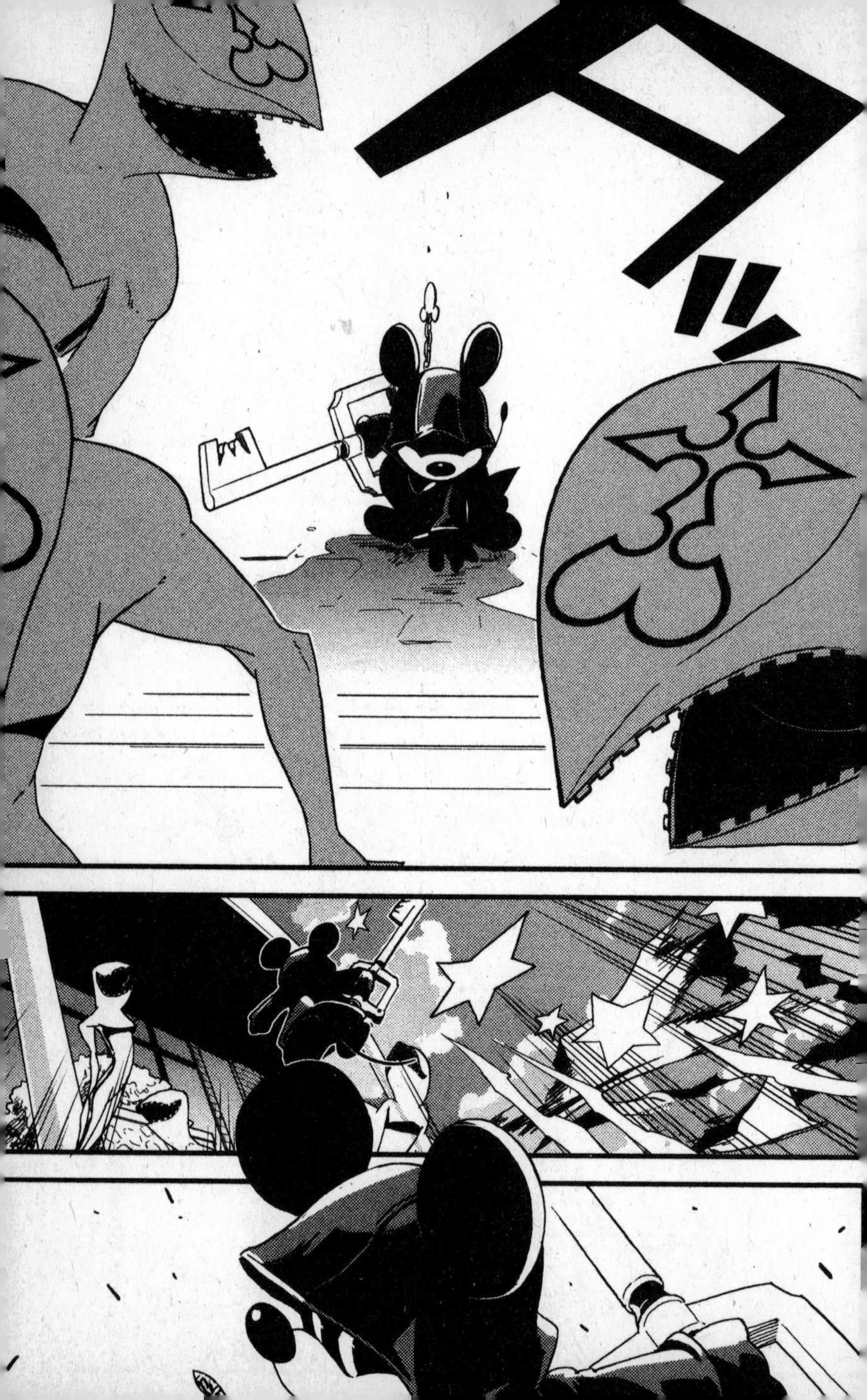
ダッ

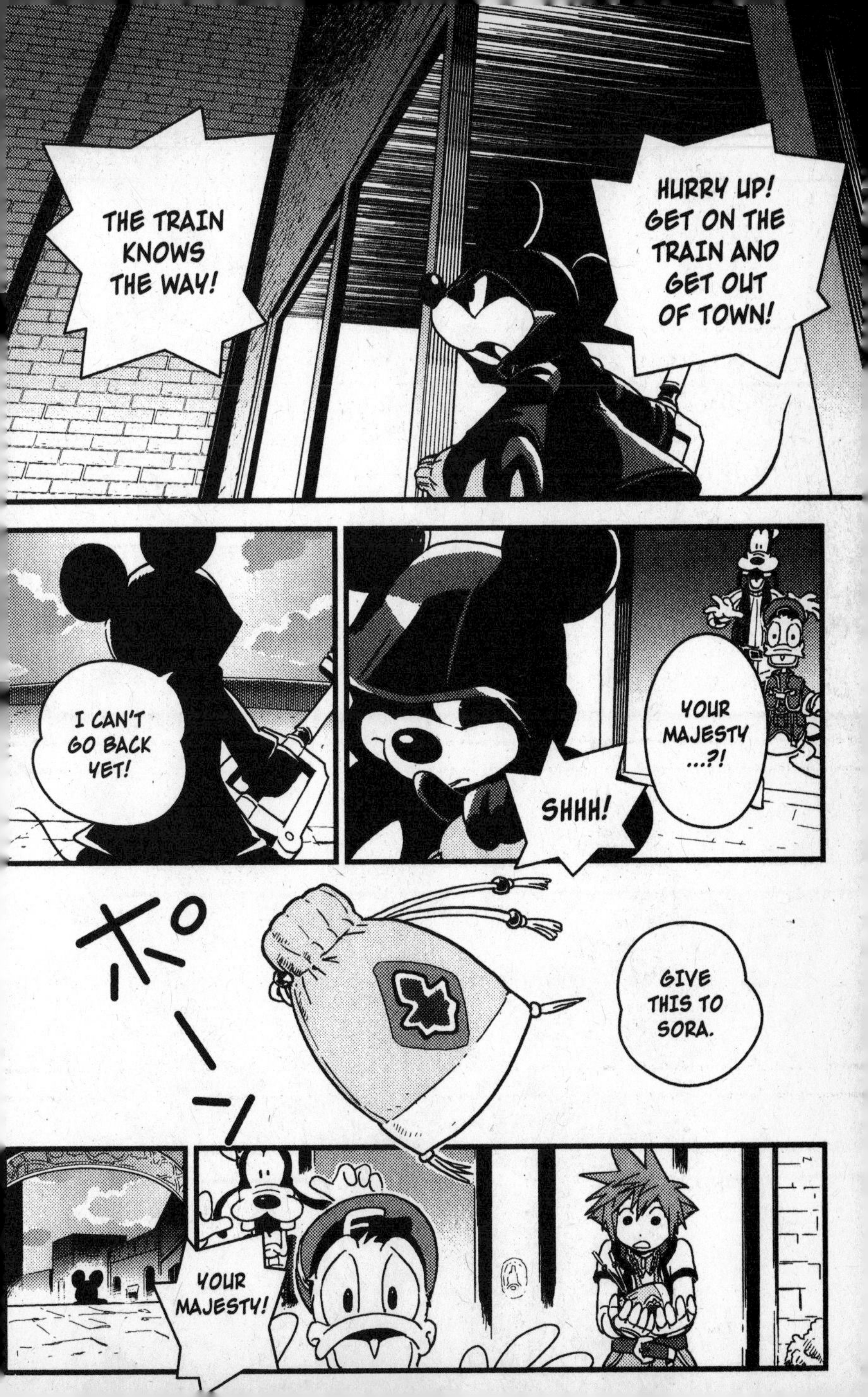
HURRY UP! GET ON THE TRAIN AND GET OUT OF TOWN!
THE TRAIN KNOWS THE WAY!
YOUR MAJESTY ...?!
SHHH!
I CAN'T GO BACK YET!
GIVE THIS TO SORA.
YOUR MAJESTY!

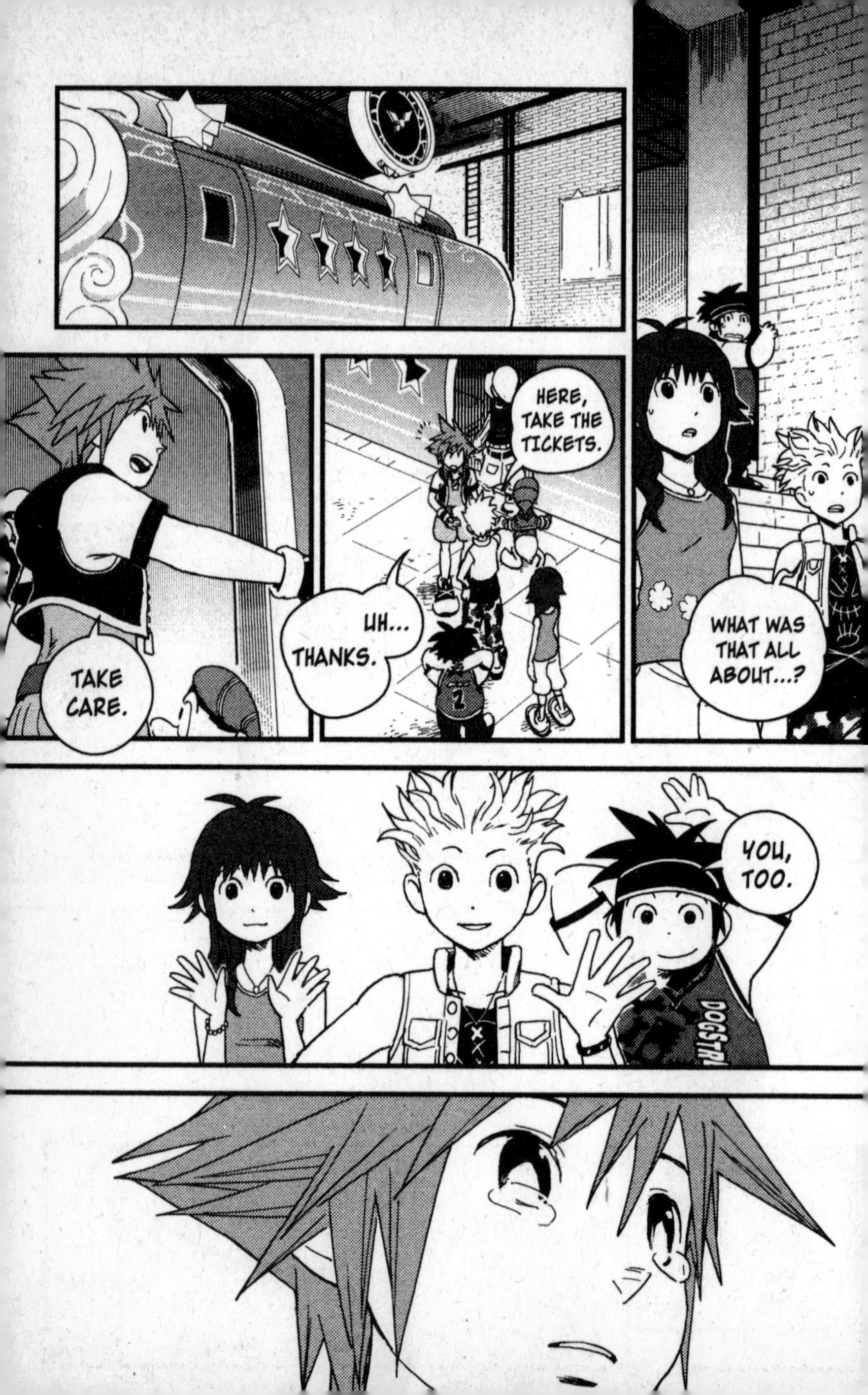
WHAT WAS THAT ALL ABOUT...?
HERE, TAKE THE TICKETS.
UH... THANKS.
TAKE CARE.
YOU, TOO.

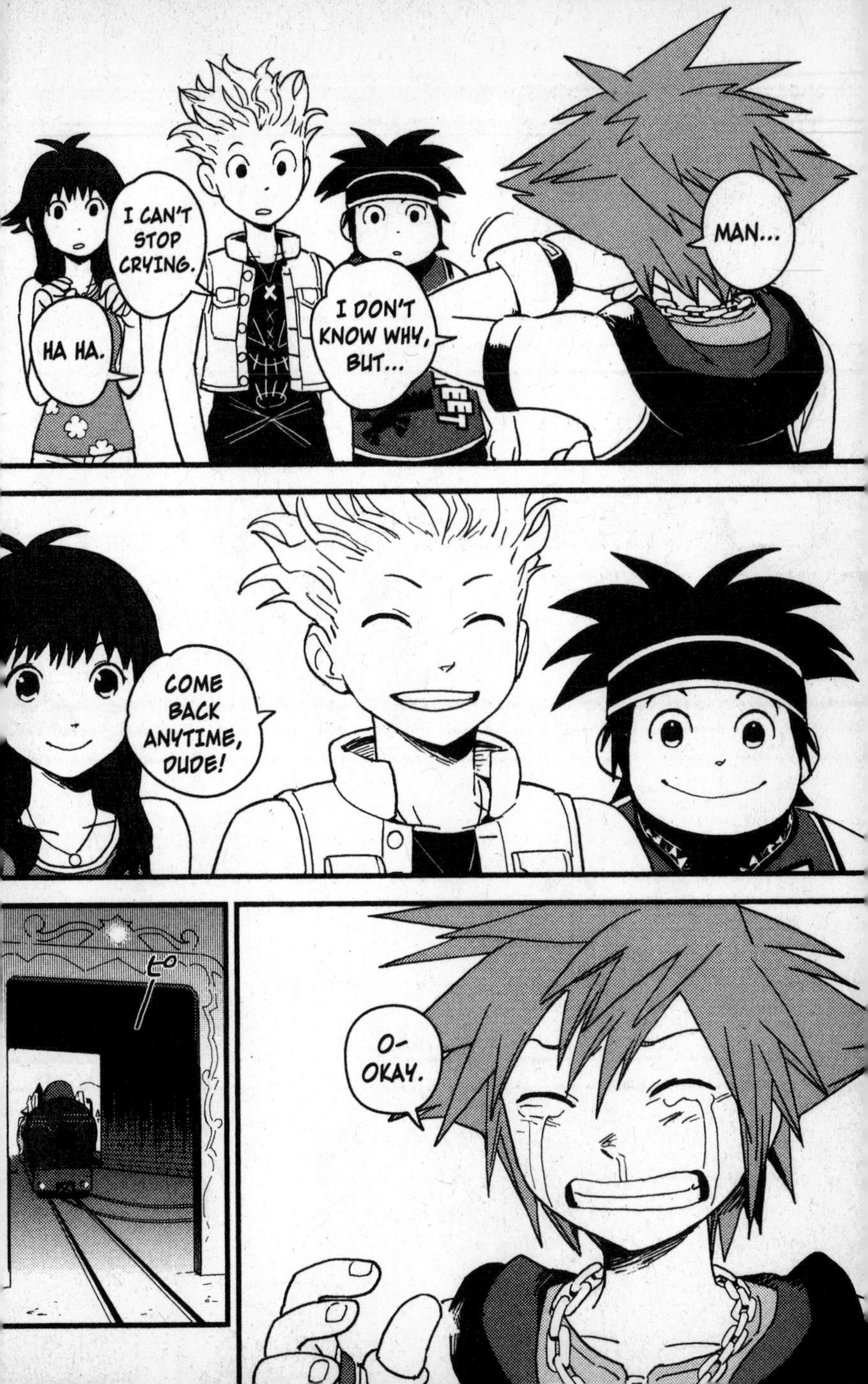
MAN...
I DON'T KNOW WHY, BUT...
I CAN'T STOP CRYING.
HA HA.
COME BACK ANYTIME, DUDE!
O-OKAY.

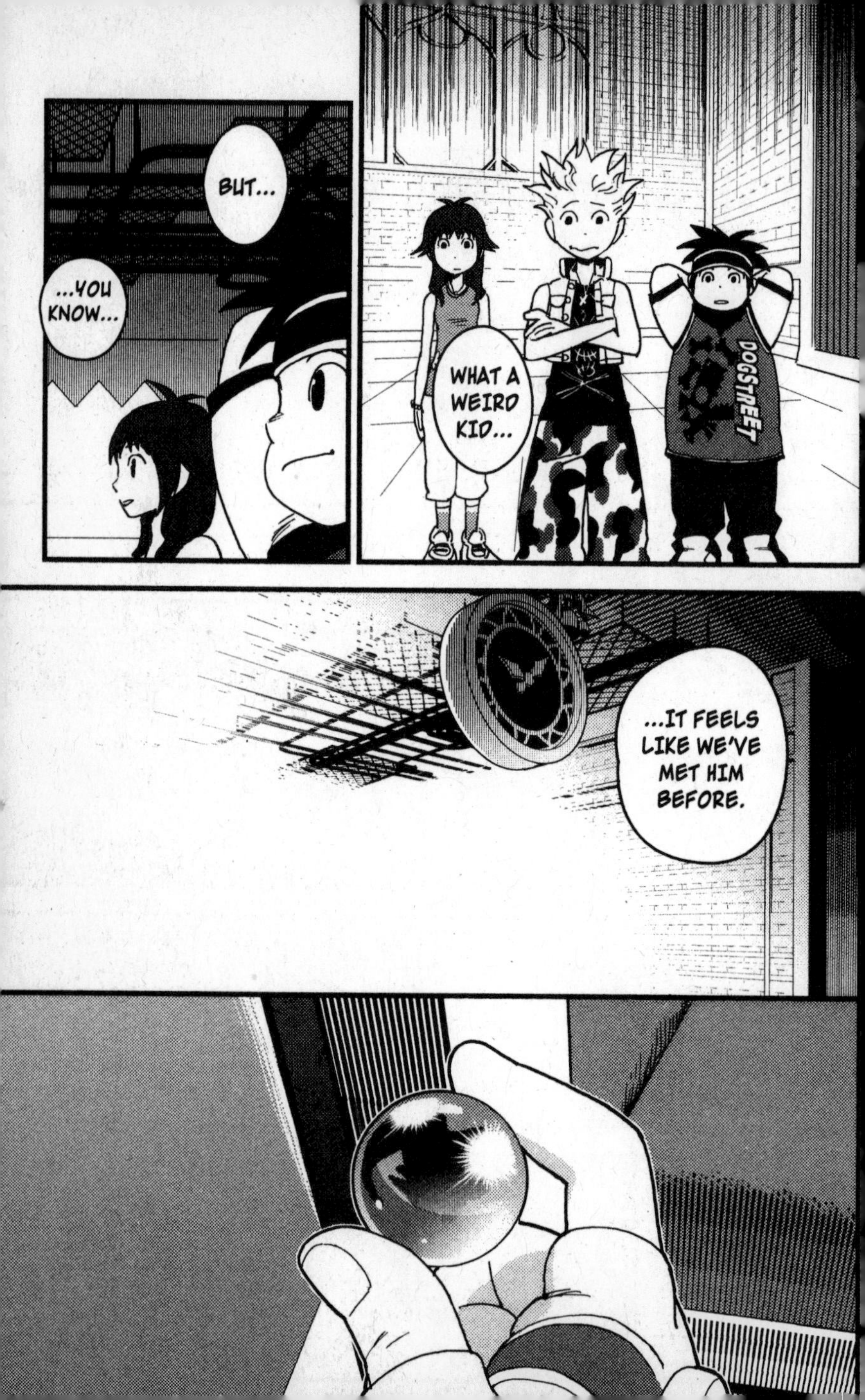
WHAT A WEIRD KID...
DOGSTREET
BUT...
...YOU KNOW...
...IT FEELS LIKE WE'VE MET HIM BEFORE.

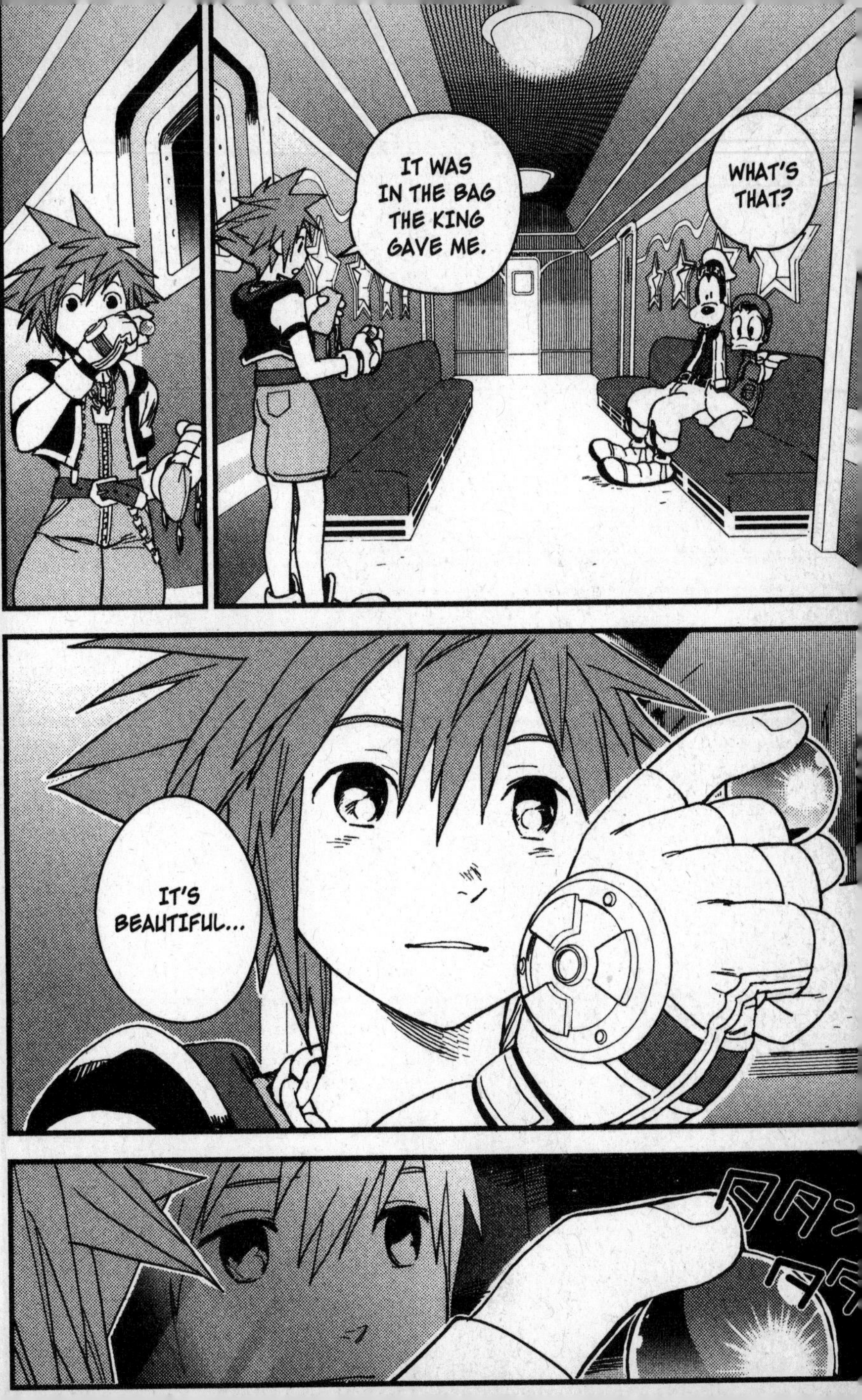
WHAT'S THAT?
IT WAS IN THE BAG THE KING GAVE ME.
IT'S BEAUTIFUL...

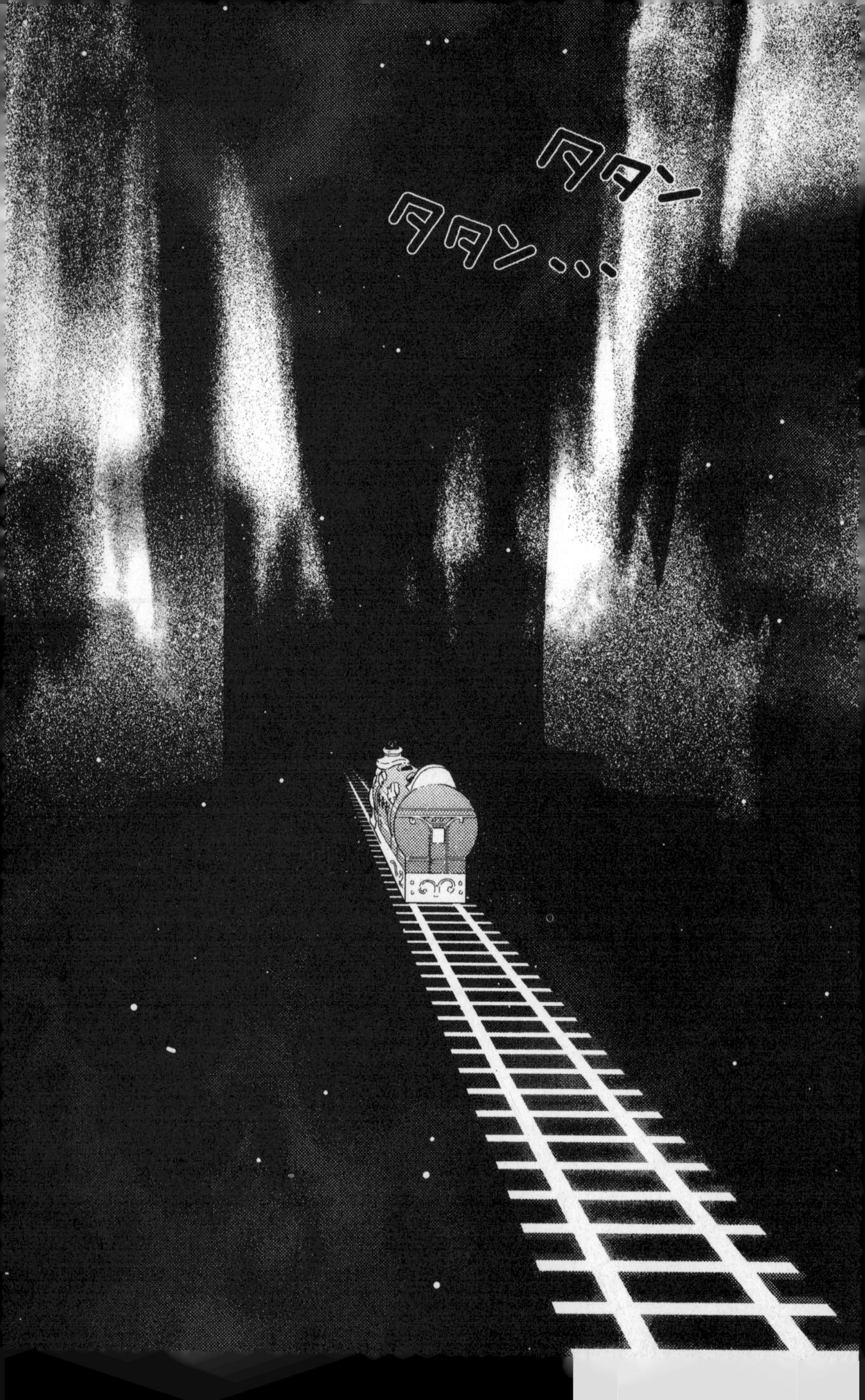
タタン
タタン…

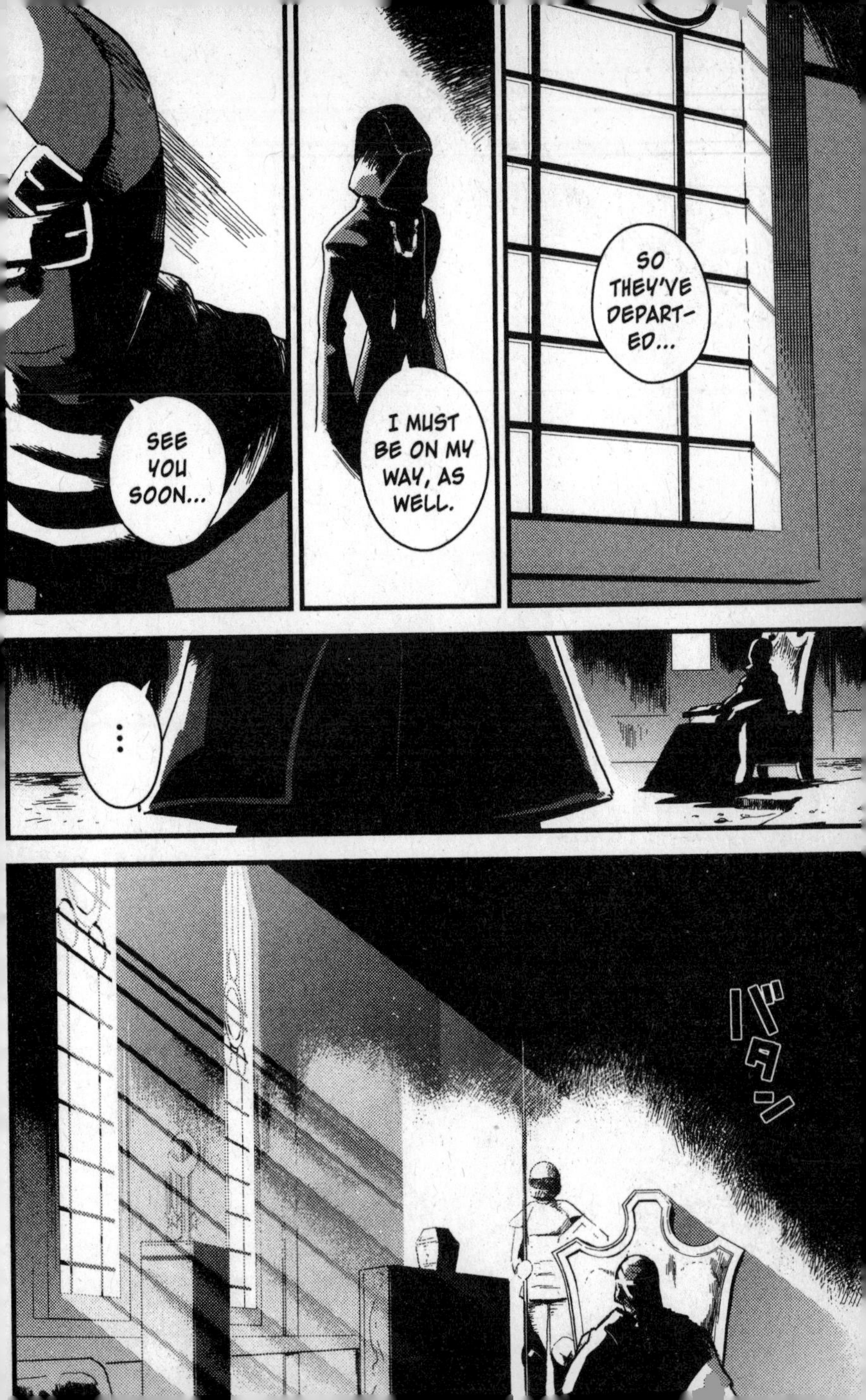
SO THEY'VE DEPART-ED...
I MUST BE ON MY WAY, AS WELL.
SEE YOU SOON...
...
バタン

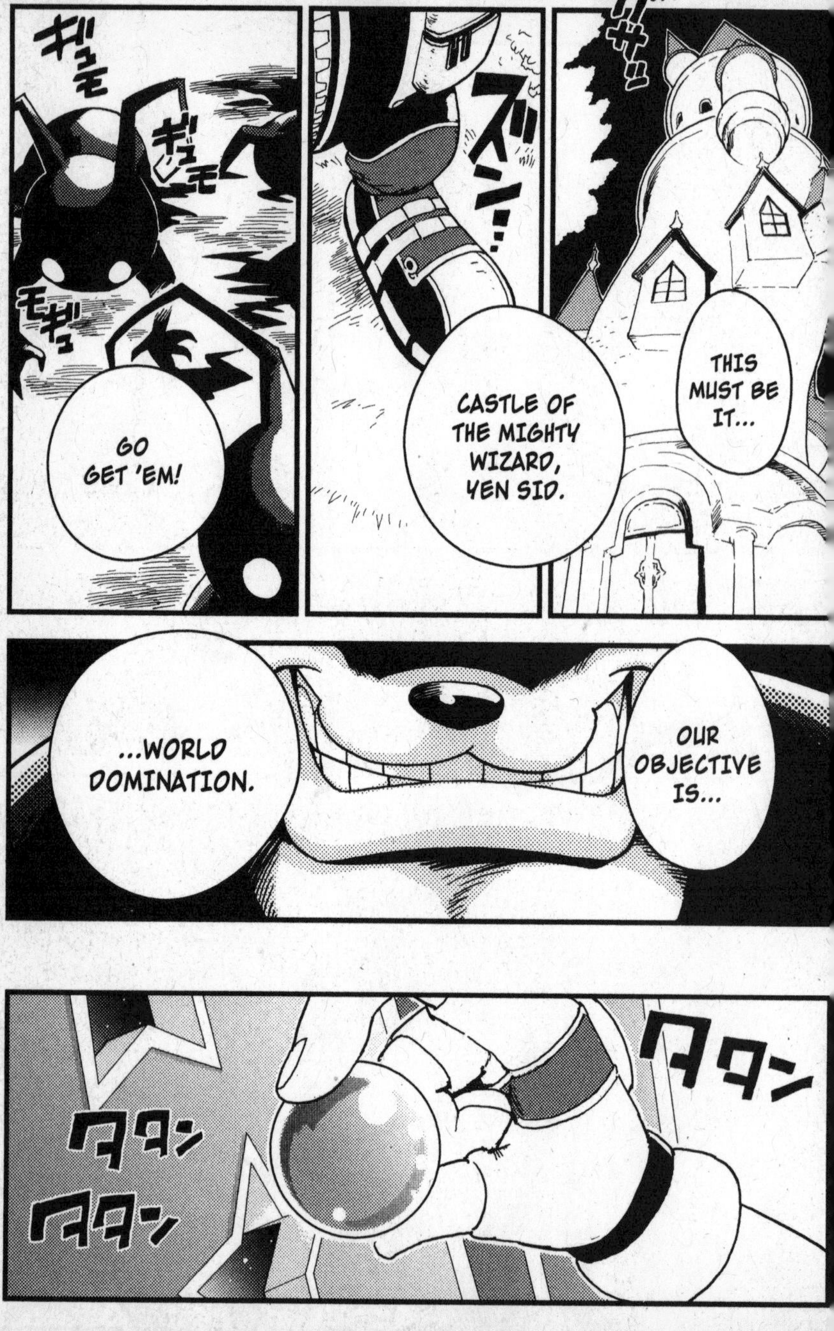
THIS MUST BE IT...
CASTLE OF THE MIGHTY WIZARD, YEN SID.
GO GET 'EM!
OUR OBJECTIVE IS...
...WORLD DOMINATION.

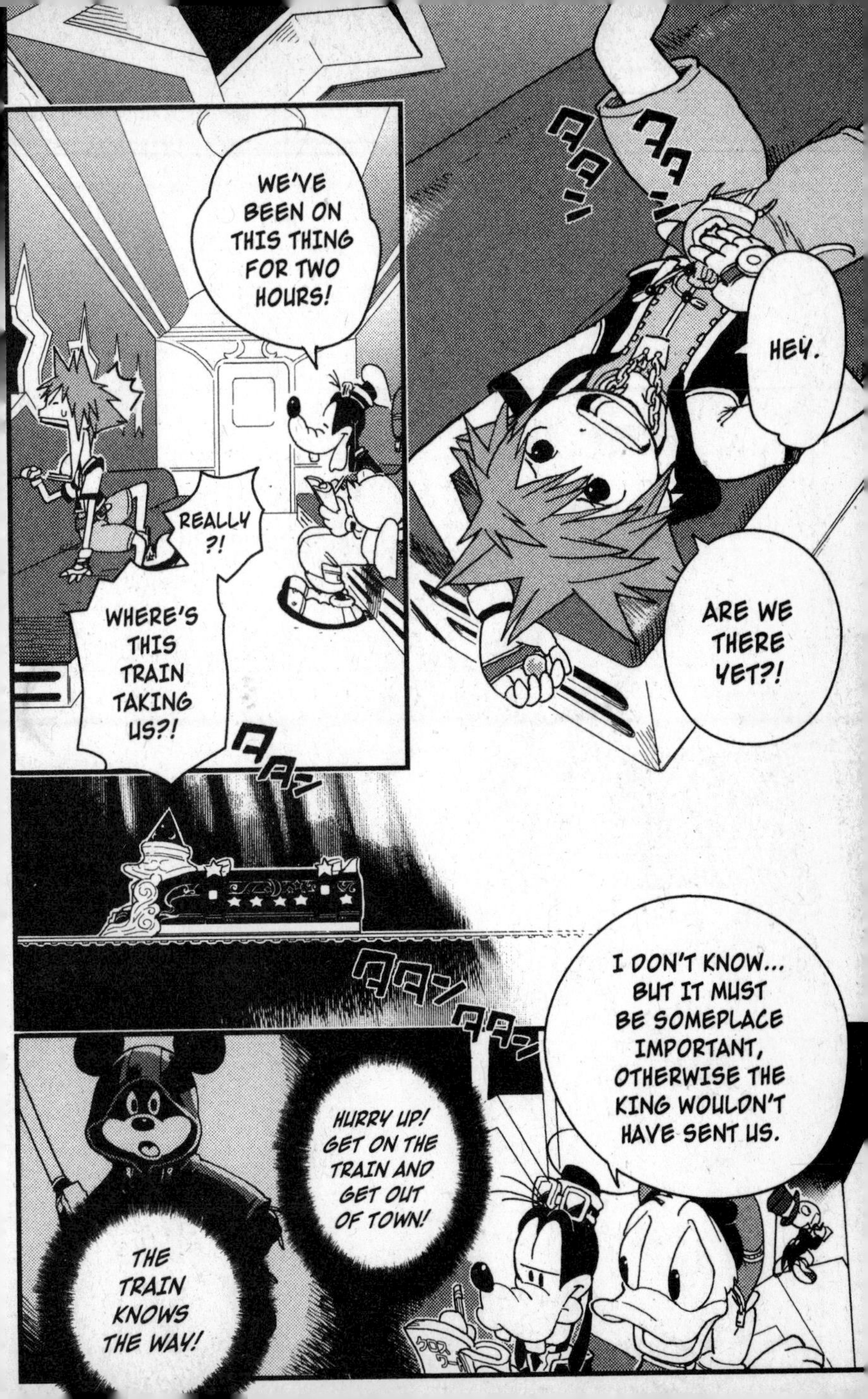
タタン
タタン
HEY.
ARE WE THERE YET?!
WE'VE BEEN ON THIS THING FOR TWO HOURS!
REALLY?!
WHERE'S THIS TRAIN TAKING US?!
タタン
タタン タタン
I DON'T KNOW... BUT IT MUST BE SOMEPLACE IMPORTANT, OTHERWISE THE KING WOULDN'T HAVE SENT US.
クロスワード
HURRY UP! GET ON THE TRAIN AND GET OUT OF TOWN!
THE TRAIN KNOWS THE WAY!

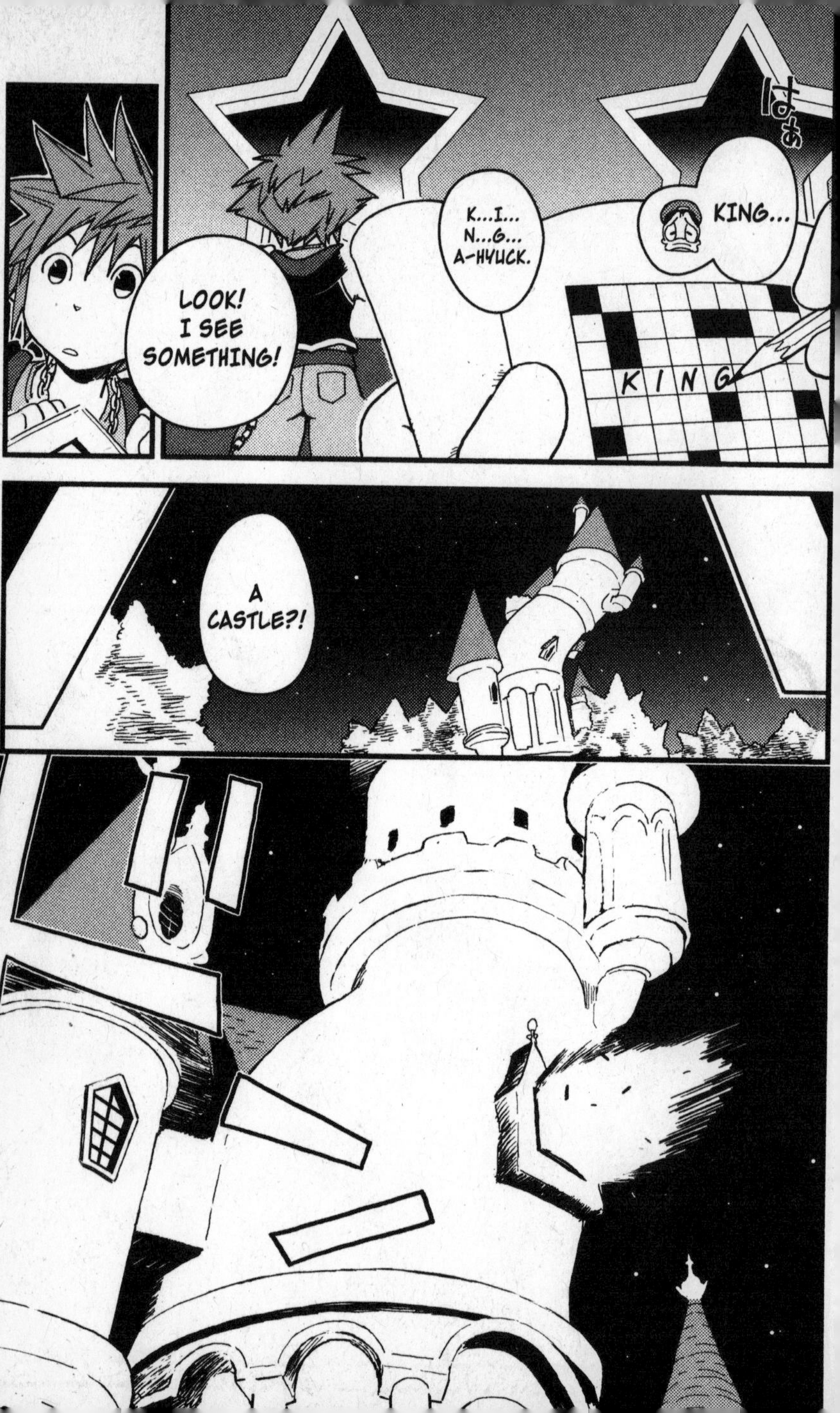
はぁ
KING...
K...I...
N...G...
A-HYUCK.
KING
LOOK!
I SEE
SOMETHING!
A
CASTLE?!

Chapter 12: Key to the Door of Light

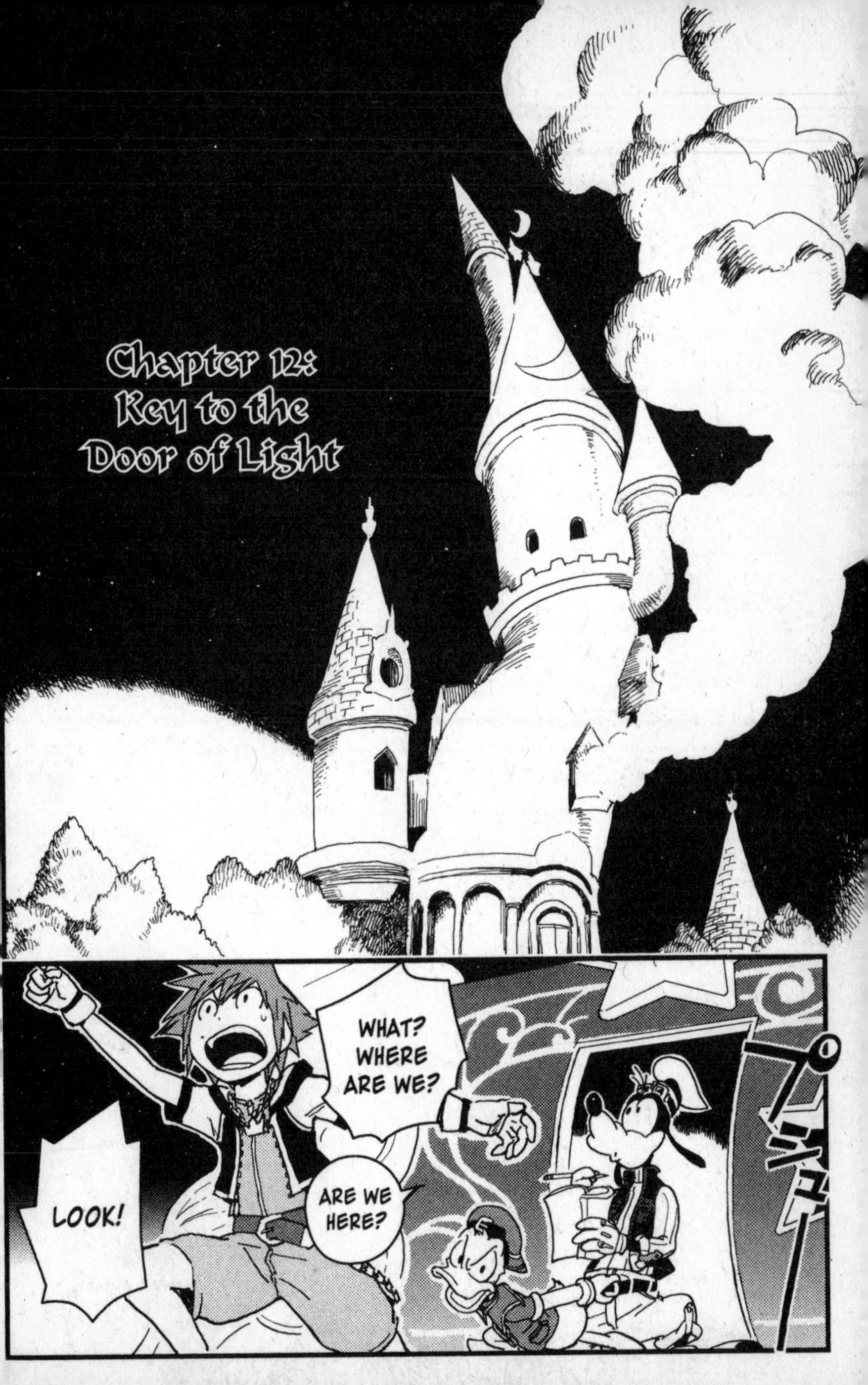
WHAT? WHERE ARE WE?
ARE WE HERE?
LOOK!

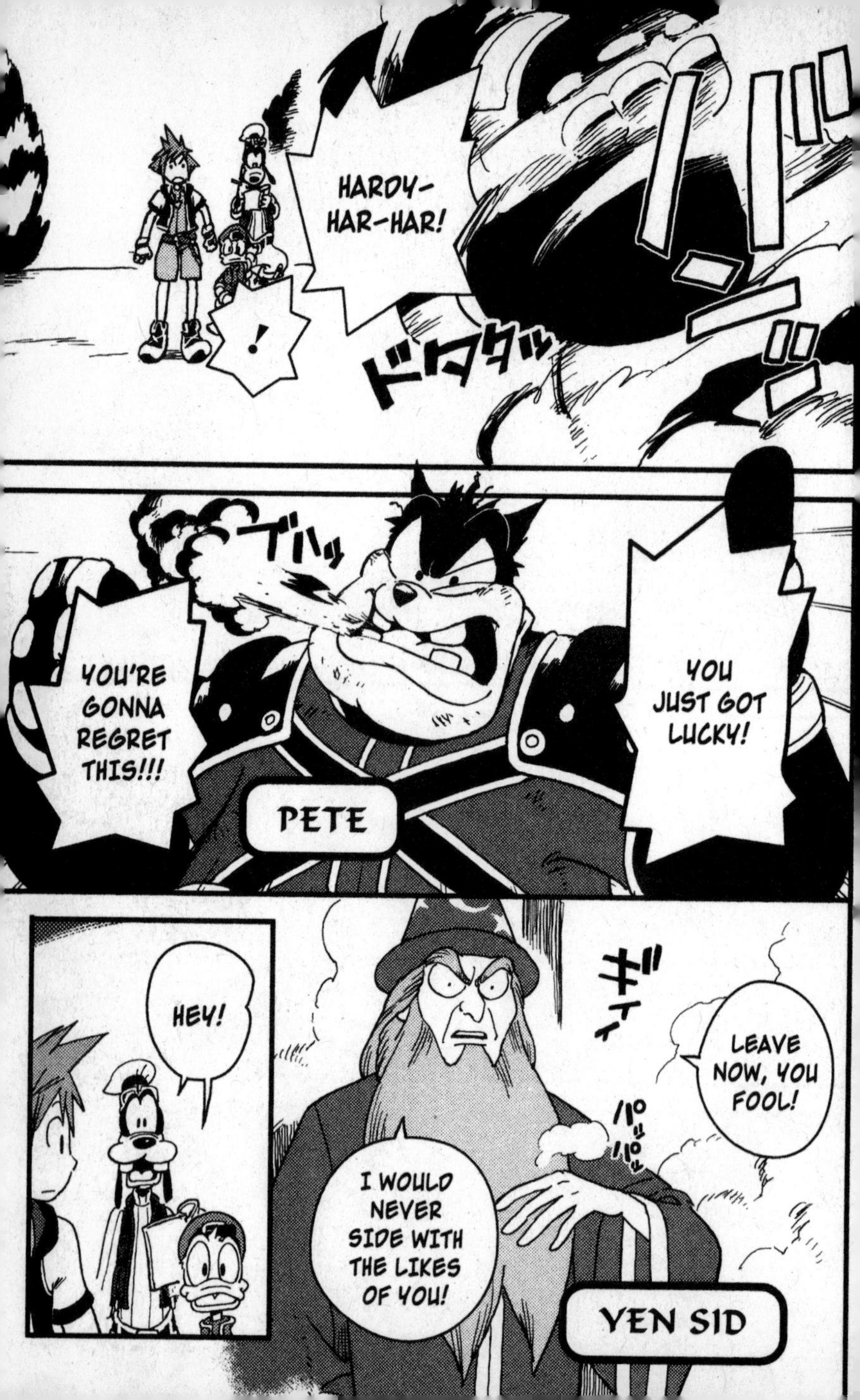
HARDY-HAR-HAR!
!
YOU JUST GOT LUCKY!
PETE
YOU'RE GONNA REGRET THIS!!!
LEAVE NOW, YOU FOOL!
I WOULD NEVER SIDE WITH THE LIKES OF YOU!
YEN SID
HEY!

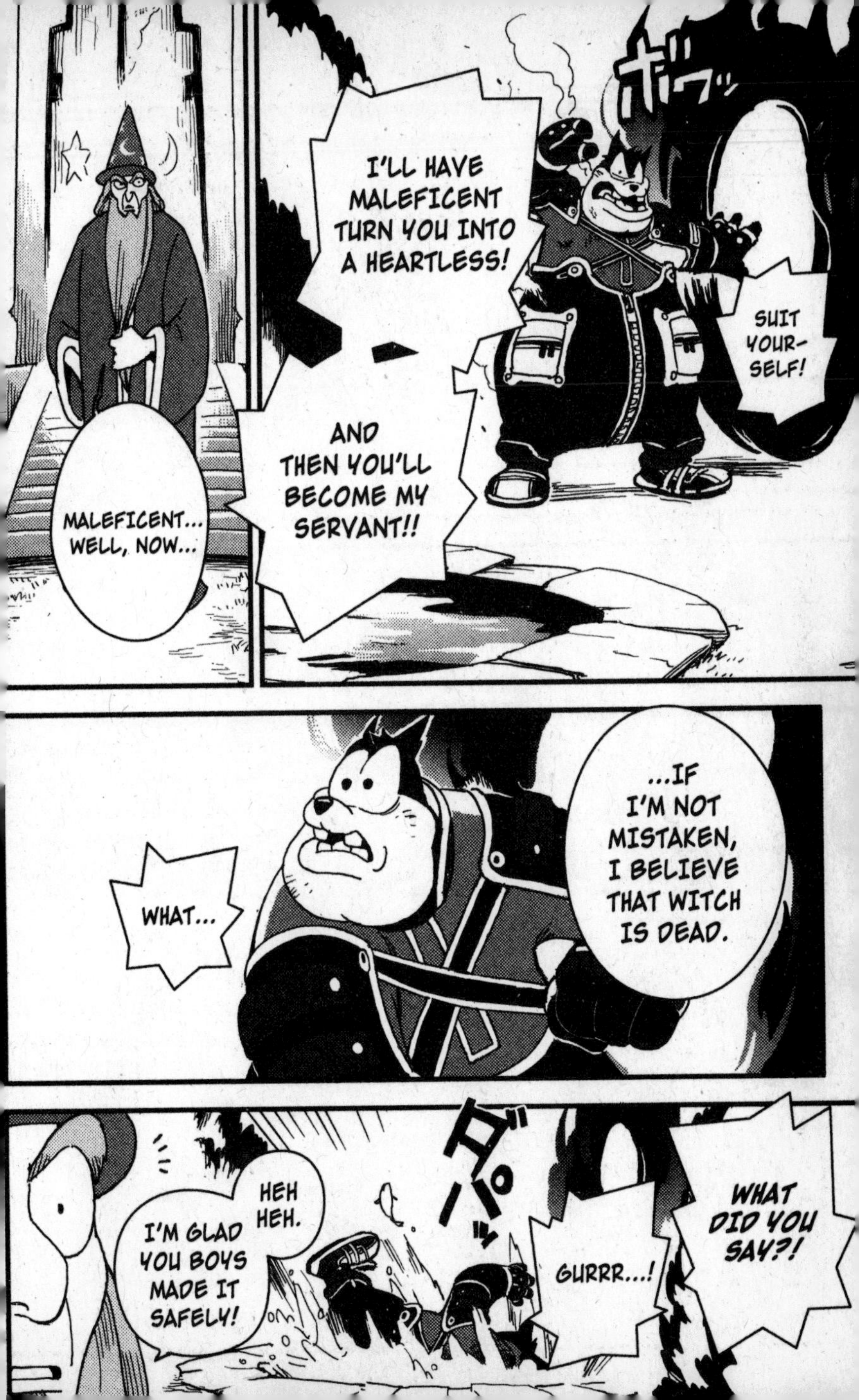
I'LL HAVE MALEFICENT TURN YOU INTO A HEARTLESS!
SUIT YOUR-SELF!
AND THEN YOU'LL BECOME MY SERVANT!!
MALEFICENT... WELL, NOW...
...IF I'M NOT MISTAKEN, I BELIEVE THAT WITCH IS DEAD.
WHAT...
WHAT DID YOU SAY?!
GURRR...!
HEH HEH.
I'M GLAD YOU BOYS MADE IT SAFELY!

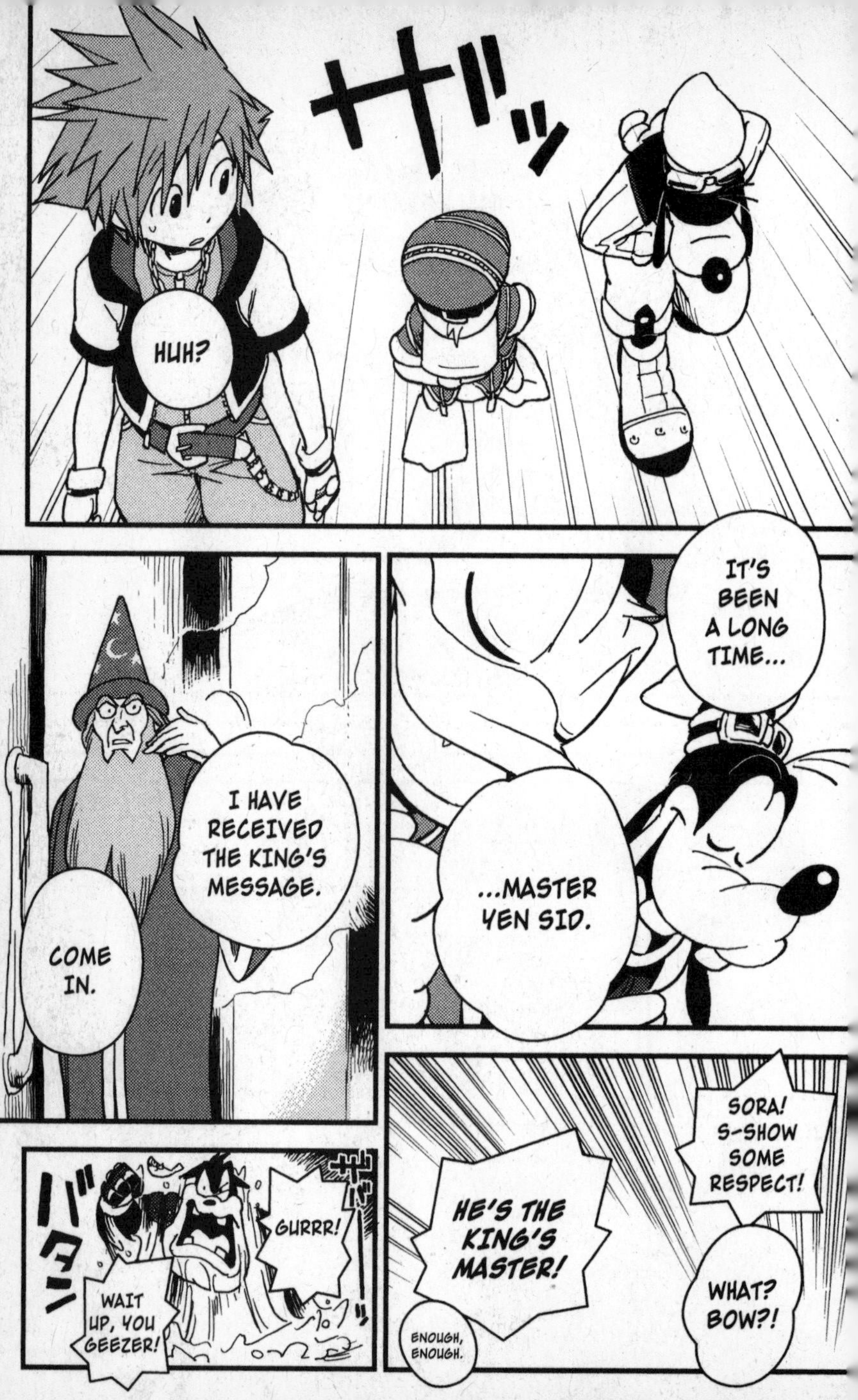
ザッ
HUH?
IT'S BEEN A LONG TIME...
...MASTER YEN SID.
I HAVE RECEIVED THE KING'S MESSAGE.
COME IN.
SORA! S-SHOW SOME RESPECT!
HE'S THE KING'S MASTER!
WHAT? BOW?!
ENOUGH, ENOUGH.
GURRR!
WAIT UP, YOU GEEZER!

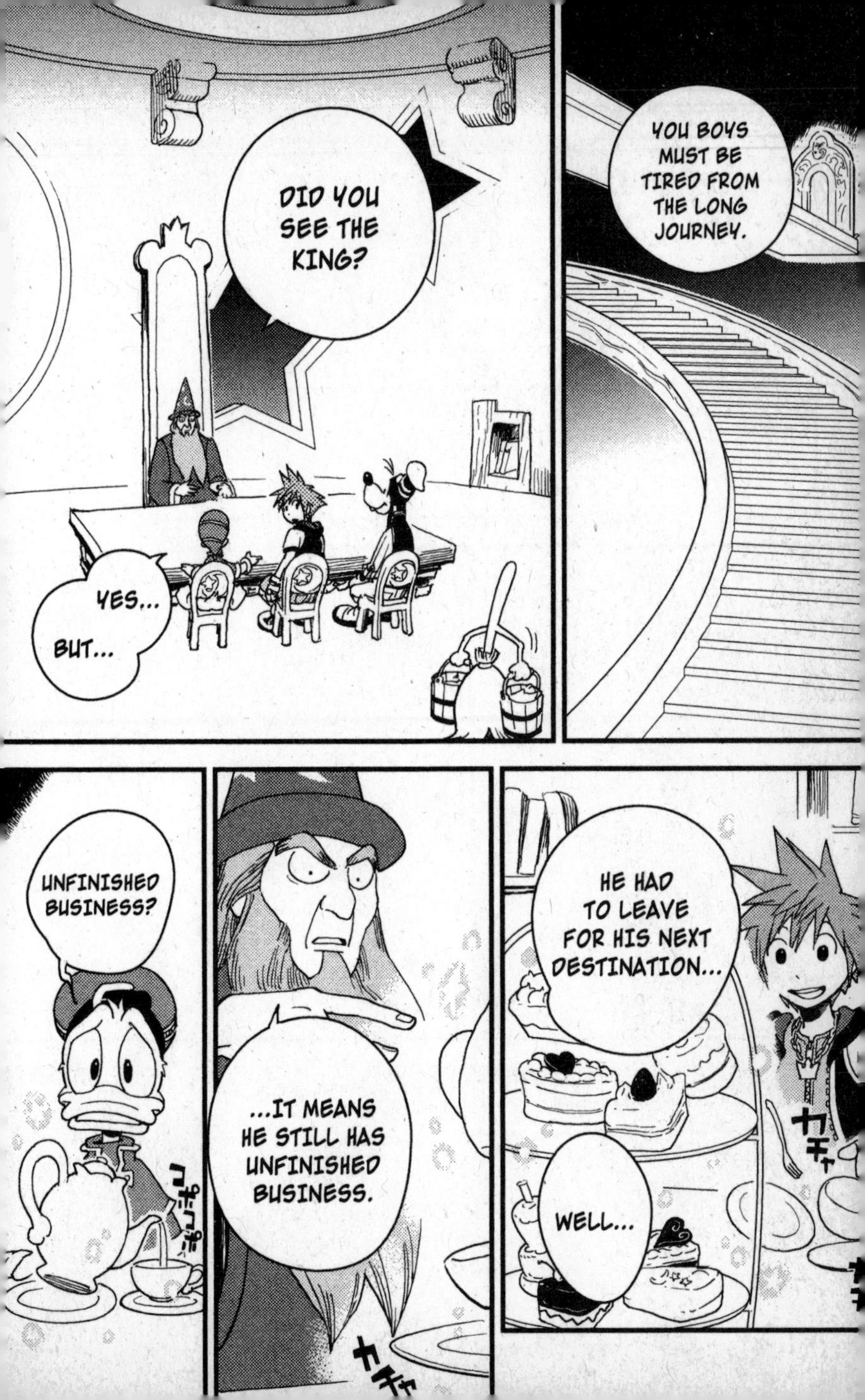
YOU BOYS MUST BE TIRED FROM THE LONG JOURNEY.
DID YOU SEE THE KING?
YES...
BUT...
HE HAD TO LEAVE FOR HIS NEXT DESTINATION...
カチャ
WELL...
...IT MEANS HE STILL HAS UNFINISHED BUSINESS.
カチャ
UNFINISHED BUSINESS?
コポコポ

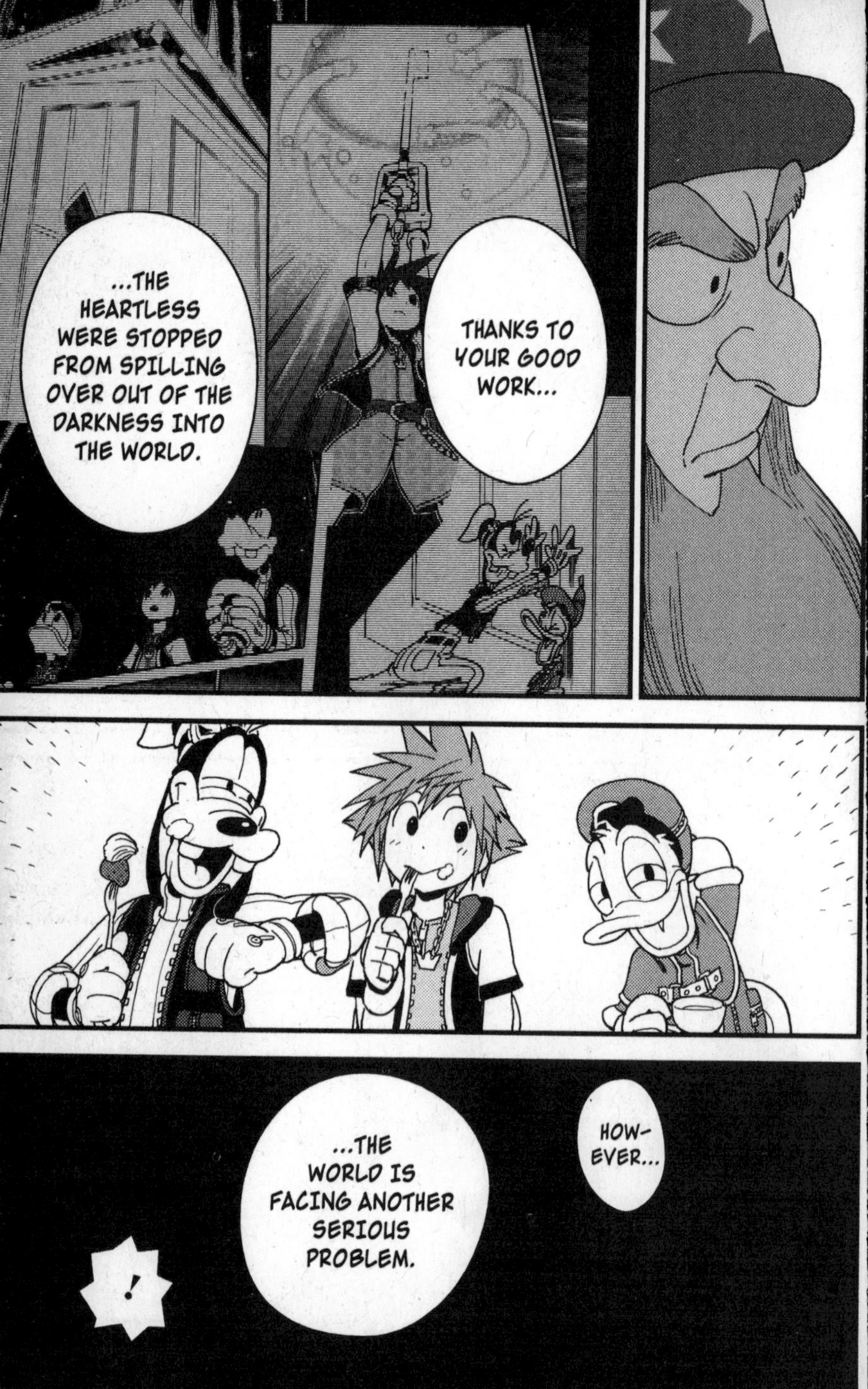
THANKS TO YOUR GOOD WORK...
...THE HEARTLESS WERE STOPPED FROM SPILLING OVER OUT OF THE DARKNESS INTO THE WORLD.
HOW-EVER...
...THE WORLD IS FACING ANOTHER SERIOUS PROBLEM.
!

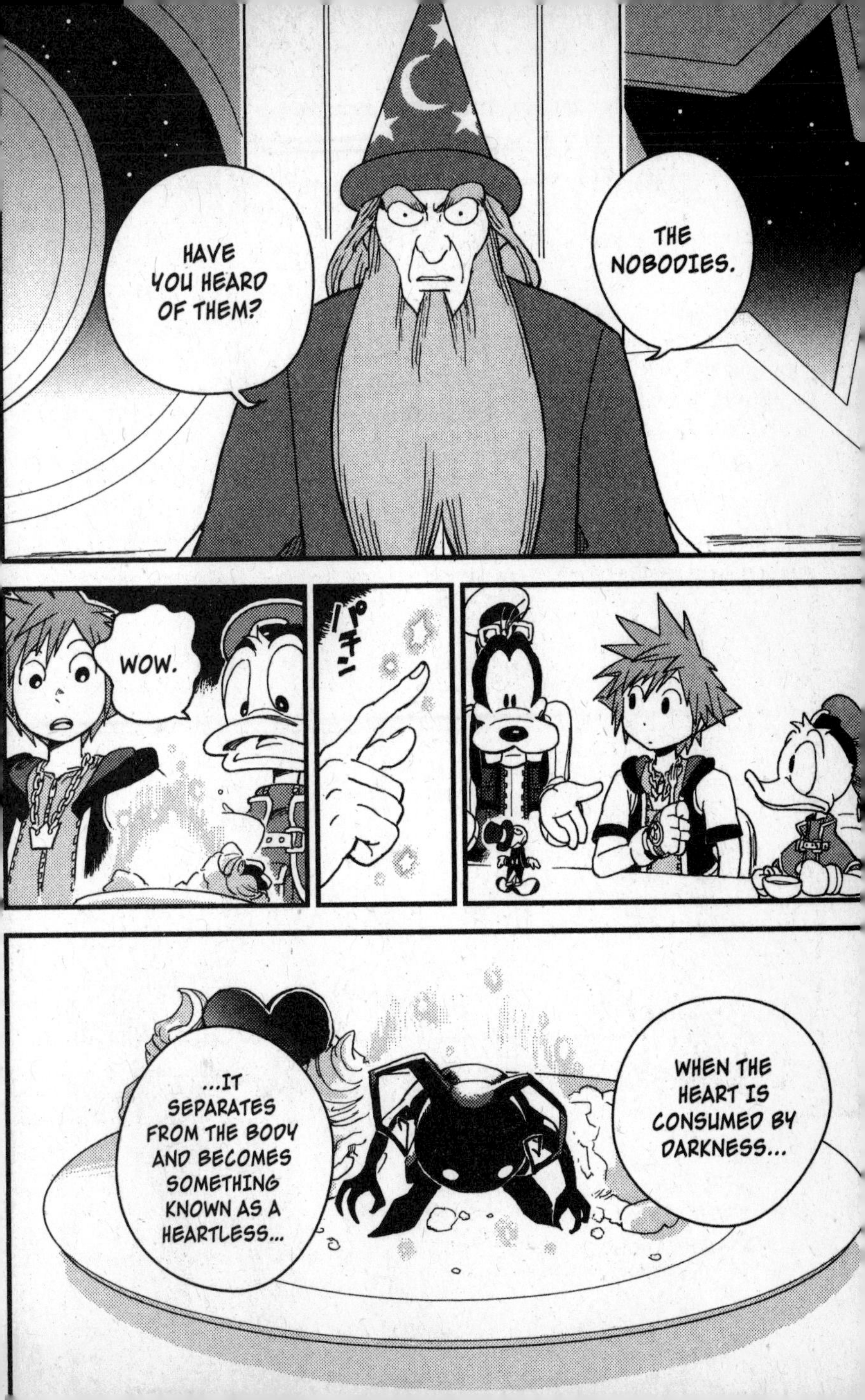
THE NOBODIES.
HAVE YOU HEARD OF THEM?
パチン
WOW.
WHEN THE HEART IS CONSUMED BY DARKNESS...
...IT SEPARATES FROM THE BODY AND BECOMES SOMETHING KNOWN AS A HEARTLESS...

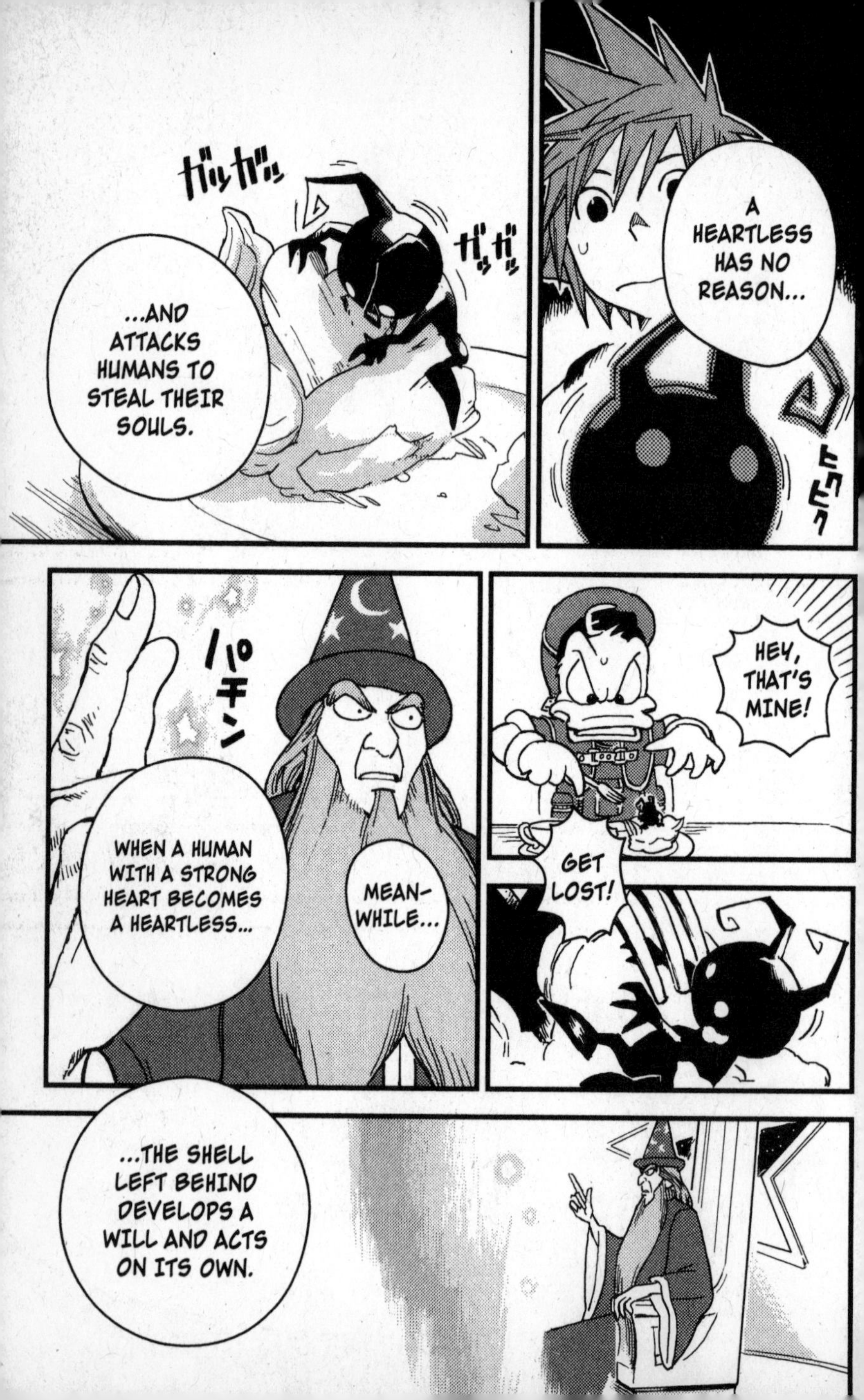
A HEARTLESS HAS NO REASON...
...AND ATTACKS HUMANS TO STEAL THEIR SOULS.
HEY, THAT'S MINE!
GET LOST!
パチン
WHEN A HUMAN WITH A STRONG HEART BECOMES A HEARTLESS...
MEAN-WHILE...
...THE SHELL LEFT BEHIND DEVELOPS A WILL AND ACTS ON ITS OWN.

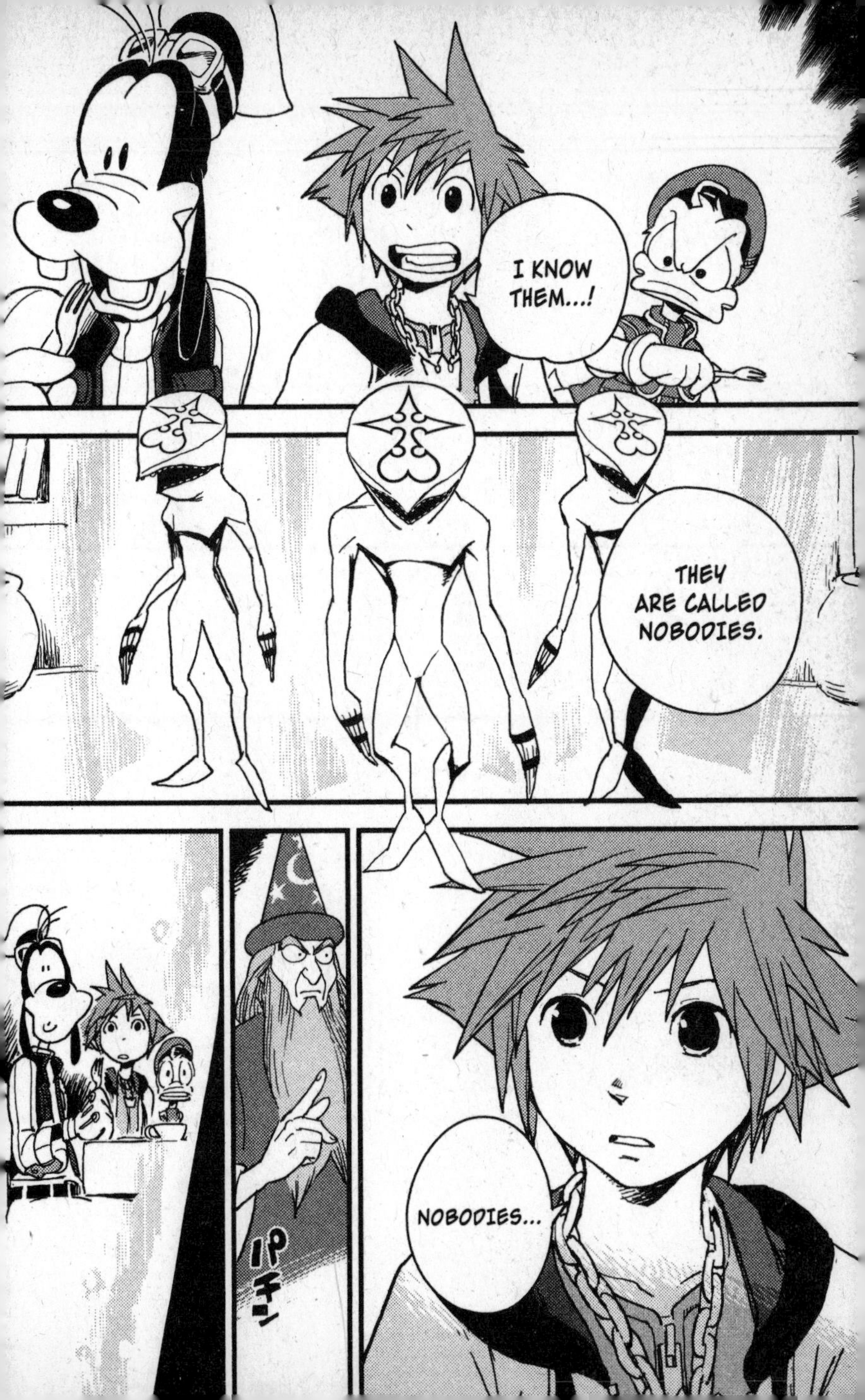
I KNOW THEM...!
THEY ARE CALLED NOBODIES.
NOBODIES...
パチン

THERE ARE SOME AMONG THEM THAT POSSESS INTELLECT AND LOOK LIKE HUMANS.
THEY'VE FORMED AN ALLIANCE AND CONTROL THE NOBODIES.
THEY CALL THEMSELVES "ORGANIZATION XIII."

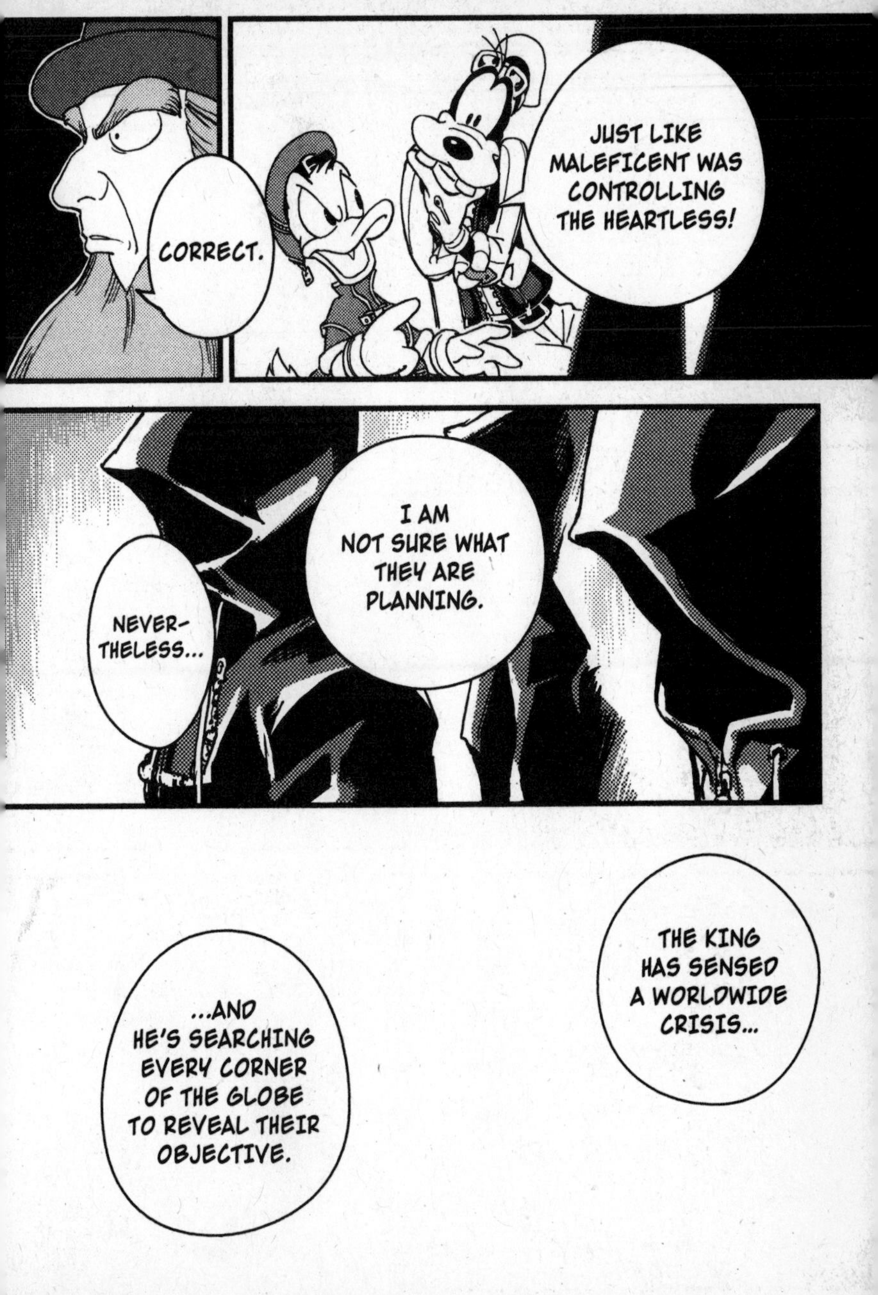
JUST LIKE MALEFICENT WAS CONTROLLING THE HEARTLESS!
CORRECT.
I AM NOT SURE WHAT THEY ARE PLANNING.
NEVER-THELESS...
THE KING HAS SENSED A WORLDWIDE CRISIS...
...AND HE'S SEARCHING EVERY CORNER OF THE GLOBE TO REVEAL THEIR OBJECTIVE.

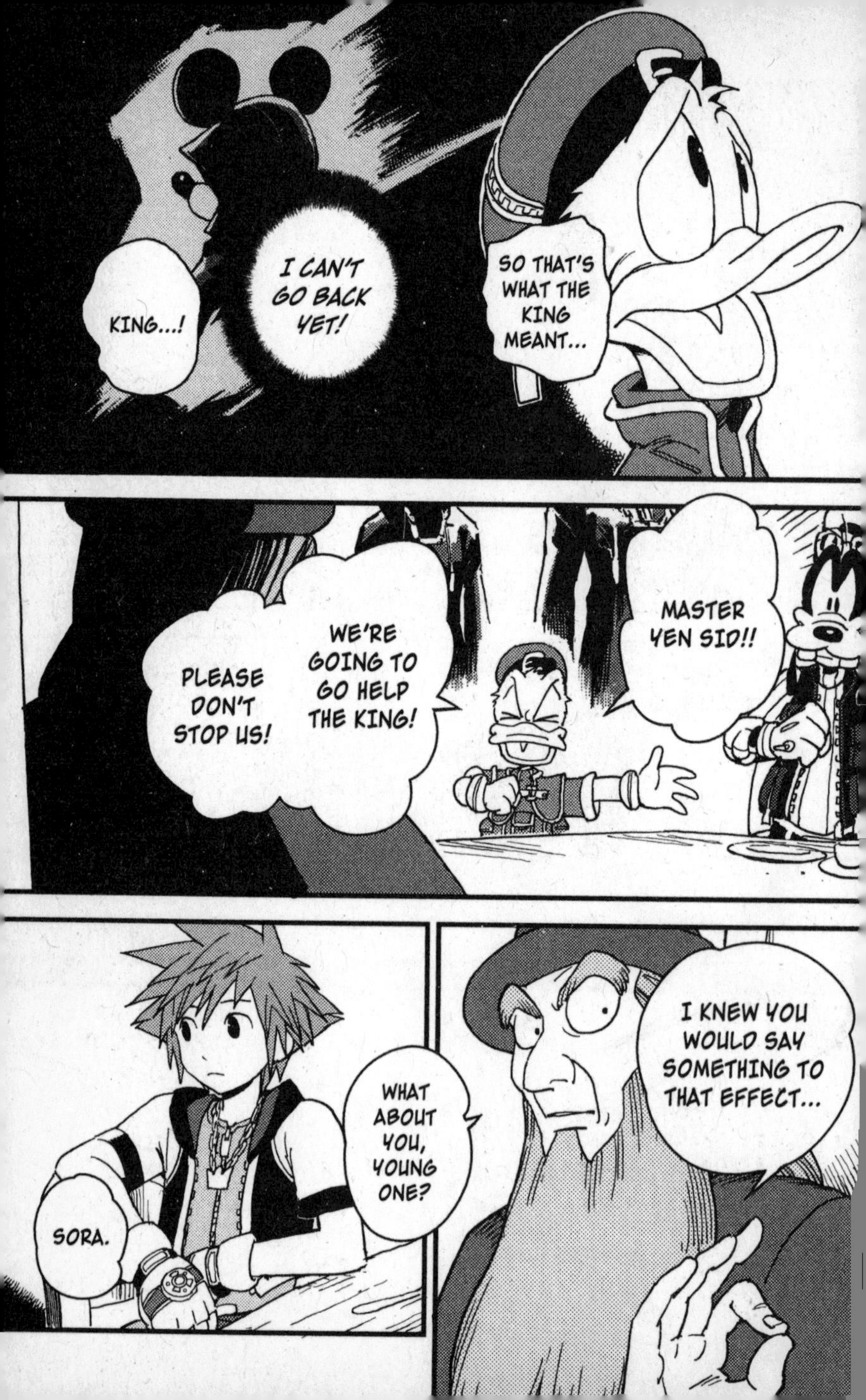
SO THAT'S WHAT THE KING MEANT...
I CAN'T GO BACK YET!
KING...!
MASTER YEN SID!!
WE'RE GOING TO GO HELP THE KING!
PLEASE DON'T STOP US!
I KNEW YOU WOULD SAY SOMETHING TO THAT EFFECT...
WHAT ABOUT YOU, YOUNG ONE?
SORA.

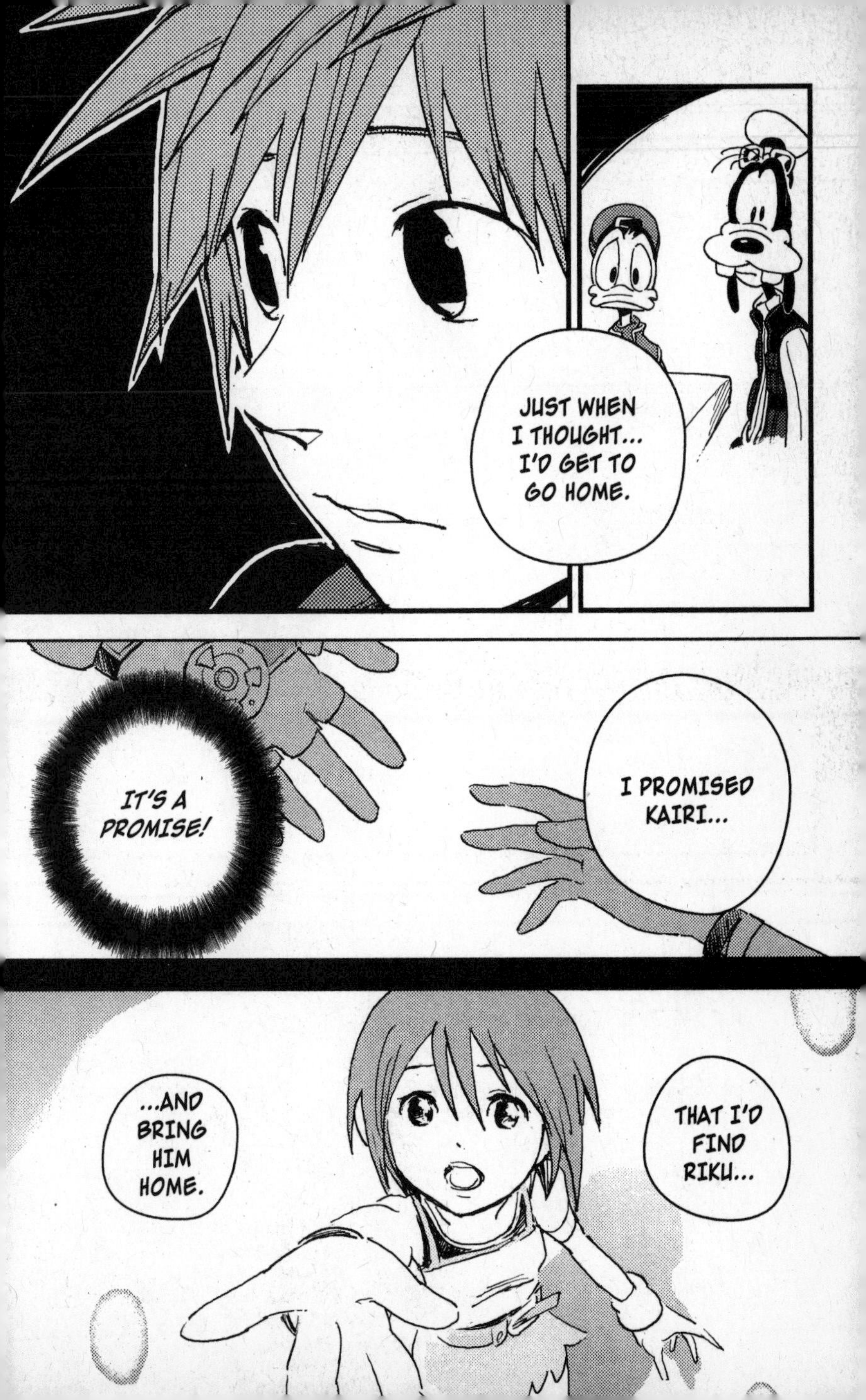
JUST WHEN I THOUGHT... I'D GET TO GO HOME.
I PROMISED KAIRI...
IT'S A PROMISE!
THAT I'D FIND RIKU...
...AND BRING HIM HOME.

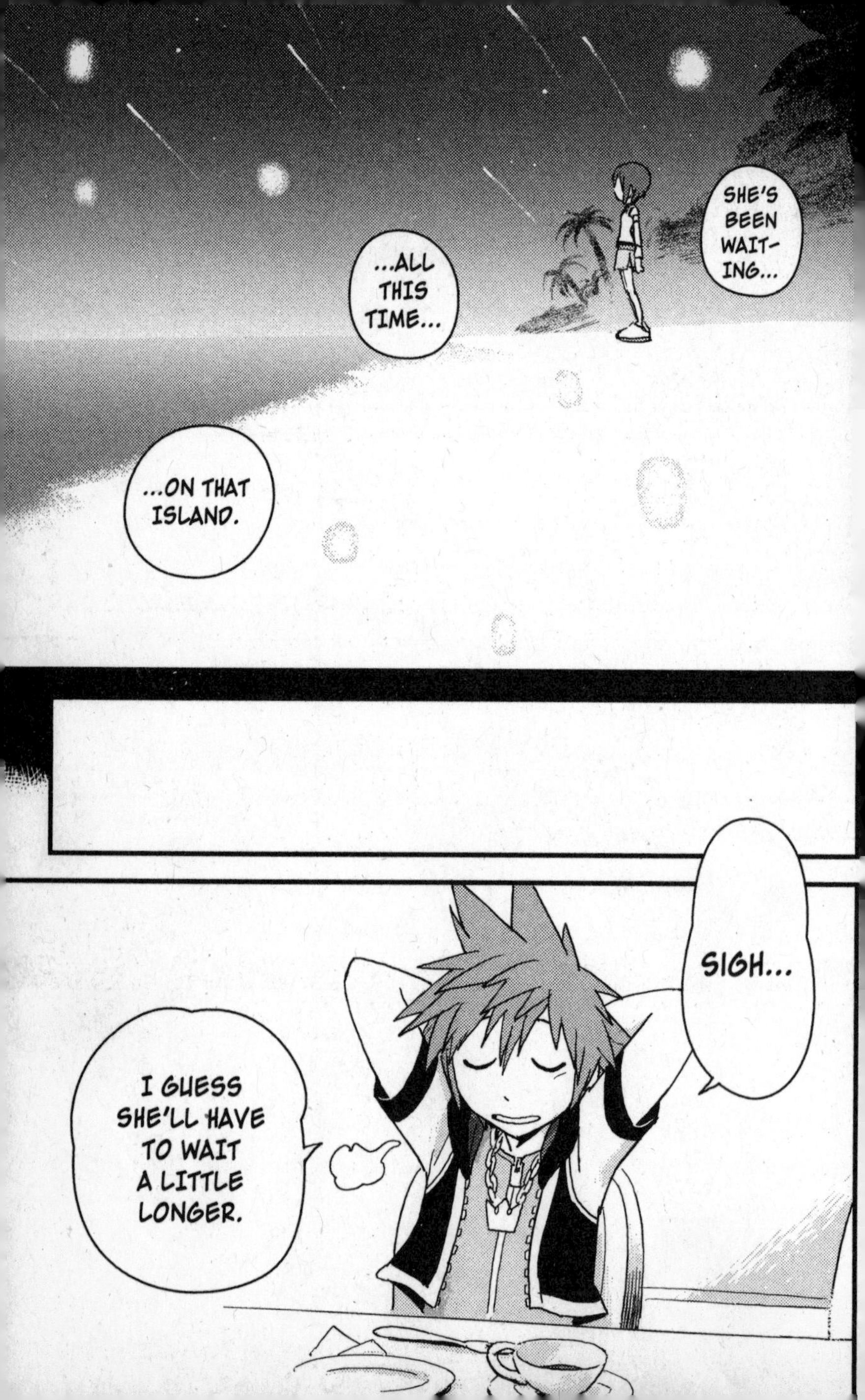
SHE'S BEEN WAIT-ING...
...ALL THIS TIME...
...ON THAT ISLAND.
SIGH...
I GUESS SHE'LL HAVE TO WAIT A LITTLE LONGER.

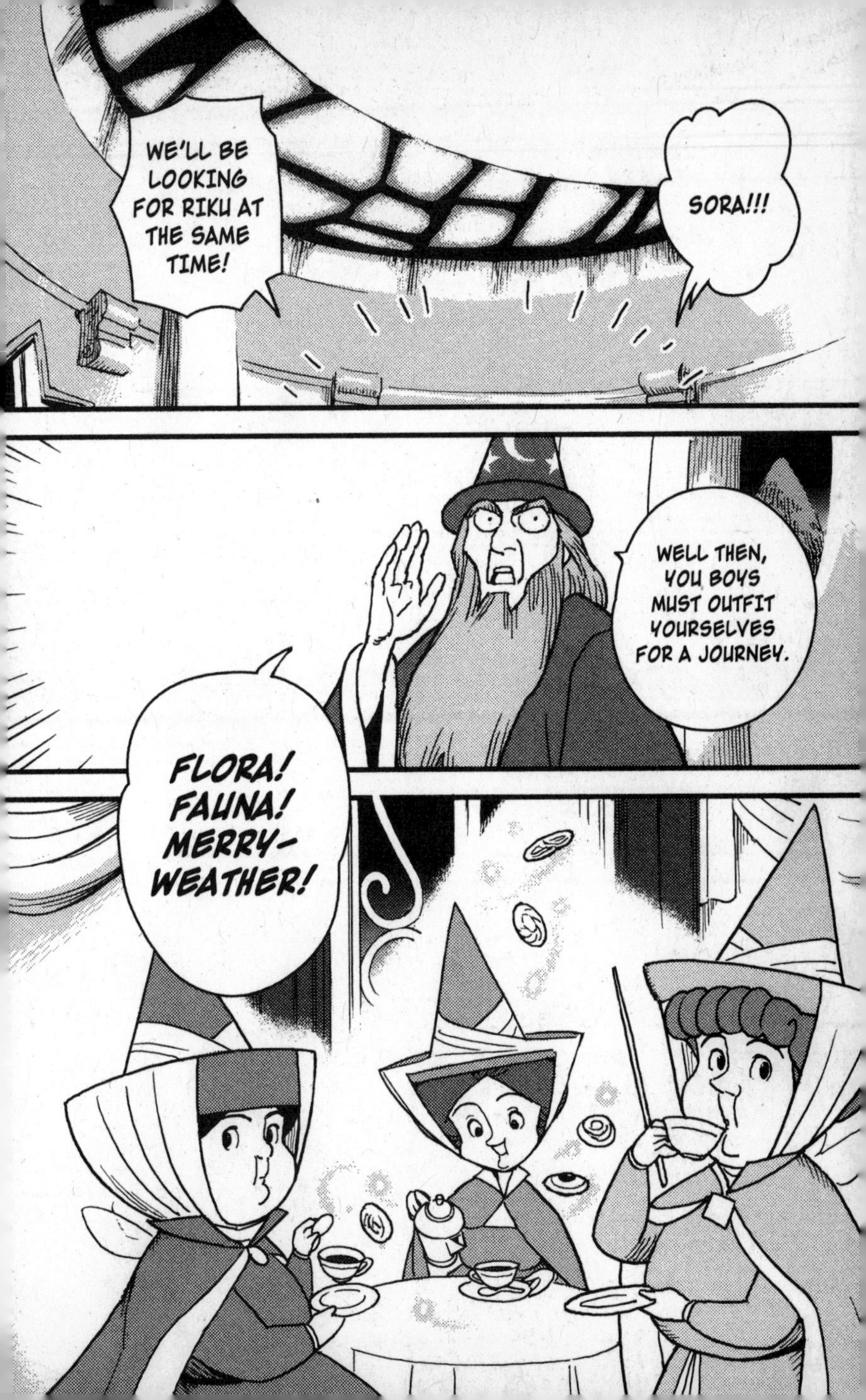
SORA!!!
WE'LL BE LOOKING FOR RIKU AT THE SAME TIME!
WELL THEN, YOU BOYS MUST OUTFIT YOURSELVES FOR A JOURNEY.
FLORA! FAUNA! MERRY-WEATHER!

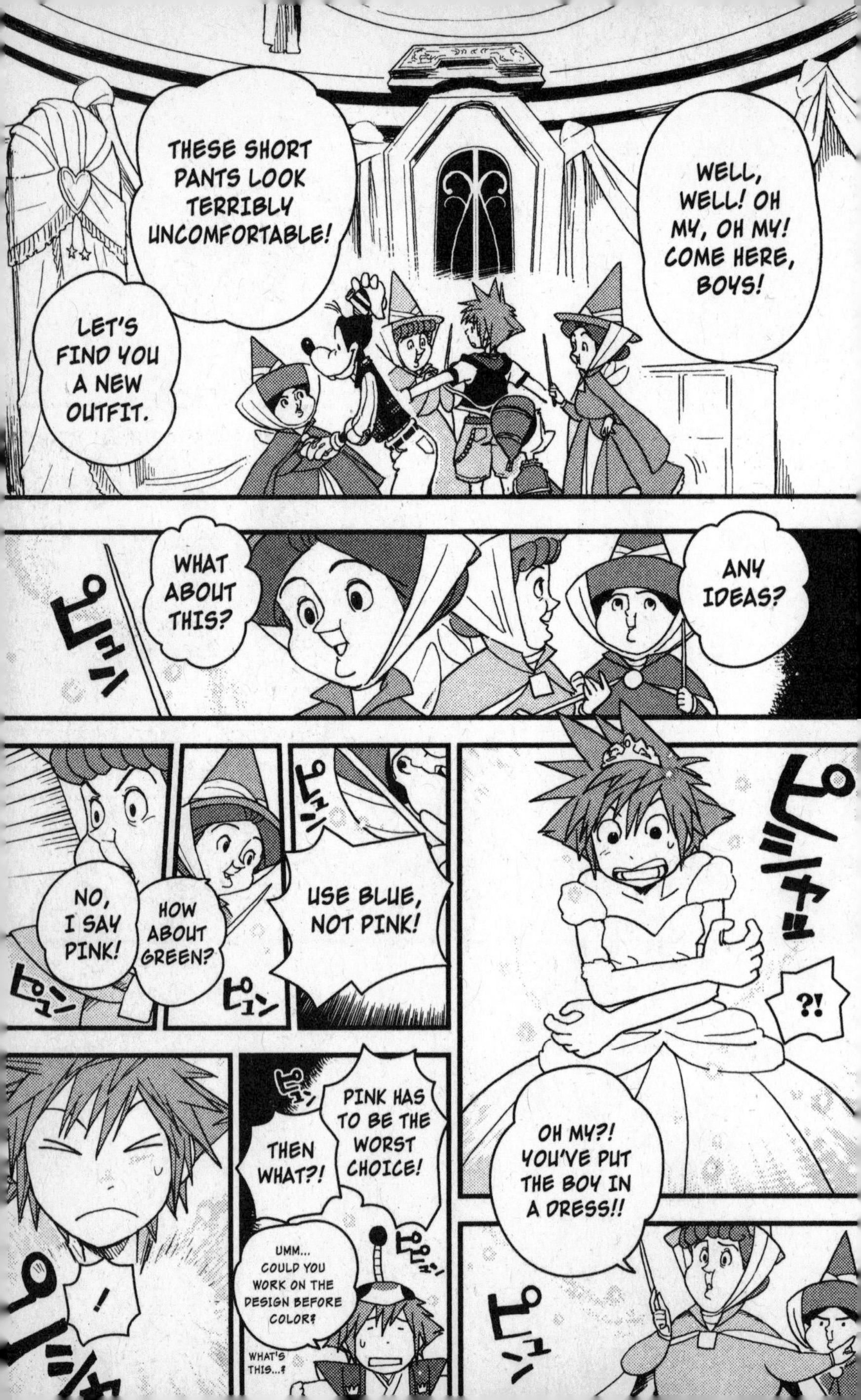

WELL, WELL! OH MY, OH MY! COME HERE, BOYS!
THESE SHORT PANTS LOOK TERRIBLY UNCOMFORTABLE!
LET'S FIND YOU A NEW OUTFIT.
ANY IDEAS?
WHAT ABOUT THIS?
?!
OH MY?! YOU'VE PUT THE BOY IN A DRESS!!
USE BLUE, NOT PINK!
HOW ABOUT GREEN?
NO, I SAY PINK!
PINK HAS TO BE THE WORST CHOICE!
THEN WHAT?!
UMM... COULD YOU WORK ON THE DESIGN BEFORE COLOR?
WHAT'S THIS...?
!

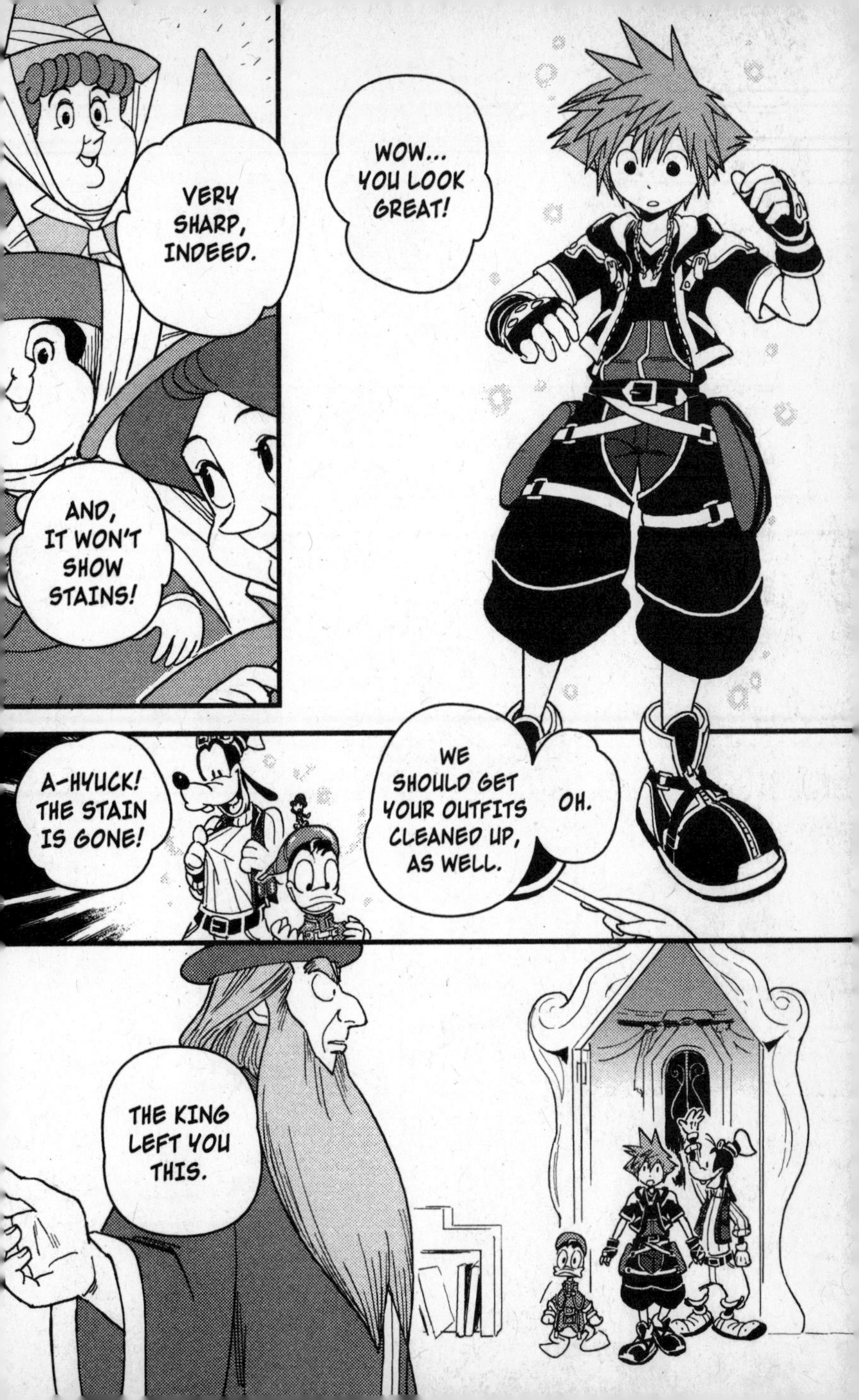
WOW... YOU LOOK GREAT!
VERY SHARP, INDEED.
AND, IT WON'T SHOW STAINS!
WE SHOULD GET YOUR OUTFITS CLEANED UP, AS WELL.
OH.
A-HYUCK! THE STAIN IS GONE!
THE KING LEFT YOU THIS.

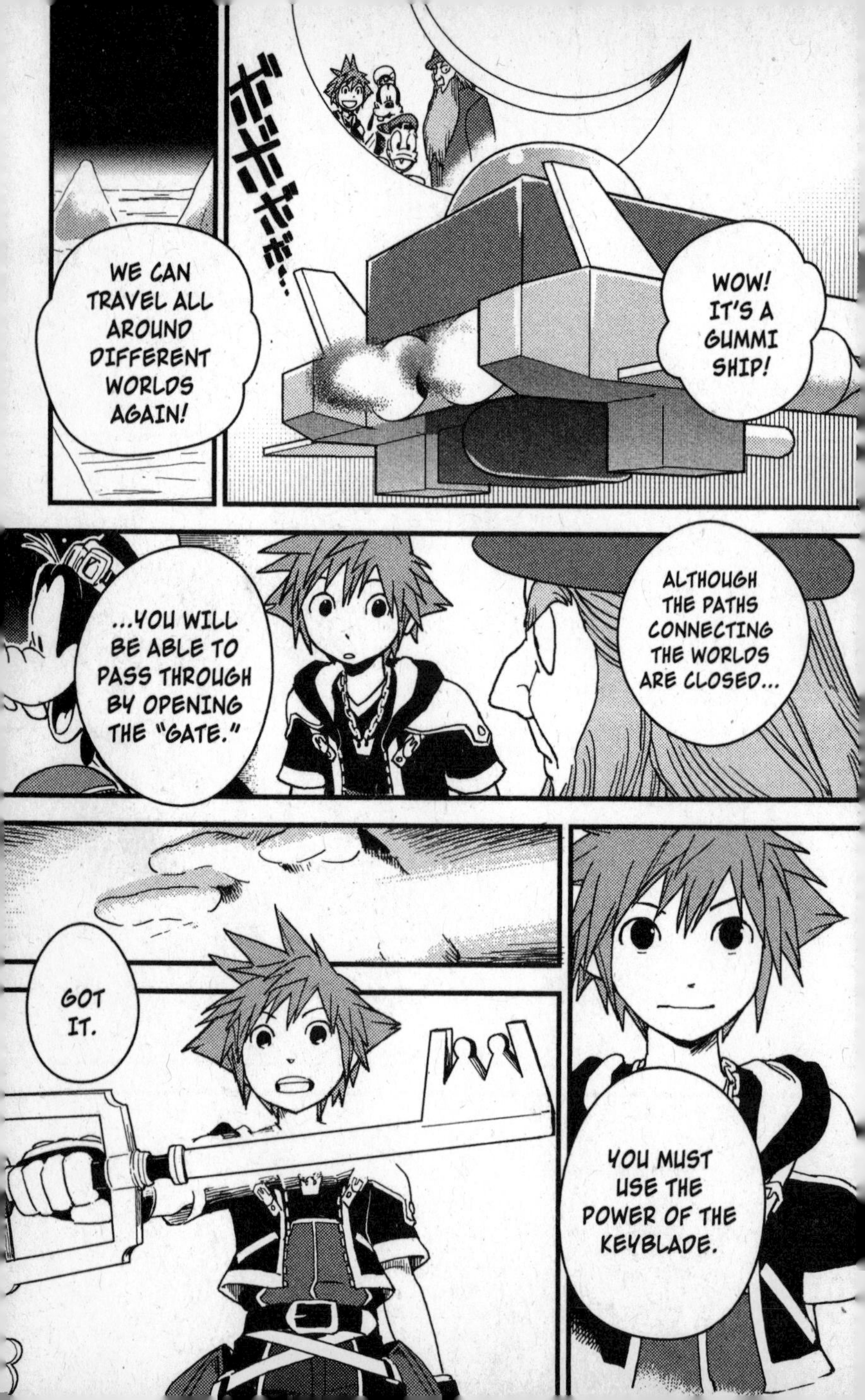
WOW! IT'S A GUMMI SHIP!
ボボボボボ…
WE CAN TRAVEL ALL AROUND DIFFERENT WORLDS AGAIN!
ALTHOUGH THE PATHS CONNECTING THE WORLDS ARE CLOSED...
...YOU WILL BE ABLE TO PASS THROUGH BY OPENING THE "GATE."
YOU MUST USE THE POWER OF THE KEYBLADE.
GOT IT.

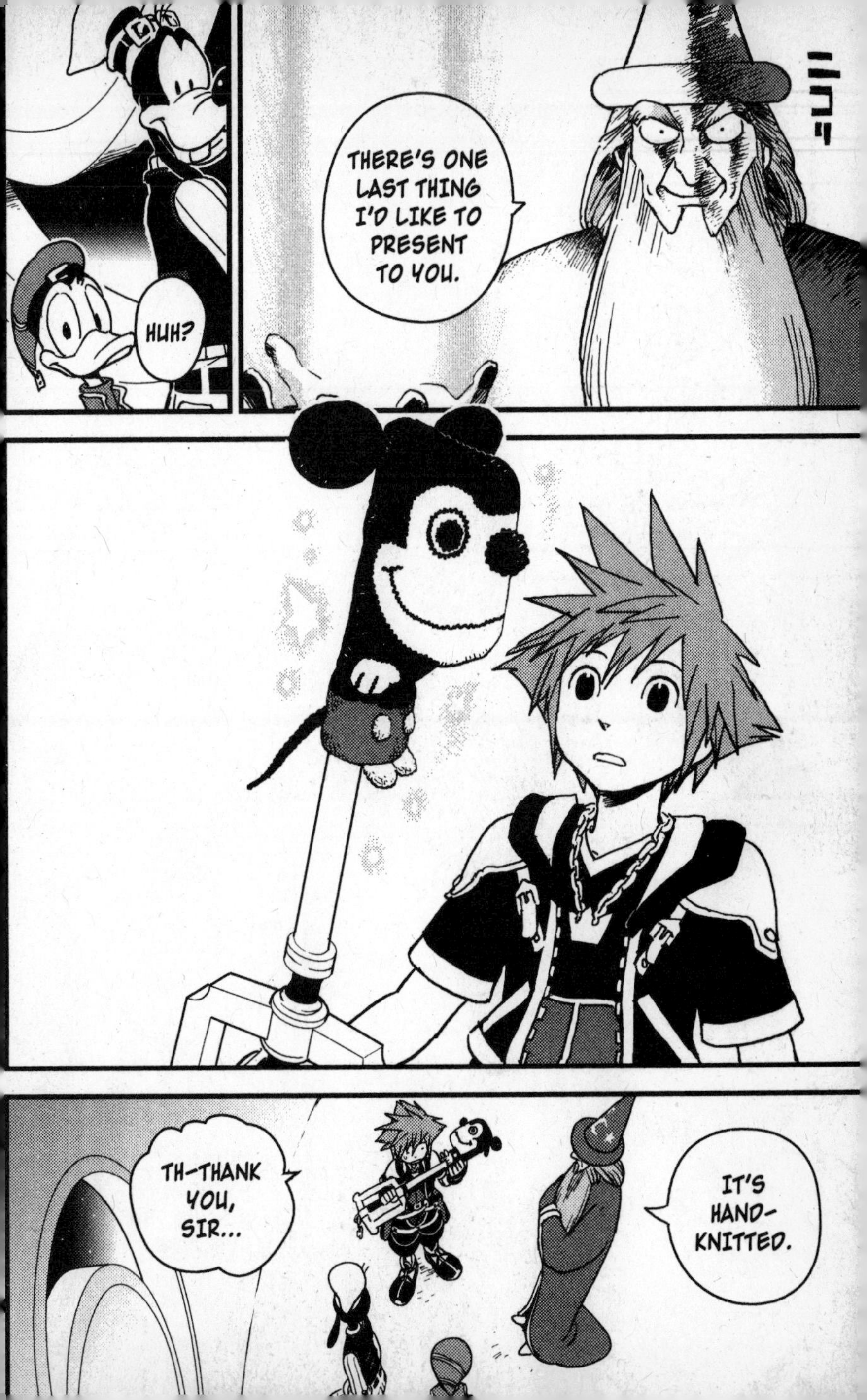
THERE'S ONE LAST THING I'D LIKE TO PRESENT TO YOU.
HUH?
IT'S HAND-KNITTED.
TH-THANK YOU, SIR...

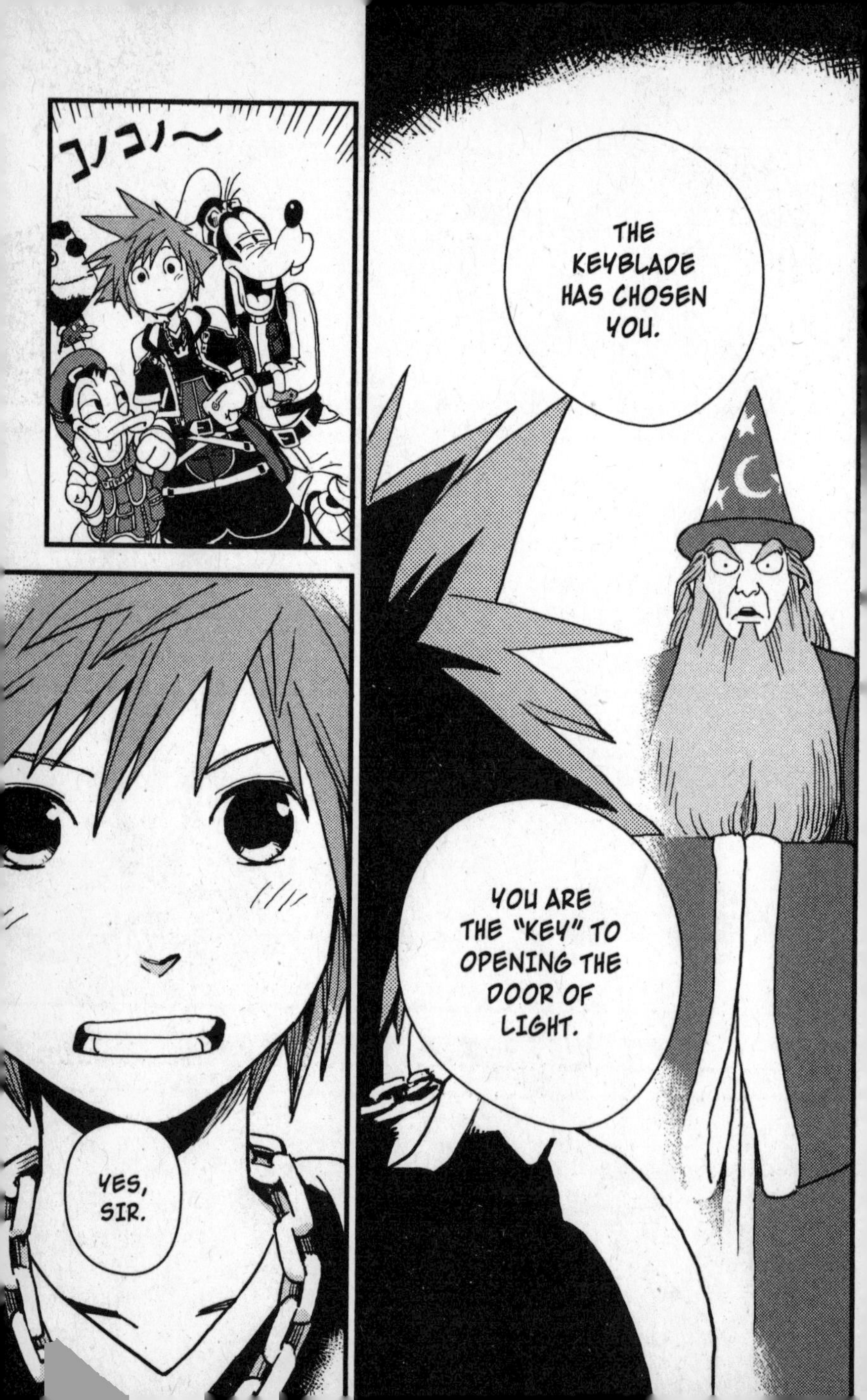
THE KEYBLADE HAS CHOSEN YOU.
YOU ARE THE "KEY" TO OPENING THE DOOR OF LIGHT.
コノコノ～
YES, SIR.

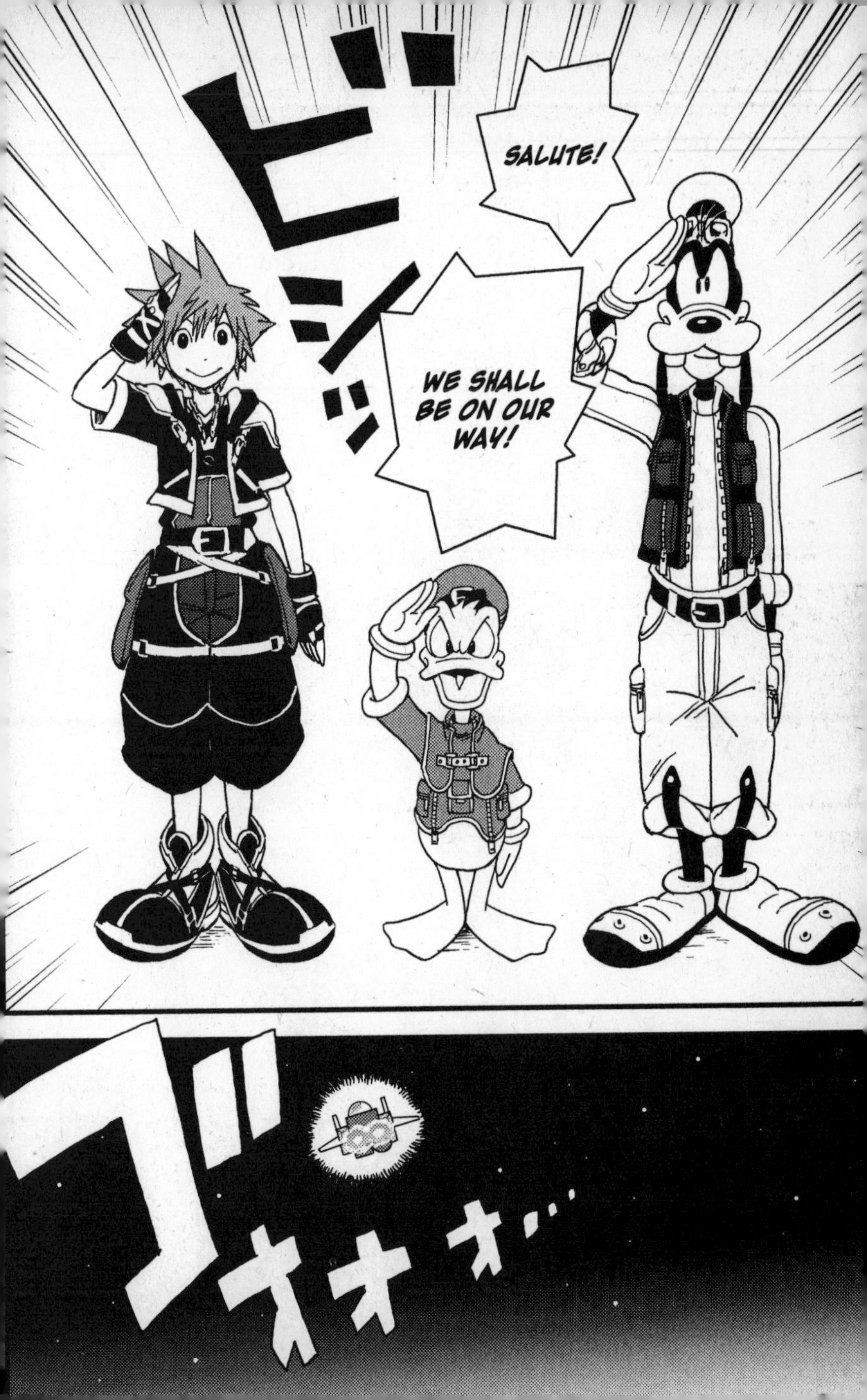
SALUTE!
WE SHALL BE ON OUR WAY!
ビシッ
ゴオオオ…

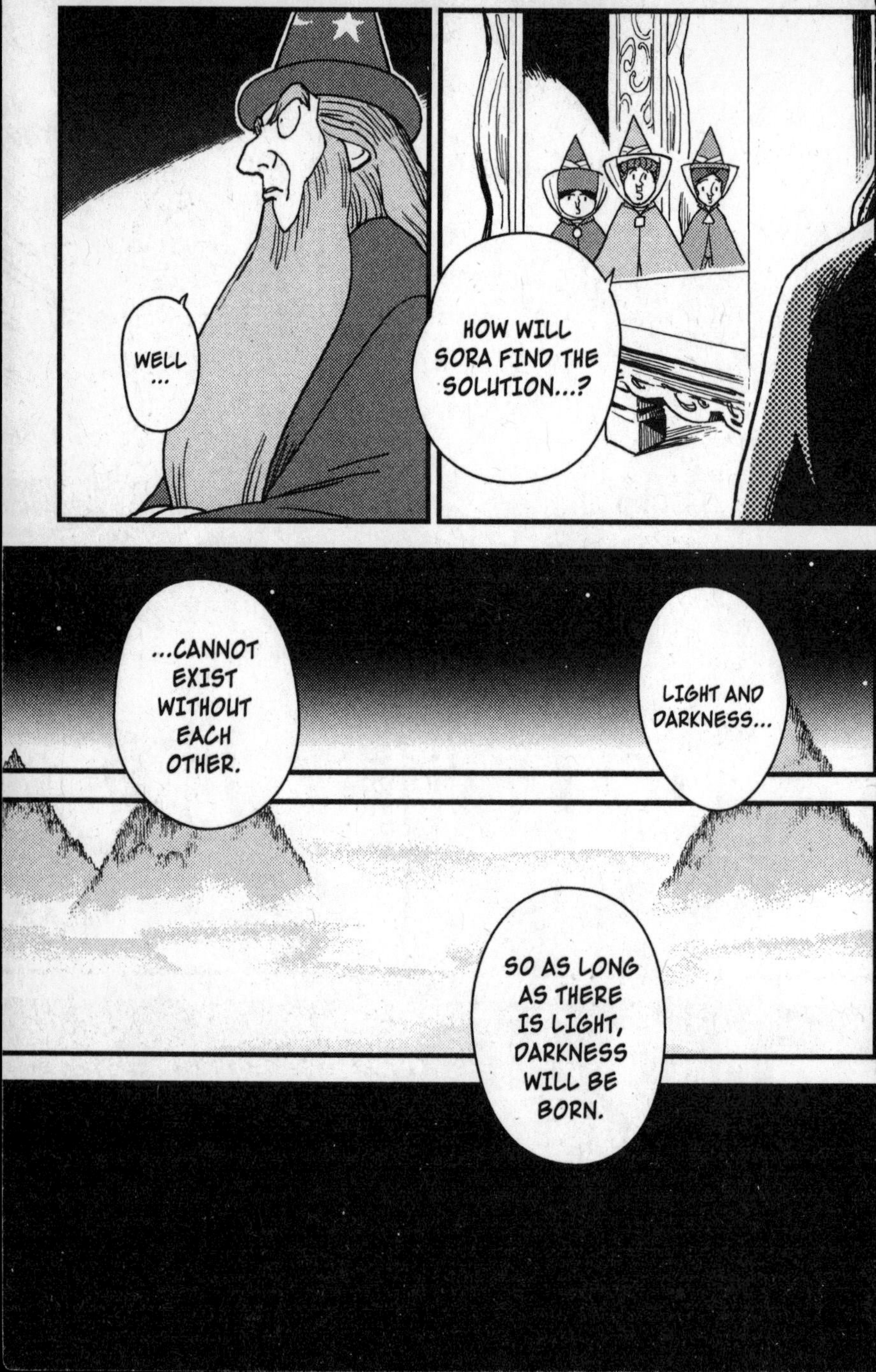
HOW WILL SORA FIND THE SOLUTION...?
WELL...
LIGHT AND DARKNESS...
...CANNOT EXIST WITHOUT EACH OTHER.
SO AS LONG AS THERE IS LIGHT, DARKNESS WILL BE BORN.

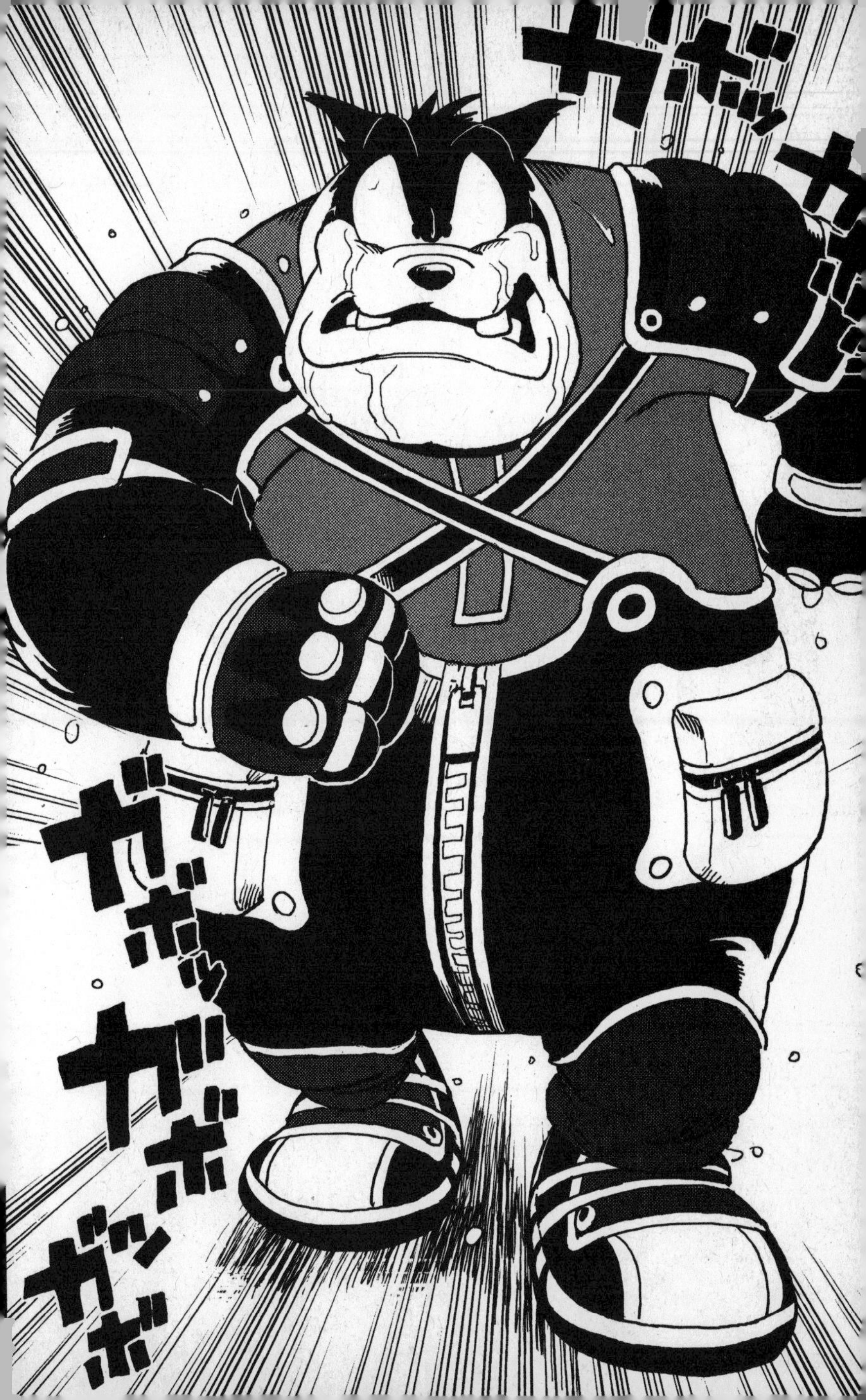
ガボッガボ
ガボッガボガッボ

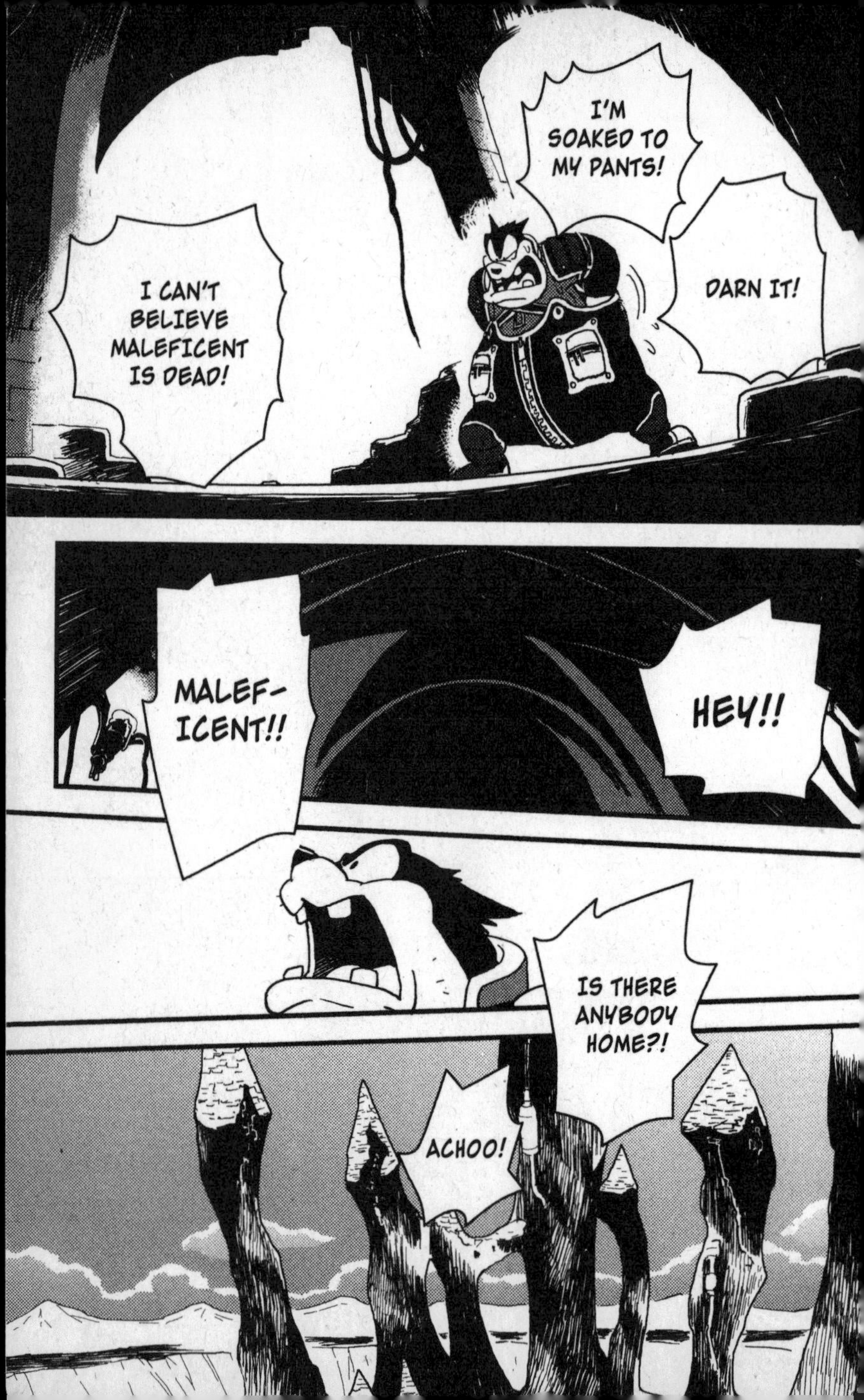
I'M SOAKED TO MY PANTS!
DARN IT!
I CAN'T BELIEVE MALEFICENT IS DEAD!
HEY!!
MALEF-ICENT!!
IS THERE ANYBODY HOME?!
ACHOO!

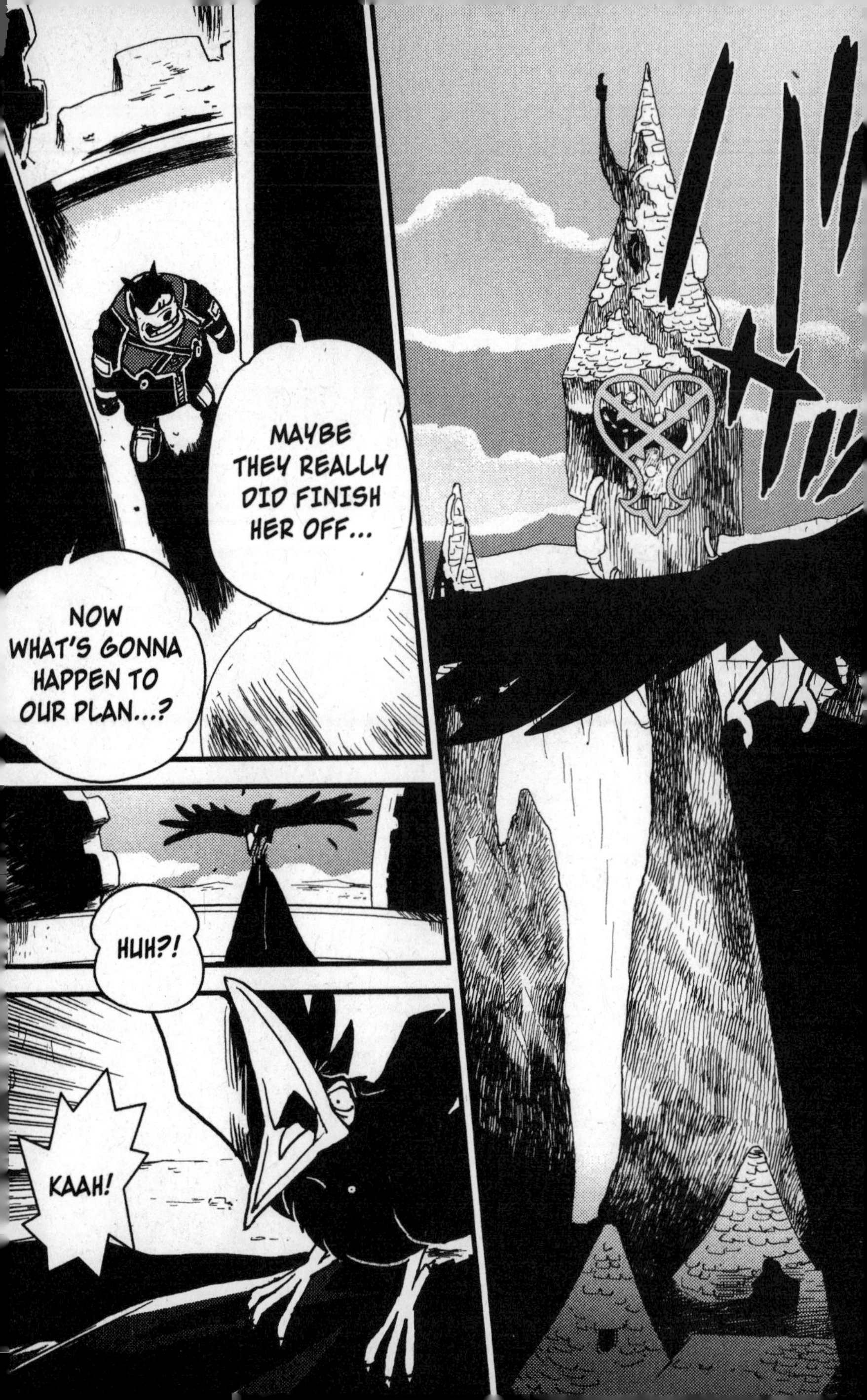
MAYBE THEY REALLY DID FINISH HER OFF...
NOW WHAT'S GONNA HAPPEN TO OUR PLAN...?
HUH?!
KAAH!

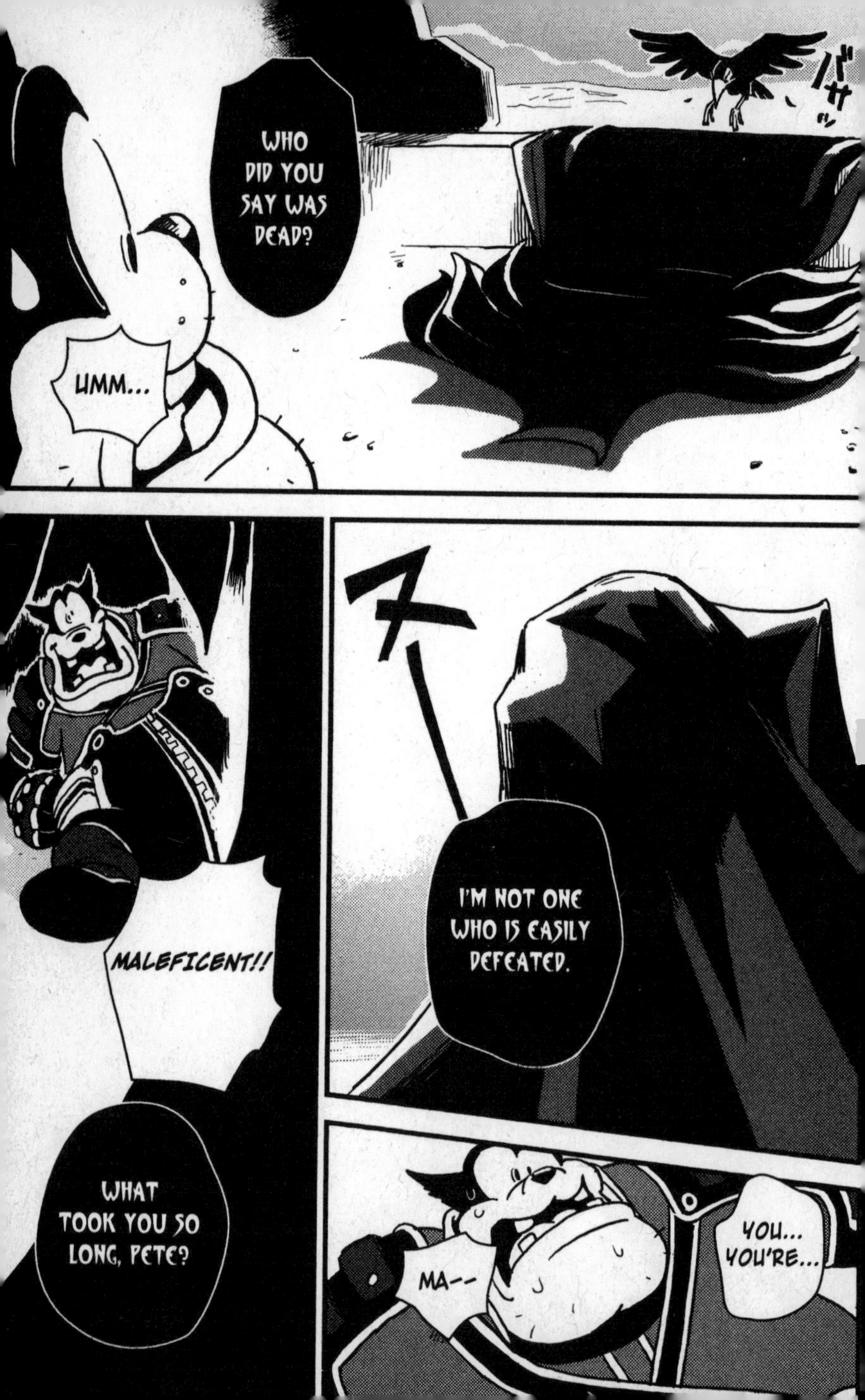
バサッ
WHO DID YOU SAY WAS DEAD?
UMM...
I'M NOT ONE WHO IS EASILY DEFEATED.
YOU... YOU'RE...
MA--
MALEFICENT!!
WHAT TOOK YOU SO LONG, PETE?

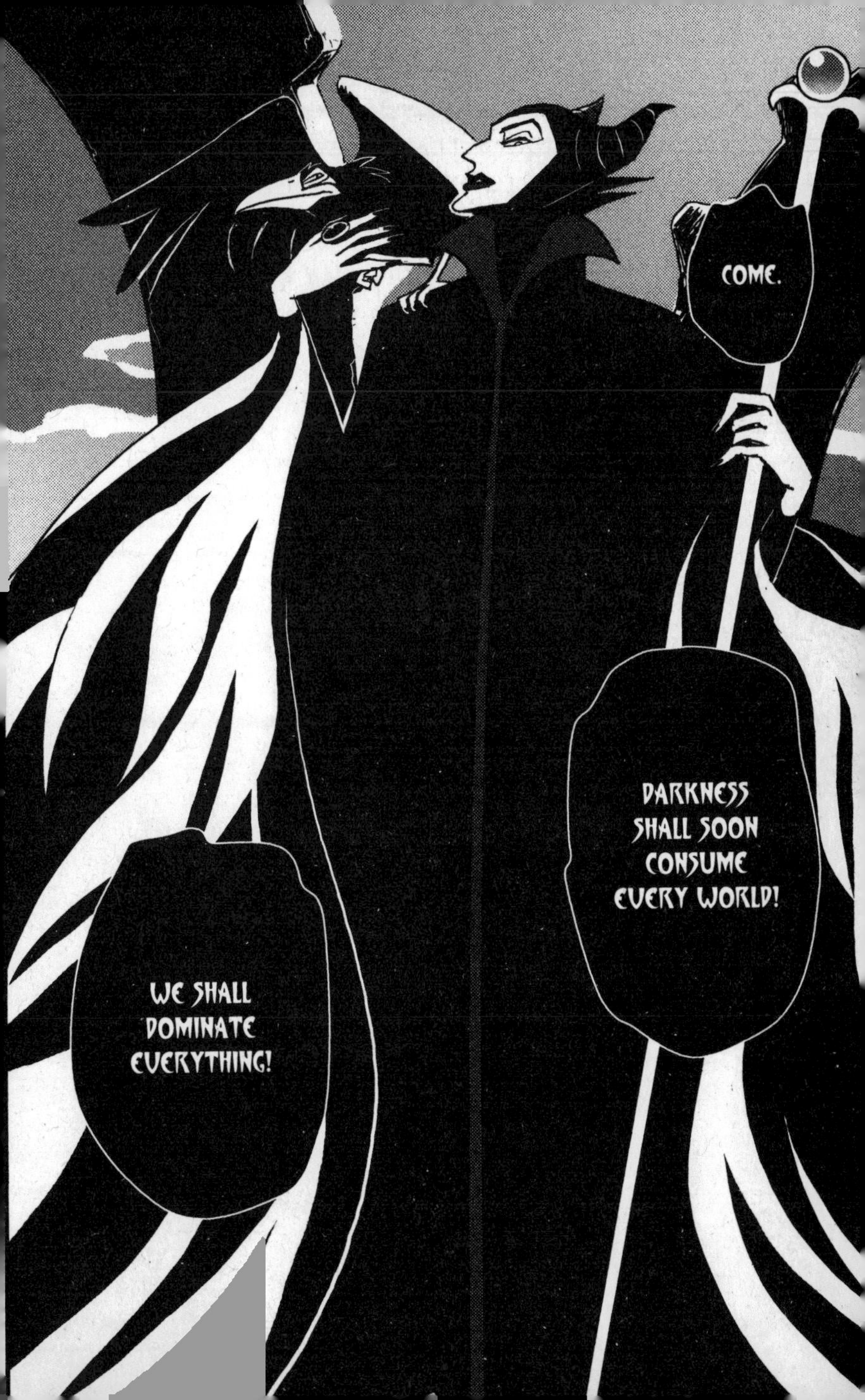
COME.
DARKNESS SHALL SOON CONSUME EVERY WORLD!
WE SHALL DOMINATE EVERYTHING!

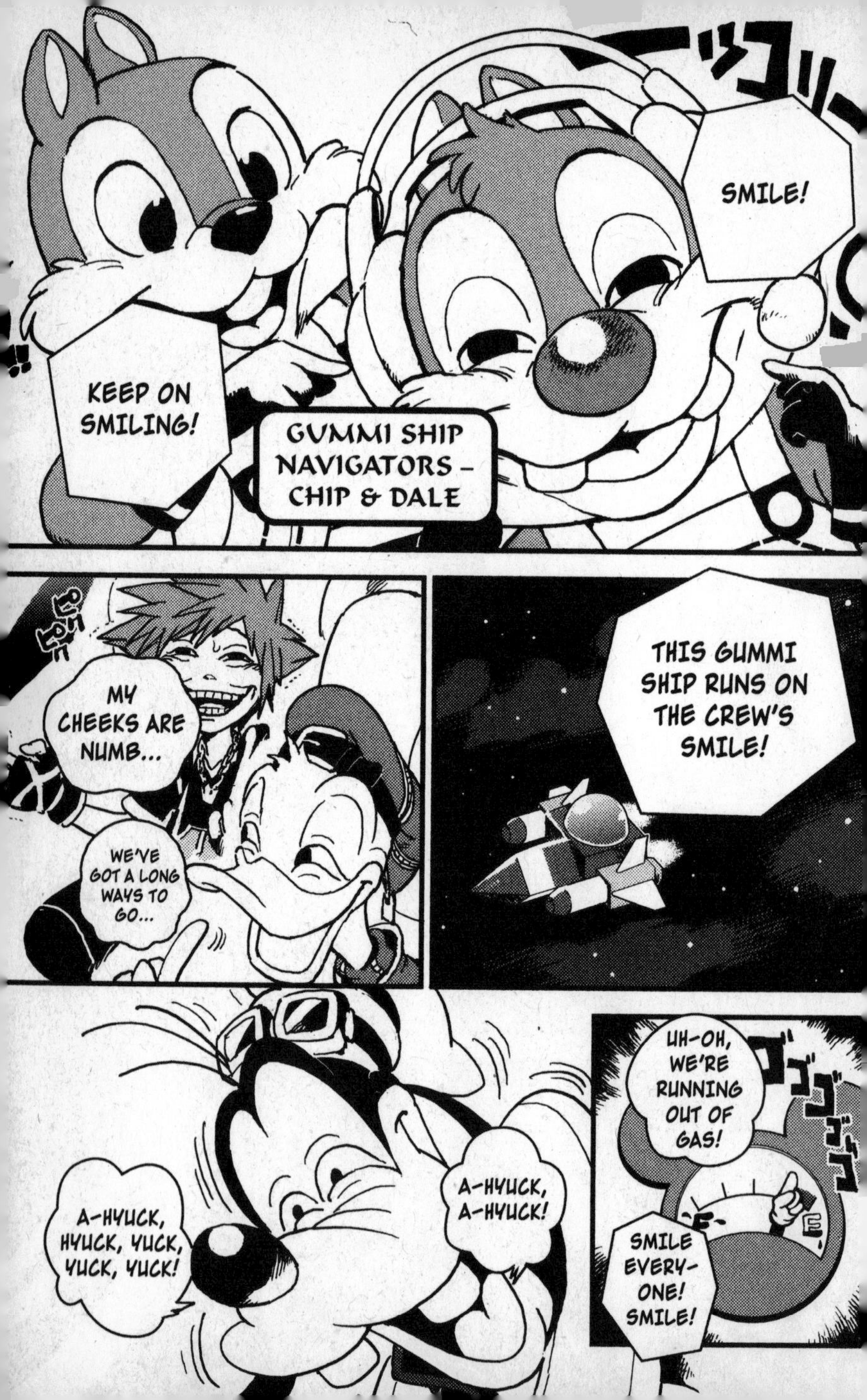
SMILE!
KEEP ON SMILING!
GUMMI SHIP NAVIGATORS – CHIP & DALE
THIS GUMMI SHIP RUNS ON THE CREW'S SMILE!
MY CHEEKS ARE NUMB...
WE'VE GOT A LONG WAYS TO GO...
UH-OH, WE'RE RUNNING OUT OF GAS!
SMILE EVERY-ONE! SMILE!
A-HYUCK, A-HYUCK!
A-HYUCK, HYUCK, YUCK, YUCK, YUCK!

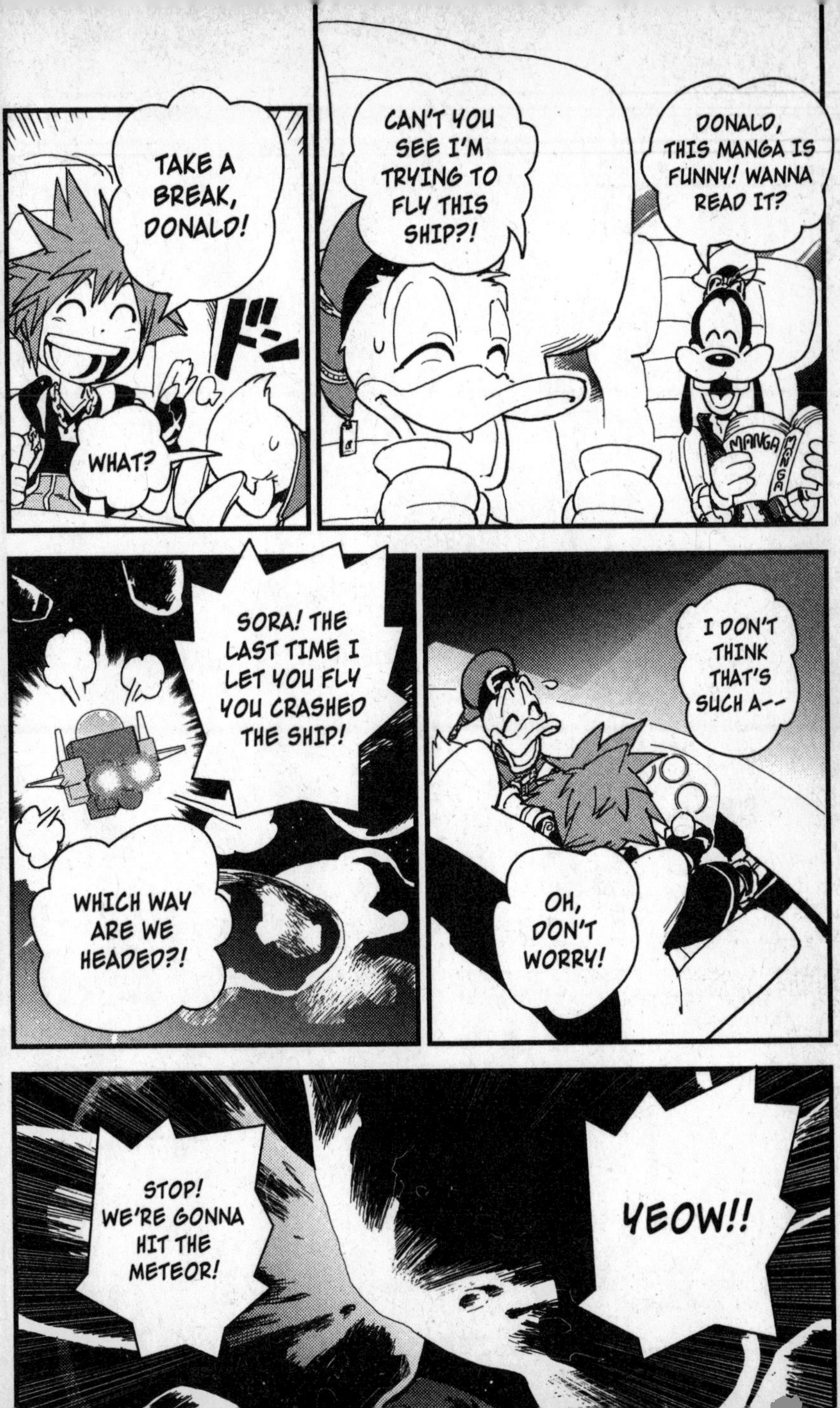
DONALD, THIS MANGA IS FUNNY! WANNA READ IT?
MANGA
MANGA
CAN'T YOU SEE I'M TRYING TO FLY THIS SHIP?!
TAKE A BREAK, DONALD!
ドン
WHAT?
I DON'T THINK THAT'S SUCH A--
OH, DON'T WORRY!
SORA! THE LAST TIME I LET YOU FLY YOU CRASHED THE SHIP!
WHICH WAY ARE WE HEADED?!
YEOW!!
STOP! WE'RE GONNA HIT THE METEOR!

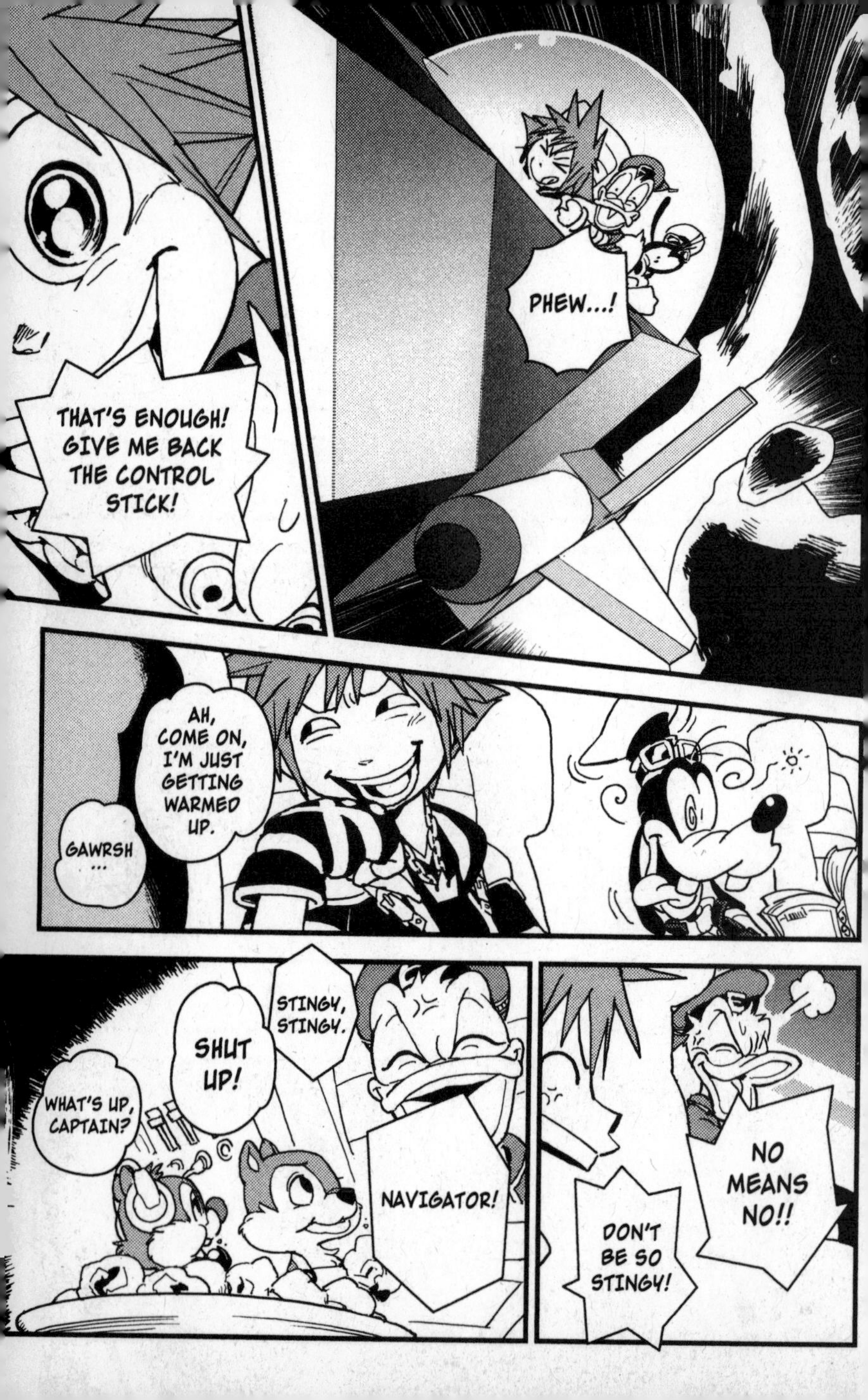
PHEW...!
THAT'S ENOUGH! GIVE ME BACK THE CONTROL STICK!
AH, COME ON, I'M JUST GETTING WARMED UP.
GAWRSH ...
NO MEANS NO!!
DON'T BE SO STINGY!
STINGY, STINGY.
SHUT UP!
NAVIGATOR!
WHAT'S UP, CAPTAIN?

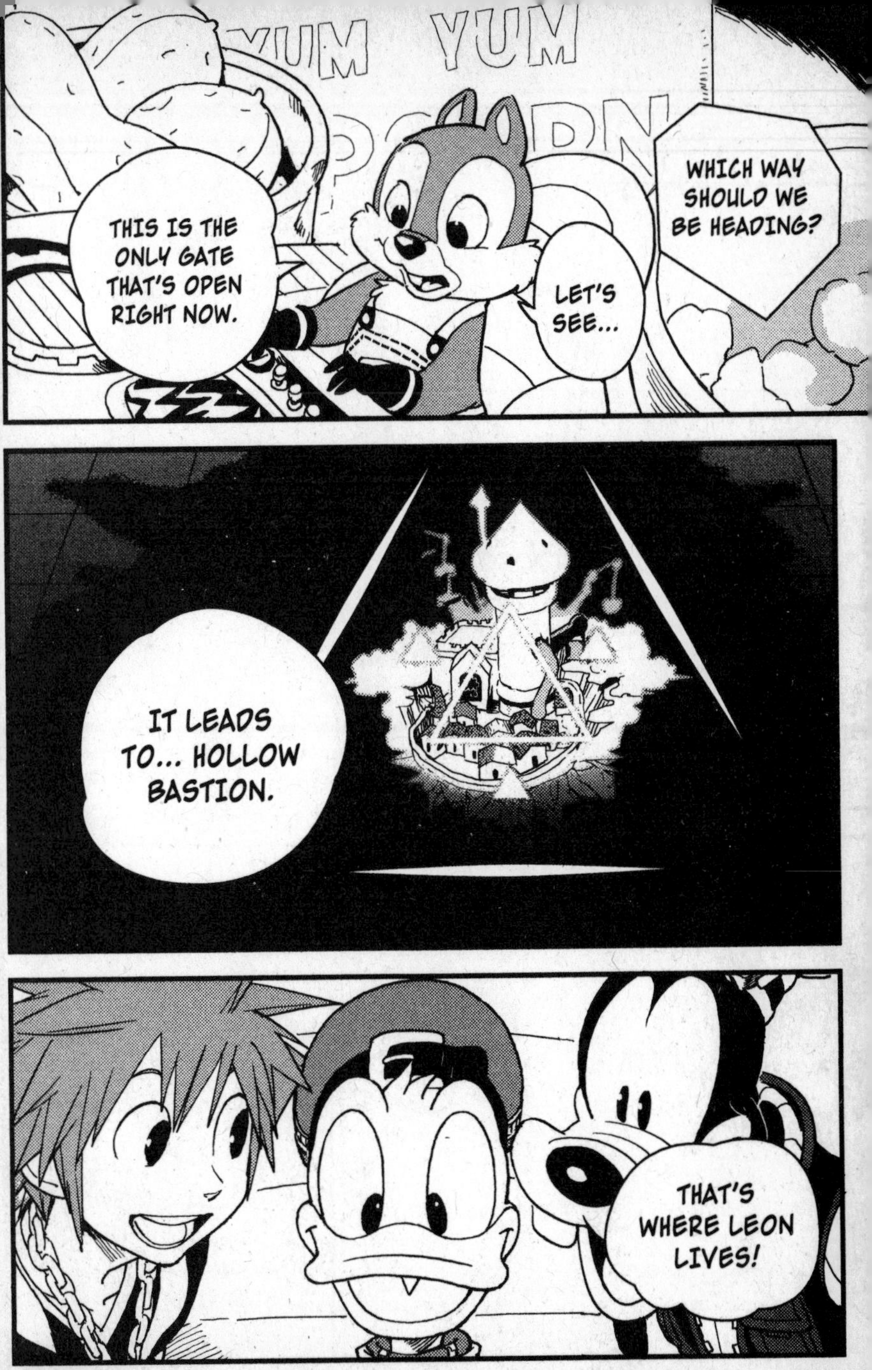
YUM YUM
WHICH WAY SHOULD WE BE HEADING?
LET'S SEE...
THIS IS THE ONLY GATE THAT'S OPEN RIGHT NOW.
IT LEADS TO... HOLLOW BASTION.
THAT'S WHERE LEON LIVES!

Chapter 13: Rendezvous at Hollow Bastion

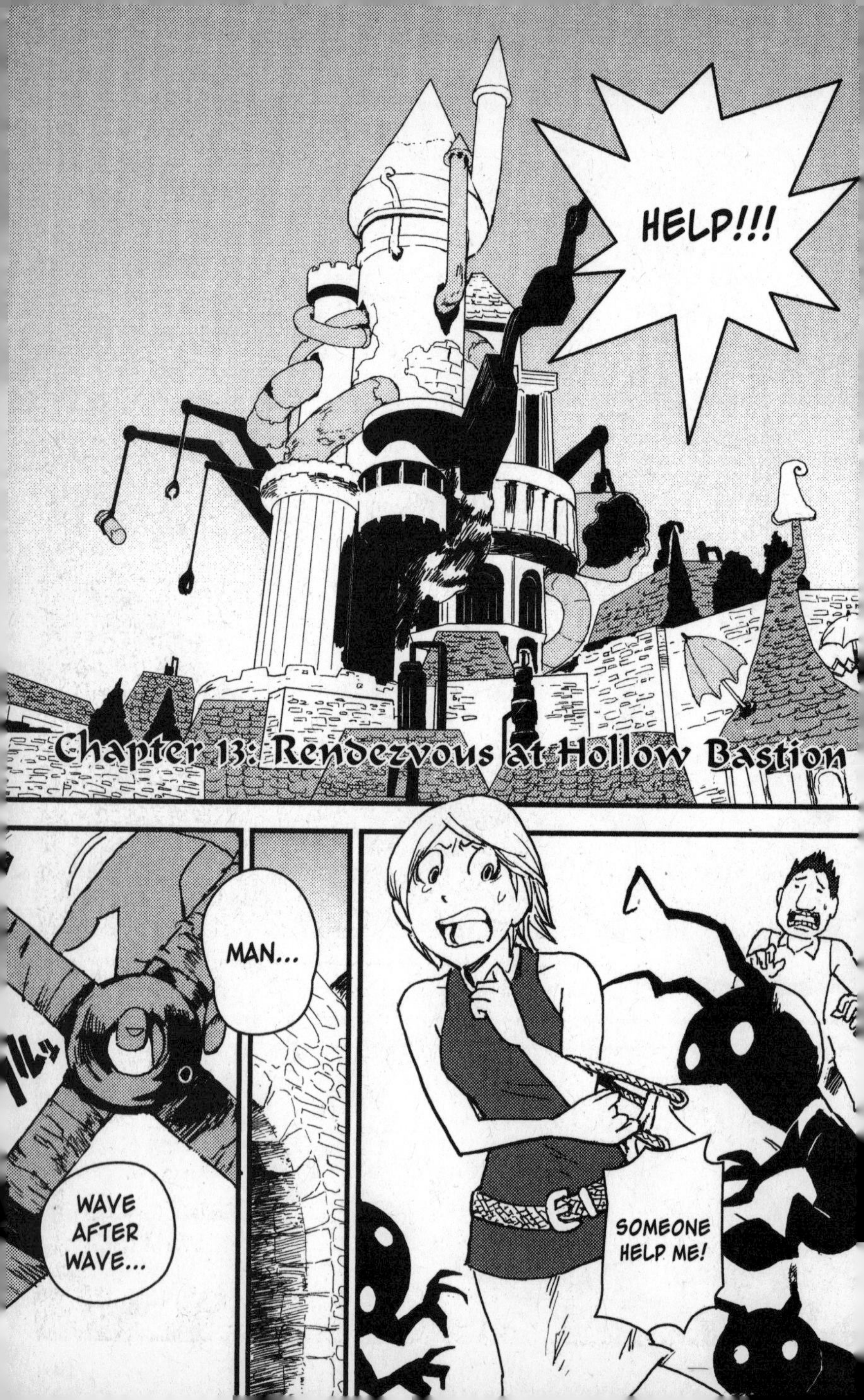
HELP!!!
Chapter 13: Rendezvous at Hollow Bastion
SOMEONE HELP ME!
MAN...
WAVE AFTER WAVE...

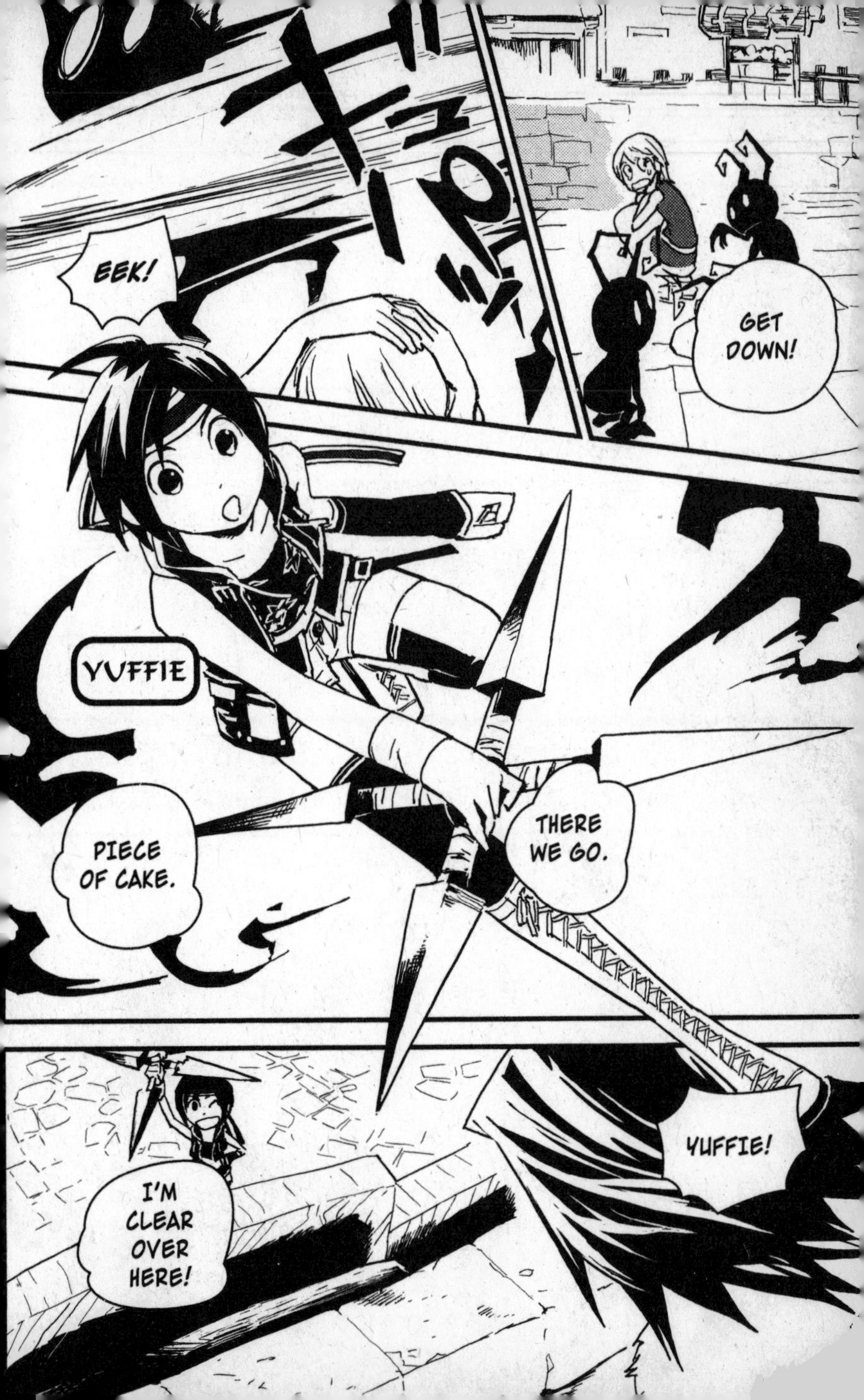
GET DOWN!
EEK!
YUFFIE
THERE WE GO.
PIECE OF CAKE.
YUFFIE!
I'M CLEAR OVER HERE!

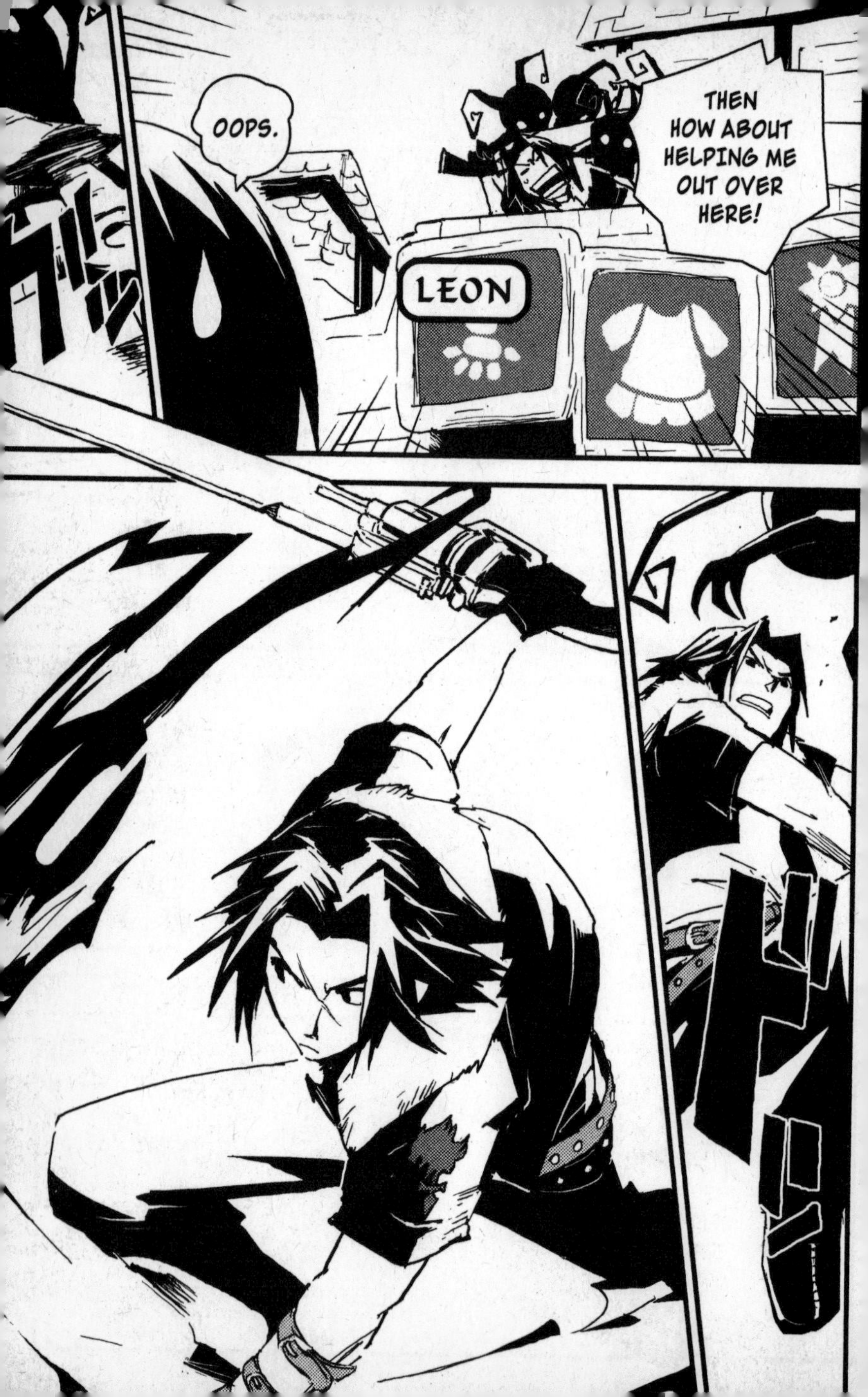
THEN HOW ABOUT HELPING ME OUT OVER HERE!
OOPS.
LEON

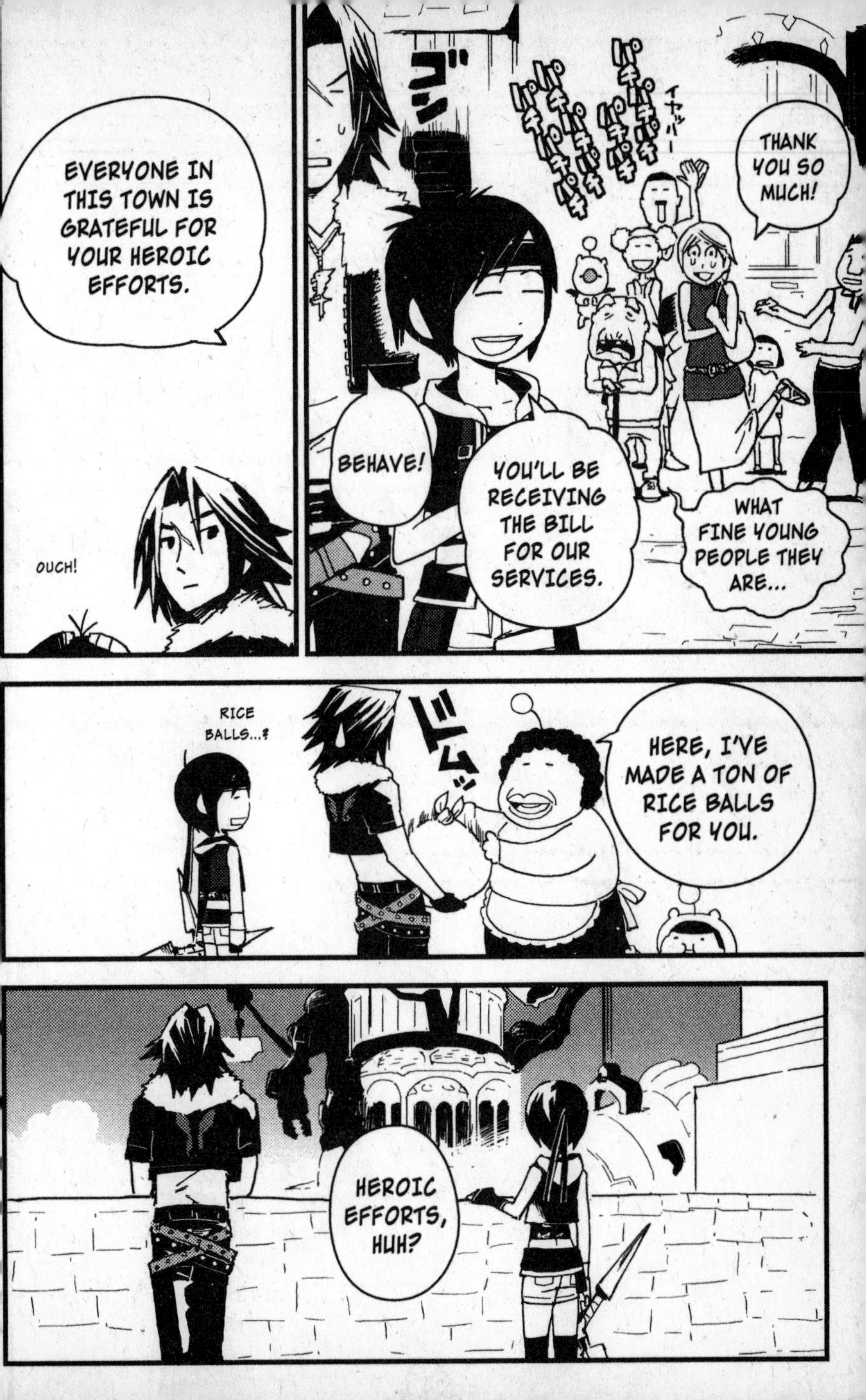
THANK YOU SO MUCH!
イヤッバー
パチパチパチパチ
パチパチパチパチ
ゴン
WHAT FINE YOUNG PEOPLE THEY ARE...
YOU'LL BE RECEIVING THE BILL FOR OUR SERVICES.
BEHAVE!
EVERYONE IN THIS TOWN IS GRATEFUL FOR YOUR HEROIC EFFORTS.
OUCH!
HERE, I'VE MADE A TON OF RICE BALLS FOR YOU.
ドムッ
RICE BALLS...?
HEROIC EFFORTS, HUH?

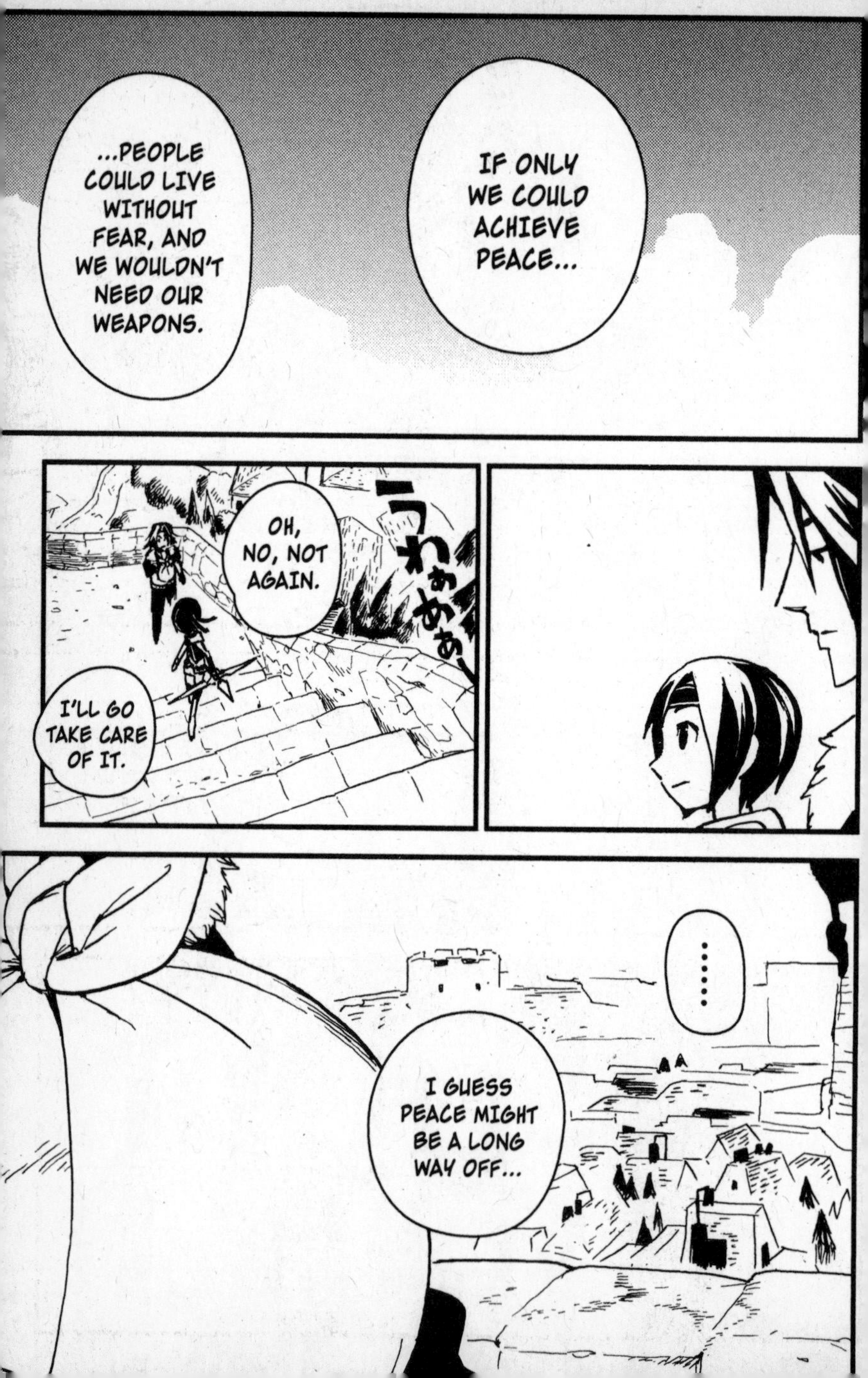
IF ONLY WE COULD ACHIEVE PEACE...
...PEOPLE COULD LIVE WITHOUT FEAR, AND WE WOULDN'T NEED OUR WEAPONS.
うわぁぁぁ
OH, NO, NOT AGAIN.
I'LL GO TAKE CARE OF IT.
......
I GUESS PEACE MIGHT BE A LONG WAY OFF...

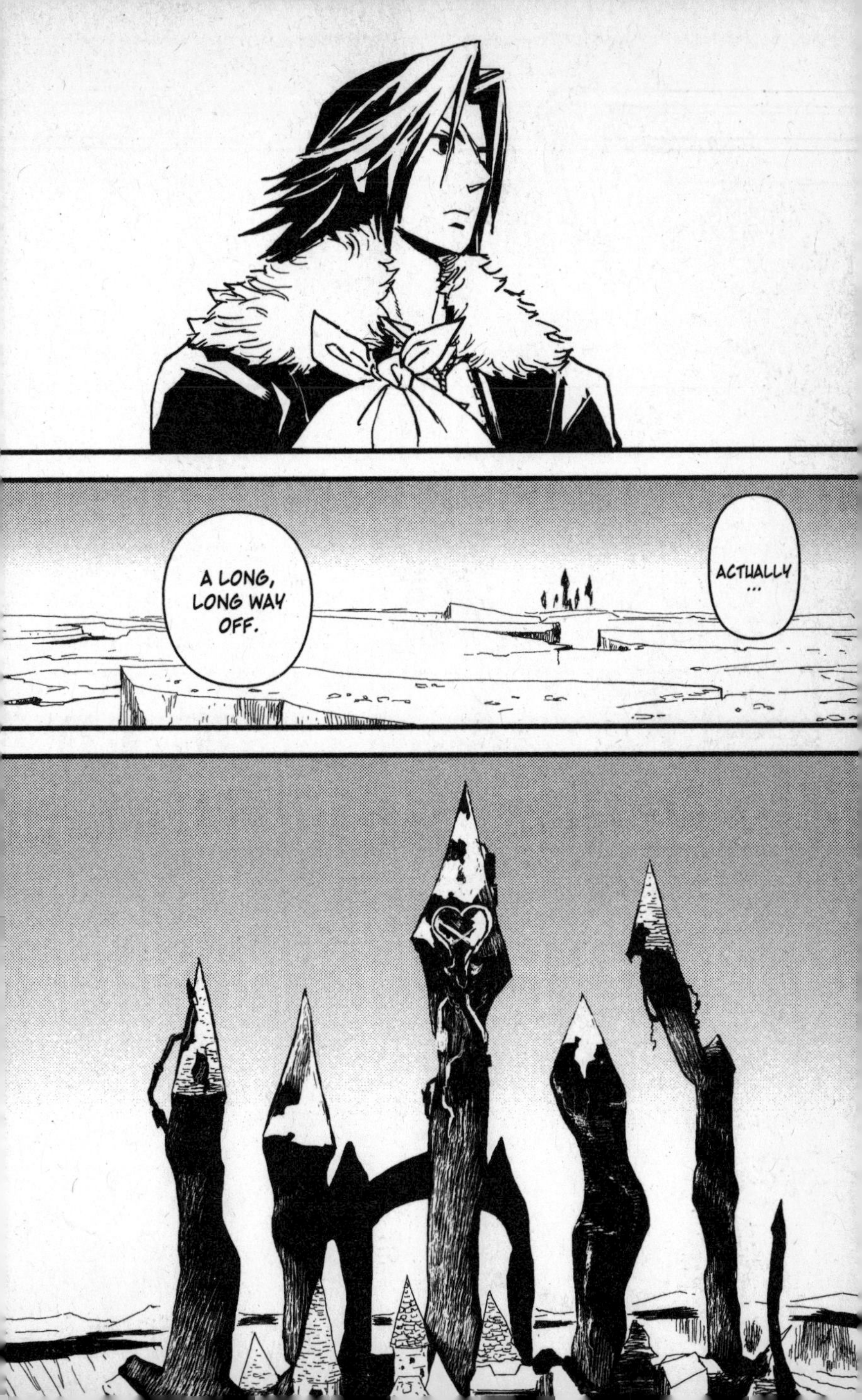
ACTUALLY...
A LONG, LONG WAY OFF.

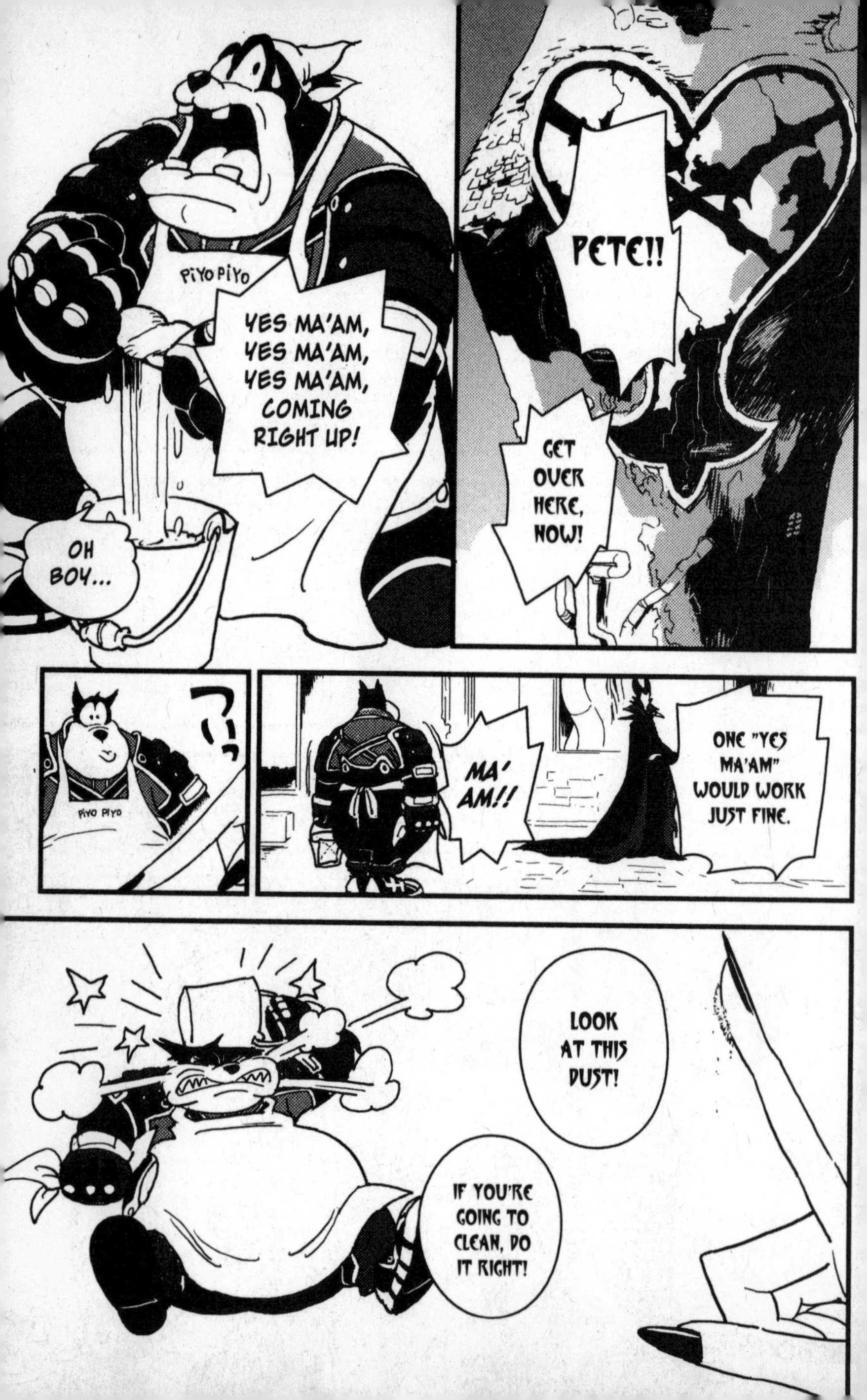
PETE!!
GET OVER HERE, NOW!
YES MA'AM, YES MA'AM, YES MA'AM, COMING RIGHT UP!
PIYO PIYO
OH BOY...
ONE "YES MA'AM" WOULD WORK JUST FINE.
MA'AM!!
PIYO PIYO
LOOK AT THIS DUST!
IF YOU'RE GOING TO CLEAN, DO IT RIGHT!

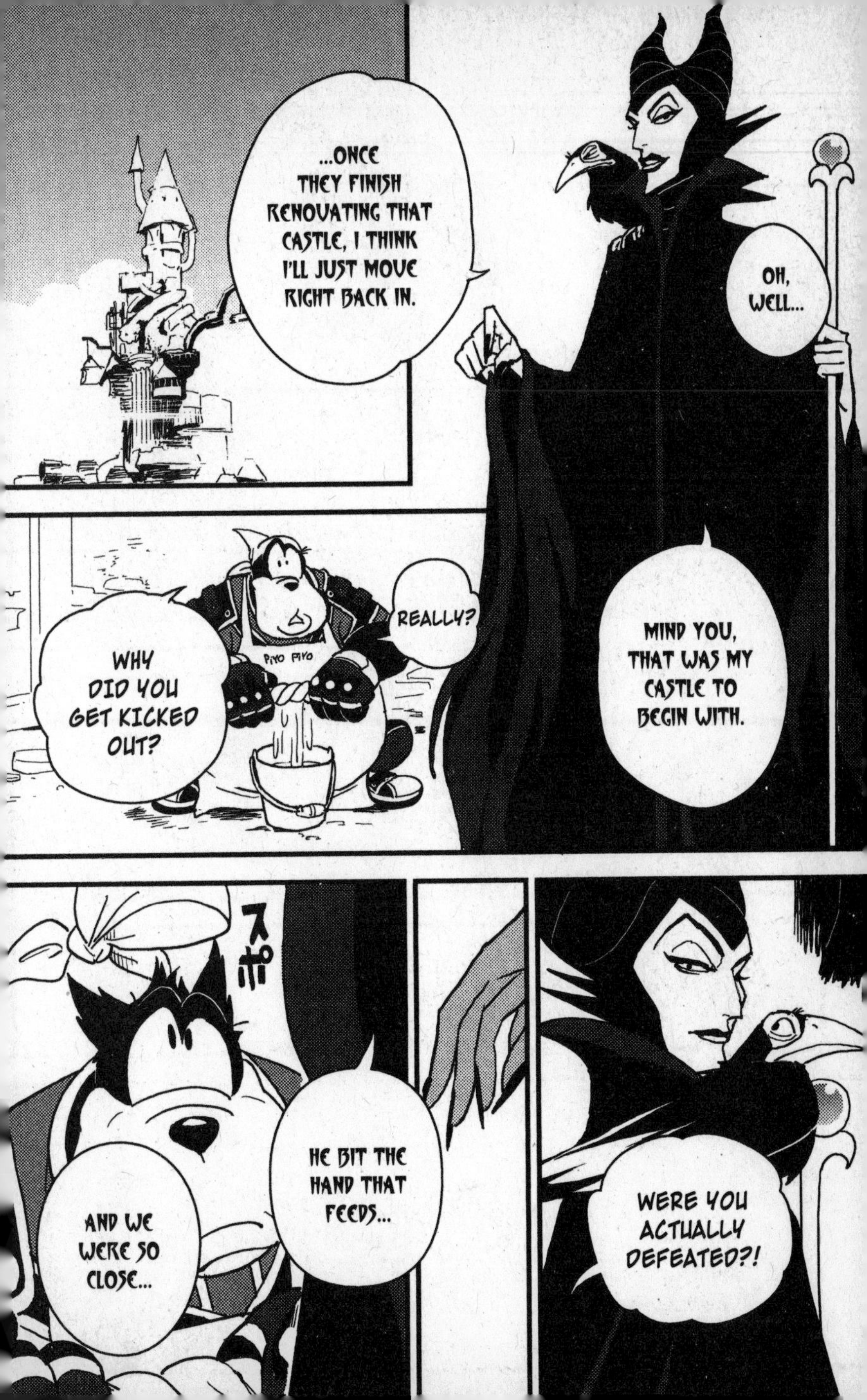
OH, WELL...
MIND YOU, THAT WAS MY CASTLE TO BEGIN WITH.
...ONCE THEY FINISH RENOVATING THAT CASTLE, I THINK I'LL JUST MOVE RIGHT BACK IN.
REALLY?
WHY DID YOU GET KICKED OUT?
PIYO PIYO
WERE YOU ACTUALLY DEFEATED?!
スポ
HE BIT THE HAND THAT FEEDS...
AND WE WERE SO CLOSE...

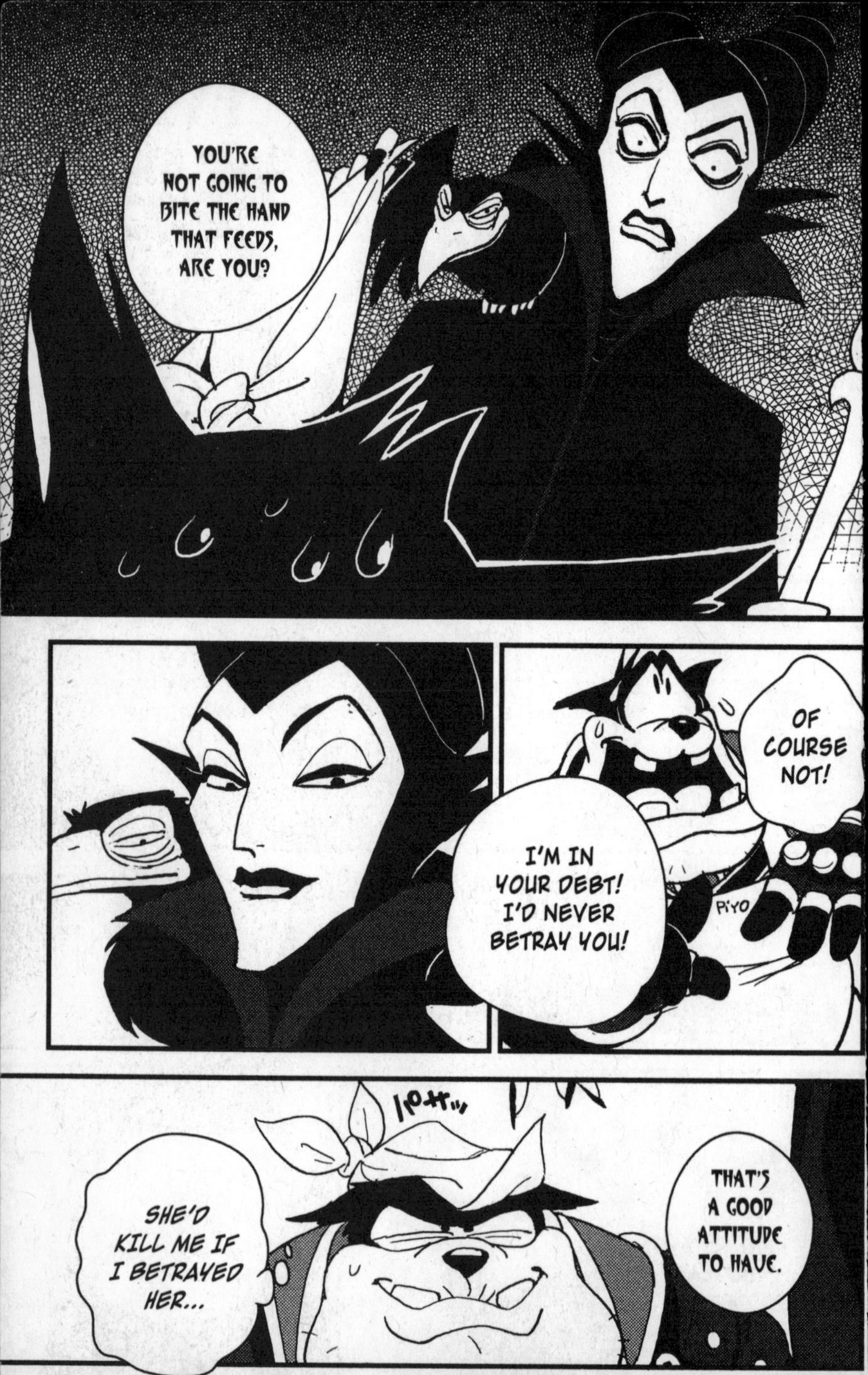
YOU'RE NOT GOING TO BITE THE HAND THAT FEEDS, ARE YOU?
OF COURSE NOT!
I'M IN YOUR DEBT! I'D NEVER BETRAY YOU!
PiYO
THAT'S A GOOD ATTITUDE TO HAVE.
SHE'D KILL ME IF I BETRAYED HER...

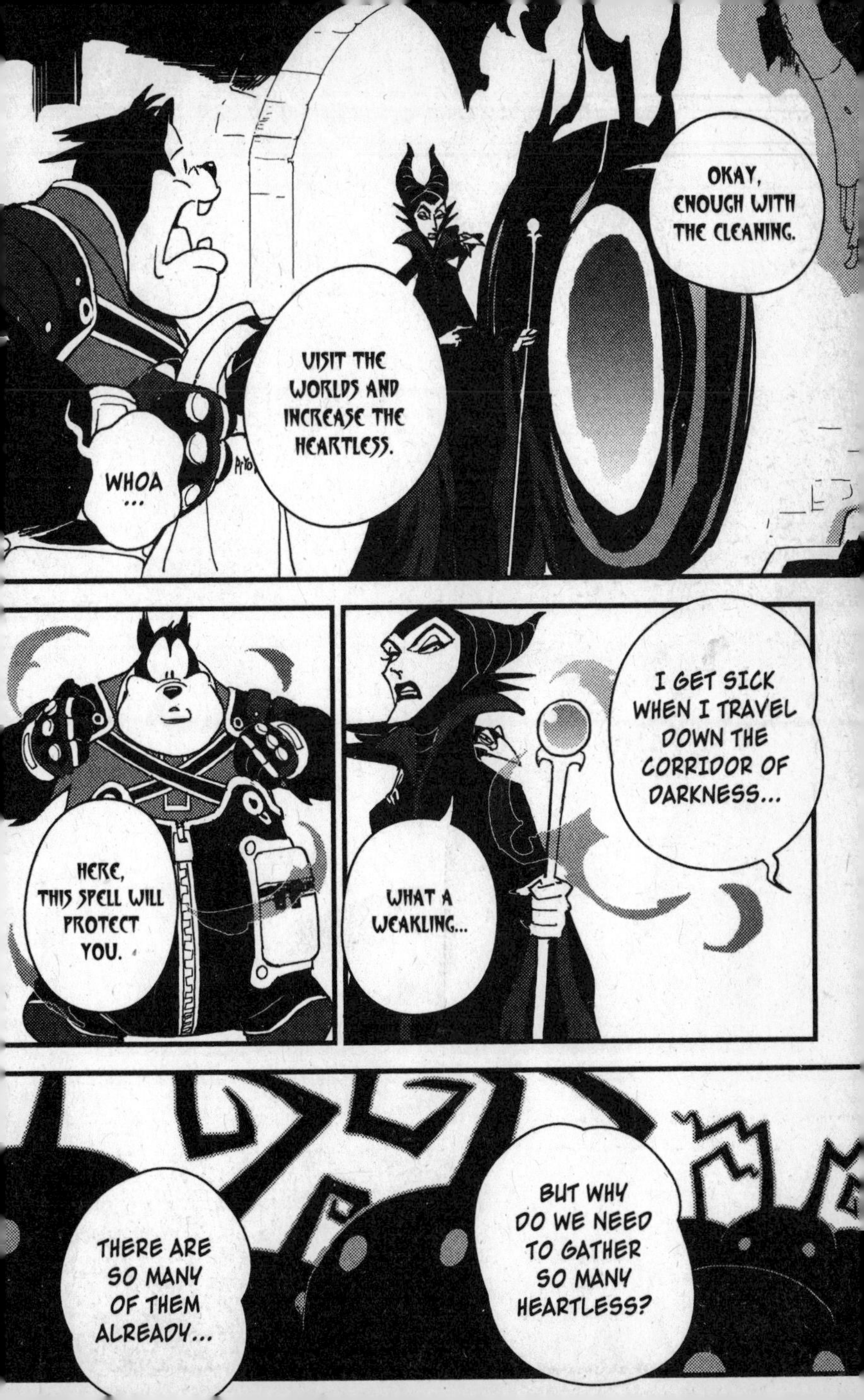
OKAY, ENOUGH WITH THE CLEANING.
VISIT THE WORLDS AND INCREASE THE HEARTLESS.
WHOA ...
I GET SICK WHEN I TRAVEL DOWN THE CORRIDOR OF DARKNESS...
WHAT A WEAKLING...
HERE, THIS SPELL WILL PROTECT YOU.
BUT WHY DO WE NEED TO GATHER SO MANY HEARTLESS?
THERE ARE SO MANY OF THEM ALREADY...

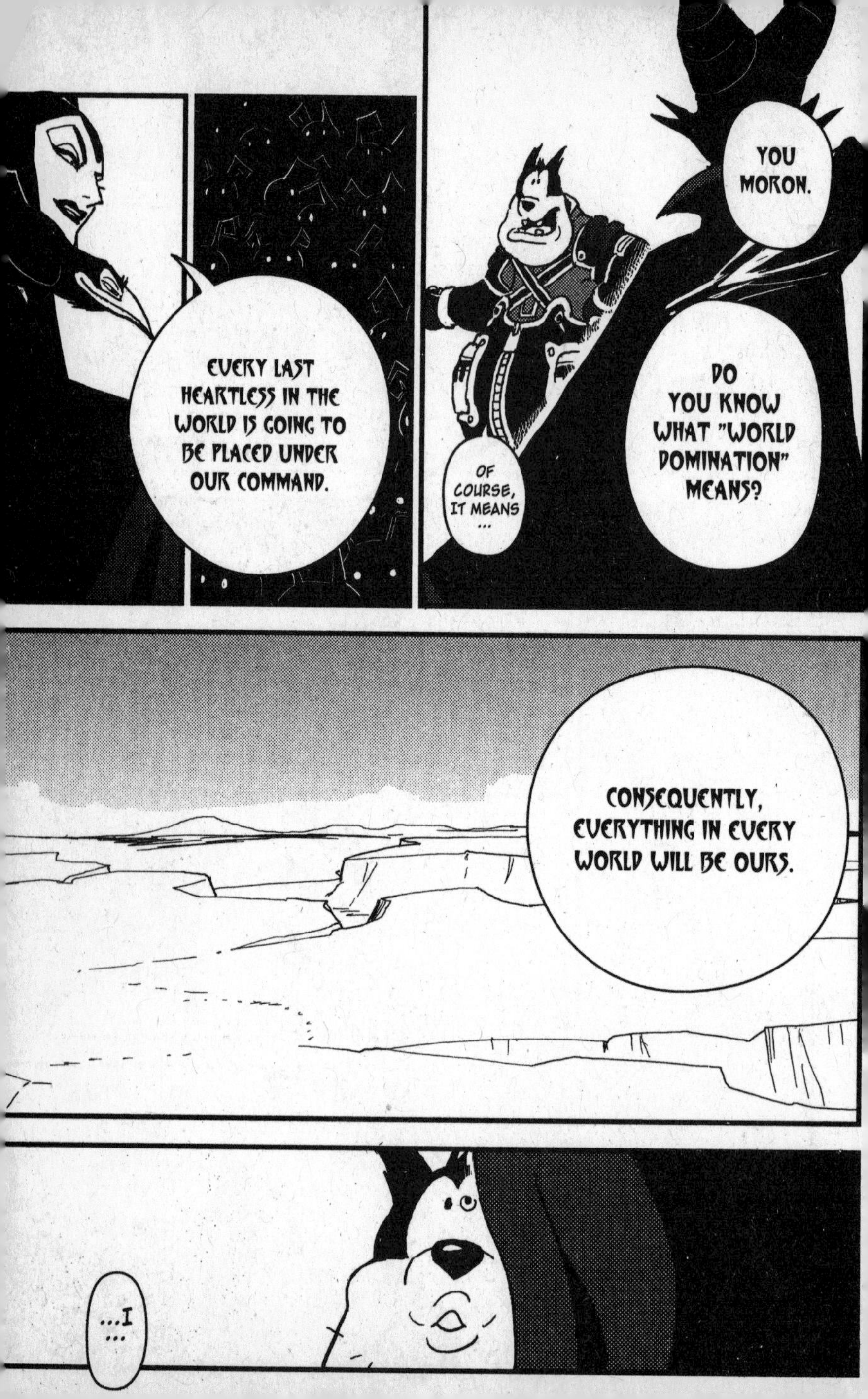
YOU MORON.
DO YOU KNOW WHAT "WORLD DOMINATION" MEANS?
OF COURSE, IT MEANS ...
EVERY LAST HEARTLESS IN THE WORLD IS GOING TO BE PLACED UNDER OUR COMMAND.
CONSEQUENTLY, EVERYTHING IN EVERY WORLD WILL BE OURS.
...I ...

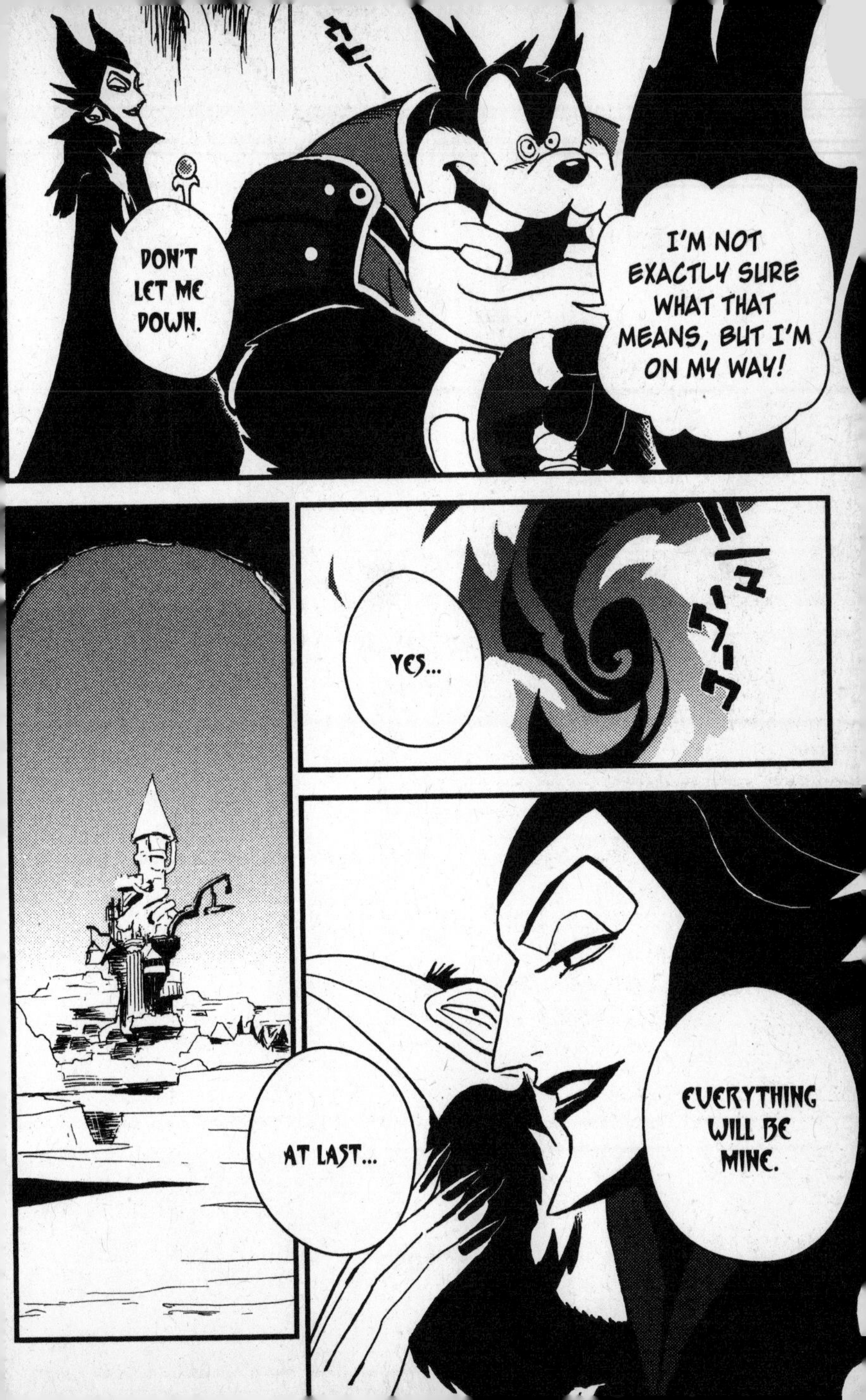
I'M NOT EXACTLY SURE WHAT THAT MEANS, BUT I'M ON MY WAY!
DON'T LET ME DOWN.
YES...
EVERYTHING WILL BE MINE.
AT LAST...

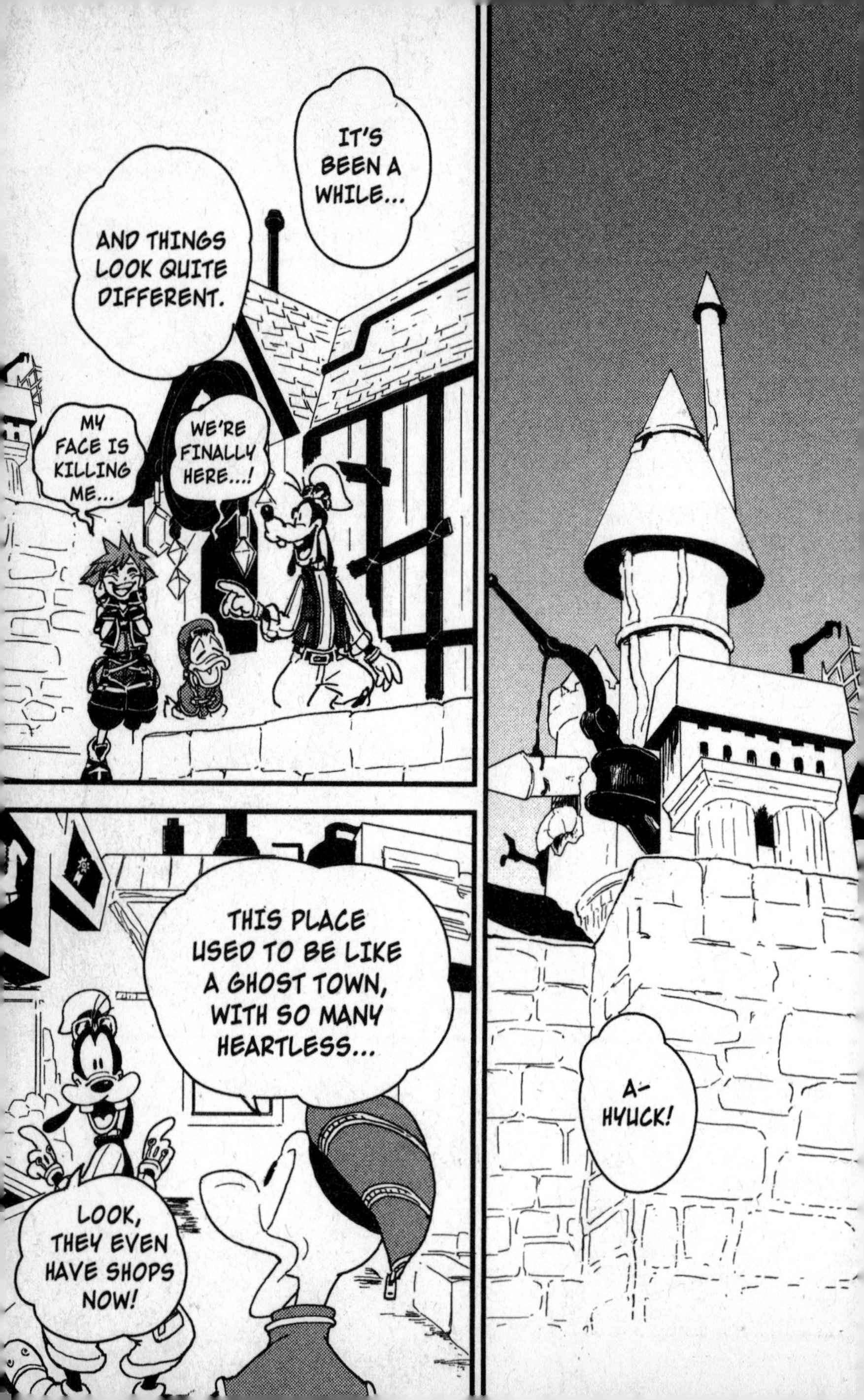
A-HYUCK!
IT'S BEEN A WHILE...
AND THINGS LOOK QUITE DIFFERENT.
WE'RE FINALLY HERE...!
MY FACE IS KILLING ME...
THIS PLACE USED TO BE LIKE A GHOST TOWN, WITH SO MANY HEARTLESS...
LOOK, THEY EVEN HAVE SHOPS NOW!

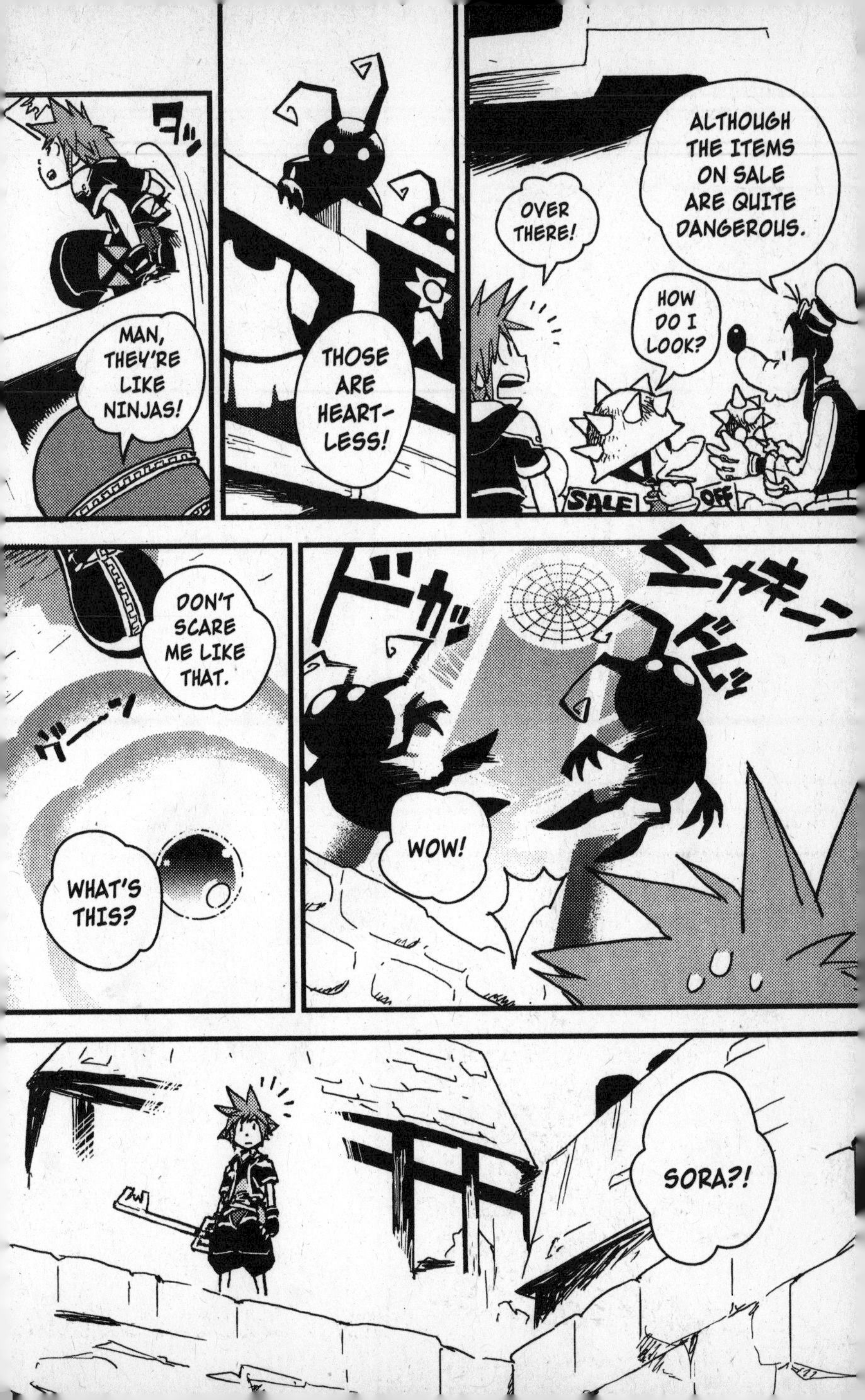
ALTHOUGH THE ITEMS ON SALE ARE QUITE DANGEROUS.
HOW DO I LOOK?
OVER THERE!
SALE
OFF
THOSE ARE HEART-LESS!
MAN, THEY'RE LIKE NINJAS!
シャキーン
ドガッ
WOW!
DON'T SCARE ME LIKE THAT.
WHAT'S THIS?
SORA?!

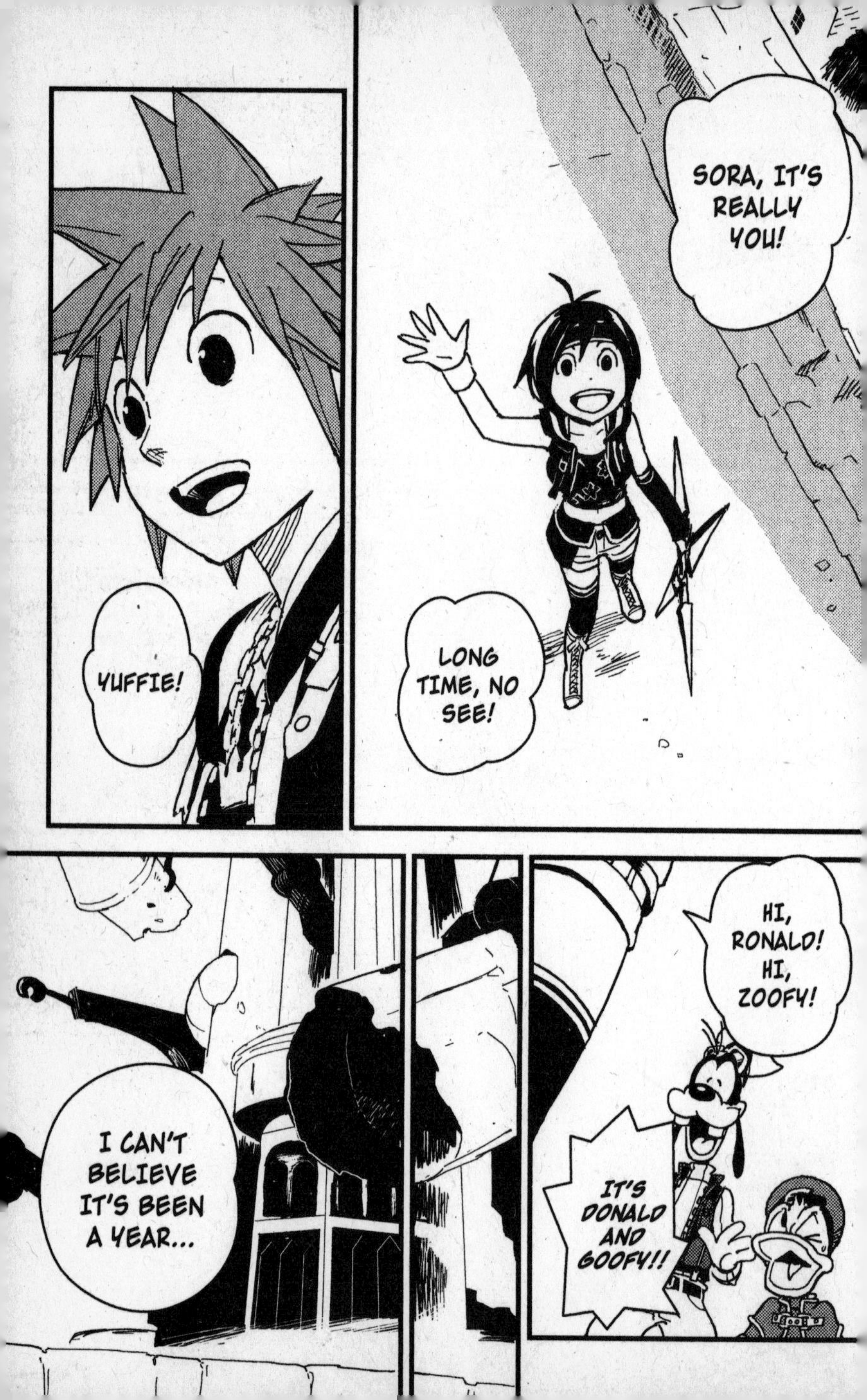
SORA, IT'S REALLY YOU!
LONG TIME, NO SEE!
YUFFIE!
HI, RONALD! HI, ZOOFY!
IT'S DONALD AND GOOFY!!
I CAN'T BELIEVE IT'S BEEN A YEAR...

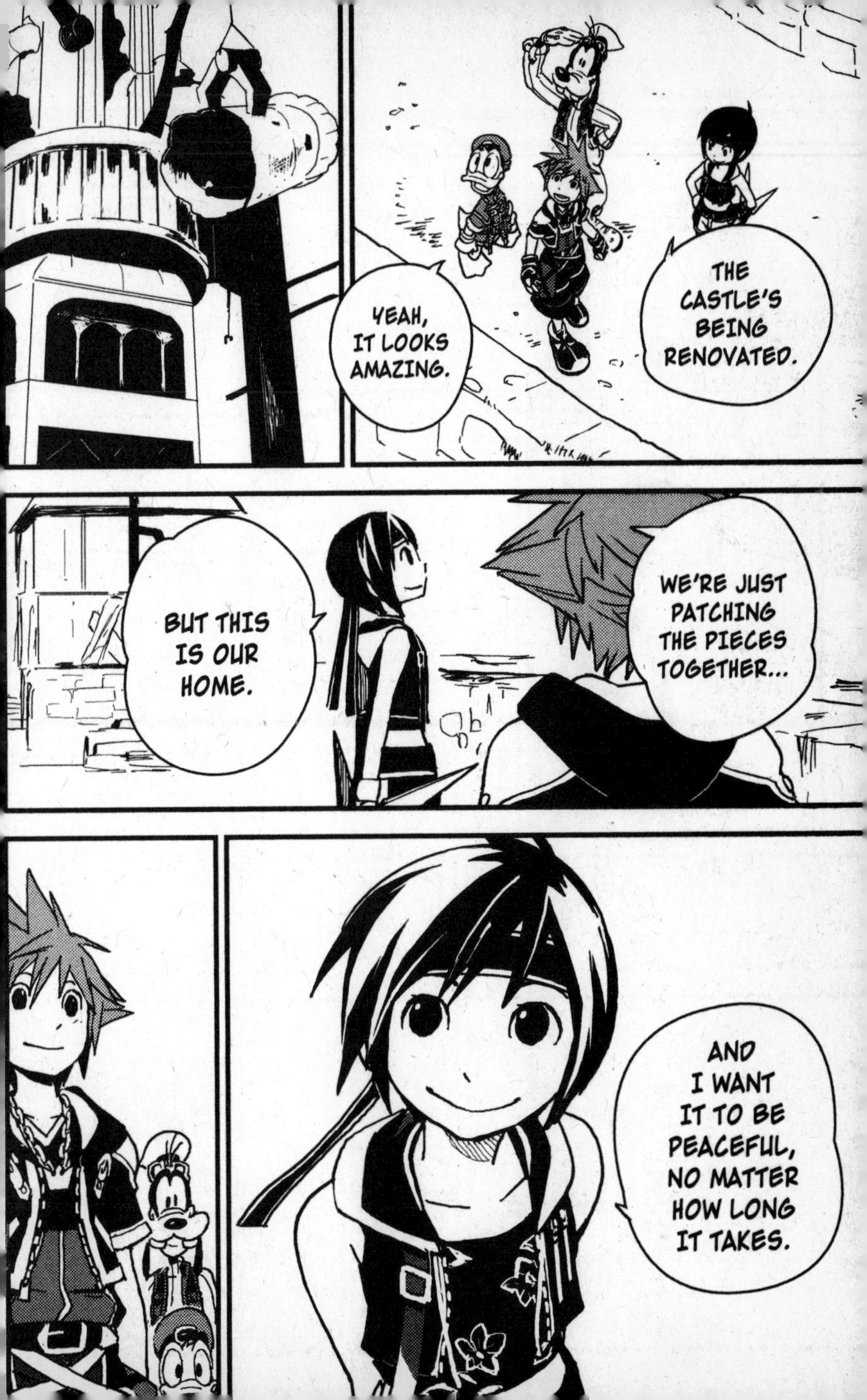
THE CASTLE'S BEING RENOVATED.
YEAH, IT LOOKS AMAZING.
WE'RE JUST PATCHING THE PIECES TOGETHER...
BUT THIS IS OUR HOME.
AND I WANT IT TO BE PEACEFUL, NO MATTER HOW LONG IT TAKES.

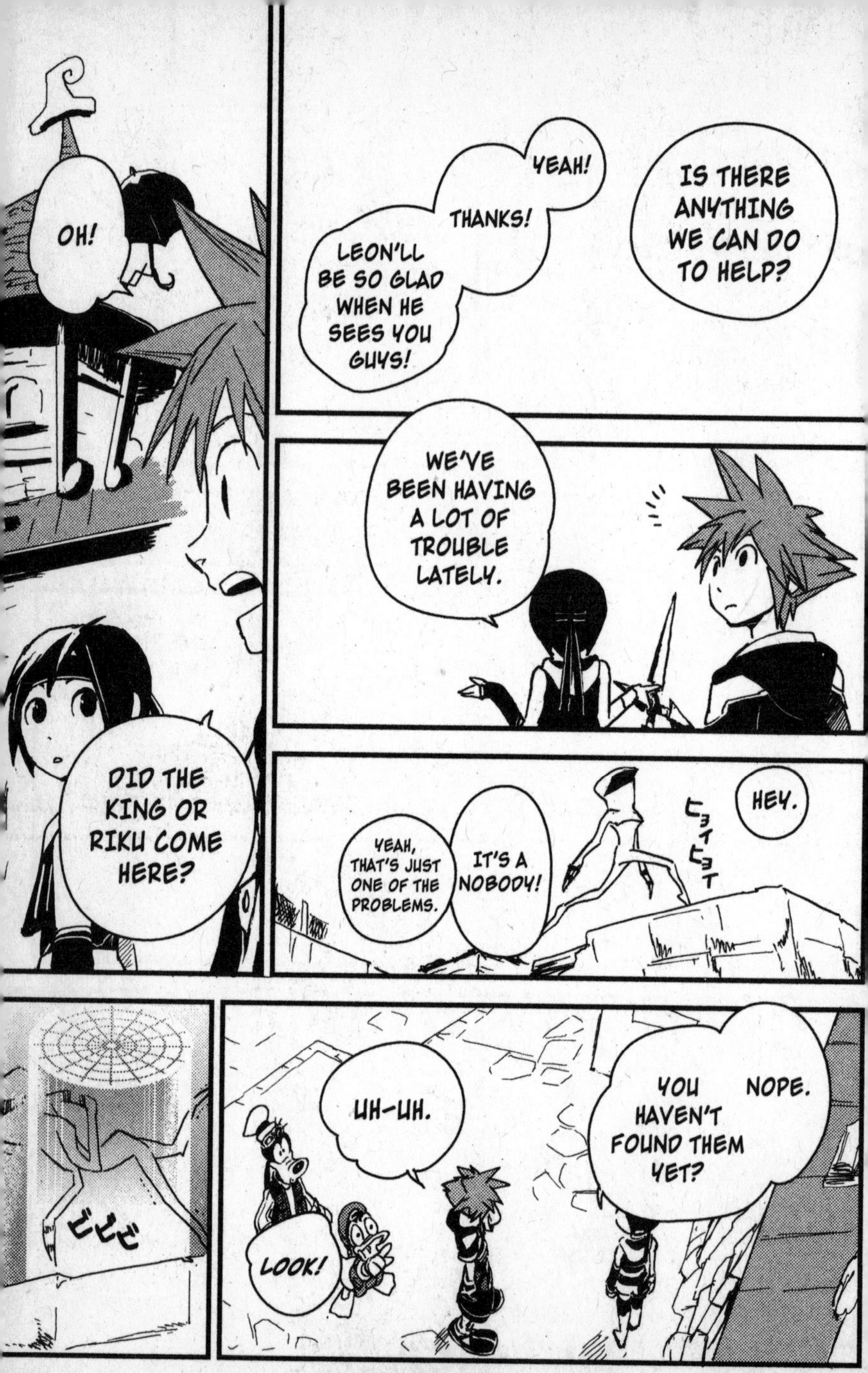
IS THERE ANYTHING WE CAN DO TO HELP?
YEAH!
THANKS!
LEON'LL BE SO GLAD WHEN HE SEES YOU GUYS!
WE'VE BEEN HAVING A LOT OF TROUBLE LATELY.
HEY.
ヒョイヒョイ
IT'S A NOBODY!
YEAH, THAT'S JUST ONE OF THE PROBLEMS.
OH!
DID THE KING OR RIKU COME HERE?
YOU HAVEN'T FOUND THEM YET?
NOPE.
UH-UH.
LOOK!
ビビビ

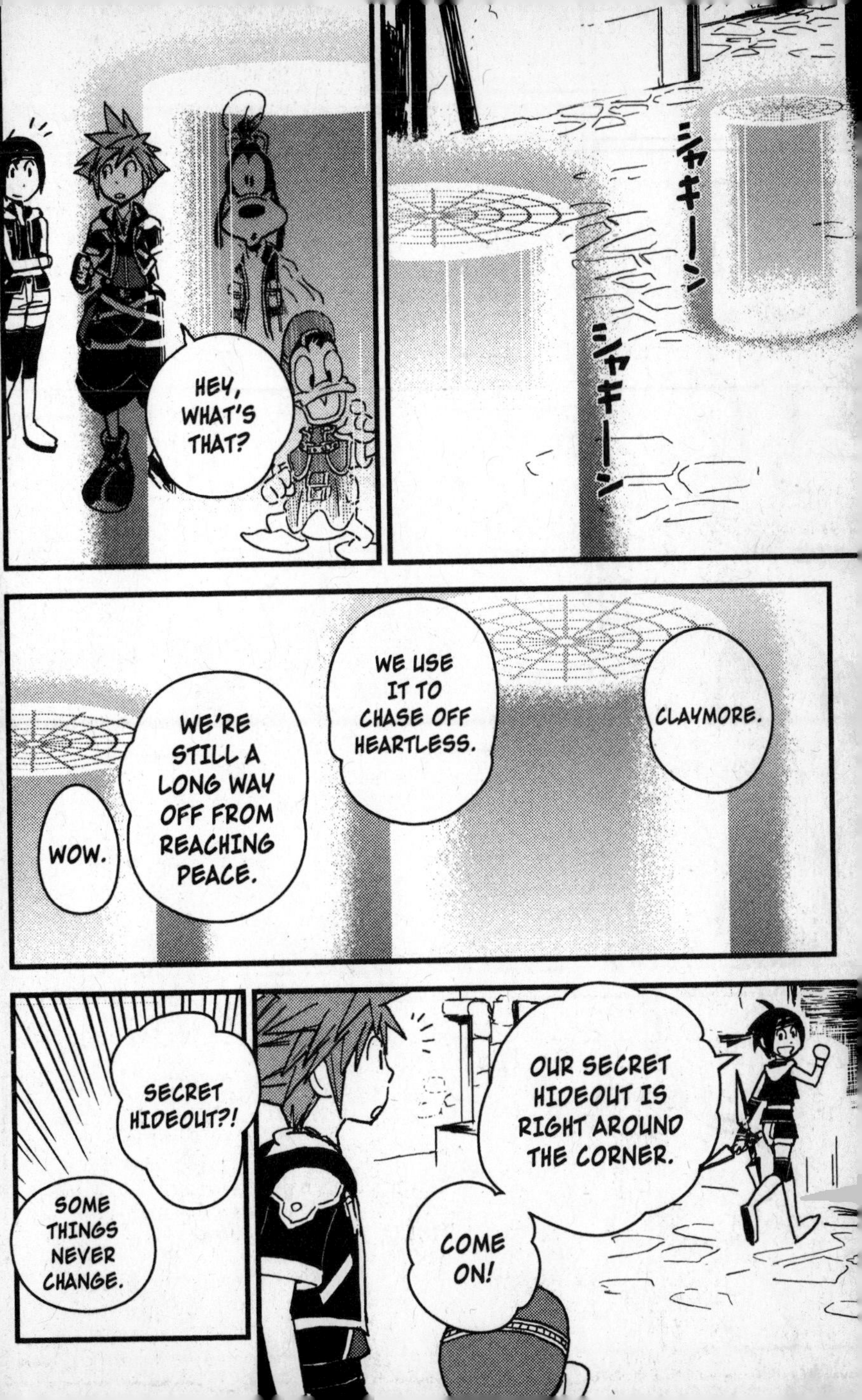
シャキーン
シャキーン
HEY, WHAT'S THAT?
CLAYMORE.
WE USE IT TO CHASE OFF HEARTLESS.
WE'RE STILL A LONG WAY OFF FROM REACHING PEACE.
WOW.
OUR SECRET HIDEOUT IS RIGHT AROUND THE CORNER.
COME ON!
SECRET HIDEOUT?!
SOME THINGS NEVER CHANGE.

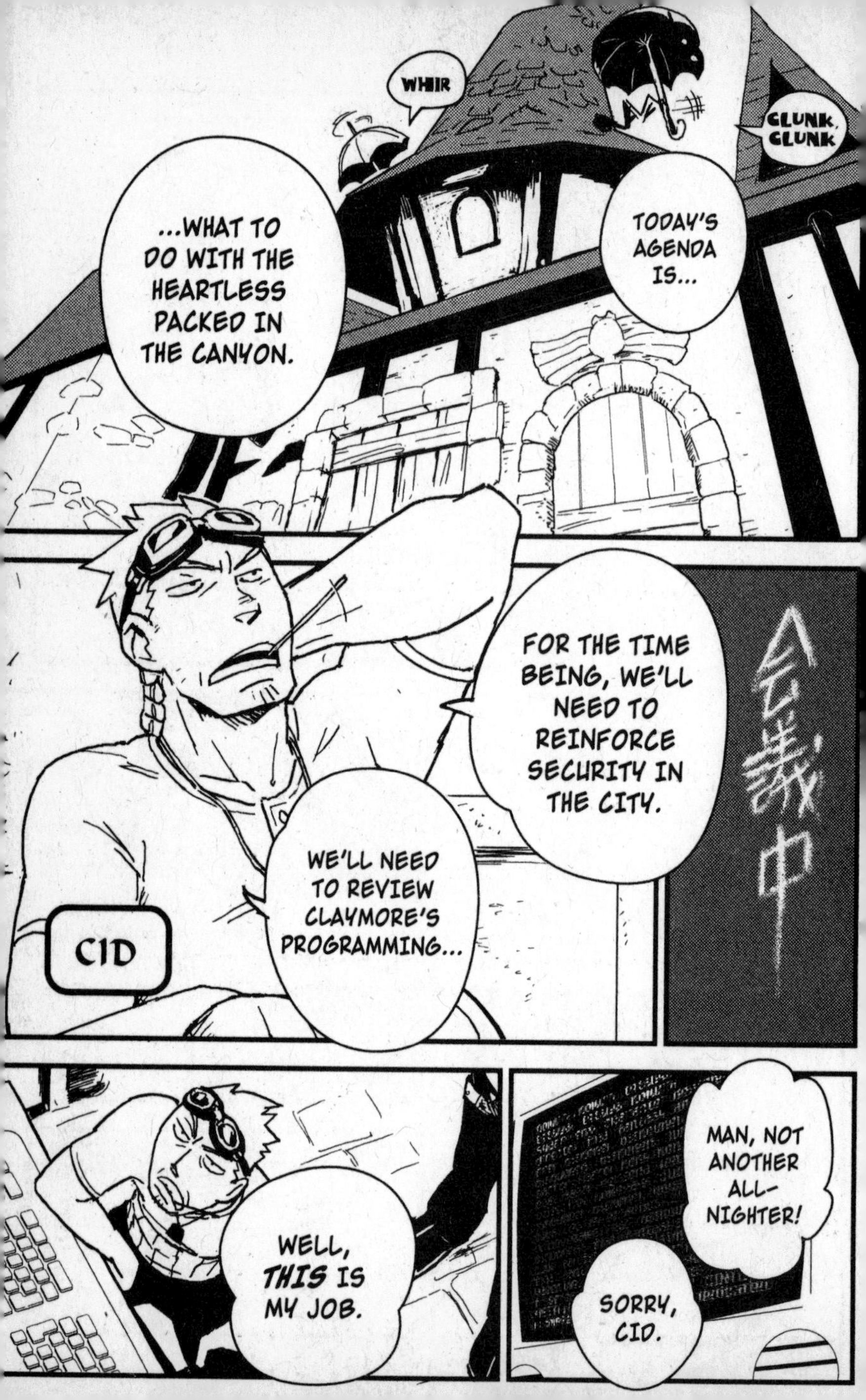
CLUNK, CLUNK
WHIR
TODAY'S AGENDA IS...
...WHAT TO DO WITH THE HEARTLESS PACKED IN THE CANYON.
会議中
FOR THE TIME BEING, WE'LL NEED TO REINFORCE SECURITY IN THE CITY.
WE'LL NEED TO REVIEW CLAYMORE'S PROGRAMMING...
CID
MAN, NOT ANOTHER ALL-NIGHTER!
SORRY, CID.
WELL, *THIS* IS MY JOB.

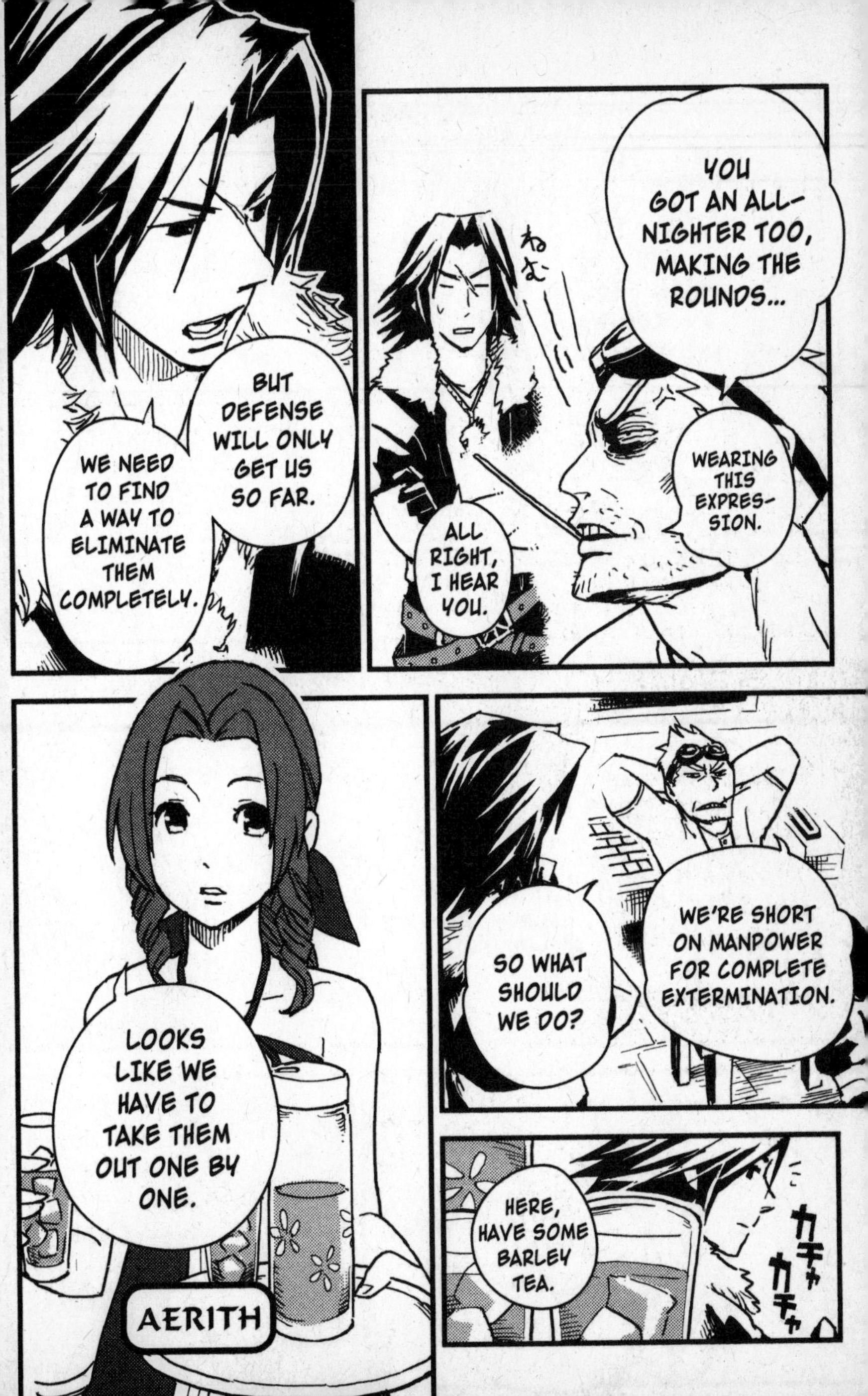
YOU GOT AN ALL-NIGHTER TOO, MAKING THE ROUNDS...
ねむ
WEARING THIS EXPRES-SION.
ALL RIGHT, I HEAR YOU.
BUT DEFENSE WILL ONLY GET US SO FAR.
WE NEED TO FIND A WAY TO ELIMINATE THEM COMPLETELY.
WE'RE SHORT ON MANPOWER FOR COMPLETE EXTERMINATION.
SO WHAT SHOULD WE DO?
HERE, HAVE SOME BARLEY TEA.
カチャ カチャ
LOOKS LIKE WE HAVE TO TAKE THEM OUT ONE BY ONE.
AERITH

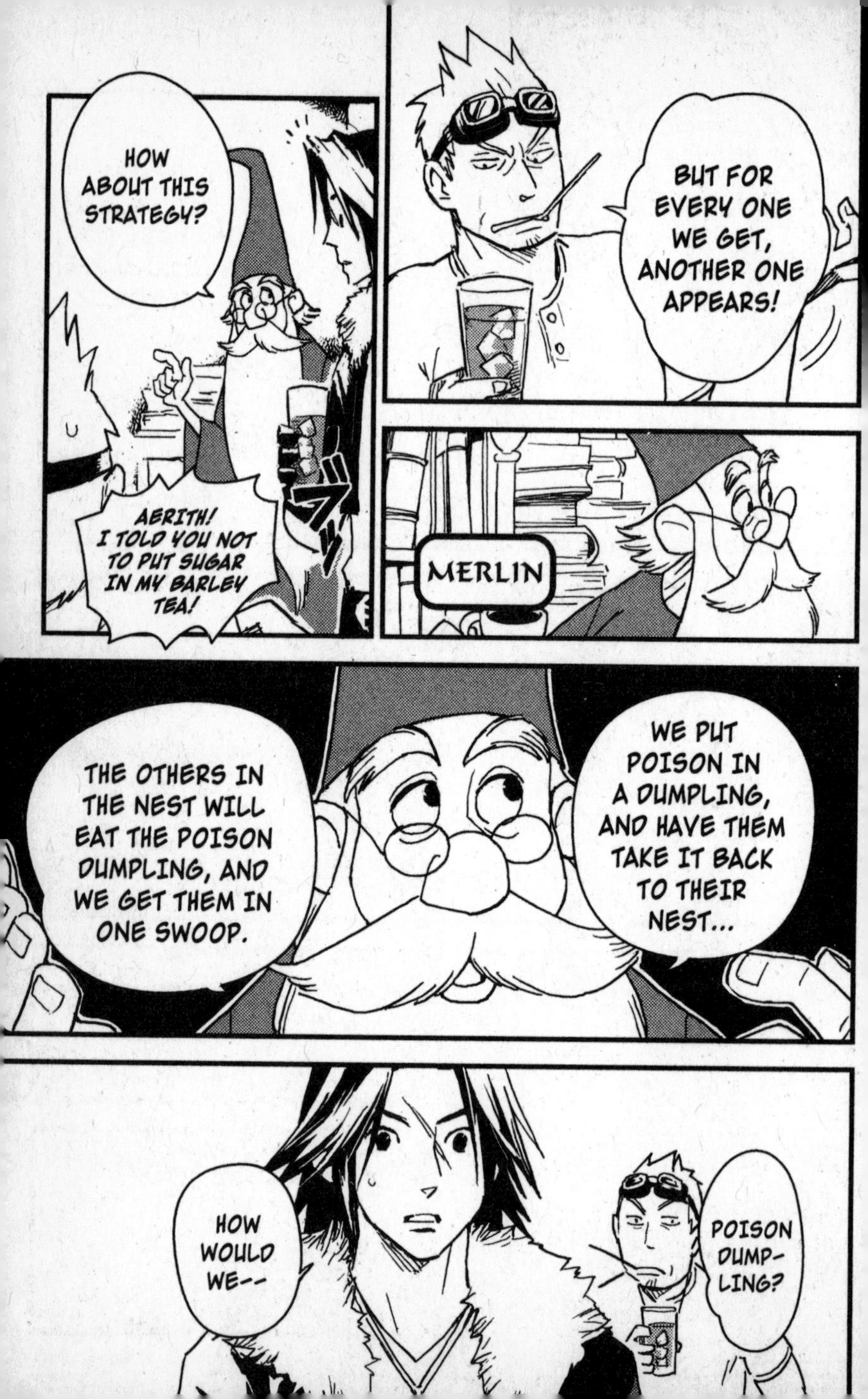
BUT FOR EVERY ONE WE GET, ANOTHER ONE APPEARS!
MERLIN
HOW ABOUT THIS STRATEGY?
AERITH! I TOLD YOU NOT TO PUT SUGAR IN MY BARLEY TEA!
WE PUT POISON IN A DUMPLING, AND HAVE THEM TAKE IT BACK TO THEIR NEST...
THE OTHERS IN THE NEST WILL EAT THE POISON DUMPLING, AND WE GET THEM IN ONE SWOOP.
POISON DUMP-LING?
HOW WOULD WE--

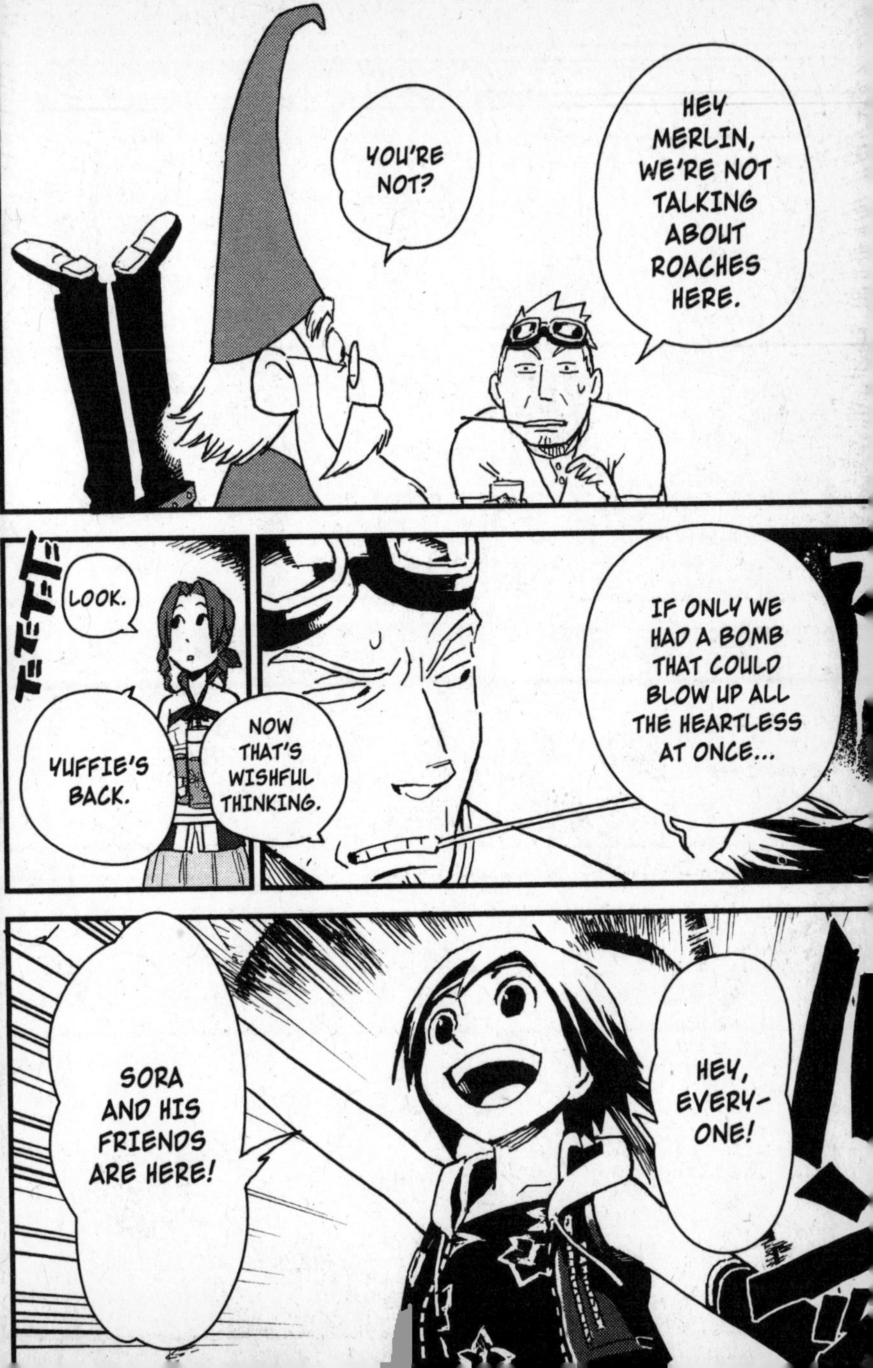
HEY MERLIN, WE'RE NOT TALKING ABOUT ROACHES HERE.
YOU'RE NOT?
IF ONLY WE HAD A BOMB THAT COULD BLOW UP ALL THE HEARTLESS AT ONCE...
NOW THAT'S WISHFUL THINKING.
LOOK.
YUFFIE'S BACK.
HEY, EVERY-ONE!
SORA AND HIS FRIENDS ARE HERE!

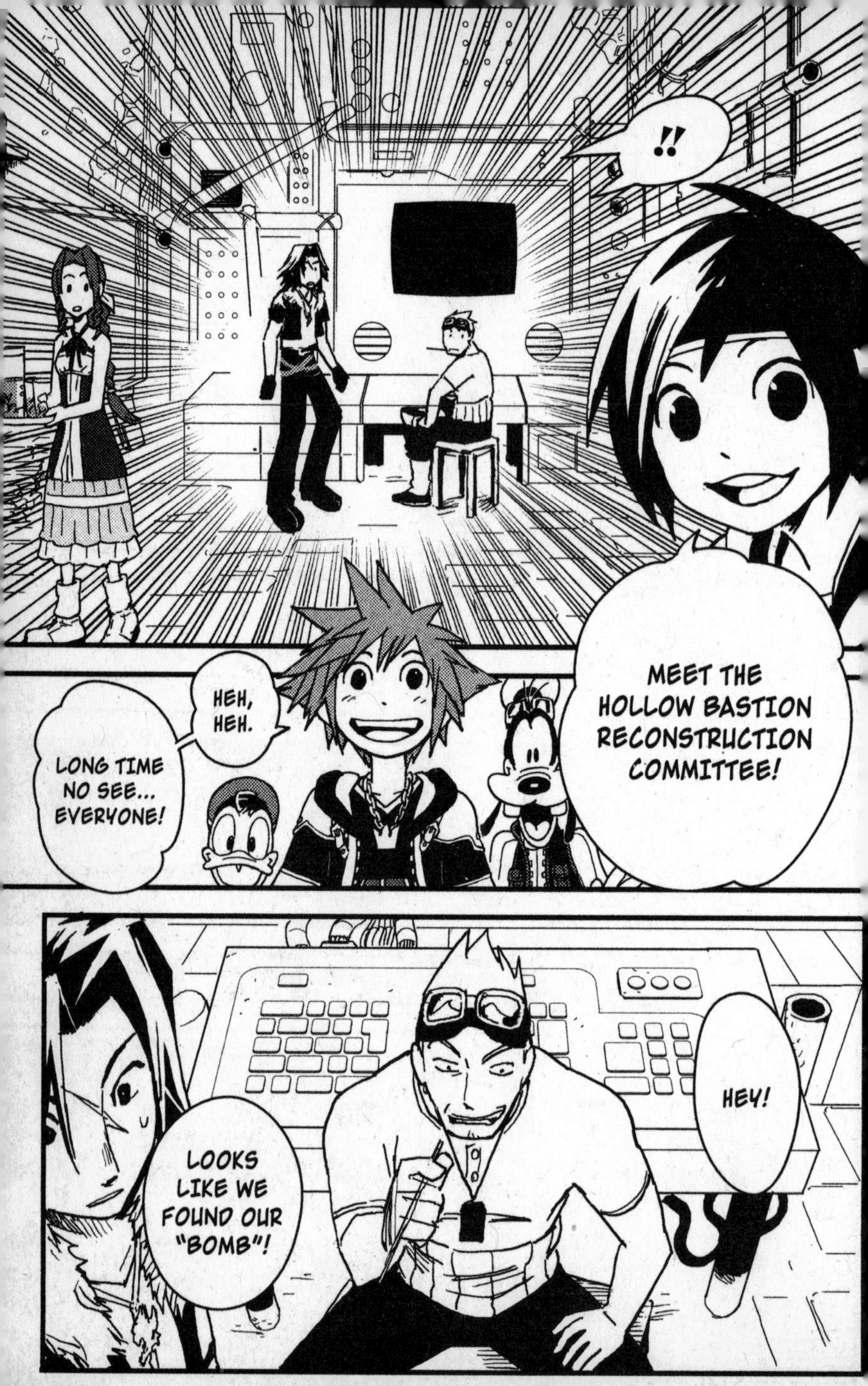
!!
MEET THE HOLLOW BASTION RECONSTRUCTION COMMITTEE!
HEH, HEH.
LONG TIME NO SEE... EVERYONE!
HEY!
LOOKS LIKE WE FOUND OUR "BOMB"!

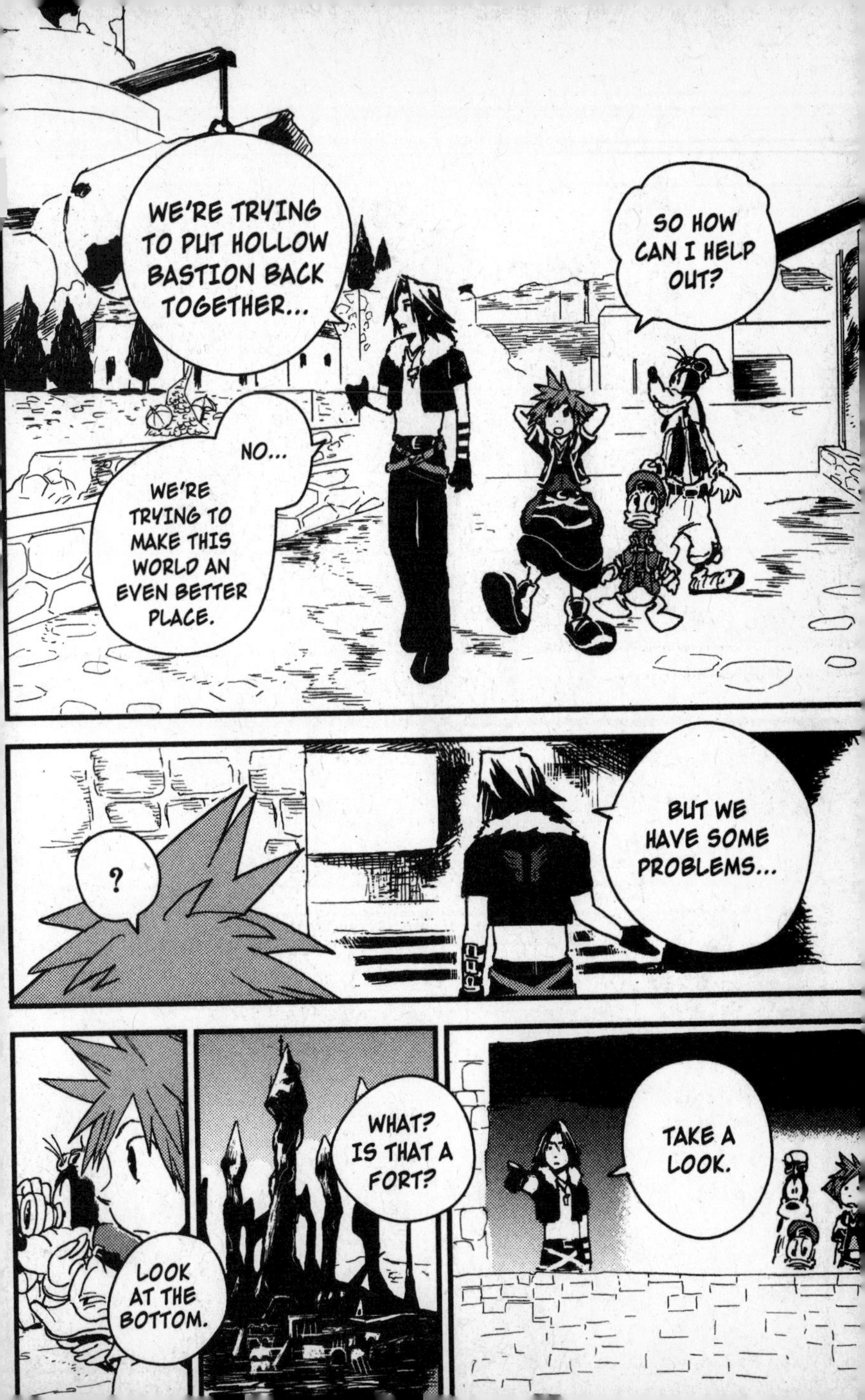
SO HOW CAN I HELP OUT?
WE'RE TRYING TO PUT HOLLOW BASTION BACK TOGETHER...
NO... WE'RE TRYING TO MAKE THIS WORLD AN EVEN BETTER PLACE.
BUT WE HAVE SOME PROBLEMS...
?
TAKE A LOOK.
WHAT? IS THAT A FORT?
LOOK AT THE BOTTOM.

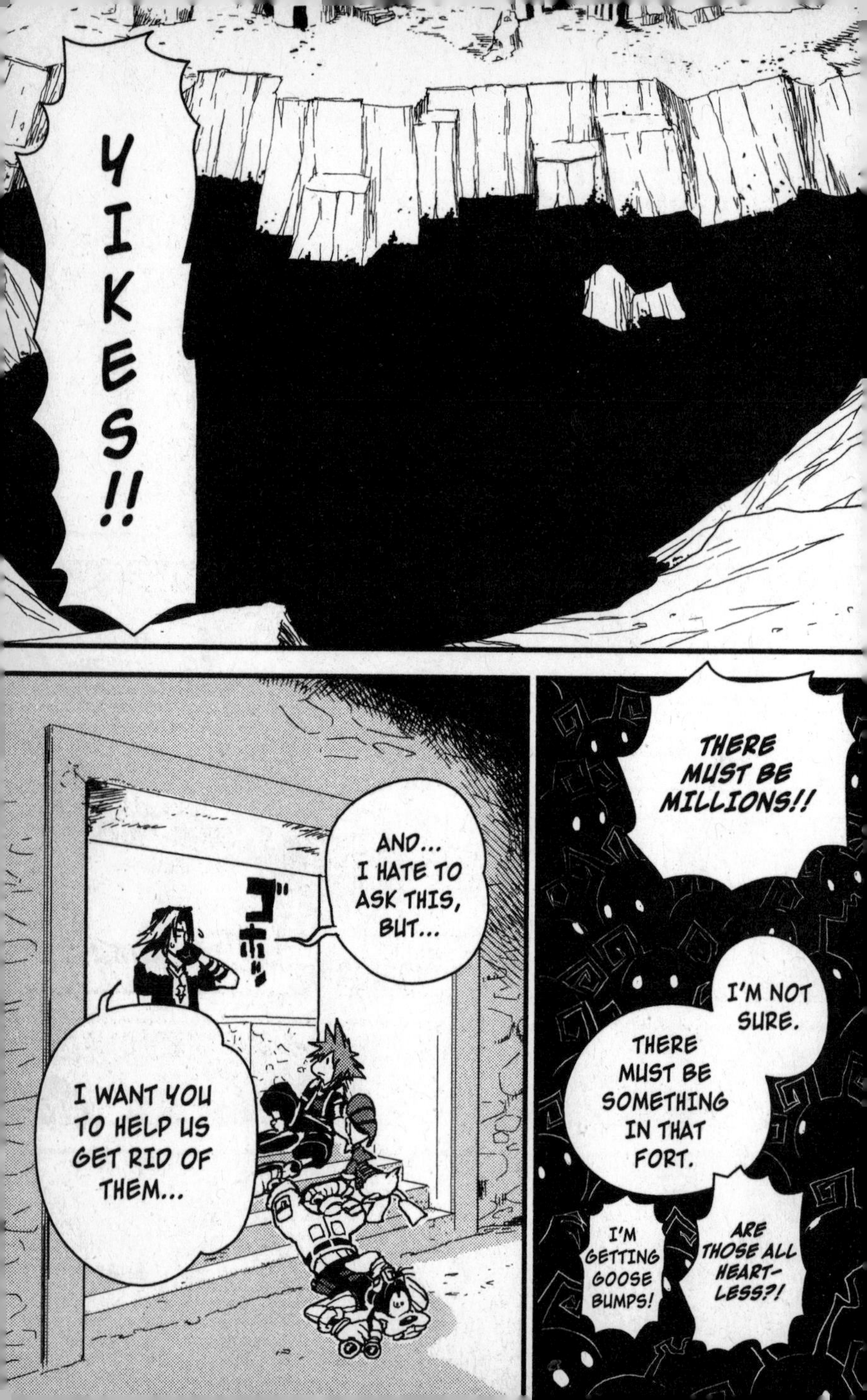
YIKES!!
THERE MUST BE MILLIONS!!
I'M NOT SURE. THERE MUST BE SOMETHING IN THAT FORT.
ARE THOSE ALL HEART-LESS?!
I'M GETTING GOOSE BUMPS!
AND... I HATE TO ASK THIS, BUT...
ゴホッ
I WANT YOU TO HELP US GET RID OF THEM...

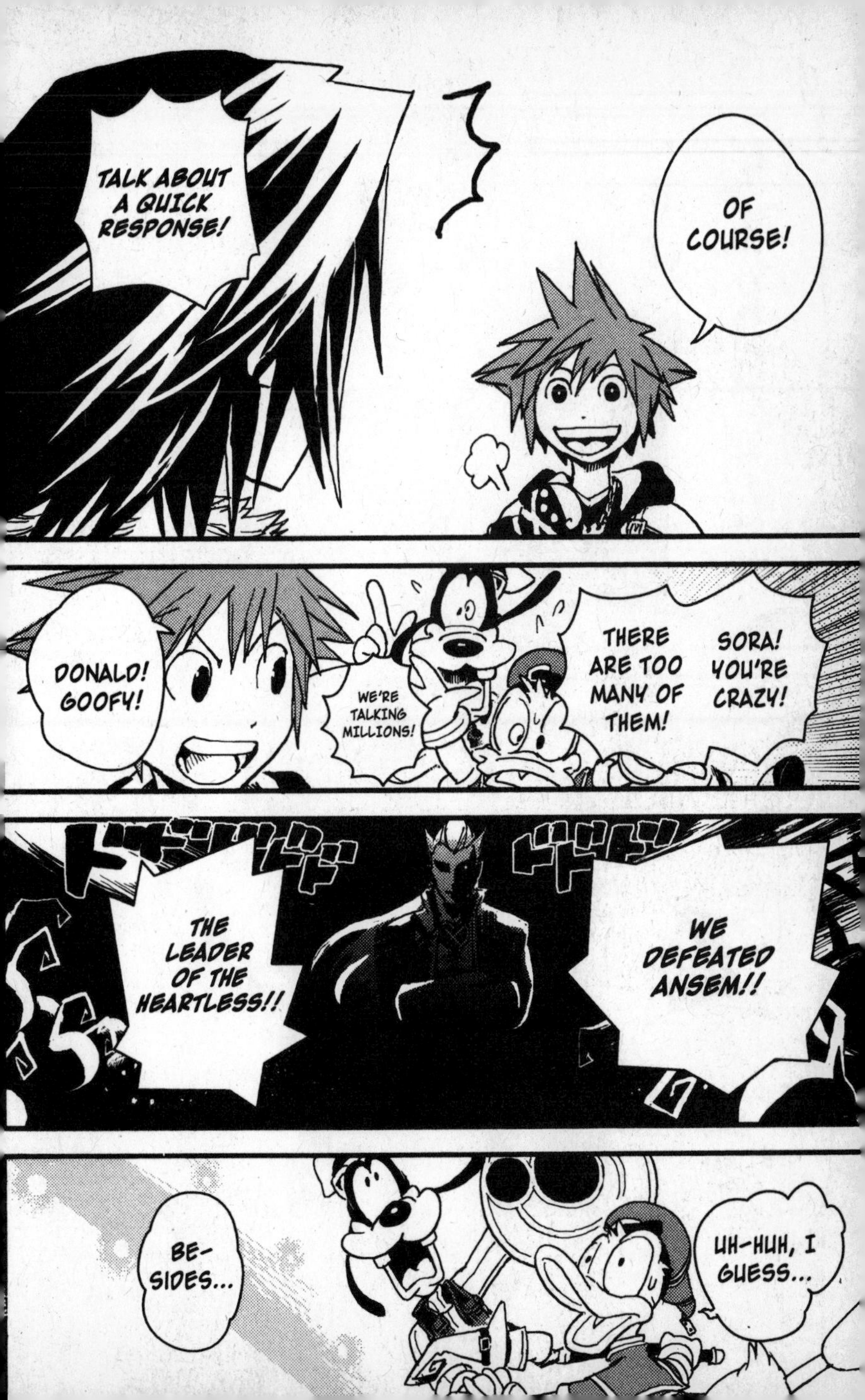
OF COURSE!
TALK ABOUT A QUICK RESPONSE!
SORA! YOU'RE CRAZY!
THERE ARE TOO MANY OF THEM!
WE'RE TALKING MILLIONS!
DONALD! GOOFY!
WE DEFEATED ANSEM!!
THE LEADER OF THE HEARTLESS!!
UH-HUH, I GUESS...
BE-SIDES...

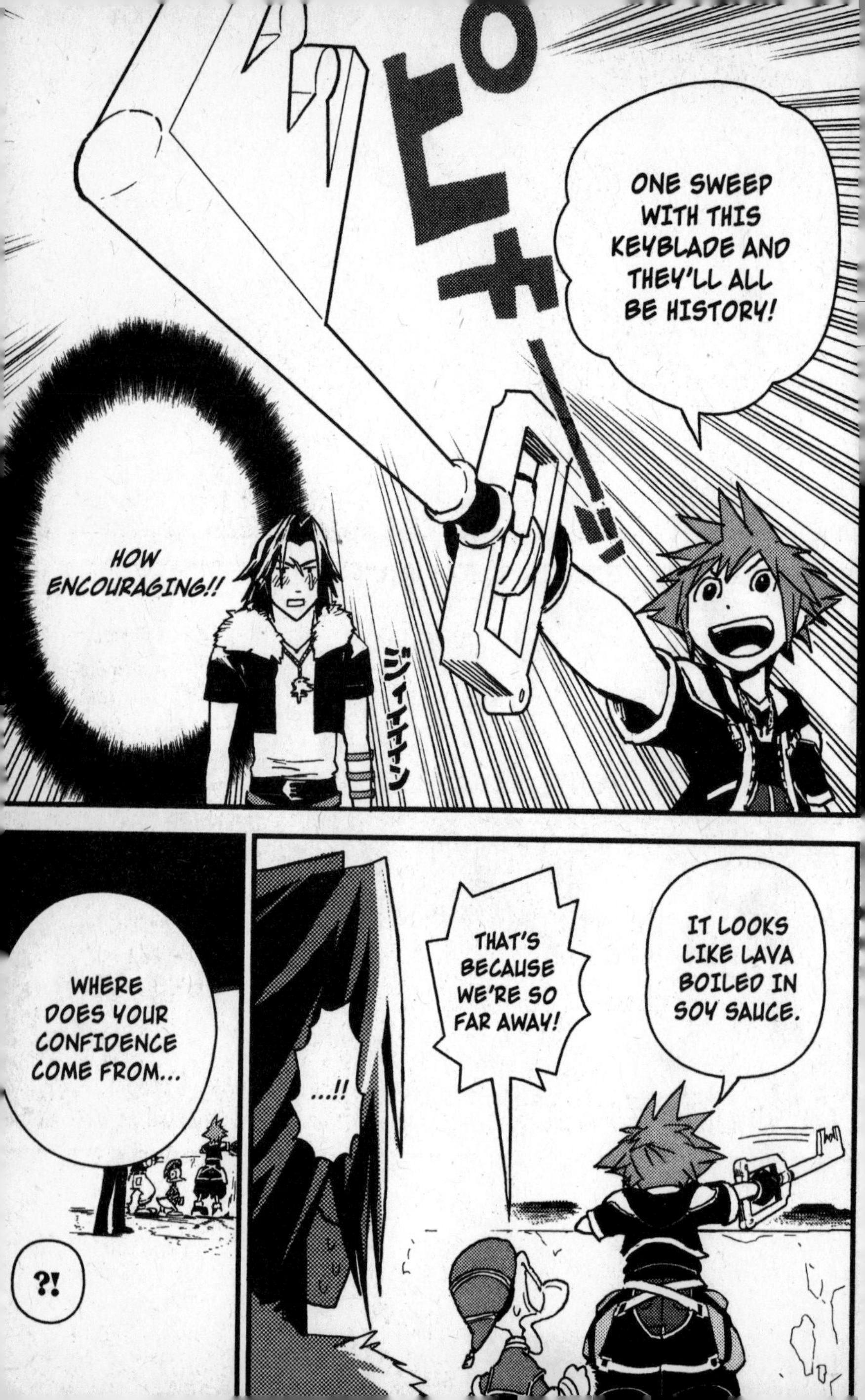
ONE SWEEP WITH THIS KEYBLADE AND THEY'LL ALL BE HISTORY!
HOW ENCOURAGING!!
IT LOOKS LIKE LAVA BOILED IN SOY SAUCE.
THAT'S BECAUSE WE'RE SO FAR AWAY!
...!!
WHERE DOES YOUR CONFIDENCE COME FROM...
?!

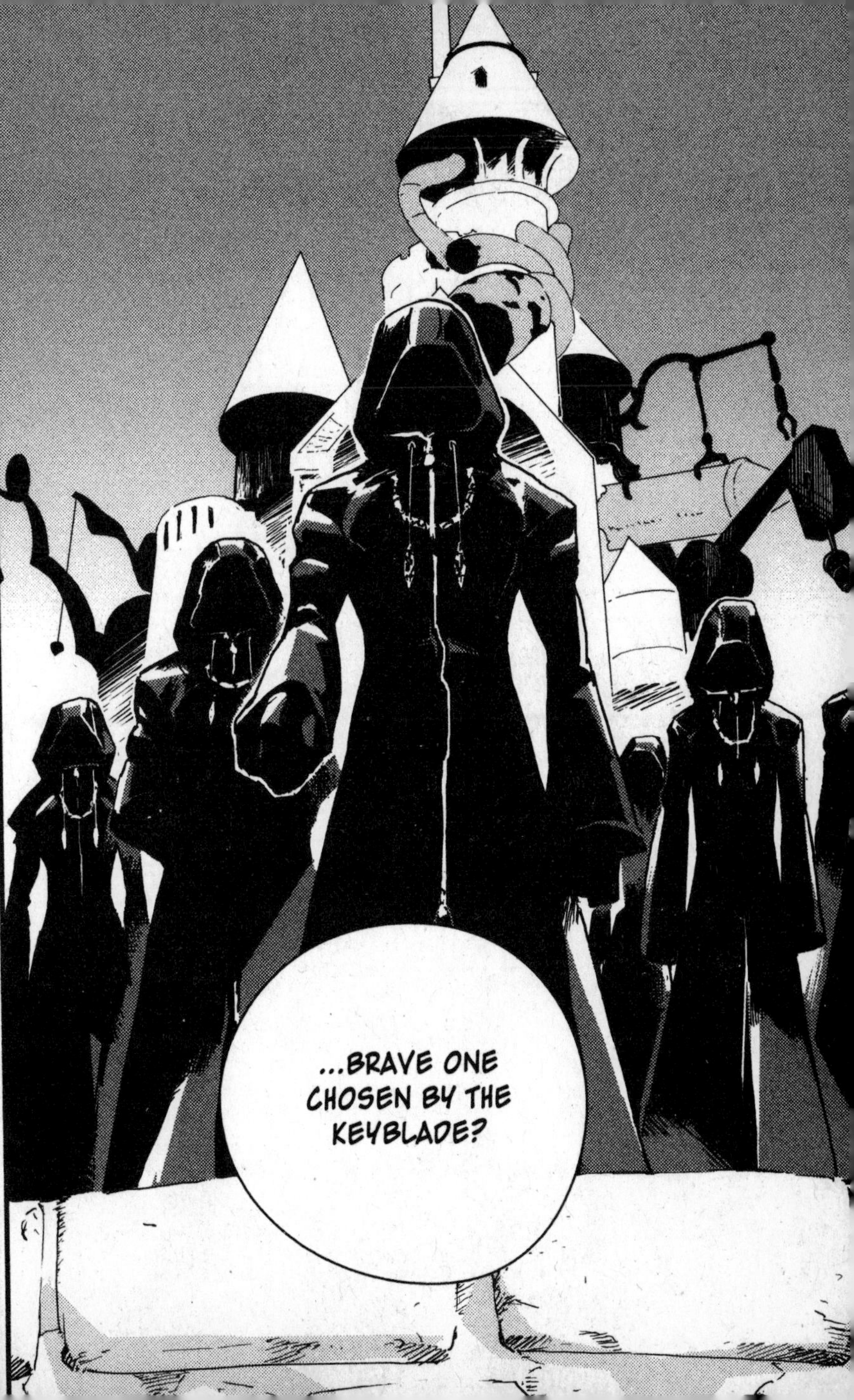
...BRAVE ONE CHOSEN BY THE KEYBLADE?

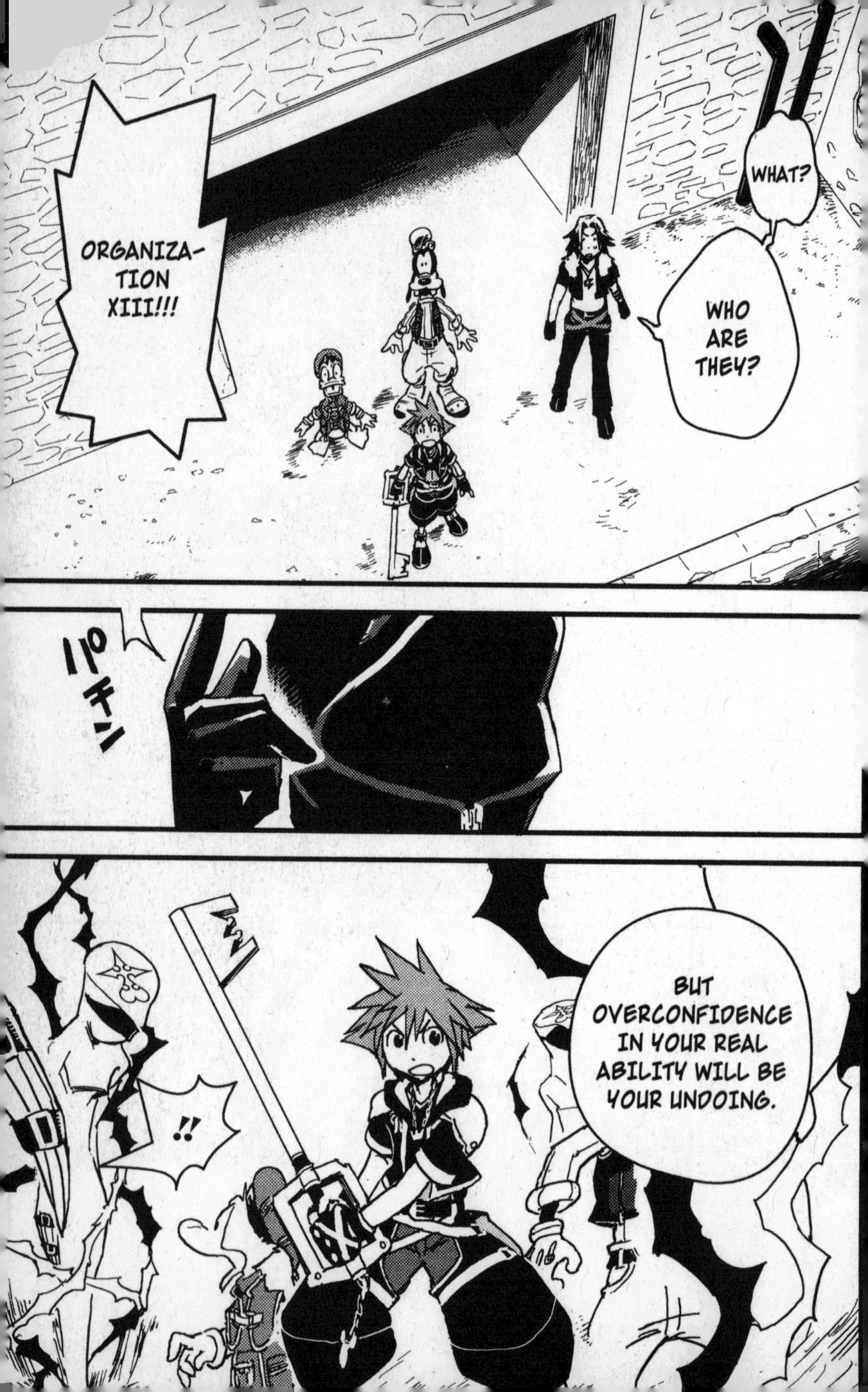
WHAT?
WHO ARE THEY?
ORGANIZATION XIII!!!
パチン
BUT OVERCONFIDENCE IN YOUR REAL ABILITY WILL BE YOUR UNDOING.
!!

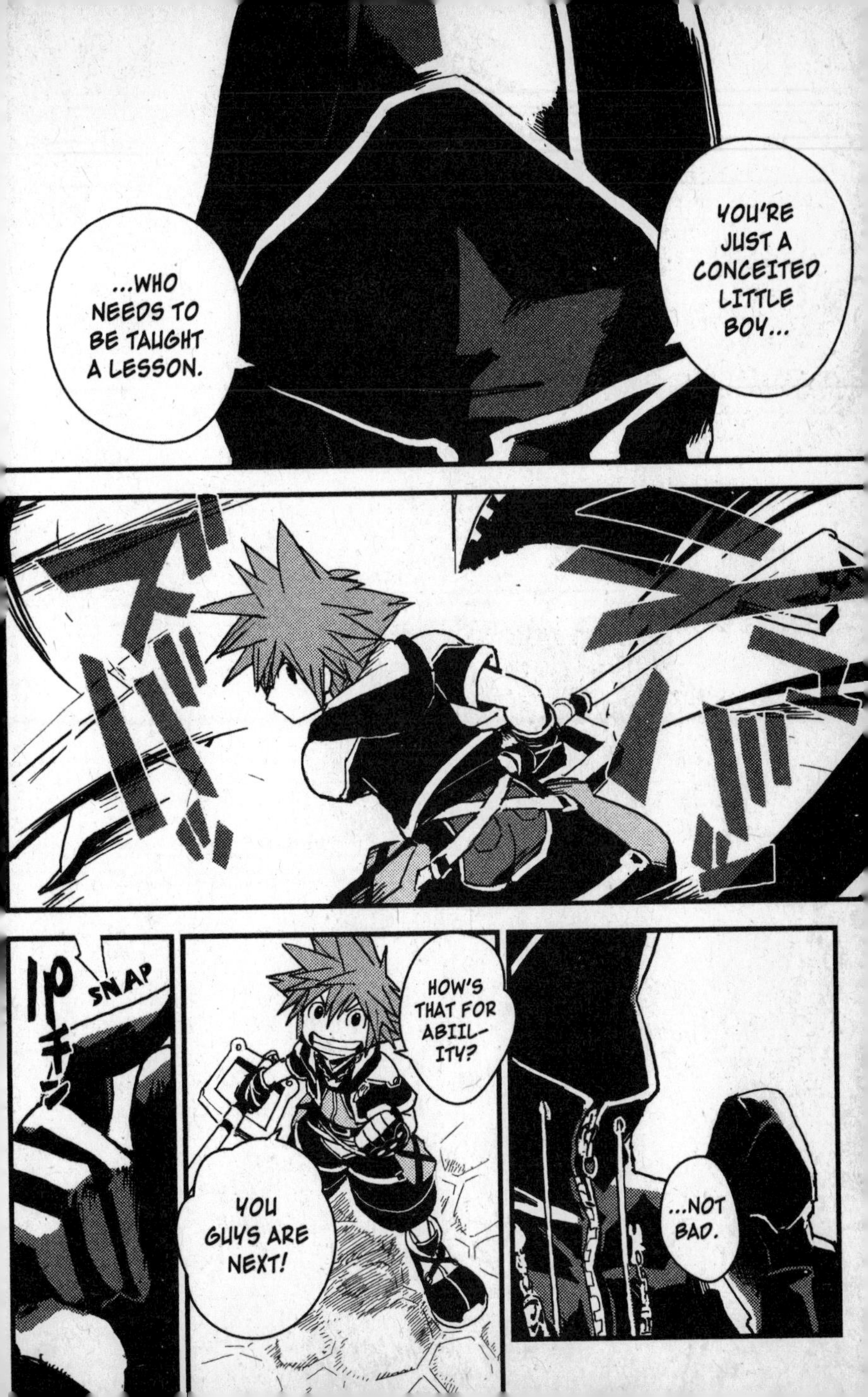
YOU'RE JUST A CONCEITED LITTLE BOY...
...WHO NEEDS TO BE TAUGHT A LESSON.
...NOT BAD.
HOW'S THAT FOR ABIIL-ITY?
YOU GUYS ARE NEXT!
SNAP

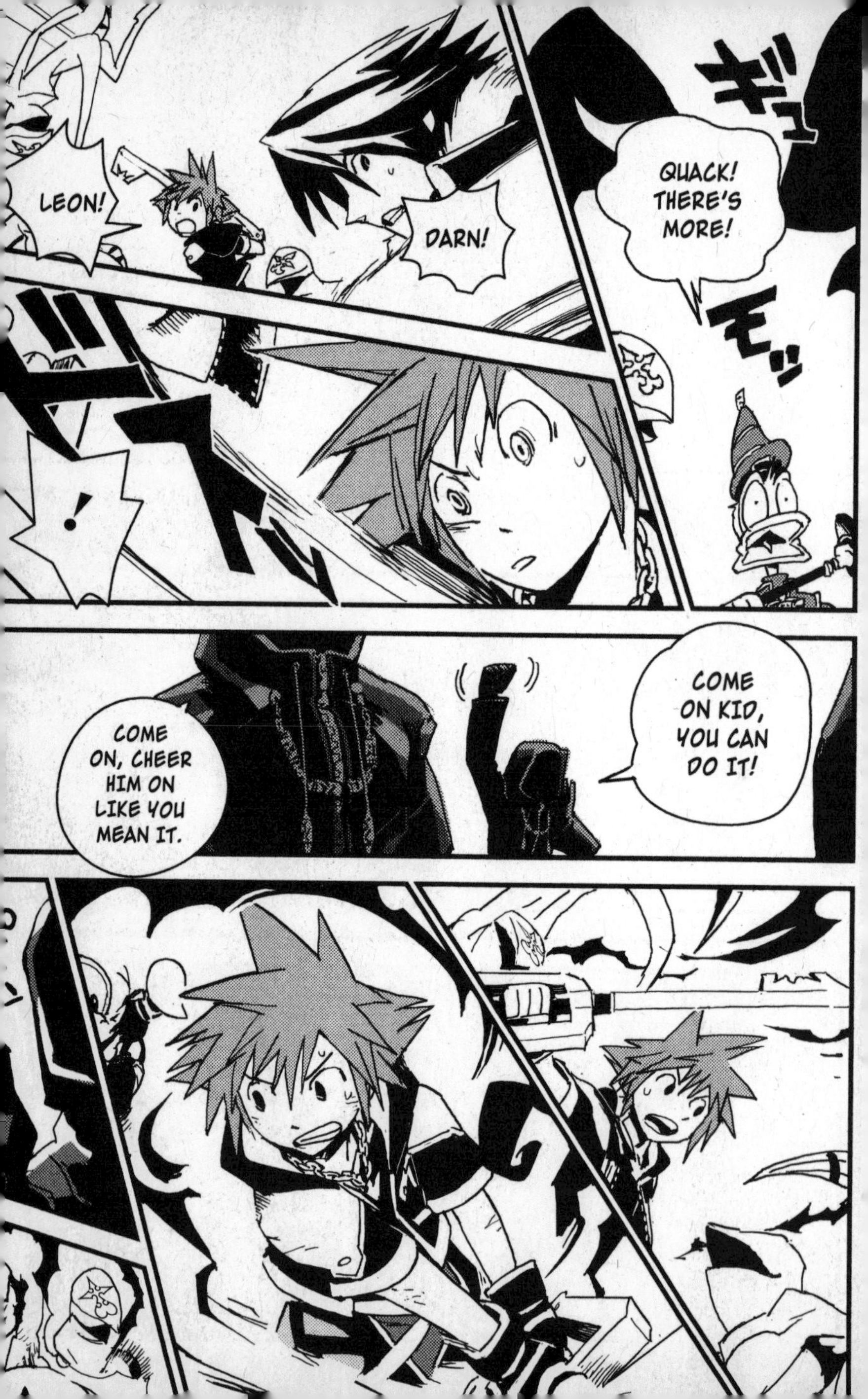
ギュ
QUACK! THERE'S MORE!
モッ
DARN!
LEON!
!
COME ON KID, YOU CAN DO IT!
COME ON, CHEER HIM ON LIKE YOU MEAN IT.

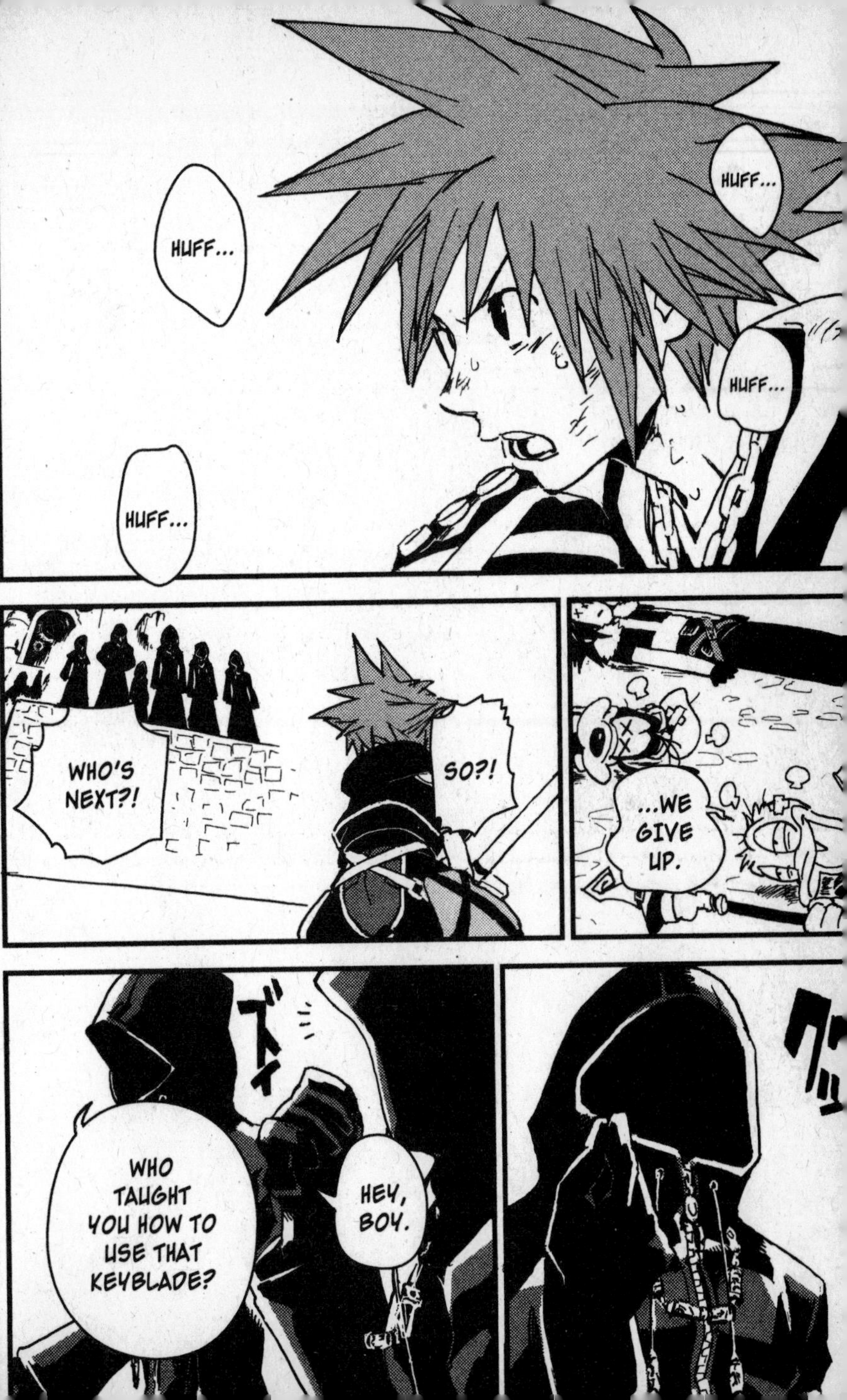
HUFF...
HUFF...
HUFF...
HUFF...
...WE GIVE UP.
SO?!
WHO'S NEXT?!
ズイ
HEY, BOY.
WHO TAUGHT YOU HOW TO USE THAT KEYBLADE?

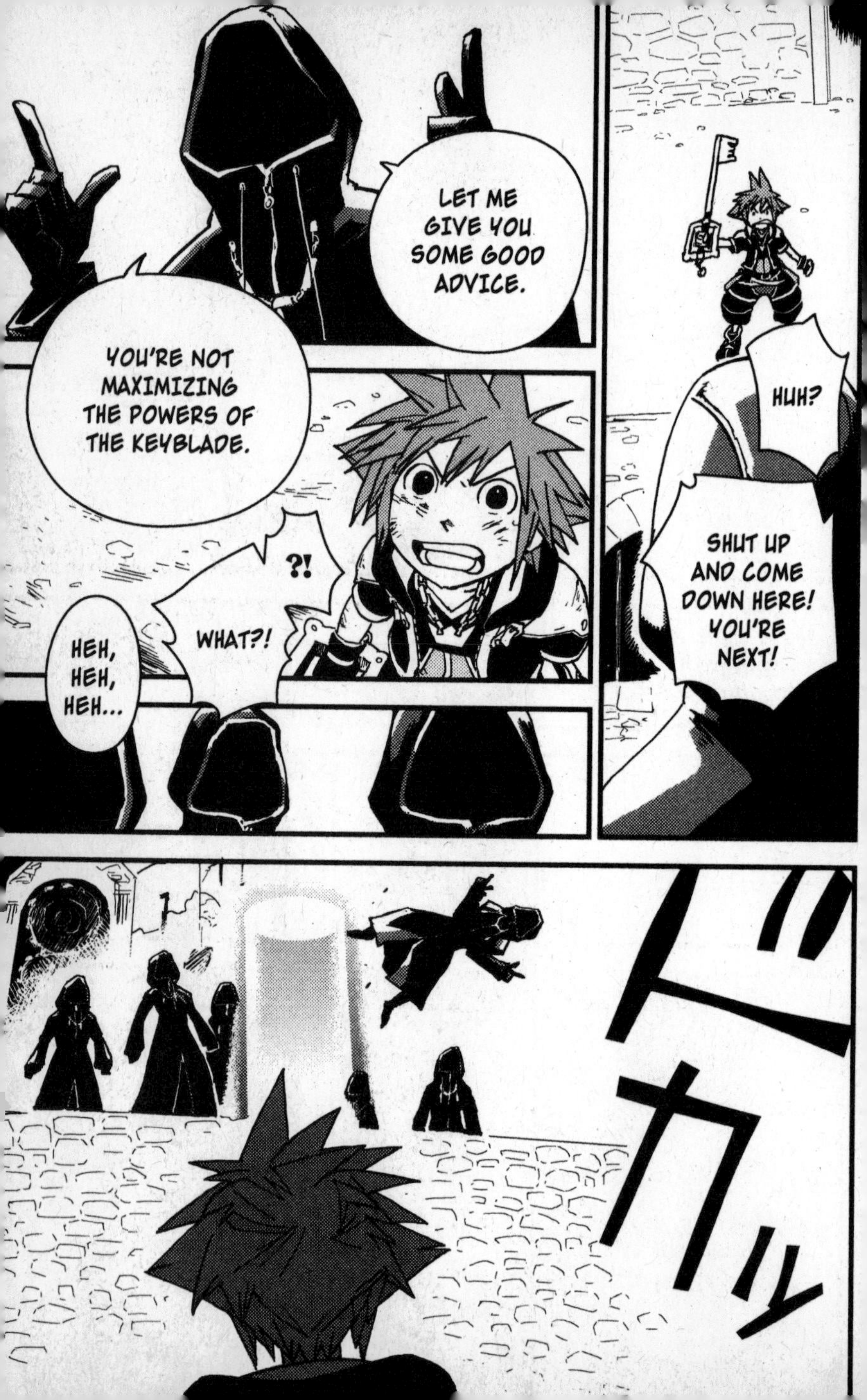
HUH?
SHUT UP AND COME DOWN HERE! YOU'RE NEXT!
LET ME GIVE YOU SOME GOOD ADVICE.
YOU'RE NOT MAXIMIZING THE POWERS OF THE KEYBLADE.
?!
WHAT?!
HEH, HEH, HEH...
ドカッ

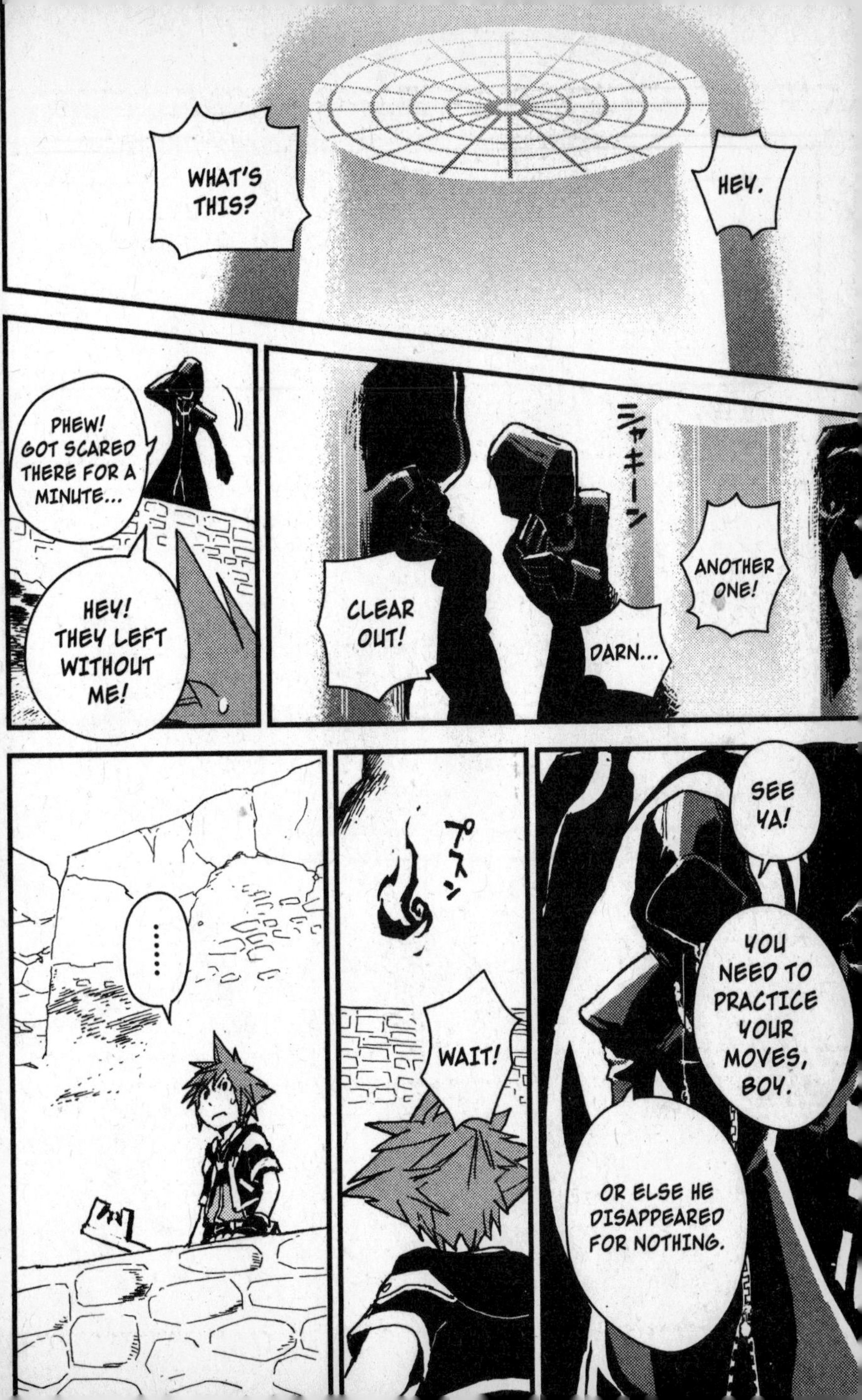
HEY.
WHAT'S THIS?
シャキーン
ANOTHER ONE!
DARN...
CLEAR OUT!
PHEW! GOT SCARED THERE FOR A MINUTE...
HEY! THEY LEFT WITHOUT ME!
SEE YA!
YOU NEED TO PRACTICE YOUR MOVES, BOY.
OR ELSE HE DISAPPEARED FOR NOTHING.
プスン
WAIT!
......

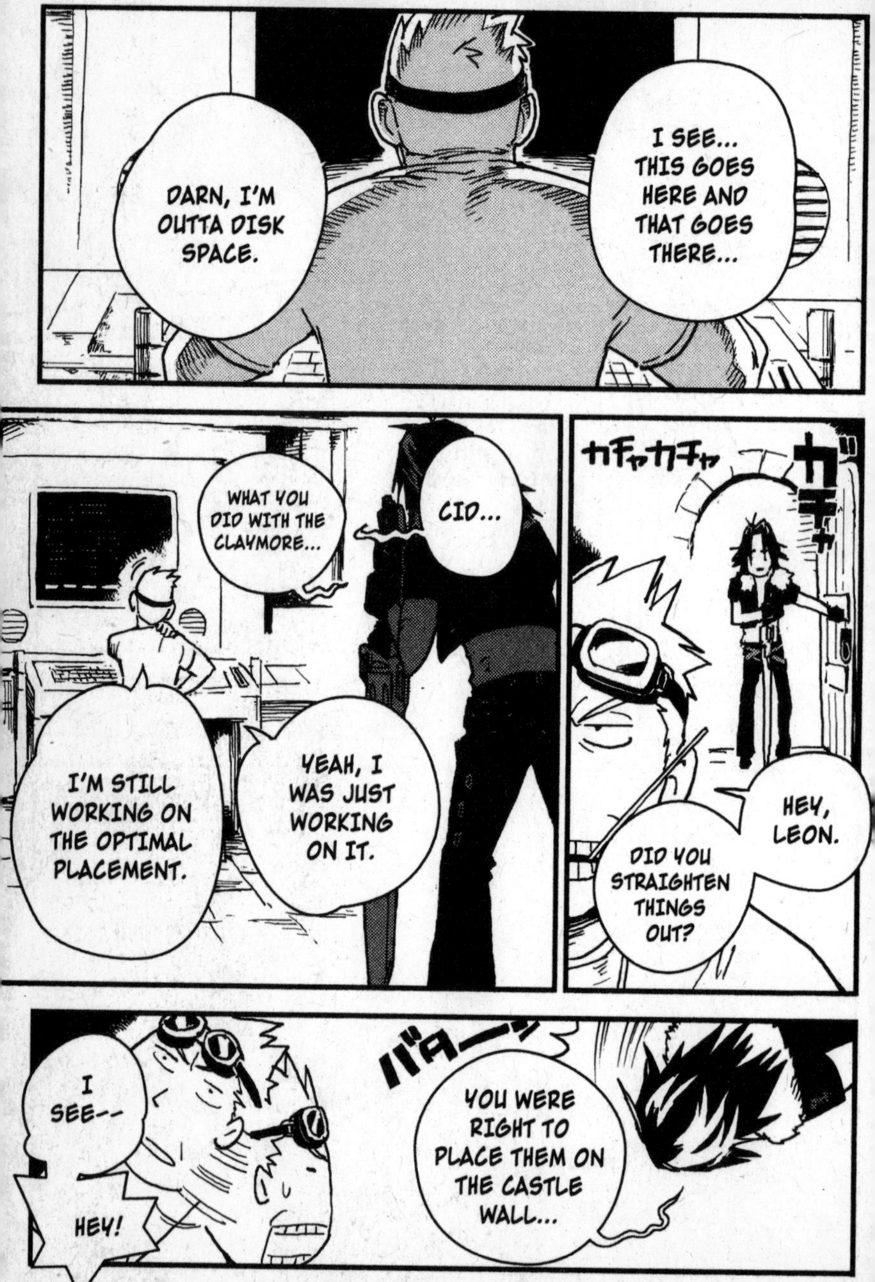
I SEE... THIS GOES HERE AND THAT GOES THERE...
DARN, I'M OUTTA DISK SPACE.
カチャカチャ
ガチャ
HEY, LEON.
DID YOU STRAIGHTEN THINGS OUT?
CID...
WHAT YOU DID WITH THE CLAYMORE...
YEAH, I WAS JUST WORKING ON IT.
I'M STILL WORKING ON THE OPTIMAL PLACEMENT.
バターン
YOU WERE RIGHT TO PLACE THEM ON THE CASTLE WALL...
I SEE--
HEY!

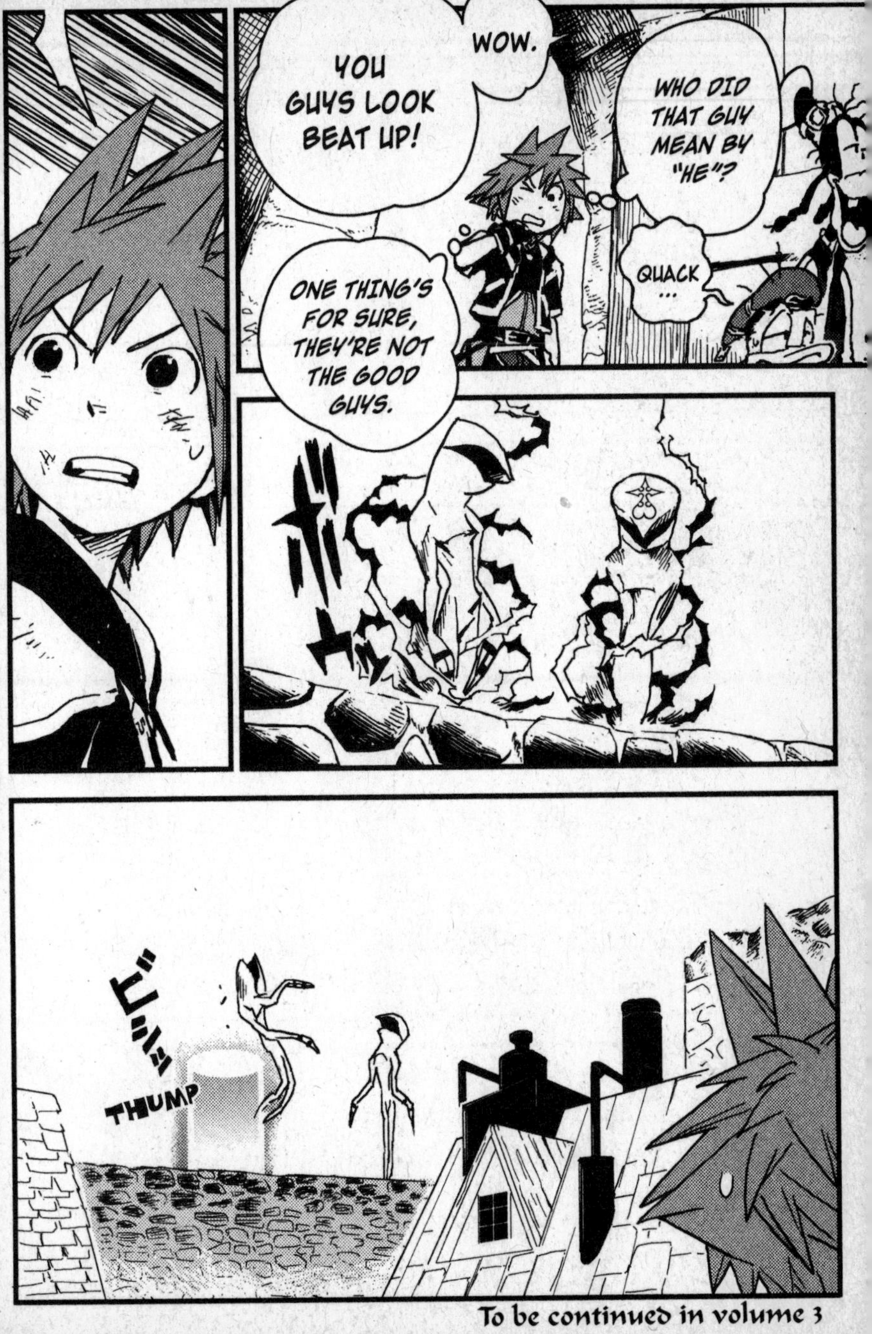
WHO DID THAT GUY MEAN BY "HE"?
QUACK ...
WOW.
YOU GUYS LOOK BEAT UP!
ONE THING'S FOR SURE, THEY'RE NOT THE GOOD GUYS.
THUMP

To be continued in volume 3

KINGDOM HEARTS II

What Dreams May Come...

Will Sora, Donald, Goofy and their allies Leon and Cid be able to turn back the hordes of Heartless in the canyon below the town? Will they uncover the true nature and intentions of the mysterious Orginazation XIII? And will Roxas regain his heart and finally join the ranks of the living, or is he fated to forever remain a nobody?

To find out the answers to these questions and more, you'll have to return for the next fantastic volume of KINGDOM HEARTS II!

KINGDOM HEARTS II CHARACTER FILE

He is the wielder of the "Keyblade" and the one charged with saving the world. He was in a deep sleep, but he has awoken to continue his journey with the "Keyblade" to find his friend Riku and save the world.

Sora

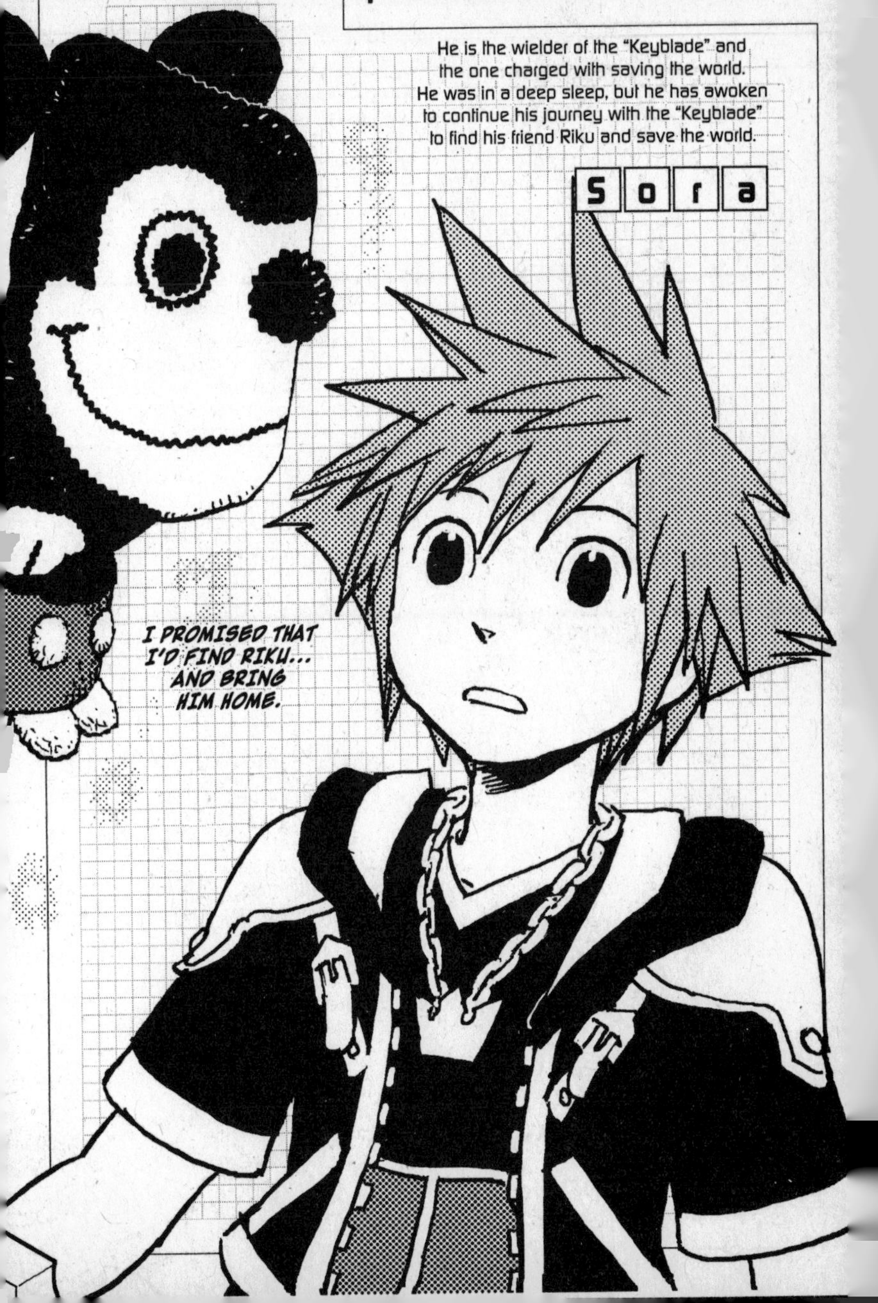
I PROMISED THAT I'D FIND RIKU... AND BRING HIM HOME.

Goofy

Together with Sora and Donald, he is searching for the missing King Mickey. Goofy is a cheerful character, and was also in a deep sleep, together with Sora and Donald.

Donald

He is a master magician who has been traveling with Sora in search of the missing King Mickey. Donald was also in a deep sleep just like Sora, but woke up at the same time as Sora.

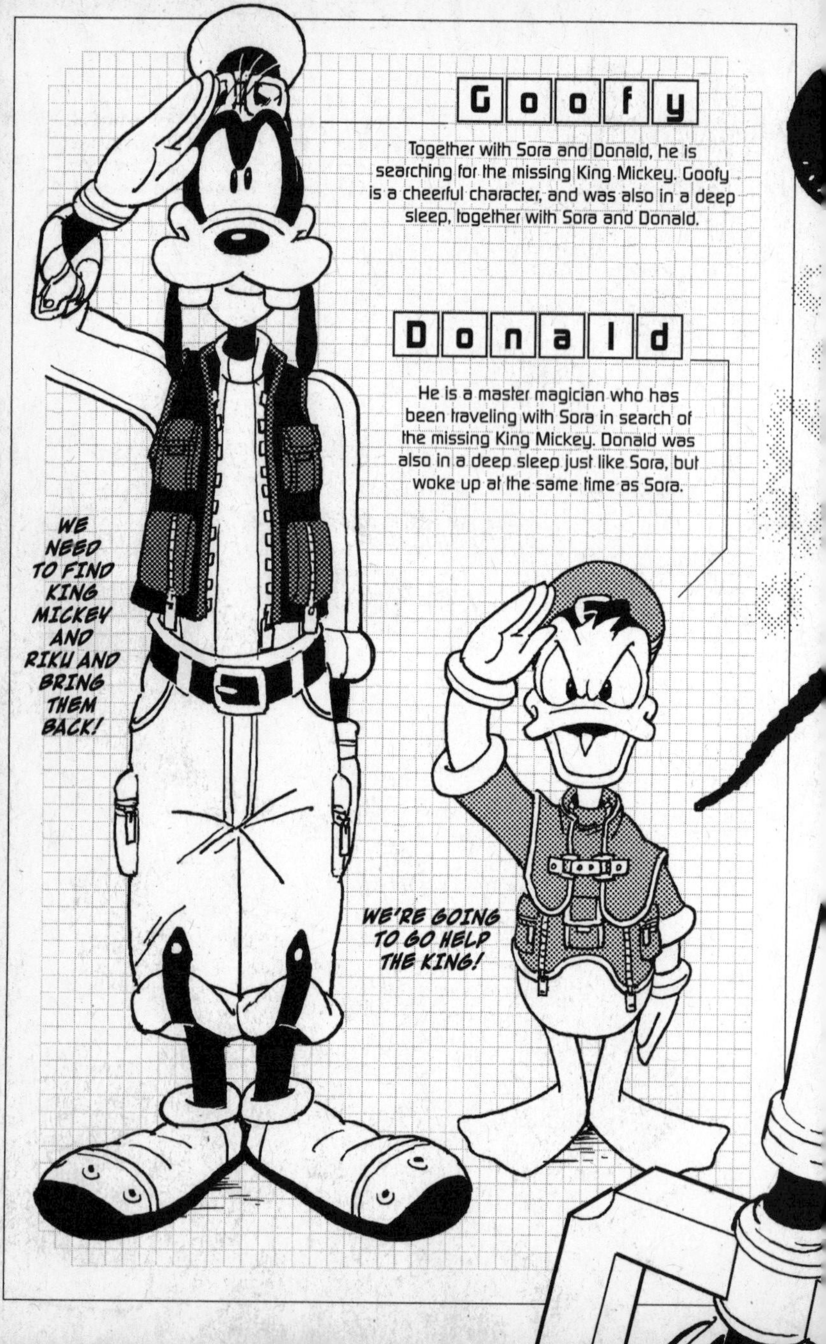
WE NEED TO FIND KING MICKEY AND RIKU AND BRING THEM BACK!
WE'RE GOING TO GO HELP THE KING!

THE QUEST TO SAVE THE WORLD
CONTINUES IN THE BEST-SELLING
MANGA FROM TOKYOPOP!

AVAILABLE WHEREVER BOOKS ARE SOLD.

www.TOKYOPOP.com

STOP!

This is the back of the book.
You wouldn't want to spoil a great ending!

This book is printed "manga-style," in the authentic Japanese right-to-left format. Since none of the artwork has been flipped or altered, readers get to experience the story just as the creator intended. You've been asking for it, so TOKYOPOP® delivered: authentic, hot-off-the-press, and far more fun!

DIRECTIONS

If this is your first time reading manga-style, here's a quick guide to help you understand how it works.

It's easy... just start in the top right panel and follow the numbers. Have fun, and look for more 100% authentic manga from TOKYOPOP®!

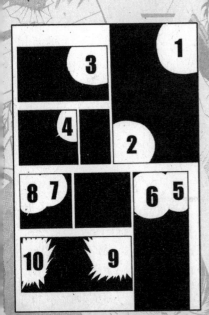